20

Twenty Decisive Battles of the World

Books by Lt. Col. Joseph B. Mitchell

Decisive Battles of the Civil War
Decisive Battles of the American Revolution
Twenty Decisive Battles of the World

Lt. Col. Joseph B. Mitchell
Sir Edward S. Creasy

ILLUSTRATED WITH MAPS

Twenty Decisive Battles of the World

20

KONECKY&KONECKY

Konecky & Konecky
72 Ayers Point Rd.
Old Saybrook, CT 06475

ISBN: 1-56852-458-7

Printed and bound in the USA

To Edward Shenton
who encouraged and aided my initial literary efforts

Contents

Foreword

WHEN Mr. Peter V. Ritner of The Macmillan Company asked me to undertake a revision of Sir Edward S. Creasy's *Fifteen Decisive Battles of the World,* and bring it up to date by adding other battles, I was delighted at the prospect. Neither Peter Ritner nor I had any conception of the magnitude of the task, but I have always appreciated his choosing me for the assignment.

It had been many years since I had first been introduced to this world-famous book and, on the occasions that I had referred to it, I had accepted its statements and conclusions with a great feeling of respect. The major portion of the job confronting me therefore seemed simply, at first glance, to decide what new battles should be chosen and described. However, the original work contained no maps, which I consider essential to descriptions of events leading to a battle. I guessed that at least one map would be necessary for each chapter. I was to find that this assumption was as greatly in error as my original assumption that the first fifteen chapters were wholly accurate.

After a very complete study of Sir Edward Creasy's book I was able to arrive at three conclusions concerning it. First, although I began to find some errors in the text, his choice of battles to be regarded as decisive to the history of mankind was excellent; his reasons were clearly stated and fundamentally sound. In fact, I found myself using his rigid clear-cut standards in the choosing of the next five battles to be added to the book. He was, in a sense, my teacher and led me in the selection of Vicksburg, rather than the more dramatic Gettysburg in the American Civil War. In like manner I chose Sadowa in the Seven Weeks' War as being more important to the rise of the German Empire than any of the battles that followed in the later Franco-Prussian War.

Also, being an American, I would have preferred to pick Normandy over Stalingrad, but could not conscientiously do so. There is no doubt of the fact that no two military historians would select exactly the same list of battles, even using the same general criteria. However, I do believe that the first author of this book would agree in principle with my selections, as I have generally agreed with his, which I did not think should be changed in this revision.

Both The Macmillan Company and I had assumed that the rewriting of a book published over a hundred years ago, involving changes in the mid-Victorian style, would present a problem. Actually I concluded quite early in the process that it would not be nearly as difficult as we had supposed. Creasy's style was much more modern than that of many of his contemporaries. But checking to see that inaccuracies in the original text did not recur and, furthermore, that the British viewpoint of a hundred years ago was brought up to date, proved to be far greater obstacles to overcome. The errors have, I hope, now been corrected. However, in criticizing such errors, it should also be remembered that in the past century a number of important historical discoveries have been made, and that we have today the benefit of a great deal of research that had not been undertaken in 1851.

My third decision, or conclusion, was that the synopses between chapters were inadequate; too many important military events had been omitted. In the long run, the preparation of entirely new synopses for all chapters proved to be far more time-consuming, and required a great deal more research, than the addition of five new battles, especially since I was already quite familiar, through previous study, with the American Revolution, the Civil War, and World War II. In turn this led to the preparation of several additional maps. I believe that towns, cities and regions referred to in any history should be spotted on a map; otherwise a great deal of the meaning and significance of the information included therein is lost. The addition of pertinent comments of a military nature to the synopses converted them into almost a short course in military history. It is my fond hope that these synopses, and the maps accompanying them, now constitute a valuable addition to the new book.

The numerous battle and campaign maps designed by me, and executed with such care and precision by Janice Downey, are intended to portray action vividly so that the casual observer can tell almost at a glance how the battle or campaign was fought.

Where there was a choice in the spelling of names, we selected that spelling we believed to be best known to American readers. Accents were retained on European names where the spellings were the same, or almost exactly so, except that accents were not used on capital letters.

I have deliberately avoided the use of footnotes in order not to interrupt the reading. Material that might have been given in footnotes was either important enough to be included somehow in the book or, if not, was omitted. Where historical quotations were used, the books from which they were obtained are included in the Bibliography.

I would like to take this opportunity to thank Mr. Peter V. Ritner for his unwavering confidence and courtesy as the book developed at a slower rate than either of us had expected. He was of great assistance to me as I kept on working, ever encouraging me in my efforts.

Special thanks are due to Mr. Robert S. Chamberlain and to Mr. Malcolm H. McGann for providing me with material for the chapters on Sadowa and Midway.

I am particularly grateful to my wife Vivienne who, throughout the preparation of this book, acted as my unofficial advisor and critic.

JOSEPH B. MITCHELL

Alexandria, Virginia
February 20, 1964

The thirty-two maps in this book, designed by the author,
were submitted in the form of pencil drawings to Janice Downey.
She then prepared careful, accurate maps,
lending her artistic skill and talent to their development,
improving the original designs in many ways.
Her invaluable contribution
is herewith gratefully acknowledged.
They were ably executed in final form
by Hagstrom Company, Incorporated, of New York.

Preface

WHEN *Fifteen Decisive Battles of the World* was published in 1851, Great Britain had been blessed by thirty-six years of peace, gained for her by the victory at Waterloo. Many people began to hope that the world had, at last, reached that point in history when it would no longer be necessary for the Great Powers to engage in a general war.

Sir Edward Creasy's Preface indicated his awareness of the spirit of the times. He was careful to explain why, in that period of peace and prosperity, he had chosen to write about battles.

During the next hundred years the nations of the world were forced into numerous great conflicts, including two world wars. Today it is not necessary to remind people of the effect that warfare can have upon their lives and upon those of succeeding generations. Yet some historians tend to treat wars and battles as simply painful interludes, interrupting for a time the steady march of progress, whereas, in the case of the world's most important battles, those which have actually been decisive have determined the route that progress would take. Creasy's original Preface, given below almost in its entirety, not only describes the fascination that accounts of battles and leaders retain for us but also emphasizes the importance of warfare by asking us to pause for a moment and ponder the course that civilization would have taken if these battles had ended differently.

"It is an honorable characteristic of the spirit of this age, that projects of violence and warfare are regarded among civilized states with gradually increasing aversion. The Universal Peace Society certainly does not, and probably never will, enroll the majority of statesmen among its members. But even those who look upon the appeal of

battle as occasionally unavoidable in international controversies, concur in thinking it a deplorable necessity, only to be resorted to when
all peaceful modes of arrangement have been vainly tried, and when
the law of self-defense justifies a state, like an individual, in using
force to protect itself from imminent and serious injury. For a writer,
therefore, of the present day to choose battles for his favorite topic,
merely because they were battles; merely because so many myriads
of troops were arrayed in them, and so many hundreds or thousands
of human beings stabbed, hewed, or shot each other to death during
them, would argue strange weakness or depravity of mind. Yet it can
not be denied that a fearful and wonderful interest is attached to
these scenes of carnage. There is undeniable greatness in the disciplined courage, and in the love of honor, which makes the combatants
confront agony and destruction. And the powers of the human intellect are rarely more strongly displayed than they are in the commander who regulates, arrays, and wields at his will these masses of
armed disputants; who, cool, yet daring in the midst of peril, reflects
on all, and provides for all, ever ready with fresh resources and designs, as the vicissitudes of the storm of slaughter require. But these
qualities, however high they may appear, are to be found in the basest
as well as in the noblest of mankind. Catiline was as brave a soldier
as Leonidas, and a much better officer. Alva surpassed the Prince of
Orange in the field; and Suwarrow was the military superior of Kosciusko. To adopt the emphatic words of Byron,

> ' 'Tis the cause makes all,
> Degrades or hallows courage in its fall.'

"There are some battles, also, which claim our attention, independently of the moral worth of the combatants, on account of their enduring importance, and by reason of the practical influence on our own
social and political condition, which we can trace up to the results of
those engagements. They have for us an abiding and actual interest,
both while we investigate the chain of causes and effects by which
they have helped to make us what we are, and also while we speculate
on what we probably should have been, if any one of those battles
had come to a different termination. Hallam has admirably expressed
this in his remarks on the victory gained by Charles Martel, between
Tours and Poictiers, over the invading Saracens.

"He says of it that 'it may justly be reckoned among those few battles
of which a contrary event would have essentially varied the drama of

the world in all its subsequent scenes; with Marathon, Arbela, the
Metaurus, Chalons, and Leipsic.' It was the perusal of this note of
Hallam's that first led me to the consideration of my present subject.
I certainly differ from that great historian as to the comparative importance of some of the battles which he thus enumerates, and also of
some which he omits. It is probable, indeed, that no two historical
inquirers would entirely agree in their lists of the Decisive Battles of
the World. Different minds will naturally vary in the impressions which
particular events make on them, and in the degree of interest with
which they watch the career and reflect on the importance of different historical personages. But our concurring in our catalogues is of
little moment, provided we learn to look on these great historical events
in the spirit which Hallam's observations indicate. Those remarks
should teach us to watch how the interests of many states are often
involved in the collisions between a few; and how the effect of those
collisions is not limited to a single age, but may give an impulse which
will sway the fortunes of successive generations of mankind.

"The reasons why each of the following fifteen battles has been selected will, I trust, appear when it is described. But it may be well to
premise a few remarks on the negative tests which have led me to
reject others, which at first sight may appear equal in magnitude and
importance to the chosen fifteen.

"I need hardly remark that it is not the number of killed and
wounded in a battle that determines its general historical importance.
It is not because only a few hundreds fell in the battle by which Joan
of Arc captured the Tourelles and raised the siege of Orleans, that the
effect of that crisis is to be judged; nor would a full belief in the largest number which Eastern historians state to have been slaughtered
in any of the numerous conflicts between Asiatic rulers, make me regard the engagement in which they fell as one of paramount importance to mankind. But, besides battles of this kind, there are many of
great consequence, and attended with circumstances which powerfully
excite our feelings and rivet our attention, and yet which appear to
me of mere secondary rank, inasmuch as either their effects were limited in area, or they themselves merely confirmed some great tendency or bias which an earlier battle had originated. For example, the
encounters between the Greeks and Persians, which followed Marathon,
seem to me not to have been phenomena of primary impulse. Greek
superiority had been already asserted, Asiatic ambition had already

been checked, before Salamis and Plataea confirmed the superiority of European free states over Oriental despotism. So Aegospotamos, which finally crushed the maritime power of Athens, seems to me inferior in interest to the defeat before Syracuse, where Athens received her first fatal check, and after which she only struggled to retard her downfall. I think similarly of Zama with respect to Carthage, as compared with the Metaurus; and, on the same principle, the subsequent great battles of the Revolutionary war appear to me inferior in their importance to Valmy, which first determined the military character and career of the French Revolution.

"I am aware that a little activity of imagination and a slight exercise of metaphysical ingenuity may amuse us by showing how the chain of circumstances is so linked together, that the smallest skirmish, or the slightest occurrence of any kind, that ever occurred, may be said to have been essential in its actual termination to the whole order of subsequent events. But when I speak of causes and effects, I speak of the obvious and important agency of one fact upon another, and not of remote and fancifully infinitesimal influences. I am aware that, on the other hand, the reproach of Fatalism is justly incurred by those who, like the writers of a certain school in a neighboring country, recognize in history nothing more than a series of necessary phenomena, which follow inevitably one upon the other. But when, in this work, I speak of probalilities, I speak of human probabilities only. When I speak of cause and effect, I speak of those general laws only by which we perceive the sequence of human affairs to be usually regulated, and in which we recognize emphatically the wisdom and power of the supreme Lawgiver, the design of the Designer."

Twenty Decisive Battles of the World

The Battle of Marathon, 490 B.C.

TWO THOUSAND four hundred and fifty-four years ago, a council of Athenian officers was summoned on the slope of one of the mountains that overlook the plain of Marathon on the eastern coast of Attica. The immediate subject of their meeting was to consider whether they should give battle to an enemy that lay encamped on the shore beneath them; but on the result of their deliberations depended not merely the fate of two armies, but the whole future progress of human civilization.

There were eleven members of that council of war. Ten were the generals who were then annually elected at Athens, one for each of the local tribes into which the Athenians were divided. Each general led the men of his own tribe, and each was invested with equal military authority. But one of the higher magistrates of the city was also associated with them in general command of the army. This magistrate was termed the Polemarch, or War Ruler; he had the privilege of leading the right wing of the army in battle, and his vote in a council of war was equal to that of any of the generals. A noble Athenian named Callimachus was the War Ruler for this year; and, as such, stood listening to the earnest discussion of the ten generals. They had indeed great cause for anxiety, though they were little aware how momentous

1

to mankind were the votes they were about to give, or how generations to come would read with interest the record of their discussions.
They saw before them the invading forces of a mighty empire that in
the last fifty years had shattered and enslaved all the kingdoms and
principalities of the then known world. They knew that all the resources
of their own country were comprised in the little army entrusted to their
guidance. They saw before them a chosen host of the Great King of
Persia, sent to wreak his special wrath on the country that had dared to
aid his rebels and burn the capital of one of his provinces. The Persian
host had already fulfilled half its mission of vengeance. Eretria, the
confederate of Athens in the bold march against Sardis eight years
before, had fallen in the last few days. The Athenian generals could dis-
cern from the heights the island where the Eretrian prisoners were
held before being led away as captives into Asia, there to hear their
doom from the lips of King Darius himself. Moreover, the men of
Athens knew that in the camp before them was their own banished
tyrant, Hippias, seeking to be restored to power.

The numerical disparity between the force the Athenian commanders
had under them and that which they were called on to encounter was
hopelessly apparent to some of the council. The historians who wrote
nearest to the time of the battle do not pretend to give any detailed
statements of the numbers engaged, but there are sufficient data for our
making a general estimate. Every free Greek was trained to military
duty and, owing to the incessant border wars between the different
states, few Greeks reached the age of manhood without having seen
some service. The muster roll of free Athenian citizens of an age fit
for military duty never exceeded 30,000 and at this epoch probably did
not amount to two-thirds of that number. Moreover, the men of the
poorer classes who served as light infantry were not so well trained
or equipped as the regular heavy infantry who fought in a solid mass
called a phalanx. Some detachments of the heavily armed troops would
be required to garrison the city itself and to man the various fortified
posts in the territory. It is therefore impossible to reckon the fully
equipped force that marched from Athens to Marathon, when the news
of the Persian landing arrived, at higher than 10,000 men.

With one exception the other Greeks held back from aiding them.
Sparta had promised assistance but religious scruples delayed the
march of the Spartan troops till the moon should have reached its full.
From one quarter only, and that from a most unexpected one, did
Athens receive aid at the moment of her great peril.

Some years before this time the little state of Plataea, being hard pressed by her powerful neighbor Thebes, had asked the protection of Athens and had owed to an Athenian army the rescue of her independence. Now, when it was made known over Greece that the Medes had come from the uttermost parts of the earth to destroy Athens, the brave Plataeans, unsolicited, marched with their whole force to assist the defense and to share the fortunes of their benefactors. The general levy of the Plataeans amounted to only 1,000 men. The reinforcement was numerically small, but this little column that joined the Athenian forces, and the gallant spirit of the men who composed it, must have made it of tenfold value to the Athenians. Its presence must have gone far to dispel the cheerless feeling of being deserted and friendless that the delay of the Spartans was calculated to create among the Athenian ranks.

This generous daring of their weak but truehearted ally was never forgotten at Athens. The Plataeans were made the civil fellow countrymen of the Athenians, except for the right of exercising certain political functions. From that time forth, in the solemn sacrifices at Athens, the public prayers were offered up for a joint blessing from Heaven upon the Athenians, and the Plataeans also. In truth, the whole career of Plataea and the friendship strong, even unto death, between her and Athens form one of the most affecting episodes in the history of antiquity. In the Peloponnesian War the Plataeans again were true to the Athenians against all risks and all calculations of self-interest; and the destruction of Plataea was the result.

After the junction of the column from Plataea, the Athenian commanders must have had under them about 11,000 fully armed and disciplined infantry, as well as some light infantry and a number of slaves who were also lightly armed. On this occasion the Athenians had no cavalry.

Contrasted with their own scanty forces, the Greek commanders saw stretched before them, along the shores of the bay, the tents and shipping of the varied nations who marched to do the bidding of the king of the Eastern world. The difficulty of finding transports and of securing provisions would form the only limit to the numbers of a Persian army. The total force that sailed under the satraps Datis and Artaphernes against Greece has been estimated at 100,000, nor is there any reason to suppose that this estimate is exaggerated. After largely deducting from this total, to allow for sailors, camp followers, and slaves, there must still have remained a land force of between 40,000 and 60,000, fearful odds for the Athenians to face. Nor could Greek generals then feel that confidence in the superior quality of their troops which after the Battle of Marathon animated Europeans in conflicts with Asiatics as, for instance, in the struggles between Greece and Persia, or when the Roman legions encountered the myriads of Mithridates and Tigranes in the Middle East. On the contrary, up to the day of Marathon, the Medes and Persians had more than once met Greek troops in Asia Minor, in Cyprus, in Egypt, and had beaten them. Nothing can be stronger than the expressions used by the early Greek writers respecting the terror the name of the Medes inspired, and the prostration of men's spirits before the apparently resistless career of Persian arms.

It is therefore not surprising that five of the ten Athenian generals shrank from the prospect of fighting a pitched battle against an enemy so superior in numbers and so formidable in military renown. Their own position on the heights was strong, and offered great advantages to a small force defending the narrow passages that led from the plain of Marathon to Athens. They deemed it foolhardy to descend into the plain to fight the invincible veterans of Cambyses and Cyrus. Moreover Sparta, the great war state of Greece, had promised help, though their religious observances had delayed their march. Would it not be wise to wait until the Spartans arrived, and to have the help of the best troops in Greece, before they exposed themselves to the shock of the dreadful Medes?

Specious as these reasons might appear, the other five generals were for speedier and bolder operations. And, fortunately for Athens and for the world, one of them was a man not only of the highest military genius but also of that energetic character which impresses its own will and ideas upon spirits feebler in conception.

Miltiades was the head of one of the noblest houses in Athens; he claimed to be descended from the great Achilles. In addition the family of Miltiades had acquired dominion of the Thracian Chersonese (the Gallipoli Peninsula), so that they were at the same time Athenian citizens and Thracian princes. About twenty-eight years before the Battle of Marathon, when his brother died in the Chersonese, Miltiades had been sent there as lord of the principality. In fact, our first knowledge of his career and character begins with his arrival on the peninsula. We find in the first act recorded of him proof of the same resolute and ruthless spirit that marked his mature age. His brother's authority had been shaken by war and revolt; Miltiades determined to rule more securely. On his arrival he remained in his house, as if mourning for his brother. The principal men of the Chersonese, hearing of this, assembled from all the towns and districts and went to see him on a visit of condolence. As soon as Miltiades had thus got them in his power, he made them all prisoners. He then asserted and maintained his own absolute authority in the peninsula, strengthening his power by marrying the daughter of the king of the neighboring Thracians.

When the Persian power was extended to the Hellespont (the ancient name for the Dardanelles) Miltiades, as prince of the Chersonese, yielded to King Darius' rule. Shortly thereafter, when Darius undertook an expedition against the Scythians, Miltiades was one of the numerous tributary rulers who led their contingents of men to serve in the Persian army. When Darius crossed the Danube and plunged into the wilds of the country that now is Russia, in vain pursuit of the ancestors of the modern Cossacks, Miltiades and the vassal Greeks of Asia Minor were left in charge of the bridge securing the line of retreat across the Danube. According to Herodotus, when Darius met with reverses in the Scythian wilderness, Miltiades proposed to his companions that they should destroy the bridge, and leave the Persian king and his army to perish by famine and the Scythian arrows. The rulers of the Asiatic Greek cities shrank from this bold and ruthless stroke against the Persian power, and Darius returned in safety. But it was known what advice Miltiades had given, and the vengeance of Darius was thenceforth specially directed against the man who had counseled such a deadly blow against his empire and his person.

The occupation of Persian forces in other quarters left Miltiades for some years after this in possession of the Chersonese, but it was precarious and interrupted. However, he availed himself of the opportunity his position gave him of obtaining the good will of his fellow countrymen at Athens. He conquered and placed under Athenian authority the island of Lemnos, to which Athens had ancient claims but which she had never previously been able to bring into subjection. At length, when the revolt of the Greek cities in Asia Minor had been suppressed and the Persian power again firmly established in that region, the Great King was ready to launch his armies and fleets against his enemies to the west. A strong squadron of Phoenician galleys was sent against the Chersonese. Miltiades, knowing that resistance was hopeless, loaded five galleys with all the treasure that he could collect, and sailed away for Athens. The Phoenicians chased him and captured one of his galleys, with his oldest son on board, but Miltiades managed to reach Athens, where he resumed his station as a free citizen of the Athenian commonwealth.

The Athenians at this time had recently expelled Hippias, the last of their tyrants. They were in the full glow of their newly recovered liberty and equality; and the constitutional changes of Cleisthenes had inflamed their republican zeal to the utmost. Miltiades had enemies at Athens and these, availing themselves of the state of popular feeling, brought him to trial for having been tyrant of the Chersonese. The charge did not necessarily imply any acts of cruelty or wrong to individuals, nor was it founded on any specific law. Actually, it appears to have been an episode in a struggle between two parties for political supremacy, with the enemies of Miltiades obviously hoping to capitalize on the Greek resentment of anyone who had exercised dominion over his fellowmen. The fact that Miltiades had been the arbitrary master of the Chersonese was undeniable, but the question the Athenians assembled in judgment must have tried was not whether he had been a tyrant, but rather if he deserved punishment as an Athenian citizen. The eminent service that he had done the state, in conquering Lemnos for it, pleaded strongly in his favor. The people refused to convict him. His acquittal was a decisive political victory for his party. When the coming invasion of the Persians was known, the people wisely elected him one of their generals.

Two other men of high eminence in history, though their renown was achieved at a later date than that of Miltiades, were also among the ten Athenian generals at Marathon. One was Themistocles, the future founder of the Athenian Navy, and the destined victor at Salamis. The other was Aristides "the Just," who afterward led the Athenian troops at Plataea, and whose integrity and popularity then acquired for his country the leadership of half the Greek city-states. It is not recorded what part either Themistocles or Aristides took in the debate of the council of war at Marathon. But from the character of Themistocles, his boldness, and his intuitive genius for extemporizing the best measures in every emergency, we may well believe that his vote was for prompt and decisive action. On the vote of Aristides it may be more difficult to speculate. His predilection for the Spartans may have made him wish to wait until they came up; but, though circumspect, he was neither timid as a soldier nor as a politician. The bold advice of Miltiades may have found in Aristides a willing, as most assuredly it found in him a candid, hearer.

Miltiades felt no hesitation as to the course the Athenians ought to pursue, and earnestly pressed his opinion on his brother generals. For several days they had stood in position, guarding the mountain passes to Athens, awaiting the arrival of the Spartans, while the Persians had also remained inactive, waiting for a signal that their friends in Athens were ready to receive them. As a practical politician Miltiades was well aware of the intrigues of those in the city who might open the gates to the invaders. Now the Persians were preparing to reembark a part of their force to make a dash on Athens, while the Greek army was absent at Marathon.

There were only two alternatives open to the Athenians. They could avoid battle and march back to Athens in order to arrive before the Persians landed, or they could attack the Persians while the enemy was in the process of dividing his army. A Greek assault would meet only the Persian covering force, remaining on the land to protect the re-embarkation. Furthermore, Miltiades was well acquainted with the organization of the Persian armies. He felt convinced of the superiority of the Greek troops if properly handled. He saw with the military eye of a great general the advantage a sudden surprise assault would have over the army now busily occupied in making preparations to embark for an attack on Athens by sea.

One officer in the council of war had not yet voted. This was Callimachus, the War Ruler. The votes of the generals were five and five, so that the voice of Callimachus would be decisive.

On that vote, in all human probability, the destiny of the nations of the world depended. Miltiades turned to him, and in simple, soldierly eloquence, the substance of which we may find faithfully reported in Herodotus, who had conversed with the veterans of Marathon, the great Athenian urged his countryman to vote for giving battle:

"It now rests with you, Callimachus, either to enslave Athens, or, by assuring her freedom, to win yourself an immortality of fame such as not even Harmodius and Aristogiton have acquired; for never, since the Athenians were a people, were they in such danger as they are in at this moment. If they bow the knee to these Medes, they are to be given up to Hippias, and you know what they then will have to suffer. But if Athens comes victorious out of this contest, she has it in her to become the first city of Greece. Your vote is to decide whether we are to join battle or not. If we do not bring on a battle presently, some factious intrigue will disunite the Athenians, and the city will be betrayed to the Medes. But if we fight, before there is anything rotten in the state of Athens, I believe that, provided the gods will give fair play and no favor, we are able to get the best of it in an engagement."

The vote of the brave War Ruler was gained; the council determined to fight immediately. There is no doubt that they made the correct decision. As the Greek army then prepared for battle, let us turn to a map of the Old World to test the comparative territorial resources of the two states whose soldiers were now about to come into conflict. The immense preponderance of the material power of the Persian king over that of the Athenian republic is more striking than any other similar contrast history can supply. It has been truly remarked that, in estimating mere areas, Attica, containing on its whole surface only about 700 square miles, shrinks into insignificance if compared with many a baronial fief of the Middle Ages, or many a colonial province of modern times. The territory of its antagonist, the Persian Empire, was bounded on the north by the Black Sea and the Caspian Sea, on the south by the waters of the Arabian Sea and the Persian Gulf. Westward it ran along the shore of the Mediterranean, including Libya, Egypt, and Thrace; eastward it stretched almost as far as the Indus River in modern Pakistan.

Nor could a European at the beginning of the fifth century B.C. look upon this huge accumulation of power beneath the scepter of a single Asiatic ruler with indifference; for, as has already been remarked, before Marathon was fought the prestige of success and of supposed superiority was on the side of the Asiatic against the European. Long before any trace can be found of the inhabitants of the rest of the world having emerged from barbarism, we can perceive that mighty and brilliant empires flourished on the Asiatic continent and in the valley of the Nile. They appear before us through the twilight of history, dim and indistinct, but massive and majestic, like mountains in the early dawn.

However, instead of the infinite variety and restless change that has characterized the institutions and fortunes of European states, a monotonous uniformity pervades the histories of nearly all Oriental empires, from the most ancient down to the most recent times. They are characterized by the rapidity of their early conquests, by the

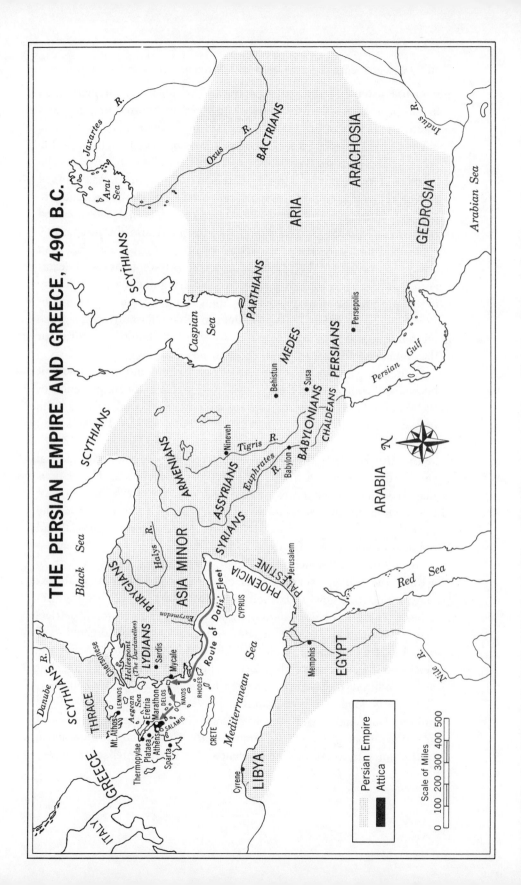

THE PERSIAN EMPIRE AND GREECE, 490 B.C.

Danube R.

Black Sea

SCYTHIANS

Jaxartes R.

Oxus R.

Aral Sea

SCYTHIANS

BACTRIANS

ARIA

ARACHOSIA

Indus R.

GEDROSIA

Arabian Sea

SCYTHIANS

Caspian Sea

PARTHIANS

MEDES

Behistun

PERSIANS

Persepolis

Persian Gulf

ARMENIANS

Nineveh

Tigris R.

Euphrates R.

Babylon

BABYLONIANS

CHALDEANS

Susa

PERSIANS

ASSYRIANS

SYRIANS

Halys R.

ASIA MINOR

PHRYGIANS

LYDIANS

Sardis

Mycale

Eurymedon

Route of Datis' Fleet

PHOENICIA

PALESTINE

Jerusalem

Red Sea

ARABIA

N

Nile R.

Memphis

EGYPT

CYPRUS

RHODES

CRETE

Mediterranean Sea

Cyrene

LIBYA

Chersonese

Hellespont (The Dardanelles)

LEMNOS

Mt. Athos

Aegean Sea

Eretria

Marathon

NAXOS

DELOS

Thermopylae

Plataea

Athens

SALAMIS

Sparta

THRACE

SCYTHIANS

GREECE

ITALY

Persian Empire

Attica

Scale of Miles

0   100 200 300 400 500

immense extent of their dominions, by an invariable degeneration in the princes of the royal house, and then by internal anarchy and insurrections that indicate and accelerate the decline and fall of these unwieldy fabrics of power. It is also a striking fact that most of the great Asiatic empires have in all ages been absolute despotisms. The practice of polygamy in almost all the nations of Inner Asia helped to support and continue this political system; fathers were ready to pay the same abject obedience to their sovereign that they exacted from their dependents. We should bear in mind also the inseparable connection between the state religion and all legislation that had always prevailed in the East. A powerful priesthood existed, exercising some check, though precarious and irregular, over the throne itself, grasping at all civil administration, claiming the supreme control of education, stereotyping the lines in which literature and science must move, and limiting the extent to which it should be lawful for the human mind to prosecute its inquiries.

With these general characteristics rightly felt and understood, it becomes a comparatively easy task to appreciate the importance of the repulse Greece gave to the arms of the East, and to judge the probable consequences to human civilization if the Persians had succeeded in bringing Europe under their yoke.

The Greeks, from their geographical position, formed the natural vanguard of European liberty against Persian ambition. The nations that dwelt in ancient times around and near the northern shores of the Mediterranean Sea were the first in Europe to receive from the East the rudiments of art and literature, and the germs of social and political organizations. Of these nations the Greeks, being the closest to Asia Minor, Phoenicia and Egypt, were among the very first to acquire the principles and habits of civilized life; and they also at once imparted a new and wholly original stamp on all that they received. Thus, in their religion, they received from foreign settlers many of their duties and their rites, but their own poets created their own beautiful mythology. No priestly caste ever existed in Greece. So, in their governments they lived long under hereditary kings, but never endured the permanent establishment of absolute monarchy. Their early kings were constitutional rulers, governing with defined prerogatives. And long before the Persian invasion the kingly form of government had given way in almost all the Greek states to republican institutions. In literature and science the Greek intellect followed no beaten track and acknowledged no limiting rules. Versatile, rest-less, enterprising, and self-confident, the Greeks presented the most striking contrast to the habitual submissiveness of the Orientals. Of all the Greeks, the Athenians exhibited these national characteristics in the strongest degree. This spirit of activity and daring had led them to join in the revolt of their fellow Greeks in Asia Minor. Now this same spirit nerved them to defy the wrath of King Darius, and to refuse to receive back at his bidding the tyrant they had some years before driven from their city.

The discoveries of comparatively recent years have confirmed by fresh evidence, and invested with fresh interest, the might of the Persian monarch who sent his troops to combat at Marathon. Scholars had long known of the existence of cuneiform (wedge-shaped) writ-ing but it is only within the last 130 years that archaeologists have been able to decipher the ancient inscriptions found at Persepolis, Susa, and at other places formerly ruled over by the Persian kings. The inscription, in three kinds of cuneiform writing, carved by order of King Darius on the sacred rock of Behistun near the western borders of Media furnished the key, as did the Rosetta Stone to the hiero-glyphic. Copied by Major Henry C. Rawlinson of the East India Com-pany, deciphered by him and other scholars, these records allow the Persian monarch to speak to us himself, telling us the names of the nations that obeyed him, the revolts that he suppressed, his victories, his piety, and his glory. These indisputable monuments of Persian fame confirm and even increase the feeling with which Herodotus inspires us of the vast power that Cyrus the Great founded, Cambyses increased, and Darius augmented.

With the exception of the Chinese Empire and India, all the great kingdoms which we know to have existed in ancient Asia, were in Darius' time, blended into the Persian. The Assyrians, the Syrians, the Babylonians, the Chaldeans, the Phoenicians, the nations of Palestine, the Armenians, the Bactrians, the Lydians, the Phrygians, the Parthians and the Medes all obeyed the Great King. The Medes stood next to the native Persians in honor, and the empire was frequently spoken of as that of the Medes and Persians. Egypt and Cyrene were Persian provinces. The Greek colonists in Asia Minor were Darius' subjects and their gallant but unsuccessful attempts to throw off the Persian yoke had only served to rivet it more strongly. Darius' Scythian war had brought about the subjugation of Thrace, so that from the Indus to the mouth of the Danube all was his.

We may imagine the wrath with which the lord of so many nations must have heard, eight years before the Battle of Marathon, that a strange nation toward the setting sun called the Athenians had dared to help his Greek rebels in Asia Minor against him and that they had plundered and burned the capital of one of his provinces. Before the burning of Sardis, Darius seems never to have heard of the existence of Athens, but his satraps in Asia Minor had for some time seen Athenian refugees at their provincial courts imploring assistance against their fellow countrymen. When Hippias was driven from Athens in 510 B.C., the banished tyrant had eventually gone to Sardis to obtain aid. There Hippias had pleaded with the satrap Artaphernes to reinstate him as the tyrant of Athens; he would then become a tributary vassal of Darius. When the Athenians learned of this, they sent envoys to Sardis to ask the Persians not to take up the quarrel of the Athenian refugees.

Artaphernes greeted the envoys with a command to take the hated Hippias back as their tyrant if they wished to live in safety. The Athenians resolved not to purchase peace at such a price, and rejected the satrap's terms. Then the Ionian Greeks who lived in Asia Minor implored the assistance of their European brethren to enable them to recover their independence from Persia. Athens and the city of Eretria alone consented. Twenty Athenian and five Eretrian galleys crossed the Aegean Sea and, by a bold and sudden march upon Sardis, the Athenians and their allies succeeded in capturing the capital city of the satrapy. They were pursued and defeated on their return to the coast. Athens took no further part in the Ionian war but the insult to the Persian power was speedily known throughout that empire, never to be forgiven nor forgotten.

In the emphatic simplicity of the narrative of Herodotus, the wrath of the Great King is thus described: "Now when it was told to King Darius that Sardis had been taken and burned by the Athenians and Ionians, he took small heed of the Ionians, well knowing who they were, and that their revolt would soon be put down; but he asked who, and what manner of men, the Athenians were. And when he had been told, he called for his bow; and, having taken it, and placed an arrow on the string, he let the arrow fly toward heaven; and as he shot it into the air, he said, 'Oh! Supreme God, grant me that I may avenge myself on the Athenians.' And when he had said this, he appointed one of his servants to say to him every day as he sat at meat, 'Sire, remember the Athenians.' "

Some years were occupied in the complete reduction of the Ionian revolt, but, when this was effected, Darius ordered his victorious forces to proceed to punish Athens and Eretria, and to conquer European Greece. In 492 B.C., a Persian army crossed the Hellespont and advanced through Thrace, while the navy followed along the coast. The attempt was a failure. The Persian army suffered heavy losses in fighting with the wild inhabitants of southern Thrace, and the fleet was wrecked in a storm off Mount Athos. A larger army was ordered to be collected, and requisitions were sent to the maritime cities of the Persian Empire for ships of war, and for transports to carry cavalry as well as infantry across the Aegean. In 490 B.C. the army destined for the invasion was assembled and a fleet of 600 ships collected. A Median general named Datis, and Artaphernes, the son of the former satrap of Sardis, were placed in joint command of the expedition. From the way in which the Greek writers speak of him, the real supreme authority was probably given to Datis alone. We know no details of the previous career of this officer, but there is every reason to believe that his ability and bravery had been proved by experience, or his Median birth would probably have prevented his being placed in such high command by Darius. Datis received instructions to complete the subjugation of Greece, and special orders were given him with regard to Athens and Eretria. He was to take these two cities, and he was to lead the inhabitants away captive, and bring them as slaves into the presence of the Great King.

Datis embarked his forces, coasted along the shores of Asia Minor, then turned westward to Naxos. Ten years before, the Naxians had successfully withstood a Persian siege, but they were now too terrified to offer any resistance. They fled to the hills while the enemy burned their town and laid waste their lands. Datis then sailed to Delos and from there onward toward Eretria. There the citizens repulsed the assaults of the Persians for six days, but on the seventh they were betrayed by two of their own chiefs, and the Persians occupied the city. The temples were burned in revenge for the burning of Sardis, and the inhabitants were carried away as captives.

Flushed with success, and with half his mission thus accomplished, Datis reembarked his soldiers and crossed from Eretria to the mainland of Greece. He encamped on the Attic coast at Marathon, drawing up his galleys on the shelving beach, as was the custom of the Mediterranean navies of antiquity. The conquered islands behind him served as places of deposit for his provisions and military stores. The position at Marathon seemed advantageous for two reasons. The level plain would provide excellent grazing for the Persian cavalry horses. If the Greeks moved to Marathon, Athens would then be exposed to a sudden attack by sea, which would be aided by sympathizers within the city.

Hippias, who accompanied Datis, and acted as the invaders' guide, had recommended Marathon as the best place for a landing for these very reasons. Probably Hippias was also influenced by the recollection that many years previously he, with his father Pisistratus, had crossed with an army from Eretria to Marathon and had won an easy victory over their Athenian enemies on that very plain, which had restored them to tyrannic power. The omen seemed cheering; the place was the same. For, although the majority of the Athenian citizens were filled with hatred for the foreign invader and were violently opposed to the restoration of their domestic tyrant, it is true that there was a faction in Athens, as at Eretria, who were willing to purchase a party triumph over their fellow citizens at the price of their country's ruin. Communications were opened between these men and the Persian camp, which might have led to a catastrophe like that of Eretria.

After waiting several days for the expected signal from their friends in Athens, the Persians decided to move on the city before the Spartans arrived on the battlefield, even though the message had not come. Datis therefore began to reembark part of his army; it was then that Miltiades persuaded Callimachus to engage in battle.

When Callimachus arrayed his men for action, he staked on the outcome of one battle, not only the fate of Athens, but that of all Greece. For, if Athens had fallen, no other Greek state except that of the Spartans would have had the courage to resist. The Spartans, though they might have died in their ranks to the last man, never could have successfully withstood the victorious Persians and the numerous Greek troops which would have been forced to march under the Persian satraps had they prevailed over Athens.

Nor was there any power to the westward of Greece that could have offered an effectual opposition to Persia had she conquered Greece and made that country a base for further military operations. Rome was at this time far too weak to resist a great invasion. She had just driven out her powerful kings; her infant commonwealth was reeling under the attacks of her neighbors from without, while fierce dissensions between the patricians and the plebeians divided her within. Nor were any of the other Italian states any match for Persia. Certainly none of the Greek colonies in Sicily or elsewhere could hope to exist freely when their parent states had perished. The Phoenician colony of Carthage, the future rival of Rome, would surely have become as submissive to the Persian power as the Phoenician cities themselves. If we turn to Spain or northern Europe, we find nothing at that period but savage tribes. Had Persia beaten Athens at Marathon, nothing would have stood in her way. The infant energies of Europe would have been trodden out beneath universal conquest. The history of the world, like the history of Asia, would have become for centuries a mere record of the rise and fall of despotic dynasties, of the incursions of barbarous hordes, and of the mental and moral prostration of millions beneath the diadem, the tiara, and the sword.

Great as the preponderance of the Persian over the Athenian power at that crisis seems to have been, it would be unjust to impute wild rashness to Callimachus, Miltiades, and those who voted with them in the Athenian council of war. For, if they were to engage in battle at all, their great opportunity lay before them. A large part of the Persian force, including probably most of the enemy's cavalry, was reembarking. Only the covering force, designed to protect the withdrawal and to hold the Athenians at Marathon while their city was being attacked, would be immediately ready for battle. A sudden, fierce assault delivered with complete surprise might well succeed, even though the covering force still far outnumbered the Greek army. Furthermore, the Greek generals well knew that, while their phalanx formation was practically irresistible to the front on level ground, it was vulnerable on the flanks, particularly to cavalry attacks. Yet here, on the plain below them, the Persians were taking most of their cavalry away for the dash on Athens.

In addition Miltiades, as has been mentioned, had seen service in the Persian armies. He knew from personal observation how many elements of weakness lurked beneath their imposing show of strength. He must certainly have advised Callimachus that the bulk of their troops no longer consisted of the hardy shepherds and mountaineers who had won Cyrus' battles, but that unwilling contingents from conquered nations now filled their ranks, fighting more from compulsion than from any zeal in the cause of their masters. The Greek generals certainly knew that a swift, unexpected assault upon such a varied mixture, many of whom could not speak one another's language, would heighten the chances of success.

Above all, the Athenian generals felt and trusted the enthusiasm of those they led. These soldiers had proved their valor in recent wars, and now they had a special reason for fighting gallantly. Hippias, the foe they hated most, was in the enemy's camp. They were now free men, fighting for a free commonwealth, liberty, and equality of civic right. Whatever treachery might lurk among some of the higher-born and wealthier Athenians, the rank and file were ready to do their utmost for the cause. With regard to future attacks from Asia, the generals might reasonably hope a victory would inspire all Greece to combine against the common foe. Then eventually the seeds of revolt and disunion in the Persian Empire might burst forth and paralyze its energies, thus leaving Greek independence secure.

With these hopes, Callimachus, on a September day, 490 B.C., gave the word for the Athenian army to prepare for battle. There were many local associations connected with those mountain heights which were calculated powerfully to excite the spirits of the men. Marathon itself was a region sacred to Hercules; the very plain on which they were to fight was the scene of exploits of their national hero, Theseus. These traditions were not merely cloudy myths or idle fictions, but matters of implicit, earnest faith to the men of that day. Many a fervent prayer arose from the Athenian ranks to the heroic spirits who, while on earth, had striven and suffered on that very spot and who were believed now to be heavenly powers, looking down with interest on their still-beloved country, and capable of interposing with super-human aid in its behalf.

According to old national custom the warriors of each tribe were arrayed together. Neighbor thus fought beside neighbor, friend by friend, competing with each other, while responsible for each other's safety. Callimachus led the right wing, for it was at that time a rule with the Athenians to give the place of honor to the War Ruler. Then came the tribes in order, with the Plataeans on the extreme left. The line consisted of the heavily armed spearmen only, for at that time the Greeks paid little attention to light infantry in a pitched battle, using them primarily in skirmishes or for pursuit of a de-

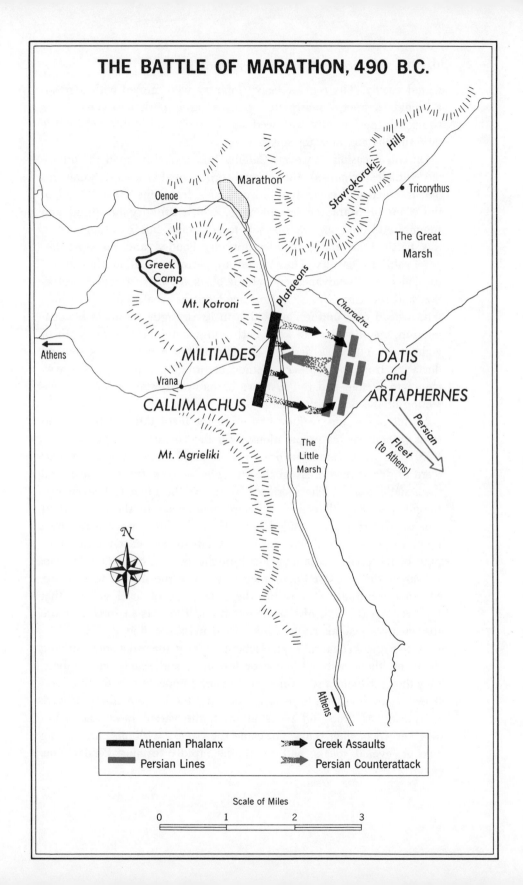

THE BATTLE OF MARATHON, 490 B.C.

Oenoe

Marathon

Stavrokoraki Hills

Tricorythus

The Great Marsh

Greek Camp

Mt. Kotroni

Plataeans

Charadra

Athens

MILTIADES

DATIS
and
ARTAPHERNES

Vrana

CALLIMACHUS

Persian Fleet
(to Athens)

Mt. Agrieliki

The Little Marsh

N

Athens

Athenian Phalanx

Greek Assaults

Persian Lines

Persian Counterattack

Scale of Miles

0   1   2   3

feated enemy. The regular heavy infantry were armed with a spear, a shield, helmet, breastplate, greaves, and a short sword. Thus equipped, they usually advanced slowly and steadily into action in a uniform phalanx of eight spears deep.

On this occasion, however, Callimachus, probably upon the advice of Miltiades, changed the normal order of battle, extending his line to equal and cover the entire Persian front line. At each end of the plain of Marathon are marshes, which are dry in spring and summer and then offer no obstacle to horsemen, but in autumn, when this battle took place, they are usually flooded and therefore impracticable for cavalry. Thus the terrain permitted Callimachus to rest the flanks of his advance on natural obstacles that provided protection and security. This extension involved the weakening of his line; but, instead of a uniform reduction in its strength, he made his center thin, enabling him to keep both wings with their usual depth of eight men. This was perhaps the first instance of a Greek general deviating from the ordinary method of bringing a phalanx of spearmen into action, and the first use of natural obstacles for the protection of the flanks of a large army.

In this order, and availing himself of the inequalities of the ground so as to conceal his preparations from the enemy until the last possible moment, Callimachus drew up the 11,000 infantry whose spears were to decide this crisis in the struggle between the European and the Asiatic worlds. The sacrifices by which the favor of heaven was sought, and its will consulted, were announced to show propitious omens. The trumpet sounded for action; the little army bore down upon the host of the foe. Instead of advancing at the usual slow pace of the phalanx, Callimachus brought his men on at double time. It was of the greatest importance to achieve the utmost in surprise, to cross as rapidly as possible the mile or so of level ground that lay between the foot of the mountain and the Persian forces, before the enemy's generals could deploy their masses in line.

"When the Persians," says Herodotus, "saw the Athenians running down on them, without horse or bowmen, and scanty in numbers, they thought them a set of madmen rushing upon certain destruction." They began, however, to receive them, and the Eastern chiefs arrayed, as quickly as time and place allowed, the varied races and tribes who served in their ranks. On came the Greeks with one unwavering line of leveled spears, and struck the rapidly forming Persian line.

The front rank of the Asiatics must have gone down to a man at the first shock, but they still strove by individual gallantry and weight of numbers to bear back the shallow line of Europeans.

On the wings the Greeks quickly routed the enemy opposing them, but in the center, where the native Persians fought, the Greeks were less successful. The Persians broke through the weakened Greek line and drove the Athenians back over the plain to their starting point, following closely in pursuit. At a trumpet signal the two victorious Greek wings wheeled inward and struck both flanks of the advancing Persians. Meanwhile the Greek center rallied and renewed the struggle.

Datis' veterans strove hard to keep their ground but, attacked from three sides at once, they fought at a tremendous disadvantage. Although not so well armed or well trained as the Greeks, the native Persians were not inferior to their opponents in personal courage or bodily activity. The struggle was long and obstinate. While their rear ranks poured an incessant shower of arrows over their heads, the foremost Persians kept rushing forward upon the projecting spears of the Greeks, striving to force lanes into the phalanx, to bring their shorter weapons into play.

At last the Persians broke and fled; the Greeks followed in pursuit to the water's edge, where the invaders sought to launch their galleys. The Athenians attacked and sought to set fire to the fleet. Here the Asiatics resisted desperately, and the principal loss sustained by the Greeks was in the assault on the ships. Here fell the brave War Ruler Callimachus. Seven galleys were secured; but the Persians succeeded in saving the rest.

Leaving Aristides and the troops of his tribe to guard the spoil, the Athenians then marched rapidly back across the mountains to Athens to protect the city. When the Persians arrived and saw the victors of Marathon arrayed on the heights above, they made no attempt to land. All hope of further conquest in Europe for the time was abandoned, and the baffled armada returned to the Asiatic coasts.

After the battle had been fought but while the dead bodies were yet on the ground, the promised reinforcement from Sparta arrived. Two thousand spearmen, starting immediately after the full moon, had marched the 150 miles between Athens and Sparta in the incredibly short time of three days. Though too late to share in the action, they requested to be allowed to behold the Medes. They continued their march to Marathon, gazed on the dead bodies of the invaders, then, praising the Athenians for their achievements, returned to Sparta.

The number of the Persian dead was said to be 6,400. The Athenian loss was given as 192; whether or not this includes the Plataeans is not known; but, as they fought on the Greek left flank where the phalanx was not broken, their losses cannot have been large. The apparent disproportion between the losses of the two armies is not surprising. As long as the heavily armed Greek spearmen stood firm in their ranks and while natural obstacles protected them from flank attacks, it was difficult to inflict heavy slaughter upon them by sword or lance. On the other hand the Persians, attacked from three sides, were forced to flee. Military history is full of examples of fleeing troops suffering disproportionately heavy casualities, but particularly was this true in ancient times. As soon as soldiers, armed with spear or sword, turned their backs on an enemy they were utterly defenseless.

This decisive defeat, however, did not stop the Persian drive toward the West. Ten years later Xerxes, King of Persia, the son of Darius, led a third expedition into Greece. The land and naval battles of Thermopylae, Salamis, and Plataea that followed also became world famous. They resulted in greater loss of life; the Persians penetrated deeper into Greece; Athens was pillaged and set afire; two years passed before the Persians were defeated and their invasions of Greece ended forever. But, mighty and momentous as these battles were, they do not rank with Marathon in importance. They only confirmed the Greek superiority in battle that had already been asserted at Marathon. It was the critical battle that broke forever the legend of Persian invincibility which had previously paralyzed men's minds. It generated among the Greeks the spirit that later defeated Xerxes and resulted in securing for mankind the intellectual treasures of Athens, the growth of free institutions, the liberal enlightenment of the Western world, and the gradual ascendancy for many ages of the great principles of European civilization.

Notes on the Battle of Marathon

Herodotus seems to have assumed that the Athenian command organization in 490 B.C. was somewhat similar to that of the time in which he wrote, which was several years later. However, more recent research indicates that he was mistaken in assuming that the various generals took command of the army on successive days and that Miltiades waited until his turn came before beginning the battle. At the time of Marathon, the Polemarch, or War Ruler, was the supreme commander, although certain decisions were made by a vote of the generals, each of whom had an equal vote with the Polemarch. Therefore this account has been written to reflect the fact that Callimachus was the commanding general and that Miltiades was the strongest and most capable of the ten generals.

The fact that Herodotus makes no mention of the Persian cavalry, which was excellent, and rightly feared by the Greeks, has also been explained by recent research, which shows that the greater part of the cavalry was probably reembarking for the dash on Athens. The Greek delay in opening the battle, which Herodotus attributes to the fact that Miltiades was waiting for his turn to command the army, was due to different reasons. As long as the Greeks remained on the mountain heights, guarding the passes to Athens, they could wait for the arrival of the Spartans. They thus avoided having to fight the entire Persian army, including the cavalry. However, when Callimachus and Miltiades saw a large part of their enemy reembarking, they could not afford to throw away this opportunity of attacking the Persians while they were thus engaged, and while the major portion of the cavalry would be loading onto the ships.

Synopsis of Events Between the Battle of Marathon, 490 B.C., and the Defeat of the Athenians at Syracuse, 413 B.C.

490–486. All Asia is filled with the preparations by King Darius for a new expedition against Greece.

486. Egypt revolts against the Persians and delays the expedition against Greece.

485. Darius dies and Xerxes, his son, becomes King of Persia.

484. The Persians suppress the Egyptian revolt.

480. Xerxes invades Greece. The Persians attack the pass at Thermopylae, heroically defended by 1,400 Greeks, of whom 300 were Spartans. The Athenians abandon Attica; Athens is looted and burned. The Greeks win the great naval victory of Salamis. Xerxes returns to Asia, leaving Mardonius to carry on the war in Greece.

479.   Mardonius and his army are destroyed by the Greeks at the Battle of Plataea, ending the Persian invasion. The Greeks land in Asia Minor and defeat a Persian force at Mycale.

478.   The Delian League is formed, with Athens as its leader, to expel the Persians from the islands in the Aegean Sea, and to free the Greek colonies in Asia Minor.

466.   Cimon defeats the Persians at the Eurymedon, the final battle to liberate the Greeks in Asia Minor from Persian rule. In succeeding years Athens, under the leadership of Pericles, converts the Delian League into an Athenian Empire. Fear of the growth of Athenian power provokes the opposition of Sparta, Corinth, Thebes, and other Greek cities.

431.   The great Peloponnesian War begins, primarily a contest between sea power and land forces, between the maritime empire of Athens and the league of states headed by Sparta. Strong Spartan armies yearly invade and ravage Attica, but the people take refuge in Athens and behind the "long walls" connecting the city with the harbor of Piraeus; food supplies are brought to them by ship.

430.   Athens is visited by a pestilence, which sweeps off large numbers of her population.

429.   The death of Pericles.

427.   Plataea is destroyed by Sparta and Thebes.

425.   The Athenians under Cleon and Demosthenes gain a victory at Sphacteria, an island off the southwestern coast of Greece.

424–422.   The Spartan general Brasidas leads an expedition to Thrace, and conquers many of the most valuable Athenian possessions in that region. Brasidas and Cleon are both killed in battle.

421.   The Peace of Nicias is negotiated to last for fifty years, but sporadic fighting continues.

418.   Sparta wins a crushing victory at the Battle of Mantinea.

415.   The Athenians send an expedition to conquer Sicily.

2

Defeat of the Athenians at Syracuse, 415–413 B.C.

The Romans knew not, and could not know, how deeply the great-
ness of their own posterity, and the fate of the whole Western world,
were involved in the destruction of the fleet of Athens in the harbor of
Syracuse. Had that great expedition proved victorious, the energies of
Greece during the next eventful century would have found their field
in the West no less than in the East; Greece, and not Rome, might
have conquered Carthage; Greek instead of Latin might have been at
this day the principal element of the language of Spain, of France,
and of Italy; and the laws of Athens, rather than of Rome, might be the
foundation of the law of the civilized world.

—ARNOLD

FEW CITIES have undergone more memorable sieges during ancient and
medieval times than has the city of Syracuse. Athenian, Carthaginian,
Roman, Saracen, Byzantine, and Norman have attacked her walls; and
the resistance which she successfully opposed to some of her early
assailants was of the greatest importance, not only to the generations
then alive, but also to the later development of civilization. Her triumphant repulse of the great Athenian expedition against her was of widespread and enduring importance. It formed a decisive epoch in the
strife for universal empire in which all the great states of antiquity successively engaged.

At Marathon we saw Athens struggling for self-preservation against
the invading armies of the East. At Syracuse she appears as the ambitious and oppressive invader of others. In the intervening years she had
rapidly grown into a conquering and dominant state, the chief of
a thousand tributary cities, and the mistress of the most powerful navy
that the Mediterranean had yet beheld. In 415 B.C. Athens had decided

23

to embark on an expedition against the city of Syracuse in Sicily, staking the flower of her forces and the accumulated fruits of seventy years of glory on one bold throw for the dominion of the Western world. By the late spring of 414 B.C. the venture appeared to have every chance of success. The Athenian navy was threatening the coast of Syracuse. An Athenian army had defeated the native troops and begun the investment of the city. A blockading wall, which would cut the Syracusans off from all aid from the interior of Sicily, was being rapidly constructed. When completed, the city would be left to the mercy of the Athenian generals.

As Napoleon from Mont Cœur de Lion pointed to St. Jean d'Acre and told his staff that the capture of that town would decide his destiny and would change the fate of the world, so the Athenian officers must have looked down on Syracuse, and felt that with its fall all the known powers of the earth would fall beneath them. Yet, knowing what a supreme effort had been required to send this force, they must have felt also that, if repulsed there, Athens must pause forever in her career of conquest, and sink from an imperial republic into a ruined and subservient community.

After the successful repulse of the Persian invaders in 479 B.C., a confederacy known as the Delian League had been formed, with Athens as its leader. Its announced purposes were to expel the Persians from the islands in the Aegean Sea and to free the Greek colonies in Asia Minor. At first the league had a general assembly that met on the island of Delos and controlled league policy, but it soon became dominated by Athens, who used the league as a means of increasing her maritime power. She protected the smaller cities from piracy and the Persian power, but she exacted in return implicit obedience to herself. She claimed and enforced the right to tax at her discretion, and proudly refused to be accountable for expending supplies. Objections against her tax assessments were treated as disloyalty, and refusal to pay was promptly punished as revolt. Permitting and encouraging her subject allies to furnish all their contingents in money, instead of part consisting of ships and men, the sovereign republic gained the double object of training her own citizens by constant and well-paid service in her fleets, while her confederates lost their skill and discipline by inaction, and became more and more passive and powerless under her yoke. Their towns were often dismantled, while the imperial city herself was fortified with the greatest care. The accumulated revenues from her tributaries served to strengthen and adorn her docks, her arsenals, her theaters, and her shrines, and to array her in that architectural magnificence whose ruins still bear witness to the glory of her age and people.

Many great powers that have acquired supremacy over other nations have ruled them selfishly and oppressively, but few openly acknowledged their system of doing so with the candor the Athenians displayed. They frankly admitted that they trusted solely to force to uphold their empire. To be safe, they must be powerful; and to be powerful, they must coerce their neighbors. They never dreamed of sharing with their dependents, but monopolized every command and all political and judicial power. But they exposed themselves to every risk with unflinching gallantry, embarked readily on every ambitious scheme, and never allowed difficulty or disaster to shake their purpose of acquiring unbounded empire for their country. The thirty thousand citizens who made up the sovereign republic devoted themselves almost exclusively to military occupations and to those brilliant sciences and arts in which Athens had already reached such heights of intellectual splendor.

Her great political dramatist speaks of the Athenian Empire as including a thousand states. The language of the stage must not be taken literally, but the number of the dependencies of Athens was undoubtedly very great. With only a few exceptions, all the islands of the Aegean and all the Greek cities, which in that age fringed the coasts of Asia Minor, the Hellespont and Thrace, paid tribute to Athens and implicitly obeyed her orders. The Aegean Sea was an Attic lake. Westward of Greece her influence, though strong, was not equally predominant. She had colonies and allies among the wealthy and populous Greek settlements in Sicily and south Italy, but she had no organized system of confederates in those regions, and her galleys brought her no tribute from the Western seas. The extension of her empire over Sicily was one of the favorite projects of her ambitious orators and generals.

When, in 431 B.C., the Peloponnesian War began and a league was formed of five-sixths of the continental Greeks, all animated by jealousy and hatred of Athens, when Spartan armies poured into Athenian territory and laid it waste to the city walls, the general opinion was that the city would be reduced in two or three years at the most. However, her strong fortifications and the "long walls" connecting with the harbor of Piraeus, gave her, in those ages, almost all the advantages of an insular position. Athens' leader, Pericles, had made her trust to her empire of the seas. Every Athenian in those days was a practiced seaman. Indeed, so small a state could only have acquired such naval dominion by zealously training all its sons to service in its fleets. In order to man the numerous galleys she sent out, she necessarily employed large numbers of hired seamen and slaves at the oars, but the staple of the crews was Athenian and all posts of command were held by native citizens. It was by reminding them of this, of their long practice in seamanship and the certain superiority their discipline gave them, that their great minister Pericles encouraged them to resist the combined power of Sparta and her allies. He taught them that Athens might thus reap the fruit of her zealous devotion to maritime affairs. He taught that the rule of the sea gave her dominion over land beyond the waves, safe from the Spartans who might harass Attica, but could not subdue the capital city.

Athens accepted the war rather than descend from her pride of place, and though the awful visitation of the plague came upon her and swept away more of her citizens than the enemy laid low, including the trusted leader Pericles, she held her own gallantly against her enemies. Though the enemy armies in irresistible strength laid waste every spring her cornlands, her vineyards, and her olive groves with fire and sword, she retaliated on their coast with her fleets. Some of her subject allies revolted, but these were in general sternly and promptly quelled. The genius of one enemy general, Brasidas, indeed inflicted heavy blows on her power in Thrace that she was unable to remedy. When he and the Athenian leader Cleon fell in battle in the tenth year of the war, both sides grew weary of the conflict. In 421 B.C. a truce for fifty years was concluded. The Peace of Nicias, named for its author, was ill kept. Hostilities continued in many parts of Greece, but Athenian territory was protected from the ravages of enemies, and Athens was enabled to rebuild her treasury. So also, as a few years passed, the havoc the pestilence and the sword had made was repaired. By 415 B.C. Athens was full of bold and restless spirits who longed for some distant field where they might distinguish themselves. These men concluded that, when Sparta had wasted their territory, she had done her worst. The fact that it was always in their enemy's power to do so seemed a strong reason for seeking to enlarge the overseas dominion of Athens.

The West was now the quarter toward which the thoughts of every

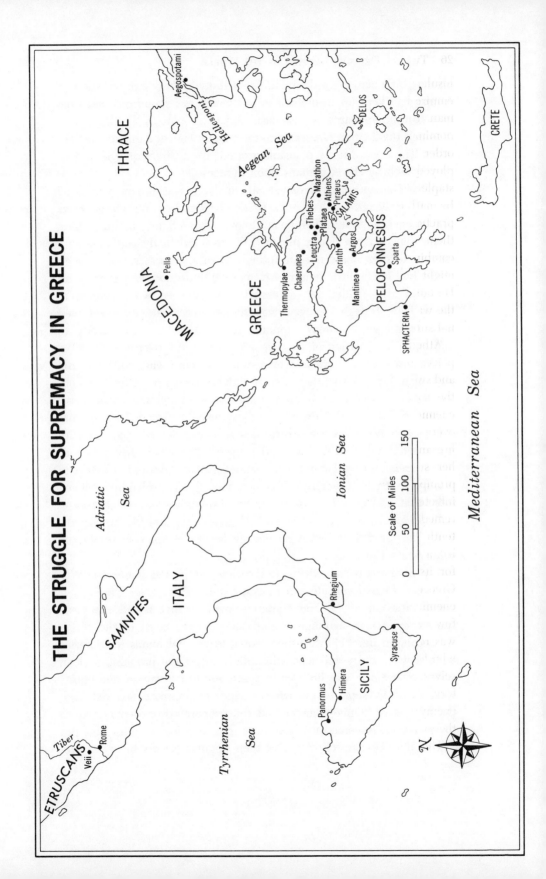

THE STRUGGLE FOR SUPREMACY IN GREECE

THRACE

Hellespont

Agospotami

Aegean Sea

DELOS

MACEDONIA

Pella

GREECE

Thermopylae

Chaeronea

Thebes

Marathon

Plataea

Athens

Leuctra

Piraeus

SALAMIS

Corinth

Argos

PELOPONNESUS

Mantinea

Sparta

SPHACTERIA

CRETE

ITALY

ETRUSCANS

Tiber

Rome

Veii

SAMNITES

Adriatic Sea

Ionian Sea

Rhegium

Tyrrhenian Sea

SICILY

Panormus

Himera

Syracuse

Mediterranean Sea

Scale of Miles

0   50   100   150

N

aspiring Athenian were directed. From the very beginning of the war Athens had kept up an interest in Sicily, and her squadrons had from time to time appeared on its coasts and taken part in the dissensions in which the Sicilian Greeks were universally engaged one against another. There were fairly plausible grounds for a direct quarrel and an open attack by the Athenians upon Syracuse.

With the capture of Syracuse, all Sicily, it was hoped, would be secured. Italy and Carthage were then to be attacked. With large levies of mercenaries, Athens then meant to overwhelm Sparta and her allies. There can be little doubt that, if Syracuse and Sicily could be conquered, neither Rome nor any other Italian state was strong enough at the end of the fifth century B.C. to have withstood an attack by an Athenian army, aided by mercenaries and flushed with triumph in Sicily. The strategic concept was sound, and the war could well have ended with Athens supreme in the Mediterranean, ready to undertake an invasion of the Persian Empire at its leisure.

The force which Athens sent against Syracuse was worthy of the state that formed such projects of universal empire. The fleet consisted of 134 galleys and a large number of supply ships and boats. A powerful army of 5,100 of the best heavily armed infantry that Athens and her allies could furnish was sent on board, together with a smaller number of archers and slingers. The whole force, including laborers and workmen, totaled about 27,000. Although deficient in cavalry strength, it was by far the most costly and splendid Hellenic force that had ever been sent out by a single city up to that time, with private as well as public wealth eagerly lavished on the expedition. The fated fleet began its voyage for the Sicilian shores in the summer of 415 B.C.

The Syracusans themselves at the time of the Peloponnesian War were a bold and turbulent democracy, tyrannizing over the weaker Greek cities in Sicily, and trying to gain in that island the same supremacy Athens maintained along the eastern coast of the Mediterranean. In numbers they were equal to the Athenians but inferior to them in military and naval discipline. When the probability of an Athenian invasion was first publicly discussed at Syracuse, and efforts were made by some of the wiser citizens to improve their defenses, the rumors of coming danger and the proposals for preparations to meet it were received by the mass of the citizens with scornful incredulity. The speech of one of their popular orators has been preserved for us by Thucydides. It provides an excellent example of the arguments that have been used over the centuries by many well-meaning people to oppose the necessity of providing adequate forces for national defense. The Syracusan orator dismissed with scorn the visionary terrors that he claimed a set of designing men were striving to excite, in order to get power and influence in their own hands. He argued that Athens would not be likely to attack them and that, even if she did come, her destruction would be inevitable. He contended that the Athenians could not possibly cross the sea with adequate supplies and a force large enough to undertake such an enormous operation as the conquest of Syracuse and Sicily.

Such assertions pleased the Syracusan assembly; but the invaders did come, and if they had promptly attacked, the Syracusans would surely have lost their city. The Athenians, however, had entrusted command of their expedition to three generals, with equal authority: Nicias, a feeble and vacillating individual who had opposed the venture; Alcibiades, an ambitious, scheming politician who had been its chief advocate; and Lamachus, an honest, straightforward soldier. At a council of war Lamachus had proposed an immediate attack, but it was decided, before undertaking such an operation, that efforts should be made in Sicily to gain friends among the other cities and foment rebellion against Syracuse. These efforts proved fruitless; and while they were in progress, Alcibiades' enemies had him recalled to Athens to stand trial for his life. With most of his political friends absent on the great expedition, Alcibiades knew that death awaited him; he managed to escape, and fled to Sparta. Eventually Nicias and Lamachus did land and win a victory, but so much time had been wasted that winter came upon them. They sailed away to wait until spring. Belatedly the people of Syracuse began to strengthen their walls and attend to the training and equipment of their forces.

During this lull in operations Nicias sent a galley back to Athens asking for money and for cavalry reinforcements, and Alcibiades reached Sparta, furious and thirsting for revenge against his native city. A skillful soldier, a talented diplomat, and a gifted orator, Alcibiades was one of the most complete examples of genius without principle that history has ever produced. When envoys arrived from Syracuse, Alcibiades joined them in urging the Spartans to send immediate assistance to Syracuse. It was his speech to the Spartan assembly that persuaded them to take action. He outlined in detail the plans that he himself had prepared in Athens to conquer Syracuse and Sicily, subdue Italy and attack Carthage. Then he described how Athens planned to descend with a large force of Greeks and hired mercenaries on Sparta and her allies.

Alcibiades urged the Spartans to send galleys to Sicily, with troops on board who would be able to row the ships and serve as heavy infantry the moment they landed. Most important of all, he recommended that they send a Spartan to take over the Sicilian command, to discipline the forces already at hand, and to encourage others to join. The renegade then urged the Spartans to carry on the war more openly in Greece itself, to march their armies into Attica and take up a permanent fortified position in that country.

Convinced that they were listening to the one man who, above all others, knew the plans of their enemies, the Spartans voted to take immediate action, and appointed Gylippus to be the commanding general in Sicily. His country gave him neither men nor money, but she gave him her authority and the influence of her name; the Corinthians and others began to equip a squadron to act under him for the rescue of Sicily. As soon as a few galleys were ready, he hurried with them to the coast of Italy. En route he received reports that Syracuse was already completely invested, but kept on in the hope that he could at least save Italy from the Athenians.

The ancient city of Syracuse extended across a knob of land that projects into the sea on the eastern coast of Sicily, between the Bay of Thapsus to the north and the Great Harbor of the city to the south. A small island or peninsula (for such it was soon rendered) lies at the southeastern extremity of this knob of land. It stretches almost entirely across the mouth of the Great Harbor, separating it from the Little Harbor. This island was the site of the original settlement of the first Greek colonists from Corinth, who founded Syracuse in 734 B.C. By the fifth century B.C., the growing wealth and population of the Syracusans had led them to occupy and include within their city walls portion after portion of the mainland lying north of their little isle, so that at the time of the Athenian expedition a large section of the land between the bay and the harbor was occupied and fortified. This section of land, which constituted the major portion of the city, was called the Achradina.

From the center of the Achradina westward toward the interior of Sicily, the land slopes upward from the sea to form a plateau called Epipolae. The fortified city wall crossed the eastern end of this plateau, denying direct access to the city. However the plateau of Epipolae continues westward for about three miles, rising to greater heights to dominate the city. Its northern and southern flanks were steep and precipitous, making an approach to the top of the plateau very difficult from either direction. But at the far western end, at Euryalus, where the plateau terminates in a long, narrow ridge, there was an entrance that was to prove useful to both sides during the siege.

South of the commanding ground of Epipolae and west of the Great Harbor is the Plain of Anapus and the river of the same name. It was in the southern part of this plain that the Athenians, in the autumn of 415 B.C., had made their first landing, then sailed away, not to return again until late the following spring.

In the spring of 414 B.C., the Athenians had returned to attack the city. The Syracusans had, during the winter, built an additional wall across Epipolae but neglected to fortify Euryalus. Landing at Leon on the northern coast, the Athenians seized Euryalus and advanced across Epipolae, defeating the Syracusans and driving them behind their walls. Promptly the invaders began the investment, building a central fort called the "Circle." From this they started construction of walls to north and south. To prevent their city from being completely cut off from all aid, the Syracusans began construction of a counterwall west of Temenites, which the Athenians rushed and destroyed, meanwhile wrecking the pipes that carried drinking water to the city. A second counterwall farther south, near the Great Harbor, met the same fate, although in the battle leading to its destruction the Athenian general Lamachus was killed, an irreparable loss to the besiegers, for it left Nicias in sole command. However the land investment was almost complete, and the Athenian fleet had sailed around into the Great Harbor itself.

So utterly desperate had the state of Syracuse seemingly become, that an assembly of the citizens was actually convened, and they were discussing the terms on which they should offer to capitulate when a galley was seen dashing into the Great Harbor, making her way toward the town with all the speed her rowers could supply. From her shunning the part of the harbor where the Athenian fleet lay and making straight for the Syracusan side, it was clear that she was a friend. She touched the beach, and a Corinthian captain springing on shore was eagerly conducted to the people's assembly.

The sight of actual help, and the promise of more, revived the drooping spirits of the Syracusans. They felt that they were not left alone to perish, and the news that a Spartan was coming to command them strengthened their resolution to continue to resist. Gylippus was already near the city. He had learned that the first reports which had reached him of the condition of the siege of Syracuse were exaggerated, that the city was not completely invested, and that it was still possible for a relieving army to effect an entrance. Gylippus landed on the northern coast of Sicily and there began to collect from the Greek cities an army, of which the regular troops he had brought with him formed the nucleus. Such was the influence of the name of Sparta, and so vigorous were his own activities, that he succeeded in raising a force of 2,000 heavily armed infantry and a large number of irregular troops. Nicias made no attempt to counteract his operations nor, when Gylippus marched toward Syracuse, did the Athenian commander make any effort to stop him. In fact, he even left Euryalus unguarded so that Gylippus was able to use that same route to ascend Epipolae and march into the besieged town. Joining forces with the Syracusans, Gylippus began construction of a third counterwall from Syracuse westward across Epipolae. When completed it blocked the Athenian wall just north of the "Circle," thus preventing investment of the city. Nicias made no real effort to break the counterwall, but instead relied more heavily than ever for supplies upon the Athenian fleet, and established a large naval base at Plemmyrium at the southern entrance to the Great Harbor. Summer was now over; the tables had been almost completely turned. Nicias complained that on land the besiegers had become the besieged.

The attention of all Greece was now fixed on Syracuse, and every enemy of Athens felt the importance of the opportunity now offered of checking her ambition and perhaps of striking a deadly blow at her power. Large reinforcements from Corinth and other Greek cities reached Syracuse, while the baffled and dispirited Athenian general earnestly asked that he be recalled, and represented the further prosecution of the siege with the forces available as hopeless.

But Athens had made it a maxim never to let difficulty or disaster drive her back from any enterprise once undertaken, so long as she possessed the means of making any effort, however desperate. She decided to send a second expedition to Syracuse, although her enemies near home had now renewed open warfare against her, and by occupying her territory had severely distressed her people and were pressing her with almost all the hardships of an actual siege. She

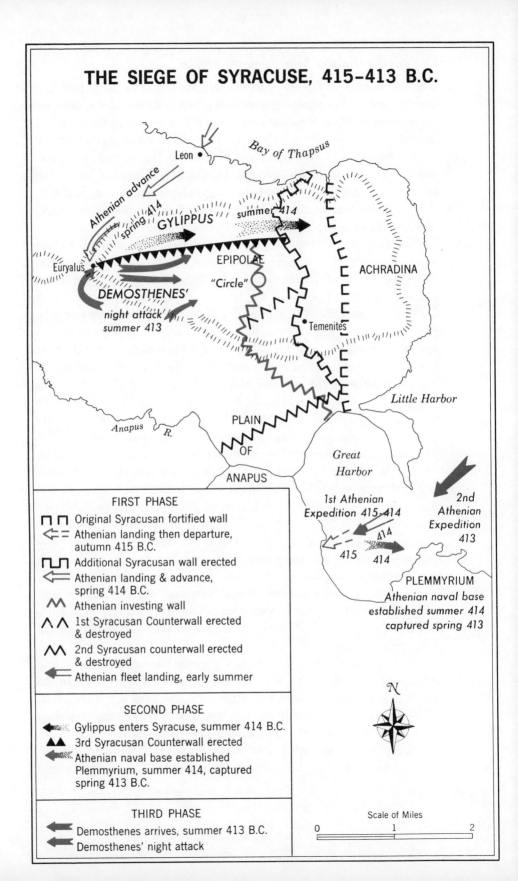

THE SIEGE OF SYRACUSE, 415–413 B.C.

Leon

Bay of Thapsus

Athenian advance

spring 414

summer 414

GYLIPPUS

Euryalus

EPIPOLAE

ACHRADINA

"Circle"

DEMOSTHENES'

night attack
summer 413

Temenites

Little Harbor

PLAIN

Anapus R.

OF

*Great
Harbor*

ANAPUS

1st Athenian
Expedition 415–414

2nd
Athenian
Expedition
413

414

415

414

PLEMMYRIUM
*Athenian naval base
established summer 414
captured spring 413*

FIRST PHASE

⊓ ⊓ Original Syracusan fortified wall

⇐= Athenian landing then departure, autumn 415 B.C.

⊓⊔ Additional Syracusan wall erected

⇦ Athenian landing & advance, spring 414 B.C.

ᴧᴧ Athenian investing wall

∧∧ 1st Syracusan Counterwall erected & destroyed

ᴧᴧ 2nd Syracusan counterwall erected & destroyed

⬅ Athenian fleet landing, early summer

SECOND PHASE

◄▪▪ Gylippus enters Syracuse, summer 414 B.C.

▲▲▲ 3rd Syracusan Counterwall erected

◄▪▪ Athenian naval base established Plemmyrium, summer 414, captured spring 413 B.C.

THIRD PHASE

⬅ Demosthenes arrives, summer 413 B.C.

⬅ Demosthenes' night attack

N

Scale of Miles

0   1   2

still was mistress of the sea, and she sent forth another large fleet and another army, thus draining almost the last reserves of her military population, to try if Syracuse could not yet be won and the honor of Athenian arms preserved. Hers was indeed a spirit that might be broken but would never bend. At the head of the second expedition she wisely placed her best general, Demosthenes. He was one of the most distinguished officers that the long Peloponnesian War had produced; if he had originally held the Sicilian command, he surely would soon have brought Syracuse to submission.

The fame of Demosthenes the general has been dimmed by the superior luster of his great countryman, Demosthenes the orator. When the name of Demosthenes is mentioned, it is the latter alone that is thought of. The soldier has found no biographer. Yet of the long list of great men the Athenian republic produced, there are few who deserve to stand higher than this brave though finally unsuccessful leader of her fleets and armies in the Peloponnesian War. His most celebrated exploit had been the capture of the Spartan forces on the isle of Sphacteria, the severest blow dealt to Sparta throughout the war and the principal reason for her agreeing to make a truce with Athens. Demosthenes was as honorably unknown in the war of party politics at Athens as he was eminent in the war against her enemies. We read of no intrigues of his on either the aristocratic or the democratic side. His private character was free from any of the stains which polluted that of Alcibiades. On all these points the silence of the comic dramatist is decisive evidence in his favor. He had also the moral courage to do his duty to his country, irrespective of any odium that he himself might incur, and was unhampered by any petty jealousy of those who were associated with him in command. There are few men named in ancient history of whom posterity would gladly know more, or with whom we sympathize more deeply in the calamities that befell them, than Demosthenes who in the spring of 413 B.C. left Piraeus at the head of the second Athenian expedition against Sicily.

His arrival was critically timed; Gylippus had opened the spring offensive by attacking the Athenians by sea as well as by land. In the first battle he had captured the Athenian naval base at Plemmyrium, while in the second battle he had actually defeated the Athenian navy itself in its own element, winning for Syracuse the initiative at sea. Gylippus was preparing to follow up his advantage by fresh attacks on the Athenians when the arrival of Demosthenes completely changed the situation and restored the superiority to the invaders. With seventy-three war galleys in the highest state of efficiency and brilliantly equipped, with a force of 5,000 picked men of the regular infantry of Athens and her allies, and a still larger number of archers and slingers, totaling about 15,000 men on board, Demosthenes entered the Great Harbor. His arrival dramatically changed the newborn hopes of the Syracusans and their confederates into the deepest consternation. The resources of Athens seemed inexhaustible, and resistance to her hopeless. They had been told that she was reduced to the last extremities and that her territory was occupied by an enemy, yet here they saw her sending forth a second armament almost as formidable as the first.

With the intuitive decision of a great commander, Demosthenes at once saw that the possession of Epipolae was the key to the capture of Syracuse. He resolved to make a prompt and vigorous attempt to recover that position while his force was unimpaired and while the consternation its arrival had produced was at its height. Promptly clearing his enemy from the Plain of Anapus, Demosthenes launched an assault upon the third counterwall across Epipolae. Could he succeed in storming this outwork and reestablishing the Athenian troops on the plateau, he might fairly hope to complete the investment of the city and become the conqueror of Syracuse.

Because the first attack on the counterwall failed, when darkness set in, Demosthenes reformed his army, issued five days' provisions to each soldier, and led them westward along the southern flank of Epipolae into the interior of Sicily. He too had recognized the pre-eminent importance of Euryalus. When the head of the column reached that point, he wheeled to the right and sent his men rapidly upward along the paths that wind along the face of the cliff. His night attack achieved complete surprise. The Syracusan outpost was captured, and the Athenians marched eagerly onward down the slope toward the town, routing some detachments that were posted along the plateau.

All at first favored the attack; the Syracusans abandoned the third counterwall, which was seized by other Athenian troops advancing northward from the Plain of Anapus, who began to dismantle it. In vain Gylippus brought reinforcements to check the assault. The Athenians broke them and drove them back, continuing to press hotly forward in the full confidence of victory, eager to achieve complete success. Amid the general confusion that is often common to night fighting, one body of defending infantry stood firm. One brigade of Greek infantry, undismayed by the current of flight around them, repulsed the advancing Athenians, then counterattacked. This was the crisis of the battle. The Athenian van, disorganized by its own previous successes and yielding to the unexpected charge thus made by troops in perfect order, was driven back in confusion upon the other divisions of the army that still continued to press forward.

When once the tide was thus turned, the Syracusans passed rapidly from the extreme of panic to the extreme of vengeful daring, and with all their forces they now attacked the retreating Athenians. In vain did the officers of the latter strive to reform their lines. Amid the din and shouting of the fight, and the confusion inseparable upon a night engagement, especially one where many thousands fought in a narrow and confined space, reorganization was impossible. Although many units still fought on desperately, wherever the moonlight showed them a foe, they fought without direction or control. Not infrequently, amid the chaos, Athenian troops assailed each other. Keeping their ranks close, the Syracusans and their allies pressed on against the disorganized masses of the besiegers. At length they drove them with heavy slaughter over the cliffs, which an hour or two before they had scaled full of hope and apparently certain of success.

This defeat was decisive; the Athenians afterward struggled only to protect themselves from the vengeance of their enemies. A series of sea fights followed in which the Athenian galleys were destroyed or eventually captured. The mariners and soldiers who escaped death in these disastrous engagements, and in a vain attempt to retreat into the interior of the island, became prisoners of war. Nicias and Demosthenes were put to death in cold blood. Their men either perished miserably in the Syracusan dungeons or were sold into slavery.

All danger from Athens to the independent nations of the West was now and forever at an end. She indeed continued to struggle against her combined enemies and her allies, who revolted against her, with unparalleled gallantry. Many more years of varying warfare passed away before she surrendered to their arms. But no success in subsequent contests could ever restore her to the preeminence in enterprise, resources, and maritime skill that she had acquired before her fatal reverses in Sicily. Nor among the rival Greek republics, whom her own rashness aided to crush her, was there any capable of reorganizing her empire or resuming her schemes of conquest. The dominion of Western Europe was left for Rome and Carthage to dispute two centuries later, in conflicts still more terrible, and with even higher displays of military daring and genius than Athens had witnessed either in her rise, her glory, or her fall.

Synopsis of Events Between the Defeat of the Athenians at Syracuse, 413 B.C., and the Battle of Arbela, 331 B.C.

412–411. Although many of her subject allies revolt and Persia enters the war against her, Athens by strenuous efforts raises another fleet. After involved intrigues with Sparta, with the Persian satraps in Asia Minor, and with various citizens in Athens, Alcibiades is given command of the Athenian Navy.

410. Alcibiades defeats a joint Spartan and Persian force. Sparta actually suggests that peace be declared, but Athens refuses.

409. The Carthaginians attack and seize cities in Sicily.

408. Darius II, King of Persia, sends his younger son Cyrus to govern Asia Minor, with orders to help Sparta against Athens.

406. The Carthaginians extend their conquests in Sicily.

405. The Spartan admiral Lysander almost totally destroys the last Athenian fleet while it is drawn up on the beach at Aegospotami. Athens is closely besieged. Dionysius becomes the ruler of Syracuse.

404. Athens surrenders. The Peloponnesian War ends with Sparta supreme in Greece.

401–400. Cyrus the Younger leads an expedition against his elder brother, Artaxerxes, who had succeeded to the throne of Persia. Cyrus is defeated and killed in battle, but the Greek mercenaries whom he had taken with him are victorious in their part of the field. The 10,000 Greeks who remain after the battle defy the whole Persian Army, then make a long and difficult march through many hostile nations and finally arrive on the shores of the Black Sea. (This historic "Retreat of the Ten Thousand" was described by Xenophon in his immortal *Anabasis*. This remarkable achievement demonstrated the internal weakness of the Persian Empire, and the superiority of an army of well-trained Greeks, a lesson Alexander the Great was to remember.)

399. In this and the five following years the Spartans carry on war against the Persian satraps in Asia Minor.

397. Syracuse is besieged by the Carthaginians and successfully defended by Dionysius.

396.   Rome makes the first great stride in her career of conquest by destroying the Etruscan city of Veii.

394–393.   The Athenian admiral Conon, in conjunction with a Persian fleet, defeats the Spartans, then restores the fortifications of Athens.

390.   The nations of northern Europe now first appear in authentic history. The Gauls overrun a great part of Italy and burn Rome. Rome recovers from the blow, but many of her old enemies to the north are left completely crushed by the Gallic invaders.

387–386.   Peace is concluded among the Greeks with the aid of the Persian king.

378–371.   Fresh wars break out in Greece. Epaminondas raises Thebes to be the leading city of Greece, and the supremacy of Sparta is destroyed at Leuctra. (At this battle in 371 B.C., Epaminondas, for the first time in recorded history, used mass tactics to drive home a main blow.)

362.   Athens and Sparta form an alliance against Thebes. Epaminondas gains a victory at Mantinea, but is killed, and the power of Thebes rapidly declines.

359.   Philip II, who had been kept as a hostage at Thebes and was a great admirer and student of Epaminondas, founds the kingdom of Macedonia. He immediately begins the thorough organizing and training of the Macedonian Army.

343.   Rome begins her wars with the Samnites which last for more than fifty years and secure for her the dominion of central Italy.

338.   Philip defeats the armies of Athens and Thebes at the Battle of Chaeronea and the Macedonian supremacy over Greece is firmly established.

336.   Philip is assassinated; his son Alexander the Great becomes King of Macedonia. He gains several victories over the northern barbarians, but rumors of his death in battle become the signal for several Greek cities to rise in revolt. Alexander marchs rapidly southward and in an astonishingly swift campaign destroys Thebes. The other cities promptly submit to his authority.

334.   Alexander crosses the Hellespont and wins the Battle of the Granicus.

333.   Alexander defeats the Persian king, Darius III, at the Battle of Issus and lays siege to Tyre in Phoenicia.

332.   Alexander captures Tyre and Gaza, occupies Egypt, and founds the city of Alexandria.

3

The Battle of Arbela, 331 B.C.

Alexander deserves the glory which he has enjoyed for so many centuries and among all nations: but what if he had been beaten at Arbela, having the Euphrates, the Tigris, and the deserts in his rear, without any strong places of refuge, nine hundred leagues from Macedonia!

—NAPOLEON

Asia beheld with astonishment and awe the uninterrupted progress of a hero, the sweep of whose conquests was as wide and rapid as that of her own barbaric kings; . . . but, far unlike the transient whirlwinds of Asiatic warfare, the advance of the Macedonian leader was no less deliberate than rapid: at every step the Greek power took root, and the language and the civilization of Greece were planted from the shores of the Aegean to the banks of the Indus; . . . to exist actually for nearly a thousand years, and in their effects to endure forever.

—ARNOLD

No TWO HISTORIANS would entirely agree on their lists of Decisive Battles of the World, but there are a few battles that are automatically included on such lists. Arbela is one of these. If Alexander the Great had been defeated, the cultural, scientific, and religious history of mankind in Europe, North Africa and most of Asia would have developed along radically different lines.

The enduring importance of Alexander's conquests is to be estimated not by the duration of his own life and empire, or by the duration of the kingdoms his generals, after his death, formed out of the fragments of that mighty dominion. In every region of the world that he traversed, Alexander planted Greek settlements and founded cities in which the Greek element at once asserted its predominance. Among his successors, the Selucidae and the Ptolemies imitated their great

39

captain in blending schemes of civilization, of commercial intercourse, and of literary and scientific research with their military enterprises and with their systems of civil administration. Such was the ascendancy of the Greek genius, so wonderfully comprehensive and assimilating its culture, that, within thirty years after Alexander crossed the Hellespont, the Greek language was spoken in every country from the shores of the Aegean to the Indus, and throughout Egypt. It became the language of every court, of literature, law, and politics, and formed a medium of communication throughout these far-flung regions of the Old World. In Asia Minor, Syria, and Egypt, the Hellenic character that was thus imparted remained in full vigor down to the time of the Mohammedan conquests. The infinite value of this to humanity has often been pointed out, and the workings of Providence have been gratefully recognized by those who have observed how the early growth and progress of Christianity were aided by that diffusion of the Greek language and civilization throughout Asia Minor, Syria, and Egypt, which had been caused by the Macedonian conquest of the East.

In Asia, beyond the Euphrates, the direct and material influence of Greek ascendancy was more short-lived. Yet, during the existence of the Hellenic kingdoms in these regions, the Grecian spirit affected the intellectual tendencies and tastes of these countries, and its influence continued to be felt for many generations.

So also, when the armed disciples of Mohammed began their triumphal career of conquest nearly a thousand years later, acquiring many of the provinces conquered by Alexander, the learning and science of the Arabians were greatly modified by Greek philosophy and Greek knowledge. It is well known that Western Europe in the Middle Ages drew its philosophy, its arts and its science to a great extent from Arabian teachers. Thus the intellectual influence of ancient Greece, poured on the Eastern world by Alexander's victories, was then brought back to medieval Europe by the spread of the Saracen power. The basic elements of modern civilization in the Western world were thus derived through this powerful though indirect channel, as well as by the more obvious effects of the remnants of classic civilization that survived in Italy, Gaul, Britain and Spain after the eruption of the Germanic nations.

These considerations invest the Macedonian triumphs in the East with never-dying interest. Whether the old Persian Empire that Cyrus founded could have survived much longer, even if Darius III had been victorious at Arbela, may be safely disputed. The satraps often rebelled against the central power, and Egypt in particular was frequently in a state of insurrection. There was no longer any effective central control. The historic "Retreat of the Ten Thousand" Greeks after the Battle of Cunaxa in 401 B.C. had demonstrated the internal weakness of the empire. Persia was evidently due to fall; but, had it not been for Alexander's invasion, she would most probably have fallen beneath some other Oriental power, simply substituting one Eastern regime for another. Alexander's victory at Arbela not only overthrew an Oriental dynasty but also established European rulers in its stead. It broke the monotonous rule of the Eastern world by the impression of Western energy and civilization.

Alexander succeeded to the throne of Macedonia in 336 B.C. upon the death by assassination of his father King Philip II. During the next two years he conducted campaigns against the northern barbarians and thoroughly crushed a revolt of the Greek states, which ended all thoughts of a Greek uprising and thus established a firm base from which he could launch an invasion of Persia.

In 334 B.C. Alexander crossed the Hellespont with an army of about 30,000 infantry and 5,000 cavalry, defeated a hastily gathered force of Persian troops at the Granicus River, and turned southward. After consolidating his position in Asia Minor, he next turned his attention to the Phoenician coast where, by capturing the Persian naval bases, he could gain control of the sea. En route Alexander defeated Darius III at the Battle of Issus, 333 B.C. and then laid siege to the city of Tyre. Seven months passed before he finally captured it; the combatants on both sides showed amazing ingenuity and inventiveness during the siege, as well as the most dogged determination. Moving south along the coast, Alexander took Gaza after a two-month siege, then occupied Egypt and founded the city of Alexandria. He was now master of the eastern Mediterranean and his communications with Greece were entirely secure. In 331 B.C. Alexander was ready to strike at the heart of the Persian Empire; he marched north again, through Syria, toward Darius and destiny.

Arbela, the city that has furnished its name to the decisive battle which gave Asia to Alexander, lies some sixty miles from the actual scene of conflict. The battle is sometimes referred to as Gaugamela, the name of the little village near the spot where the armies met, but the more euphonious name of Arbela is generally used. The battle-ground is located in one of the wide plains that lie between the Tigris and the mountains of Kurdistan. A few undulating hillocks diversify the surface of the sandy track; but the ground is generally level and admirably qualified for the evolutions of cavalry, and also calculated to give the larger of the two armies the full advantage of numerical superiority. The Persian king (who before he came to the throne had proved his personal valor as a soldier and his skill as a general) had wisely selected this region for the third and decisive encounter between his forces and the invader. The previous defeats of his troops, however severe they had been, were not looked on as ir-reparable. The Granicus had been fought by his generals, and though Darius himself had commanded and been beaten at Issus, that defeat might be attributed to the disadvantageous nature of the ground. He would not be caught a second time in a restricted space where, between the mountains, the river, and the sea, the huge numbers of the Persians confused and clogged alike the general's skill and the soldiers' prowess, and their very strength had been made their weakness. Here on the broad plains there was scope for Asia's largest host to array its lines, to wheel, to skirmish, to maneuver, and to charge at will. Should Alexander and his scanty band dare to plunge into that sea of war, their destruction seemed inevitable.

Darius felt, however, the critical nature to himself as well as to his adversary of the coming encounter. He could not hope to retrieve the consequences of a third defeat. The great cities of Mesopotamia and the central provinces of the Persian Empire would then be at the mercy of the victor. He knew the Asiatic character well enough to be aware that it would yield to the prestige of success and the apparent career of destiny. He felt that the diadem was now either to be firmly replaced on his own brow or be irrevocably transferred to his European conqueror. Therefore, during the long interval left him after the Battle of Issus while Alexander was subjugating Syria and Egypt, Darius assiduously busied himself in selecting the best troops his vast empire supplied, and in training his varied forces to act together with some uniformity of discipline and system. The numbers of the Persian army, as stated by different historians, vary from 200,000 infantry and 45,000 cavalry to 1,000,000 foot soldiers and 100,000 horsemen. Darius also had with him 200 scythed chariots and fifteen war elephants.

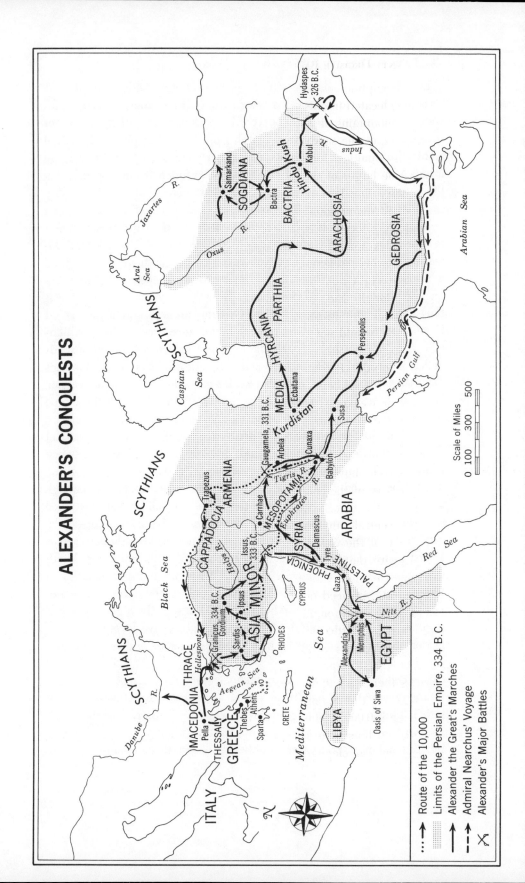

ALEXANDER'S CONQUESTS

Scale of Miles

0   100   300   500

······· Route of the 10,000

Limits of the Persian Empire, 334 B.C.

⟶ Alexander the Great's Marches

⇢ Admiral Nearchus' Voyage

✗ Alexander's Major Battles

The position of the Persian king was chosen with skill. It was certain that Alexander, on his return from Egypt, must march northward through Syria before he could attack the central provinces of the empire. A direct eastward march from the lower part of Palestine across the desert was then, as ever, utterly impracticable for a large army. Marching eastward from Syria, Alexander would, on crossing the Euphrates, arrive at the vast Mesopotamian plains. The wealthy capitals of the empire, Babylon, Susa, and Persepolis, would then lie to the south. If Alexander marched down through Mesopotamia to attack them. Darius might reasonably hope to follow the Macedonians with his immense force of cavalry, and without even risking a pitched battle, to harass and finally destroy them. We may remember that three centuries later a Roman army under Crassus was thus overwhelmingly defeated by Oriental archers and horsemen at Carrhae in these very plains and that the ancestors of the Parthians who thus vanquished the Roman legions served by the thousands under King Darius. If, on the contrary, Alexander should defer his march against Babylon, and first seek an encounter with the Persian army, the country on each side of the Tigris provided the best type of battleground for such an army as Darius commanded.

On came his great antagonist across the Euphrates at the head of an army which Arrian, who wrote his history of Alexander when Hadrian was emperor of the Roman world, states to have consisted of 40,000 foot and 7,000 horse. This estimate seems reasonable enough when we take into account both the losses Alexander had sustained and the reinforcements he had received since he left Europe. The disparity of numbers between the Persians and the Macedonians seems at first glance incredible, but it will be recalled with what mere handfuls of men English generals defeated large numbers of Asiatics at Plassey and at Assaye in India. Furthermore, the army Alexander now led was wholly composed of veteran troops in the highest possible state of equipment and discipline, enthusiastically devoted to their leader and full of confidence in his military genius and his victorious destiny.

The celebrated Macedonian phalanx formed the main strength of his infantry. This force had been raised, organized, and trained by his father, Philip. The phalangite soldier was fully equipped in the armor and with the weapons of the regular Greek infantry, but the pike, or *sarissa*, that he carried was doubled, to a length of twenty-one feet.

When leveled for action it reached fifteen feet in advance, and the spears of the four files behind him projected in front of each front-rank man. Thus there were five banks of spearpoints in front of the alignment. Under Alexander the phalanx was brought to the height of efficiency. The men were trained to advance one or both wings to envelop the flanks of the enemy; to refuse one or both flanks for defense; to form a wedge for penetration; and to form pincers in which the center was drawn back in inverted wedge form to receive and crush an enemy wedge. In addition the Macedonian phalanx was trained to wheel, countermarch, and march by the flank. It was practically irresistible to the front on level ground, but was vulnerable on the flanks. If broken up by movement on uneven ground, it could be penetrated and was then vulnerable to determined troops. However, Alexander also had light and heavily armed infantry, who could be used to protect the flanks of the phalanx as well as for offensive movements.

Alexander had more cavalry, and used it more effectively, than any Greek prior to his time. His finest mounted troops were the Companions, who were made up of young Macedonian nobles, and the Thessalian cavalry. These were heavily armed and were primarily for shock action. Other regiments of cavalry were less heavily armed, and there were several bodies of light horsemen, whom Alexander's conquests in Egypt and Syria had enabled him to mount superbly.

A little before the end of August, Alexander crossed the Euphrates, a small corps of Persian cavalry retiring before him. Alexander was too prudent to march down through the Mesopotamian deserts, and continued to advance eastward with the intention of passing the Tigris, finding Darius, and bringing him to action.

Darius, finding that his adversary was not to be enticed into the march through Mesopotamia against his capital, determined to remain on the battleground he had chosen. There, if Alexander met a defeat or was checked, the destruction of the invaders would be more certain with two such rivers as the Euphrates and the Tigris in their rear. The Persian king availed himself to the utmost of every advantage in his power. He caused a large space of ground to be carefully leveled for the operation of his scythe-armed chariots; and he deposited his military stores in the town of Arbela, about sixty miles in his rear. Simply because Darius was defeated, the writers of later ages have loved to describe him as unintelligent, but a fair examination of his generalship in this his last campaign shows he was a worthy opponent.

On learning that Darius was east of the Tigris, Alexander hurried forward and crossed that river without opposition. The fact that an eclipse of the moon occurred on that day has enabled us to fix the date of Alexander's crossing as September 20, 331 B.C. After giving his army a short interval of rest, he continued his march, and a few days later his advance guard reported that a body of the enemy's cavalry was in sight. He instantly formed his army in order for battle, and directing them to advance steadily, rode forward at the head of some squadrons of cavalry and charged the Persian horse whom he found before him. This was a mere reconnoitering party who broke and fled immediately, but the Macedonians made some prisoners. From these Alexander found that Darius was posted only a few miles off, and learned the strength of the army that he had with him. On receiving this news, Alexander halted and rested his troops so that they could go into action fresh and vigorous. He also fortified the camp and deposited in it all his military stores, and all the sick and disabled soldiers, intending to advance upon the enemy with the serviceable part of his army perfectly unencumbered.

Having made his preparations, he moved forward on the fourth night, under cover of darkness, hoping to attack Darius at daybreak, but he was delayed and made a new camp within sight of the Persian hosts. By the early light, Alexander saw the Persians arrayed before him, and observed traces of some engineering operations having been carried out along part of the ground in front. Not knowing that these marks had been made by the Persians leveling the ground for their war chariots, Alexander suspected that obstacles might have been placed along the line. He called a council of war. Some of the officers were for attacking instantly, at all hazards, but the more prudent opinion of the elderly Parmenio, the Second in Command, prevailed. It was determined not to advance until the battleground had been carefully surveyed.

Alexander halted his army and, taking with him some light infantry and cavalry, passed part of the day reconnoitering the enemy and observing the nature of the ground. Darius wisely refrained from moving from his position, and the two armies remained until night without molesting each other. On Alexander's return to his headquarters, he summoned his generals and senior officers together, and telling them that he knew well that their zeal wanted no exhortation, he besought them to do their utmost in encouraging and instructing those whom each commanded. They were to remind their officers and men that they were now not going to fight for a province but that they were about to decide by their swords the dominion of all Asia. Their natural courage required no long words to excite ardor; but they should be reminded of the paramount importance of steadiness in action. The silence in the ranks must be unbroken as long as silence was proper; but when the time came for the charge, the shout and the cheer must be full of terror for the foe. The officers were to be alert to receive and communicate orders; and everyone was to act as if he felt that the whole result of the battle depended on his own single good conduct.

Having thus briefly instructed his generals, Alexander ordered that the troops should be fed and take their rest for the night.

Darkness had closed over the tents of the Macedonians when Alexander's veteran general Parmenio came to him and proposed that they should make a night attack on the Persians. The king is said to have answered that he scorned to employ such tactics and that he must conquer openly and fairly. The real reason undoubtedly was that he knew the uncertainties inherent in a battle fought at night, and he wished to gain a decisive victory that would leave his rival without any excuse or apology for defeat—and without any hope of recovery.

The Persians, in fact, expected and were prepared to meet a night assault. Darius formed his troops at evening in order of battle and kept them under arms all night. Having stood thus all day and all night, the Persians were weary when morning came, while it brought their adversaries fresh and vigorous against them.

The Persian right consisted of Syrians, the Mesopotamians and the Medes, the Parthians, Hyrcanians and other tribes from the northern and eastern sections of the empire, arranged in deep masses. In front of these were the Armenian and Cappadocian cavalry, with fifty scythed chariots. In the center was Darius with the bodyguard of the Persian nobility, the brigade of Greek mercenaries who alone were considered fit to stand the charge of the Macedonian phalanx, a division of Persians, and other selected troops. These were protected by the fifteen war elephants and fifty scythe-armed chariots. The left wing consisted of the Bactrian and Arachosian cavalry, and the bulk of the native Persian infantry and cavalry. In their front were the Scythian cavalry and one hundred war chariots.

Thus arrayed, the great host of King Darius passed the night that to many thousands of them was to be their last. The morning of the first of October dawned slowly to their wearied watching, and they could hear the notes of the Macedonian trumpets sounding to arms, and could see King Alexander's forces form in order on the plain.

There was deep need of skill as well as of valor on Alexander's side; and few battlefields have witnessed more consummate general-ship than was now displayed by the Macedonian king. There were no natural barriers by which he could protect his flanks. Not only was he certain to be overlapped on either wing by the vast lines of the Persian army; he had also to guard against their circling around him and charging from the rear, as he advanced. For the coming battle he adopted a formation that could be made ready to receive an attack from any direction.

In the center of his line he placed the Macedonian phalanx of six divisions. On their right he placed a body of heavily armed infantry to connect with the Companion cavalry who constituted the main offensive strength of the right wing, which Alexander led in person. On the left wing, under the command of Parmenio, were placed the allied Greek cavalry and the Thessalian cavalry. Then in rear of each flank, at an angle to the front, Alexander posted light infantry and horsemen, so disposed that they could face quickly in any direc-tion, thus protecting his flanks against envelopment by the long Persian line. Finally, in front of the Companion cavalry, some light infantry were aligned to meet the charge of the Persian war chariots. With a squadron of the royal cavalry Alexander took the post of honor and danger in front of the right flank, while Parmenio occupied a similar position in front of the left flank. A division of Thracian in-fantry was left to guard the camp.

Conspicuous by the brilliance of his armor and by the chosen band of officers who were round his person, Alexander led his men toward the enemy. It was ever his custom to expose his life freely in battle, but he never allowed his ardor as a soldier to make him lose the cool-ness of the general.

Great reliance had been placed by the Persian king on the effects of the sycthe-bearing chariots. He intended to launch these against the Macedonian phalanx, then follow with a powerful cavalry charge. Alexander, however, did not advance straight to the front, but moved forward obliquely to the right, causing Darius to shift his line some-

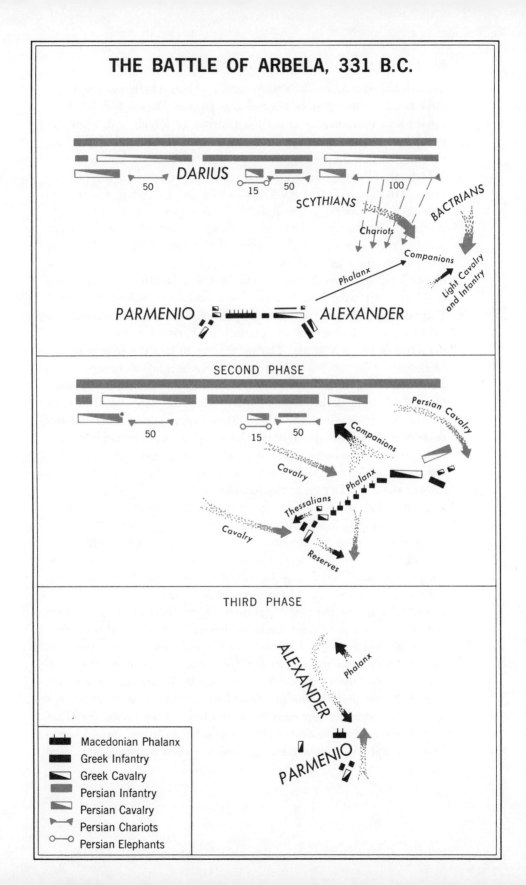

THE BATTLE OF ARBELA, 331 B.C.

DARIUS

50

15   50

100

SCYTHIANS

Chariots

BACTRIANS

Companions

Light Cavalry
and Infantry

Phalanx

PARMENIO   ALEXANDER

SECOND PHASE

50

15   50

Persian Cavalry

Companions

Cavalry

Phalanx

Thessalians

Cavalry

Reserves

THIRD PHASE

ALEXANDER

Phalanx

PARMENIO

Macedonian Phalanx
Greek Infantry
Greek Cavalry
Persian Infantry
Persian Cavalry
Persian Chariots
Persian Elephants

what to his left. Alexander's purpose was threefold. By moving to his right front he might pass beyond the ground Darius had carefully leveled and smoothed to allow the chariots to attack with their full sweep and speed. Secondly, a movement toward one end of the long Persian line would decrease the possibility of being enveloped on both flanks. Finally, he wished to strike a decisive blow with the strong Macedonian right wing first, while the left wing was refused in an oblique order of advance for as long as possible. Thus he might defeat the Persians on his right and strike a heavy blow at the center of their line before the full strength of the rest of the Persian army could be brought to bear upon his own left wing.

As Alexander moved forward, the Scythian cavalry posted in front of Darius' left wing attacked but were unable to halt the advance. This oblique movement was bringing the phalanx and the Macedonian right close to the limits of the ground the Persians had prepared for the advance of the chariots. Darius, fearing to lose the benefit of this arm, ordered his Bactrian cavalry to charge around Alexander's right wing and force it to halt. Against these assailants Alexander sent some of his light cavalry and infantry, which he had placed in position behind his right flank. As additional units successively entered the fray, a furious cavalry fight developed. The Bactrians and Scythians were far more numerous and were better armed, and the loss at first was heavier on the Macedonian side. Nevertheless, the European cavalry stood the charge of the Asiatics, and at last, by their superior discipline and by acting in squadrons that supported each other, instead of fighting in a confused mass like their opponents, the Macedonians broke their adversaries and drove them from the field.

Darius now directed the scythe-armed chariots to be driven against the phalanx and against the heavily armed infantry between it and the Companion cavalry. These formidable vehicles were accordingly sent rattling across the plain against the Macedonian line. The object of the chariots was to create unsteadiness in the ranks, and squadrons of cavalry followed close upon them to profit by the disorder. But the Asiatic chariots were rendered ineffective at Arbela by the light-armed troops, whom Alexander had especially appointed for this service. Wounding the horses and drivers with showers of arrows and javelins, running alongside to cut the traces, they ruined the effect of the charge. The few chariots that reached the phalanx passed harmlessly through the intervals the spearmen opened for them, and were easily captured in the rear. Chariots not captured or destroyed charged back into the Persian ranks, creating much confusion and disorder.

The first part of the battle was now over; the second and decisive phase was about to begin. Another mass of Persian cavalry was now collected and moved against Alexander's extreme right flank, but in so doing opened a gap in the main Persian line near the center. Alexander saw this immediately, formed his Companion cavalry in a deep wedge formation and, leaving to his subordinates the combat against the Persians on the flank, charged straight toward the gap. Pressing toward his left, he soon began to make havoc in the Persian center. The heavily armed infantry now charged also. On came four of the six divisions of the phalanx, with the irresistible might of their *sarissas* driving all before them. In the early part of the battle Darius had showed skill and energy. Now, for some time, he encouraged his men, by voice and example, to stand firm. But the lances of Alexander's cavalry and the pikes of the phalanx pressed nearer and nearer. At last Darius' nerve failed him; mounting a swift horse he galloped from the field.

While the Macedonian right wing under Alexander was achieving such startling success, the left wing was in serious difficulties. Parmenio had kept out of action as long as possible, but the advance of four of the six divisions of the phalanx had left a gap in the Macedonian line, through which a heavy column of cavalry poured, streaming toward the baggage camp in rear. At the same time the Persian cavalry had swung around Parmenio's left flank, completely outflanking him, and pressing him severely with repeated charges by superior numbers.

Parmenio had taken such action as he could, sending his reserves to attack in flank the enemy looting the camp, while holding off the massive assaults on his left flank with the Thessalian cavalry. But he was completely surrounded and needed assistance immediately.

When Parmenio's urgent call for rescue reached Alexander, he immediately turned with the Companion cavalry, to attack the Persian right. En route he encountered the enemy cavalry returning from his camp. These men, taken in flank by Parmenio's reserves and in rear by Alexander, saw that their only chance was to cut their way through. In one huge column they charged desperately upon the Macedonian regiments. There was a close hand-to-hand fight; at length Macedonian discipline and valor again prevailed. A large number of horsemen were cut down, only a few succeeding in breaking through and escaping. Relieved of these obstinate enemies, Alexander again formed his squadrons, but by this time Parmenio also was victorious. Probably the news of Darius' flight had reached the Persian right-wing cavalry, while the tidings of their comrades' success had proportionately encouraged the Macedonian forces under Parmenio. His Thessalian cavalry particularly distinguished themselves. By the time that Alexander had ridden up to Parmenio, the whole Persian army was in full flight from the field.

It was of the deepest importance to Alexander to secure the person of Darius, and he now urged on the pursuit. A river was between the field of battle and the city of Arbela. The passage of this river was even more destructive to the Persians than the losses on the battlefield itself. The narrow bridge was soon choked by the flying thousands who rushed toward it. Vast numbers of the Persians threw themselves, or were hurried by others, into the rapid stream, and perished in its waters. Darius had crossed it and had ridden through Arbela without halting. Alexander reached the city the next day and made himself master of all Darius' treasure and stores. Darius escaped, only to perish by the treachery of the Bactrian satrap, Bessus.

The losses of the Macedonians at the Battle of Arbela have been variously recorded between 100 and 300 killed, while the Persian dead have been estimated from 40,000 to as high as 300,000 killed. These figures are obviously untrustworthy.

A few days after the battle Alexander entered Babylon as its acknowledged lord and master. Before the end of the year he had occupied Susa and seized Persepolis. There were yet some campaigns of his brief and bright career to be accomplished. Many thousands of Asiatics were yet to witness the march of his phalanx, but the crisis had been reached. The great object of his mission was accomplished. The Persian Empire, which had menaced all the nations of the known world, was irreparably crushed when Alexander won his crowning victory at Arbela.

Synopsis of Events Between the Battle of Arbela, 331 B.C., and the Battle of the Metaurus, 207 B.C.

331.   The Spartans endeavor to create an uprising in Greece against the Macedonian power. They are defeated by Antipater, Alexander's governor, and their king, Agis, falls in the battle.

330. Alexander pursues Darius and occupies the Median capital of Ecbatana (modern Hamadan). Darius is assassinated by the Bactrian satrap Bessus, who attempts to succeed him as ruler of what remains of the Persian Empire.

329–328. Alexander marches through Arachosia, crosses the Hindu Kush into Bactria and Sogdiana, overcoming opposition and founding a number of Greek cities. Bessus is captured and executed.

327–326. Alexander again marches over the Hindu Kush, crosses the Indus River and encounters King Porus at the Hydaspes River. After executing a model river-crossing operation, he defeats and captures Porus. The army refuses to march farther. Leaving Porus to rule the recently conquered territory, Alexander begins his descent of the Indus.

325–324. Alexander directs his admiral Nearchus to sail round to the Persian Gulf, then conducts an appalling return march through the Gedrosian Desert.

323. Alexander dies in Babylon at the age of thirty-three.

322–301. After a long series of wars with one another, and after all the heirs of Alexander had perished, the principal surviving generals divide the empire between them. After the death of Antigonus I at the Battle of Ipsus in 301 B.C. the empire is again subdivided. (The longest-lasting dynasties were the Empire of the Seleucidae in Asia, the Empire of the Ptolemies in Egypt, and that of Antigonus Gonatus in Macedonia.)

290. The Third Samnite War ends with Rome victorious in central Italy. The Gauls in northern Italy are also driven back, leaving only some Greek cities in southern Italy to stand against her.

282–272. Wishing to confirm her dominion in southern Italy, Rome becomes entangled with the powerful Greek city of Tarentum. The Roman legions are defeated by Pyrrhus at Heraclea (280) and at Ausculum (279) then win at Beneventum (275). Tarentum surrenders, leaving Rome supreme in southern Italy.

264. The first of the three Punic Wars between Rome and Carthage begins. The primary cause is the desire of both to possess themselves of Sicily. Rome has become the controlling state in Italy; Carthage is the chief maritime power in the western Mediterranean; neither can permit the other to acquire Sicily.

260. Realizing that she cannot defeat Carthage without gaining control of the sea, Rome builds a fleet and wins a naval victory at the Battle of Mylae by an ingenious method of letting down a large hook and a bridge for Roman soldiers to board and seize the enemy ships.

256. A Roman invasion fleet en route to Africa defeats the Carthaginians in the naval Battle of Ecnomus. After the Romans land in Africa, the Carthagenians sue for peace, but the consul Regulus' terms are so harsh that Carthage continues the struggle.

255. Regulus is defeated and captured. The Roman forces are withdrawn from Africa.

254–241. The First Punic War develops into a struggle for Sicily where the military genius of Hamilcar Barca sustains the Carthaginian cause. Finally, in the twenty-third year of the war, the Romans by magnificent exertions build a new fleet, financed by private subscription. In a battle off the Aegusa Islands, the Romans win a decisive victory, and Carthage sues for peace. The Carthaginian territory in Sicily becomes the first Roman province.

240–220. The Carthaginian mercenaries, brought back from Sicily to Africa, mutiny and nearly succeed in destroying Carthage. After a desperate struggle Hamilcar Barca crushes them. During this season of Carthaginian weakness, Rome invades Sardinia and forces Carthage to cede Corsica to her also.

Hamilcar Barca forms the project of seeking to compensate for losses by acquiring Spain, thus enabling Carthage to renew the struggle with Rome. He takes his young son Hannibal with him, founds Cartagena (New Carthage) and begins the development of Spain. Upon Hamilcar's death the command passes to his son-in-law Hasdrubal, who continues his work. When he dies the command is given to Hannibal, who is then only twenty-six years old.

During this interval Rome has to sustain a storm from the North. The Cisalpine Gauls form an alliance with one of the fiercest tribes of their brethren north of the Alps, and wage a furious war against the Romans that lasts four years. The Romans give them several severe defeats and take from them part of their territories near the Po, but have no opportunity to establish themselves securely in the area. As a result, when Hannibal later invades this region he finds the natives hostile to Rome, ready to join him in his march upon their common enemy.

219. Hannibal attacks Saguntum, a city Rome claims as an ally, and captures it after a siege lasting eight months.

218. Rome declares war. Hannibal marches from Cartagena, crosses the Pyrenees, moves through southern Gaul over the Rhône River, eluding the Romans, then effects his dramatic, daring march over the Alps down onto the plains of northern Italy. Before the end of the year he defeats a Roman force on the Ticinus River and routs a Roman army at the Battle of the Trebia.

217. Hannibal ambushes and destroys the Romans at the Battle of Lake Trasimene.

216. Hannibal annihilates the Roman army of G. Tarentius Varro and L. Aemilius Paulus in the extraordinary Battle of Cannae, the world's most famous example of a battle won by a double envelopment of the enemy's force. (It has been truly said that no army in history was ever more magnificently handled than was Hannibal's army at Cannae.) Some of Rome's Italian allies, including Capua, the second greatest city in Italy, desert her.

215–209. Rome adopts the "Fabian" policy of attrition advocated by Quintus Fabius Maximus, known as the "Cunctator," or "Delayer." Although Hannibal captures Tarentum in 212 B.C., he is practically unsupported by Carthage, and Rome gradually regains superiority in Italy, starving Capua into surrender in 211 and recapturing Tarentum in 209. In Sicily, a large Roman force commanded by M. Claudius Marcellus, baffled for many months by the ingenious mechanical devices of the great mathematician Archimedes, eventually reduces the city of Syracuse. In Spain, Publius Cornelius Scipio captures Cartagena in 209 B.C.

208. Hannibal's brother, Hasdrubal, marches with his army from Spain toward Italy.

4

The Battle of the Metaurus,
207 B.C.

ABOUT MIDWAY between Rimini and Ancona a little river called the
Metauro falls into the Adriatic. Its present Italian name, so similar to
the ancient Latin name, wakens recollections of the resolute daring of
ancient Rome and of the slaughter that stained its current two thousand one hundred and seventy-one years ago. Here the combined consular armies of Livius and Nero encountered the varied host Hasdrubal,
Hannibal's brother, was leading to aid the great Carthaginian in his
struggle against the might of the Roman Republic.

The Roman historian Livy, who termed that struggle the most
memorable of all wars, wrote in no spirit of exaggeration. For it is
not in ancient, but in modern, history that parallels for its incidents
and its heroes are to be found. The similarity between the contest that
Rome maintained against Hannibal and the one that England was
engaged in against Napoleon has not passed unobserved by historians.
"Twice," says Arnold, "has there been witnessed the struggle of the
highest individual genius against the resources and institutions of a
great nation, and in both cases the nation has been victorious. For
seventeen years Hannibal strove against Rome; for sixteen years
Napoleon Bonaparte strove against England; the efforts of the first
ended in Zama; those of the second in Waterloo." One point, however,

56

of the similarity between the two wars has not been so adequately presented, and that is the remarkable parallel between the Roman general who finally defeated the great Carthaginian and the English general who gave the final blow that overthrew the French emperor. Scipio and Wellington both held for many years commands of high importance, but distant from the main theaters of warfare. The same country was the scene of the principal military career of each. It was in Spain that Scipio, like Wellington, successively encountered and defeated subordinate generals of the enemy before being opposed to the chief champion and conqueror himself. Both Scipio and Wellington restored their countrymen's confidence in arms when shaken by a series of reverses, and each of them closed a long and perilous war by a defeat of the chosen leader of the foe.

Scipio at Zama trampled in the dust the power of Carthage, but that power had been already irreparably shattered on another field, where neither Scipio nor Hannibal commanded. When the Metaurus witnessed the defeat and death of Hasdrubal, it witnessed the ruin of Hannibal's last hope of conquering Rome. That battle was the determining crisis of the contest, not merely between Rome and Carthage, but between two great families of the world who had made Italy the arena of their struggle for preeminence.

The French historian Michelet, whose *Histoire romaine* would have been invaluable if the general industry and accuracy of the writer had in any degree equaled his originality and brilliance, eloquently remarks, "It is not without reason that so universal and vivid a remembrance of the Punic wars has dwelt in the memories of men. They formed no mere struggle to determine the lot of two cities or two empires; but it was a strife, on the event of which depended the fate of two races of mankind, whether the dominion of the world should belong to the Indo-Germanic or to the Semitic family of nations. . . . On the one side is the genius of heroism, of art, and legislation; on the other is the spirit of industry, of commerce, of navigation. The two opposite races have everywhere come into contact, everywhere into hostility. In the primitive history of Persia and Chaldea, the heroes are perpetually engaged in combat with their industrious and perfidious neighbors. The struggle is renewed between the Phoenicians and the Greeks on every coast of the Mediterranean. The Greek supplants the Phoenician in all his factories, all his colonies in the East: soon will the Roman come, and do likewise in the West. Alexander did far more against Tyre than Salmanasar or Nabuchodonosor had done. Not content with crushing her, he took care that she never should revive; for he founded Alexandria as her substitute, and changed forever the track of the commerce of the world. There remained Carthage—the great Carthage, and her mighty empire— mighty in a far different degree than Phoenicia's had been. Rome annihilated it. Then occurred that which has no parallel in history— an entire civilization perished at one blow—banished, like a falling star. The 'Periplus' of Hanno, a few coins, a score of lines in Plautus, and lo, all that remains of the Carthaginian world!

"Many generations must needs pass away before the struggle between the two races could be renewed; and the Arabs, that formidable rear-guard of the Semitic world, dashed forth from their deserts. The conflict between the two races then became the conflict of two religions. Fortunate was it that those daring Saracenic cavaliers encountered in the East the impregnable walls of Constantinople, in the West the chivalrous valor of Charles Martel and the sword of the Cid."

It is difficult, amid the glimmering light supplied by the allusions of the classical writers, to gain a full idea of the character and institutions of Rome's great rival. But we can perceive how inferior Carthage was to her competitor, and how far less fitted than Rome to become the founder of centralized and centralizing dominion, that should endure for centuries, and fuse into imperial unity the ancient races that dwelt around and near the shores of the Mediterranean Sea.

Carthage was originally neither the most ancient nor the most powerful of the numerous colonies the Phoenicians planted on the coast of northern Africa. But her advantageous position, and the commercial and political energy of her citizens, soon gave her the ascendancy over the other Phoenician cities in those regions. She finally reduced them to a condition of dependency similar to that which the subject allies of Athens occupied relative to that once imperial city. When Tyre and the other cities of Phoenicia sank from independent republics into mere vassal states of the great Asiatic monarchies, their power and their traffic declined. Then Carthage succeeded to the important maritime and commercial position which Tyre had previously maintained.

The Carthaginians did not seek to compete with the Greeks in the northeastern Mediterranean, but they maintained an active intercourse with the Phoenicians, and through them with Asia. They navigated the waters of the Atlantic and had a monopoly of all commerce carried on beyond the Straits of Gibraltar. We have still extant a supposed Greek translation of the narrative of the voyage of Hanno, one of their admirals, along the western coast of Africa as far as Sierra Leone, while their explorations northward probably took them as far as Great Britain, and possibly to the Baltic. When it is remembered that the mariner's compass was unknown in those ages, the boldness and skill of the seamen of Carthage excite our imaginations. Their achievements are certainly equal to anything that the history of modern navigation can produce.

In their Atlantic voyages along the African shores, the Carthaginians followed the double object of traffic and colonization. The numerous settlements that were planted by them along the coast provided for the needy members of the constantly increasing population of a great commercial capital, and also strengthened the influence Carthage exercised among the tribes of Africa.

Although essentially a mercantile and seafaring people, the Carthaginians by no means neglected agriculture. On the contrary, the territory around and about the city was cultivated like a garden. The fertility of the soil repaid the skill and toil bestowed on it. Every invader, from Agathocles to Scipio Aemilianus, was struck with admiration at the rich pasture lands carefully irrigated, the abundant harvests, the luxuriant vineyards, the plantations of fig and olive trees, the thriving villages, the populous towns and the splendid villas of the wealthy Carthaginians.

Although the Carthaginians abandoned the Aegean and the Black Sea to the Greeks, they were by no means disposed to relinquish to those rivals the commerce and the dominion of the coasts of the Mediterranean westward of Italy. For centuries the Carthaginians strove to make themselves masters of the islands that lie between Italy and Spain. They acquired the Balearic Islands where the principal harbor, Port Mahon, still bears, in altered form, the famous Carthaginian name Mago. The Carthaginians also succeeded in obtaining control of Sardinia and Corsica, but Sicily could never be brought into their power. They repeatedly invaded that island, and nearly overran it, but the resistance opposed to them by the Syracusans preserved the island from becoming Punic. Many of its cities remained under Carthaginian control until Rome finally settled the question by conquering Sicily for herself.

With so many elements of success, with almost unbounded wealth, with commercial and maritime activity, with a fertile territory, with a capital city of almost impregnable strength, with a constitution that ensured the blessing of social order, with an aristocracy singularly fertile in men of the highest genius, Carthage yet failed signally and calamitously in her contest for power with Rome. One of the immediate causes of this seems to have been the want of firmness among her citizens, which made them terminate the First Punic War rather than endure any longer the hardships and burdens caused by a state of warfare, although their antagonists had suffered far more severely than themselves. Another cause was the spirit of faction among their leading men, which prevented Hannibal in the second war from being properly reinforced and supported. But there were also more general causes why Carthage proved inferior to Rome. These were the relationship of the citizens of Carthage to the mass of the inhabitants of North Africa, and Carthage's habit of trusting to mercenary armies to fight her wars.

The historian Diodorus Siculus, while describing Carthage, classified the people in four different categories. First he mentioned the Phoenicians who dwelt in Carthage. Next he spoke of the Liby-Phoenicians who dwelt in many of the maritime cities and who were connected by intermarriages with the Phoenicians. Then he mentioned the Libyans, the oldest and the largest segment of the population, who hated the Carthaginians intensely because of the oppressiveness of their domination. Finally he named the Numidians, the nomadic tribes of the frontier.

It is evident from this description that the native Libyans were a subject class, without franchise or other political rights. Accordingly we find no instance specified in history of a Libyan holding political office or military command. The half-castes, the Liby-Phoenicians, seem to have been sometimes sent out as colonists; but it may be inferred, from what Diodorus says, that they did not have the rights of citizens of Carthage.

With respect to their armies, it is obvious that, though thirsting for extended empire, and though some of her leading men became generals of the highest order, the Carthaginians, as a people, were not personally warlike. As long as they could hire mercenaries to fight for them, they had little appetite for the irksome training and the loss of valuable time military service would have entailed.

As Michelet, perhaps somewhat unfairly, remarks: "The life of an industrious merchant, of a Carthaginian, was too precious to be risked, as long as it was possible to substitute advantageously for it that of a barbarian from Spain or Gaul. Carthage knew, and could tell to a drachma, what the life of a man of each nation came to. A Greek was worth more than a Campanian, a Campanian worth more than a Gaul or a Spaniard. When once this tabulation of blood was correctly prepared, Carthage began war as a commercial speculation. She tried to make conquests in the hope of getting new mines to work, or to open fresh markets for her exports. In one venture she could afford to spend fifty thousand mercenaries, in another rather more. If the returns were good, there was no regret for the capital that had been sunk in the investment; more money got more men and all went on well."

Armies composed of foreign mercenaries have in all ages been as formidable to their employers as to the enemy against whom they were directed. The largest and best-known revolt by Carthaginian mercenaries occurred after the First Punic War, which Rome had won by gaining control of the sea. The hired soldiers who had fought so long and valiantly in Sicily were brought back to Africa. Upon their arrival their Carthaginian masters refused to give them their pay; a large-scale mutiny resulted, which brought Carthage to the very brink of destruction. Hamilcar Barca finally suppressed the revolt after a long and bitter struggle. Rome, who had acquired all of Carthage's possessions in Sicily at the peace treaty, took advantage of this period of weakness to invade Sardinia and to force Carthage to give up claim to Corsica also. Yet the civil authorities at Carthage learned nothing from this revolt and made no changes whatever in their military policy. When Hamilcar went to Spain to found a new empire to take the place of the colonies lost in Sicily, Sardinia, and Corsica, he was again forced to employ mercenaries to fight his battles. When his son Hannibal invaded Italy, his army was almost entirely composed of mercenaries: Spaniards, Africans, Gauls, Numidians, a varied mixture of races and peoples, without any common bond of origin, language, tactics or cause. It is remarkable indeed that Carthage was able to wage war so successfully against the legions of Rome, composed of free citizens who regarded the bearing of arms as a privilege rather than a duty. Drawn from a hardy agricultural population, trained in the

strictest discipline, animated by the most resolute patriotism, the individual Romans were better soldiers than the mercenaries and slaves
who filled the Carthaginian armies. Whatever success in arms Carthaginian generals were able to achieve, it was in spite of the system
imposed upon them by their commercial aristocracy, not because of it.

Of all the great generals who ever led Carthaginian armies, Hannibal was undoubtedly the noblest leader, the most intelligent strategist,
and the finest tactician. Although too little is known of him, and most
of our knowledge comes from his former enemies, historians have
never hesitated to honor him as an unsurpassed military genius, one
of the great captains of the world. Hannibal's crossing of the Alps
and his victories at the Ticinus and the Trebia in 218 B.C. brought
him renown; his destruction of a Roman army at Lake Trasimene in
217 and the world-famous victory over the consul Varro at Cannae in
216 established his military fame forever, and struck terror into the
heart of Rome; but full appreciation of his splendid courage and
magnificent leadership ability came later. For fourteen long years
after Cannae, although almost neglected by Carthage, the men of his
heterogeneous army followed Hannibal, true to their leader in ad-
versity as well as in victory. Inspired by his personality, they never
wavered; no panic rout ever disgraced a division under his command;
no mutiny, or even attempt at mutiny, was ever known in his camp.
Finally, with unwavering spirit, his men followed their old leader to
Zama, with no fear and little hope. There, on that disastrous field,
they stood firm around him, his Old Guard, until through ill fortune
rather than their enemy's design, they were surrounded. Overpowered
though they were, the veteran battalians sealed their devotion to their
general with their blood.

Lest we become overly sympathetic toward Hannibal and the men
of his gallant army, it would be helpful to read Arnold's words of
caution: "But if Hannibal's genius may be likened to the Homeric god,
who, in his hatred to the Trojans, rises from the deep to rally the faint-
ing Greeks and to lead them against the enemy, so the calm courage
with which Hector met his more than human adversary in his country's
cause is no unworthy image of the unyielding magnanimity displayed
by the aristocracy of Rome. As Hannibal utterly eclipses Carthage, so,
on the contrary, Fabius, Marcellus, Claudius Nero, even Scipio himself, are as nothing when compared to the spirit, and wisdom, and
power of Rome. The Senate, which voted its thanks to its political

enemy, Varro, after his disastrous defeat, 'because he had not despaired of the commonwealth,' and which disdained either to solicit, or to reprove, or to threaten, or in any way to notice the twelve colonies which had refused their accustomed supplies of men for the army, is far more to be honored than the conqueror of Zama. This we should the more carefully bear in mind, because our tendency is to admire individual greatness far more than national; and, as no single Roman will bear comparison to Hannibal, we are apt to murmur at the event of the contest, and to think that the victory was awarded to the least worthy of the combatants. On the contrary, never was the wisdom of God's providence more manifest than in the issue of the struggle between Rome and Carthage. It was clearly for the good of mankind that Hannibal should be conquered; his triumph would have stopped the progress of the world; for great men can only act permanently by forming great nations; and no one man, even though it were Hannibal himself, can in one generation effect such a work. But where the nation has been merely enkindled for a while by a great man's spirit, the light passes away with him who communicated it; and the nation, when he is gone, is like a dead body, to which magic power had for a moment given unnatural life: when the charm has ceased, the body is cold and stiff as before. He who grieves over the battle of Zama should carry on his thoughts to a period thirty years later, when Hannibal must, in the course of nature have been dead, and consider how the isolated Phoenician city of Carthage was fitted to receive and to consolidate the civilization of Greece, or by its laws and institutions to bind together barbarians of every race and language into an organized empire, and prepare them for becoming, when that empire was dissolved, the free members of the commonwealth of Christian Europe."

The history of the Second Punic War is almost an account of the activities of the three sons of Hamilcar Barca, the most able general of the First Punic War. He boasted that he had trained his three sons, Hannibal, Hasdrubal, and Mago, like three lion's whelps, to prey upon the Romans. Hannibal, the eldest, had crossed the Alps in 218 B.C. Mago, who had fought at Cannae, had been sent to Carthage to proclaim that great victory, and then had sailed for Spain to aid Hasdrubal.

Now, in the spring of 207 B.C., the second brother, Hasdrubal, after skillfully disentangling himself from the Roman forces in Spain, and after marching through Gaul and over the Alps, had appeared in northern Italy. By this time Hannibal, with his unconquered and seemingly unconquerable army, had been over ten years in Italy, carrying out the vow which he had sworn as a child at the bidding of his father. However, Hannibal's later campaigns had not been signalized by any such great victories as marked the first three years of his invasion of Italy. The stern spirit of Roman resolution, ever highest in disaster and danger, had neither bent nor despaired beneath the merciless blows "the dire African" dealt her in rapid succession at the Trebia, Lake Trasimene and at Cannae. Rome's population was thinned by repeated slaughter in the field; poverty and actual scarcity ground down the survivors, through the fearful ravages Hannibal's cavalry spread through their cornfields, their pasture lands, and their vineyards. Many of her allies had gone over to the invader's side, and new clouds of foreign war threatened. But Rome receded not. Rich and poor among her citizens vied with each other in devotion to their country. The wealthy placed their stores, and all placed their lives, at the state's disposal. And though Hannibal could not be driven out of Italy, though every year brought its sufferings and sacrifices, Rome felt that her constancy had not been exerted in vain. If she was weakened by the continued strife, so was Hannibal. It was clear that the unaided resources of his army were unequal to the task of her destruction.

The single deerhound could not pull down the quarry he had so furiously assailed. Rome not only stood fiercely at bay, but had pressed back and gored her antagonist. She was weary and bleeding in every pore when suddenly the second hound of old Hamilcar's race appeared to aid his brother in the death grapple.

Hasdrubal had commanded the Carthaginian armies in Spain for some time with varying fortune. He had not as full authority over the Punic forces in that country as his father and brother had previously exercised. The faction at Carthage, which was feuding with his family, succeeded in fettering and interfering with his power. Then in 209 his new opponent, the recently appointed Publius Cornelius Scipio, later known to history as Scipio Africanus, surprised and captured the important city of Cartagena. However, in 208 B.C., Hasdrubal outmaneuvered Scipio and succeeded in crossing over the Pyrenees into Gaul. Scipio had carefully fortified and guarded the eastern passes of the Pyrenees, but Hasdrubal had passed these mountains near their western extremity with a considerable force of Spanish infantry, a number of African troops, and some elephants. He seemed to be in no hurry, for he halted for the winter in the territory of the Arverni, the modern Auvergne, and conciliated or purchased the goodwill of the Gauls in that region. He not only obtained winter quarters among them, but great numbers enlisted to fight under his command; and, in the year 207, on the approach of spring, marched with him to invade Italy.

As soon as the winter snows thawed, Hasdrubal commenced his march from Auvergne to the Alps. He experienced very few of the difficulties his brother had met with from the mountain tribes. Hannibal's army had been the first body of regular troops that had ever traversed these regions; and, as wild animals assail a traveler, the natives had risen against the army instinctively, in imagined defense of their own habitations. However, the fame of the war, with which Italy had been convulsed for so many years, had penetrated into the Alpine passes, and the mountaineers understood that a mighty city to the south was to be attacked by the troops whom they now saw marching among them. They not only opposed no resistance to the passage of Hasdrubal, but many of them, out of love of enterprise and plunder, or allured by high pay, took service with him.

Thus Hasdrubal advanced upon Italy with an army that gathered strength at every league. Emerging from the Alpine valleys, he crossed the river Po and marched down its southern bank toward the city of Placentia (now Piacenza). Many warriors of the Ligurian tribes joined him, but here he made the first of a series of three mistakes that would in the end prove fatal. Time was of the essence; his prime mission was to join forces with Hannibal as soon as possible. Every day that he wasted would find the armies of Rome better prepared to receive him. Hasdrubal's operations in Spain had been characterized by speed and boldness, but now that he was finally embarked upon the great adventure, he seems to have grown cautious. Instead of pushing rapidly southward, he sat down before Placentia to undertake a siege, which proved fruitless and lost many days.

In this crisis, Rome bent every effort to prepare for the encounter, but with a feeling akin to desperation. With extreme difficulty she had continued to fight against Hannibal alone. Now another son of Hamilcar had appeared who seemed even greater than Hannibal himself. Whereas Hannibal had made the seemingly impossible crossing of the Alps with difficulty, Hasdrubal had accomplished the same feat with apparent ease, gathering strength as he came.

At the beginning of the war Rome and its allies had counted a total strength of 770,000 men, of whom 70,000 were mounted. Although she retained control of the sea with a large and efficient navy, only twenty-three legions were serving under the colors in Italy, Sicily, Spain, and elsewhere. The term "legion" at this time usually meant one Roman and one allied legion, with a total strength of about 10,000 men. The fact that, in its hour of need, Rome could muster only twenty-three legions is fearfully emphatic of the extremity to which she had been reduced. Not only men, but money and military stores, were drained to the utmost, and if the armies of that year should be swept away by a repetition of the slaughters of Lake Trasimene and Cannae, all felt that Rome would cease to exist. Even if the campaign were to be marked by no decisive success on either side, her ruin seemed certain. In south Italy, Hannibal had either detached Rome's allies from her or had impoverished them by the ravages of his army. If Hasdrubal could do the same in upper Italy, Rome must sink beneath sheer starvation, for the hostile or desolated territory would yield no supplies of corn for her population, and of money to purchase it from abroad there was none. Instant victory was a matter of life or death.

Of the twenty-three legions, fifteen were in Italy. One defended Capua, two were needed to defend Rome, leaving twelve legions divided into six armies of 20,000 men each. Three of the armies were alloted to the northern forces under the consul Marcus Livius. He sent the praetor Porcius ahead with one army to meet and keep in check the advanced troops of Hasdrubal, then followed more slowly with the second army in support. The third army he held back in Etruria to overawe the Etruscans who were giving every indication of being eager to take this opportunity to desert the Roman cause. The other three armies of 20,000 each were south of Rome, facing Hannibal, under the command of the other consul, Claudius Nero.

Hannibal at this period occupied the extreme south of Italy, waiting for news from his brother. It must have been a shock when he learned that Hasdrubal was wasting valuable time besieging Placentia, when he should be marching southward with all possible speed to join forces. By this time Nero had concentrated two of his armies (40,000 men) at Venusia; the other Roman army, twenty thousand strong, was protecting the Tarentum area. Hannibal, whose army could not have been

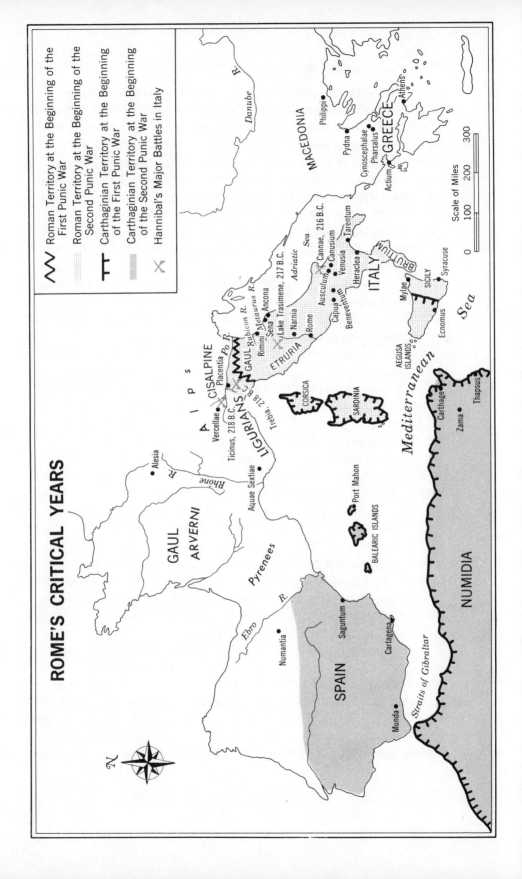

ROME'S CRITICAL YEARS

Legend:
- ∿∿∿ Roman Territory at the Beginning of the First Punic War
- ⊤⊤⊤ Roman Territory at the Beginning of the Second Punic War
- Carthaginian Territory at the Beginning of the First Punic War
- Carthaginian Territory at the Beginning of the Second Punic War
- ✗ Hannibal's Major Battles in Italy

Scale of Miles
0   100   200   300

Danube R.

MACEDONIA
Philippi
Pydna
Cynoscephalae
Pharsalus
Actium
Athens
GREECE

Adriatic Sea

ITALY
Cannae, 216 B.C.
Canusium
Tarentum
Venusia
Heraclea
Ausculum
Capua
Benevenum
Rome
Narnia
Lake Trasimene, 217 B.C.
Sena
Ancona
Rimini
Metaurus R.
Rubicon R.
Po R.
Placentia
CISALPINE
GAUL
Trebia, 218 B.C.
218 B.C.
Vercellae
Ticinus, 218 B.C.
LIGURIANS
Alps
ETRURIA
BRUTTIUM
SICILY
Syracuse
Mylae
Ecnomus

AEGUSA ISLANDS

CORSICA
SARDINIA

Mediterranean Sea

Carthage
Thapsus
Zama
NUMIDIA

Port Mahon
BALEARIC ISLANDS

Aquae Sextiae
Rhone R.
Alesia
GAUL
ARVERNI
Pyrenees
Ebro R.
Numantia
SPAIN
Saguntum
Cartagena
Munda
Straits of Gibraltar

N

much over 30,000, of whom two-thirds were Bruttians who had recently joined him, could not assume the offensive against Nero until he knew which road Hasdrubal would take to join him. Furthermore, a premature advance would mean leaving his own allies in the southern part of Italy at the mercy of the Romans near Tarentum for an unnecessarily long period of time. A movement northward, before he was informed of his brother's plans, would thus be worse than useless. Nero could retreat before him upon the other Roman troops near the capital, and Hannibal knew by experience that a mere advance upon the walls of Rome would have no effect on the fortunes of war. Nevertheless, to decrease the distance between the two Carthaginian armies and thus obtain news more rapidly, Hannibal did move northward from Bruttium. Some partial encounters took place between the two forces until Hannibal moved to Canusium in Apulia, there to await news of his brother's movements.

Meanwhile Hasdrubal had raised the siege of Placentia and was advancing toward Ariminum (now Rimini) on the Adriatic, driving before him the Roman army under Porcius. When the consul Livius came up in support, the invaders still continued their advance, pressing the Romans ever backward. Livius retreated beyond Ariminum, beyond the Metaurus as far as the little town of Sena, southeast of that river. Hasdrubal then made his second and most fatal error. He sent a group of six messengers to Hannibal with written instructions giving his proposed line of march and his complete plan of operations, calling for a junction of their armies at Narnia. The written plan should have been false, while the messengers should have had the true plan entrusted to memory. Never was a more grievous error committed. Those messengers traversed the greater part of Italy in safety but were then captured by a Roman detachment. Hasdrubal's letter, detailing his whole plan of campaign, was laid, not in his brother's hands, but in those of the commander of the Roman armies of the south.

Nero saw at once the full importance of the crisis. The two sons of Hamilcar were now within two hundred and fifty miles of each other, and if Rome were to be saved, the brothers must never meet alive. Nero instantly ordered 7,000 picked men, a thousand being cavalry, to hold themselves in readiness for a secret expedition against one of Hannibal's garrisons. As soon as night fell, he hurried forward on his bold enterprise. Starting toward the southwest, he soon amazed his officers and men, who had been given no inkling of the true destination, by wheeling around and pressing northward with the utmost rapidity.

During the preceding afternoon Nero had sent messengers to Rome, who were to give Hasdrubal's letters to the Senate. There was a law forbidding a consul to make war or march his army beyond the limits of the province assigned to him. But in such an emergency Nero did not wait for the permission of the Senate to execute his project, but informed them that he was already marching to join Livius. The Senate promptly confirmed his action, called the Capua legion to Rome, enlisted new troops to aid in the defense of the city, and sent the two legions in Rome to Narnia to defend that place against Hasdrubal in case he should march upon Rome before the consular armies could attack him.

Nero also sent horsemen forward along his line of march, with orders to the local authorities to bring stores of provisions and refreshments of every kind to the roadside, and to have relays of carriages ready to help transport the wearied soldiers. Such were the precautions he took for accelerating his march and, when he had advanced some distance from his camp, he briefly informed his soldiers of the real object of their expedition. He told them that never was there a design more seemingly audacious yet actually more safe. He said he was leading them to certain victory, for his colleague had an army large enough to balance the enemy already, so that *their* swords would decisively turn the scale. They would have all the credit of the victory and of having dealt the final decisive blow. He pointed to the enthusiastic reception they had already met on their line of march as a proof and as an omen of their good fortune. And, indeed, the entire population of the districts through which they passed, throughout their march, flocked to the roadside to see and bless the deliverers of their country. Food, drink, and refreshments of every kind were eagerly pressed upon them. Each peasant thought a favor was conferred upon him if one of Nero's chosen band accepted something from him. Veterans of former wars, and boys, too young to be ordered to the colors, fell in ranks. The soldiers caught the spirit of their leader. Night and day they pressed forward, taking their hurried meals as they advanced, resting by relays in the wagons which the zeal of the country people provided. In seven days they covered 250 miles, one of the most wonderful marches in history.

Meanwhile, at Rome, the news of Nero's expedition had caused the greatest excitement and alarm. All men felt the full audacity of the enterprise. People reasoned on the perilous state in which Nero had left the rest of his army, without a general, under the command of an untried legate named Quintus Catius, in the vicinity of the terrible Hannibal. They speculated on how long it would take Hannibal to pursue Nero and his expeditionary force. They talked over the former disasters of the war and how all these calamities had befallen them while they had only one Carthaginian general and army to deal with in Italy. Now they had two Carthaginian armies, two Hannibals in Italy. Hasdrubal was sprung from the same father; brought up in the same hostility to Rome; equally practiced in battle against their legions; and, if the comparative success with which he had crossed the Alps was a fair test, he was possibly a better general than his brother. With fear they listened to every rumor, exaggerated the strength of their enemy's forces, and criticized their own.

Fortunately for Rome, while she was thus a prey to terror and anxiety, her consul's nerves were stout and strong. He resolutely urged on his march toward Sena, where his colleague Livius and the praetor Porcius were encamped, Hasdrubal's army being in position about half a mile to their north. Nero had sent couriers forward to tell his colleague of his approach; and, by the advice of Livius, Nero so timed his final march as to reach the camp at Sena by night. By arrangement, Nero's men were received silently into the tents of their comrades, each according to his rank. Thus there was no enlargement of the camp that could betray to Hasdrubal the increase of force the Romans had received. This was considerable because of the large numbers of volunteers who had joined Nero's original 7,000 men.

A council of war was held at which some advised that time should be given for the men to refresh themselves after the fatigue of such a march. But according to the historian Livy, Nero vehemently opposed all delay, protesting: "The officer, who is for giving time to my men here to rest themselves, is for giving time to Hannibal to attack my men, whom I have left in the camp at Apulia. He is for giving time to Hannibal and Hasdrubal to discover my march, and to maneuver for a junction with each other . . . at their leisure. We must fight instantly, while both the foe here and the foe in the south are ignorant of our movements. We must destroy this Hasdrubal, and I must be back in Apulia before Hannibal awakes from his torpor." Nero's advice prevailed, and the Roman army drew up in battle array outside the camp, prepared to fight that day.

Hasdrubal had been anxious to bring Livius and Porcius to battle, though he had not judged it expedient to attack them in their lines. Now, on hearing that the Romans offered battle, he also drew up his men, and advanced toward them. No spy or deserter had informed him of Nero's arrival, nor had he received any direct information that he had more than his old enemies to deal with. But as he rode forward to reconnoiter the Roman line, he thought their numbers seemed to have increased, and that the armor of some of them was unusually dull and stained. He noticed, also, that the horses of some of the cavalry appeared to be rough and out of condition, as if they had just come from a succession of forced marches. It is said also that he heard the trumpet sound that morning once oftener than usual, as if directing the troops of some additional superior officer. It seems hard to believe that this should have occurred after all the precautions that had been taken to avoid showing any increase in the size of the camp. In any event Hasdrubal saw enough to cause him to refuse battle that day. In doubt as to what might have occurred between the armies of the south, and probably hoping that Hannibal also was approaching, he led his troops back into camp. Since the Romans did not venture an assault upon his entrenchments, the day passed uneventfully.

Hasdrubal then made his third mistake of the campaign. His mission was to join Hannibal. A bold attempt to bypass the Romans might have succeeded. It was true that a retreat would put greater distance between the two armies. However, to remain where he was, protected by his entrenchments, would have been better than to turn back. But Hasdrubal had become overcautious, and decided to effect a retreat during the night, hoping to reopen communications with Hannibal at a later date. A night withdrawal is a difficult maneuver at any time, but with troops as undisciplined as his Gallic allies who had recently joined him, it was hazardous indeed. Yet, as darkness fell, Hasdrubal led his men silently out of their camp and moved northward toward the Metaurus, in the hope of placing that river between himself and the Romans before his retreat was discovered. His guides betrayed him and, having purposely led him away from the part of the river that was fordable, made their escape in the dark. Hasdrubal and his army were left wandering in confusion along the steep bank, seeking in vain for a spot where the stream could be crossed. At last they halted, and when day dawned Hasdrubal found that many of his Gallic auxiliaries were in sorry condition. The Roman cavalry was soon seen coming in pursuit, followed at no great distance by the legions. There was no ford at hand; it was hopeless to think of continuing the retreat; he could not cross the river with the Romans almost upon him. Hasdrubal therefore ordered his men to prepare for action.

Heeren has described the general appearance of a Carthaginian army: "It was an assemblage of the most opposite races of the human species from the farthest parts of the globe. Hordes of half-naked Gauls were ranged next to companies of white-clothed Iberians, and savage Ligurians next to the far-traveled Nasamones and Lotophagi. Carthaginians and Phoenici-Africans formed the center, while innumerable troops of Numidian horsemen, taken from all the tribes of the Desert, swarmed about on unsaddled horses, and formed the wings; the van was composed of Balearic slingers; and a line of colossal elephants, with their Ethiopian guides, formed, as it were, a chain of moving fortresses before the whole army." This general description of the average Carthaginian army helps to visualize the appearance of the hosts that fought for Carthage, but Hasdrubal's army did not fit the pattern in certain respects. He seems to have been especially deficient in cavalry, and he had few African troops, though some Carthaginians of high rank were with him. His veteran Spanish infantry, armed with helmets and shields, and short cut-and-thrust swords, were the best part of his army.

After surveying the ground over which he must fight, Hasdrubal found that he was on a slight rise boardering the river. On his left was a small brook or valley which would be an obstacle to a Roman advance. Here he placed his unreliable Gauls who were armed with long javelins and huge broadswords and targets. In the center he formed his Ligurian infantry. On the right he drew up his Spanish infantry and his few Africans, under his own personal command. This arrangement would permit him to attack the Romans with his best troops on his right flank, while the rugged nature of the ground on the left flank would make it difficult for the Roman right wing to come to close quarters with those unserviceable Gauls at the opposite end of the line. This arrangement was his only chance of victory or safety, and he seems to have done everything that good generalship could do to secure victory, except to keep out an army reserve to meet unexpected contingencies, which was a practice that had not yet come into general use in warfare. He placed his ten elephants in advance of his center and right wing and caused the driver of each of them to be provided with a sharp iron spike and a mallet. The drivers were

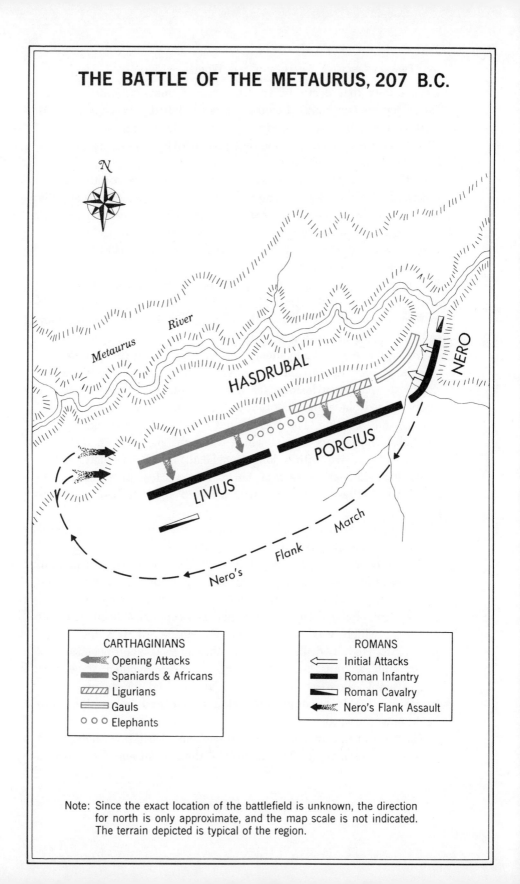

THE BATTLE OF THE METAURUS, 207 B.C.

CARTHAGINIANS
- Opening Attacks
- Spaniards & Africans
- Ligurians
- Gauls
- ○ ○ ○ Elephants

ROMANS
- Initial Attacks
- Roman Infantry
- Roman Cavalry
- Nero's Flank Assault

Note: Since the exact location of the battlefield is unknown, the direction for north is only approximate, and the map scale is not indicated. The terrain depicted is typical of the region.

given orders that every beast that became unmanageable and ran back upon his own ranks should be instantly killed. We have no trustworthy information as to the size of his army but it probably exceeded 40,000 men, which meant that the combined Roman forces outnumbered him almost five to four.

At the time of the Punic Wars, the heavy infantry of the legion consisted of three classes. The Hastati, who at that time were the troops in the first line of the legion, comprised men between twenty-five and thirty years of age; the Principes, who formed the second line, were from thirty to forty; and the Triarii, or third-line troops, were veterans from forty to forty-five. In addition, the Velites, or light infantry, consisted chiefly of young men from seventeen to twenty-five years of age who at the beginning of an engagement were posted in front of the Hastati. When the engagement became serious, they fell back to the line of the Triarii.

The equipment of the legionary was excellent. His principal weapon was the gladius, the terrible Roman sword, that may be classed as the deadliest weapon in history, for it killed millions of men. It had a double-edged blade and, like that of the Spaniards, was used for both cutting and thrusting. The Hastati and the Principes also carried two short throwing spears, one of which was light and slender, the other strong and massive with a long iron head. The Triarii had, in lieu of the heavy lance, a pike from ten to fourteen feet long and several darts. The Velites were armed with a sword and also had a number of darts.

For armor, the heavy infantry wore a leather helmet strengthened with iron, a metal and leather breastplate, greaves for the legs, and a large wooden shield, covered with leather and reinforced with iron. The greave for the right leg was stouter than that for the left, as the legionary worked always to the right, stabbing and cutting under and to the right of the shield. Each legionary occupied a front of about five feet, which was nearly twice the space allowed the Greek phalangite. He was drilled to reduce this interval when necessary, as for example, to resist a cavalry charge. This arrangement gave each soldier ample room for throwing his javelins and for the use of his sword and shield. He could step back between those behind him, who could move forward.

The tactical unit of each of the three lines, Hastati, Principes and Triarii, was the maniple. The maniple of the Hastati and the Principes numbered 120 men, twelve men front by ten deep, while the maniple of the Triarii consisted of sixty men on a frontage of six men. The maniples were normally arranged in checkerboard fashion; this was termed the quincunx order. The Hastati could therefore retire between the maniples of the Principes, or the latter could advance, without disordering either line.

The cavalry of each legion was at this period about three hundred strong. The Italian allies were similarly organized, armed and equipped, but their numerical proportion of cavalry was much larger.

Such was the nature of the forces that advanced on the Roman side to the Battle of the Metaurus. Nero commanded the right wing opposite the Gauls; the praetor Porcius faced the Ligurians in the center; the consul Livius stood opposite the Spaniards and Africans on the Roman left wing. Hasdrubal opened the battle by attacking Livius and at first made some headway, then was halted, as the fighting spread along the line to the center. The Africans and Spaniards were stout soldiers, as were the Ligurians, and they had the advantage of position on the hillside. The Romans, fighting uphill, made no progress; both sides were incurring heavy casualties.

But at last Nero, who found that Hasdrubal refused his left wing, and who could not overcome the difficulties of the ground in the area assigned to him, decided the battle by another stroke of that military genius which had inspired his march to the battle area. Leaving the Hastati to hold the line against the Gauls, he moved his Principes and Triarii in rear and completely around the left flank of the Roman army. To the utter surprise of both friend and foe, he emerged from the hills on Hasdrubal's right flank, and fiercely charged the Spaniards and Africans. The assault was as successful as it was sudden. When it came, Livius redoubled his efforts in front. Rolled back in disorder upon each other, overwhelmed by numbers, the Spaniards and Ligurians died, fighting gallantly to the last. The Gauls, who had taken little or no part in the battle, were then cut to pieces. Hasdrubal, after having, by the confession of his enemies, done all that a general could do, saw that the victory was irreparably lost. Scorning to survive the gallant host he had led, refusing to gratify as a captive Roman cruelty and pride, he spurred his horse into the midst of his enemies and, sword in hand, met death in a manner worthy of the son of Hamilcar and the brother of Hannibal.

Practically the whole Carthaginian army had been killed or captured. The Roman loss was about 8,000. Complete success had crowned Nero's enterprise. Returning as rapidly as he had advanced, he was again facing the inactive enemies in the south before they ever knew of his march. In just over two weeks Nero had marched more than 500 miles and achieved the greatest Roman victory of the entire war —but he brought with him a ghastly trophy of what he had done. In the true spirit of that savage brutality which deformed the Roman national character, Nero ordered Hasdrubal's head to be flung into his brother's camp. Ten years had passed since Hannibal had last gazed on those features. The sons of Hamilcar had then planned their war against Rome, which had so nearly succeeded. If Hasdrubal had won, it is possible that Hannibal would have conquered Rome. Year after year Hannibal had been struggling in Italy, in the hope of one day hailing the arrival of him whom he had left in Spain, and of seeing his brother's eye flash with affection and pride at the junction of their irresistible hosts. He now saw that eye glazed in death, and in the agony of his heart the great Carthaginian groaned aloud that he recognized his country's destiny.

Meanwhile, at the tidings of the great battle, Rome at once rose to the full confidence of triumph. Hannibal might retain his hold on southern Italy for a few years longer, but the imperial city and her allies were no longer in danger from his arms; and, after Hannibal's downfall, the great military republic of the ancient world met in her career of conquest no other worthy competitor.

Synopsis of Events Between the Battle of the Metaurus, 207 B.C., and Arminius' Victory over the Roman Legions under Varus, A.D. 9.

206. Scipio drives the Carthaginians out of Spain.

205–201. Scipio is made consul and carries the war into Africa. He gains several victories there, and the Carthaginians recall Hannibal from Italy to oppose him. Scipio wins the Battle of Zama in 202 and Carthage sues for peace. The Second Punic War ends, leaving Rome confirmed in her dominion over Italy, Sicily, Sardinia and Corsica, mistress of a great part of Spain, and virtually predominant in North Africa.

200–197. Rome makes war upon Philip V, King of Macedonia. Philip is defeated by Flamininus at Cynoscephalae, 197, and forced to make peace. The Macedonian influence is now destroyed in Greece and the Roman established in its stead.

192–189. Antiochus III, King of Syria, invades Greece, is driven out, then completely defeated at the Battle of Magnesia, 190, by the Romans led by L. Cornelius Scipio and his famous brother, Scipio Africanus. (This was the first battle fought by the Roman legions in Asia. In the following year Antiochus gladly accepted peace on terms that left him dependent upon Rome.)

200–190. "Thus, within the short space of ten years, was laid the foundation of the Roman authority in the East, and the general state of affairs entirely changed. If Rome was not yet the ruler, she was at least the arbitress of the world from the Atlantic to the Euphrates. The power of the three principal states was so completely humbled, that they durst not, without the permission of Rome, begin any new war; the fourth, Egypt, had already, in the year 201, placed herself under the guardianship of Rome; and the lesser powers followed of themselves, esteeming it an honor to be called the allies of Rome."—HEEREN.

171–168. War is renewed between Macedonia and Rome. After the defeat of Perseus, the Macedonian king, at Pydna in 168 by L. Aemilius Paulus, the Macedonian monarchy is ended.

149–146. Rome oppresses the Carthaginians until they are driven to take up arms, and the Third Punic War begins. After a long siege, in which the Carthaginians fight desperately with almost no resources, the city is finally taken after prolonged assault by the Romans under Scipio Aemilianus. Carthage is burned; the walls are torn down; the site is leveled, salted, and plowed over.

133. The fall of Numantia in Spain, which is reduced after a long siege by Scipio Aemilianus, marks the end of years of revolt against Roman rule.

133. A century of domestic strife begins at Rome with the attempts of the Gracchi to aid the impoverished farmer and the lower classes. It lasts until the Battle of Actium (31 B.C.), which establishes Octavian as sole master of the Roman world.

111–105. In the Jugurthine War, Numidia is conquered by Gaius Marius.

102. Two fierce Germanic tribes, the Cimbri and Teutones, after destroying several Roman armies, unite to invade Italy. The military genius of Marius here saves his country. He defeats the Teutones in a decisive battle at Aquae Sextiae (known today as Aix-en-Provence).

101. Marius defeats the Cimbri at the Battle of Vercellae. Marius is now the national hero, but during these years, owing to the changes in the character of the Roman people, he has been unable to obtain enough freeholders to fill his army. The best people of Rome are generally avoiding military service; the armies gradually cease to be armies of the nation. They become more efficient and better trained than before, but less patriotic, and more likely to become instruments of danger in the hands of their leaders.

91–88.   Several of Rome's Italian allies (*socii*) revolt and form a republic of their own. When Rome gradually concedes to the allies certain of the rights of citizenship, the Social War is brought to a close.

88–78.   Mithridates VI, called the Great, King of Pontus, declares war on Rome and overruns Asia Minor. The Roman Senate appoints Lucius Cornelius Sulla, who had distinguished himself in the Social War, to command against Mithridates. The popular party then names Marius as commander and rioting breaks out in Rome. Sulla marches on Rome, thereby becoming the first general to occupy the city with a Roman army; Marius is forced to flee. Sulla then leaves for the East, where he successfully concludes the war with Mithridates in 84 B.C. Meanwhile, Marius has returned, is elected consul for the seventh time, then dies in office. Sulla returns in 82 to defeat the popular party and establish himself as dictator; he retires in 79 B.C. and dies the following year.

74.   When the last king of Bithynia bequeathes his kingdom to Rome, Mithridates occupies it, and another war with Rome results.

73–71.   Spartacus leads a Revolt of the Gladiators which is eventually crushed, with difficulty, by M. Licinius Crassus, with some assistance from Gnaeus Pompey. The consul Lucullus defeats Mithridates, driving him to seek refuge in Armenia with his son-in-law Tigranes.

69–63.   Lucullus gains more victories against Mithridates, then is replaced by Pompey, who had won additional fame by rapidly exterminating piracy in the Mediterranean. Pompey completely defeats Mithridates and Tigranes, captures Jerusalem, and reorganizes Asia Minor and Syria.

60.   Pompey, Crassus and Julius Caesar form the First Triumvirate, which lasts until Crassus is defeated and killed at the Battle of Carrhae by the Parthians in 53 B.C.

58–51.   Caesar conquers Gaul and in the process organizes and leads in battle probably the best trained and most efficient troops for their work that the world has ever seen. (The cavalry was good and the infantry superb. Caesar's soldiers were remarkably versatile. They built and navigated ships, were adept at engineering work, building bridges, constructing roads and fortifications; they brought siegecraft to a state of development that was not equaled for hundreds of years. Their outstanding ability in this respect undoubtedly saved them in the last great revolt of Vercingetorix which ended at the Siege of Alesia in 52 B.C.)

49. Caesar crosses the Rubicon with one legion, announcing, "Alea iacta est" (The die is cast). Pompey and most of the Senate flee to Greece. Caesar, after rapidly clearing Spain of Pompey's adherents, returns to Rome, prepared to follow Pompey.

48. Caesar defeats Pompey in the decisive Battle of Pharsalus.

47–45. In turn, Caesar defeats Pharnaces, the son of Mithridates at Zela, where he sent his famous "Veni, vidi, vici" message; an army in Africa at Thapsus; and Pompey's sons at Munda in Spain.

44. Caesar is assassinated on the Ides of March.

43. Mark Antony, Lepidus and Octavian form the Second Triumvirate.

42. Brutus and Cassius are defeated by Antony and Octavian at Philippi.

31. The Battle of Actium leaves Octavian as undisputed master of the Roman world, later ruling as Augustus Caesar.

5

The Victory of Arminius over the Roman Legions under Varus, A.D. 9

WHEN AUGUSTUS CAESAR became the ruler of the Roman Empire, he faced two major problems, the reestablishment of government in a world shaken by over twenty years of civil war and anarchy, and the acquisition of suitable frontiers. The people wanted peace and asked that a strong hand guide them. In the two hundred years since the Second Punic War, Roman citizens had lost their pride in their army and now avoided the burdens of military service. Gone were the days when free men vied with each other in devotion to their country. No longer was the bearing of arms considered a privilege rather than a duty; no longer was it a disgraceful punishment to be denied that right.

Confronted with this situation which had gradually developed over the last hundred years, Augustus, while reorganizing the internal government of Italy and the provinces, instituted a number of reforms in the Roman Army. Many of these were simply adaptations or extensions of developments that had already taken place. It was now a professional army; Augustus recognized this fact, established definite rates of pay and a definite discharge bonus. The term of service was set at from 20 to 25 years, though this was elastic. Morale was secured not by appeals to patriotism but by unit *esprit de corps* and a system of rewards and punishment. Augustus also reorganized the auxiliaries, recruited from the best men of the empire who were not Roman citizens. They were less well paid than the Romans, but upon discharge they received a bounty and were granted the Roman franchise for themselves, their wives and their children. The result was a highly trained, efficient army that successfully guarded Rome against invasion for hundreds of years, but behind it there was almost nothing. Gradually the only military spirit left in the empire came to reside in the army itself, where traditions and teachings were handed down from old soldiers to recruits, many of whom were sons of former legionaries.

With this instrument Augustus set about the task of acquiring suitable defensible frontiers, but first he had to pacify and reorganize the provinces of Spain and North Africa. This task took almost ten years before the inhabitants were thoroughly subdued. In the East he arranged for the return by the Parthians of the standards captured at Carrhae (53 B.C.); he set the eastern boundaries of the empire at the upper reaches of the Euphrates and along the edges of the Arabian Desert.

This left, as the main problem, the northern frontier. As Augustus found it, this boundary was anything but satisfactory. Caesar had conquered Gaul, but the major portion of the Alps had never been subjugated. From this region and from the area north of Macedonia the wild tribes of the Alps and the Danube could easily raid northern Italy, Macedonia, and Thrace. The frontier was far too long, and the communications from Italy to Gaul and Macedonia insecure. It appeared to Augustus that the first task to undertake was the annexation of the western Alps between Italy and Gaul. When this was successfully accomplished, he turned his attention to acquiring natural frontiers farther north. The Danube was an obvious line. In 15 B.C. he sent the efficient Roman legions pouring across the Alps northward to that river, acquiring the new provinces of Rhaetia and Noricum, extending Roman control eastward almost to Vienna.

This was excellent progress, but not nearly enough. The line of the Danube must be secured all the way to the Black Sea, and furthermore the area between the upper waters of the Rhine and Danube produced a dangerous salient projecting straight toward the heart of Gaul. In addition the Rhine-Danube line was far too long, whereas the Elbe-Danube line just a little distance farther north would be much shorter and easier to defend. If this second line could be secured, innumerable problems would be solved, and if it had been reached the history of Europe would have been changed radically.

For the next twenty years the Roman commanders proceeded to carry out these plans. By A.D. 6 it appeared that the problem was almost solved. The line of the Danube had been reached to the Black Sea and the new provinces of Pannonia and Moesia annexed. In northern and central Germany the line of the Elbe had also been attained, although the country could not yet be called entirely secure. There remained only one region to be invaded, a large section of Bohemia occupied by a powerful tribe known as the Marcomanni. Plans were already underway, the orders had been issued, the troops were actually marching toward their goal when suddenly the whole of Pannonia and Illyricum burst into revolt. It took three years to suppress this insurrection, which appears to have been the most serious uprising encountered by Rome in the two hundred years since the Second Punic War. It was then, in the third year of the revolt, in A.D. 9, that Arminius struck.

When Arminius planned the general uprising of his Germanic countrymen against Rome, the prospect must have seemed dark and disheartening. Half the land was occupied by Roman garrisons; and, what was worse, many of the Germans seemed fairly content with their lot. The braver portion, whose patriotism could be relied upon, was ill armed and undisciplined, while the enemy's troops consisted of veterans in the highest state of equipment and training, familiarized with victory and commanded by officers of proved skill and valor. The resources of Rome seemed boundless.

The German chieftain knew well the gigantic power of his opponent. Arminius was no rude savage. He was familiar with the Roman language and civilization. He had served in the Roman armies; he had been admitted to the Roman citizenship, and raised to the rank of the equestrian order. It was part of the policy of Rome to confer rank and privileges on the leading families of nations that served with her in her campaigns. Among other Germanic chieftains, Arminius and his brother, who were the heads of the noblest house in the tribe of the Cherusci, had been selected for this honor. Roman refinements and dignities succeeded in denationalizing the brother, who assumed the Roman name of Flavius, and adhered to Rome throughout all her wars against his country.

Arminius remained unbought by honors or wealth, by refinement

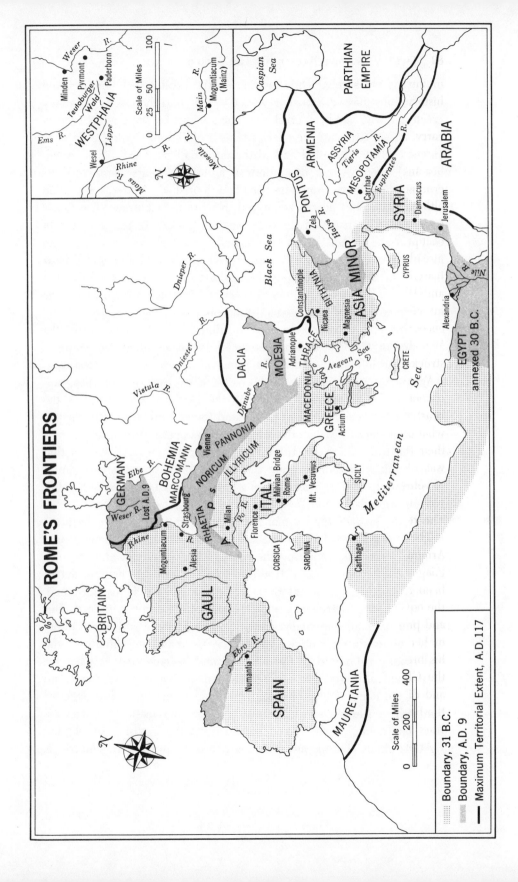

ROME'S FRONTIERS

WESTPHALIA (inset)

Weser R.
Minden
Pyrmont
Weser
Teutoburger Wald
Paderborn
Moguntiacum (Mainz)
Main R.
Ems R.
Lippe R.
Wesel
Rhine R.
Maas R.
Moselle R.

Scale of Miles
0 25 50 100

BRITAIN

GERMANY
Lost A.D. 9
Elbe R.
Weser R.
Rhine
Moguntiacum
Alesia

GAUL

SPAIN
Ebro R.
Numantia

CORSICA
SARDINIA

ITALY
Milan
Po R.
Florence
Milvian Bridge
Rome
Mt. Vesuvius
SICILY
Carthage

MAURETANIA

BOHEMIA
MARCOMANNI
Strasbourg
RHAETIA
A L P S
NORICUM
Vienna
PANNONIA
ILLYRICUM

DACIA
Danube R.
Dniester R.
Vistula R.
Dnieper R.

Black Sea

MOESIA
Adrianople
THRACE
Constantinople
Nicaea
MACEDONIA
GREECE
Actium
Aegean Sea
CRETE

Mediterranean

ARMENIA
PONTUS
Zela
Halys R.
BITHYNIA
Magnesia
ASIA MINOR
CYPRUS

Caspian Sea

PARTHIAN EMPIRE

ASSYRIA
Tigris R.
MESOPOTAMIA
Carrhae
Euphrates R.

ARABIA

SYRIA
Damascus
Jerusalem

EGYPT
annexed 30 B.C.
Alexandria
Nile R.

Scale of Miles
0 200 400

Boundary, 31 B.C.

Boundary, A.D. 9

Maximum Territorial Extent, A.D. 117

or luxury, yet surely, while meditating the exploit that immortalized him, he must have anxiously revolved in his mind the fate of the many great men who had been crushed in the attempt he was about to renew —the attempt to stay the chariot wheels of Rome. Could he hope to succeed where Hannibal and Mithridates had perished? What warning had been written one hundred and forty years before on the desolate site where Numantia once had flourished? Nor was a caution wanting in scenes nearer home and in more recent times. The Gauls had fruitlessly struggled for years against Caesar. In the last year of that war the gallant Vercingetorix had roused all his countrymen to insurrection, had cut off Roman detachments, and brought Caesar himself to the extreme of peril at Alesia—he, too, had finally succumbed, had been led captive in Caesar's triumph, and had then been killed in cold blood in a Roman dungeon.

Arminius had watched the powerful Roman armies, moving from the province of Gaul, establish a chain of fortresses along the right as well as the left bank of the Rhine and, in a series of victorious campaigns, advance their eagles as far as the Elbe. Roman fleets also, sailing from the harbors of Gaul along the German coasts and up the estuaries, had cooperated with the land forces, and seemed to display even more decisively than the armies, Rome's overwhelming superiority over the rude Germanic tribes. Yet Arminius may have known that behind this formidable facade the Roman military spirit had almost disappeared; that it was a strong line but without reserves; once broken through it might be penetrated.

Still, to persuade the Germans to combine, in spite of their frequent feuds among themselves, in one sudden outburst against Rome was a most difficult task, requiring the ultimate in persuasion and tact. To keep the scheme concealed from the Romans until the hour of action arrived and then to defeat those veteran armies with his untrained, undisciplined countrymen seemed a perilous enterprise indeed. But Arminius was an impetuous spirit who hated Rome and, in addition, had another strong motive. Among the Germans of high rank who had readily submitted to the invaders and become zealous partisans of Roman authority was a chieftain named Segestes. Arminius had sought the hand of his daughter Thusnelda in marriage, but Segestes had forbade the suit and tried to stop all communication between the two. Thusnelda, however, had baffled her father's wishes by eloping with Arminius. Disappointed in his efforts to prevent the marriage,

Segestes had then accused Arminius of plotting treason against Rome. The royal governor ignored this warning; perhaps he felt that it was only the logical result of the personal quarrel between the two men.

A change of governors had taken place three years before. The new governor, Quintilius Varus, had been proconsul of Syria, and when he arrived he began to treat his new subjects as he had treated the natives of Syria. Apparently he made no effort to understand the nature of the German national character. Furthermore he was not a trained soldier and had none of the high military talent of the commanders who had preceded him. However, the country was supposed to have been subdued, and no trouble was expected by the higher authorities in Rome.

Arminius appears to have sensed the opportunity thus presented to him. He found among the other German chiefs many who sympathized with him, and many whom private wrongs had stung deeply. There was little difficulty in collecting bold leaders for an attack, and little fear of the population not rising readily at their call. But to declare open war against Rome and to encounter Varus' army in a pitched battle would have been merely rushing upon certain destruction. Varus had five legions under his command. Of these, two were stationed on the Rhine at Moguntiacum (present-day Mainz), while the other three were quartered for the summer in Westphalia in the vicinity of modern Minden on the Weser. When winter came these three legions would return to winter quarters on the Lippe, or on the Rhine where these two rivers meet today at Wesel. They were Arminius' target. He hoped to catch them on the march but, together with their auxuliaries they numbered over 20,000 men, including their cavalry.

It was not merely the number but the quality of the force that made them formidable. No matter how contemptible Varus might be as a general, Arminius well knew how admirably the Roman armies were organized and officered, and how perfectly the legionaries understood every maneuver and every duty which the varying emergencies of a battle might require. Stratagem was therefore indispensable. It was necessary to blind Varus to their schemes until a favorable opportunity should arrive for striking a decisive blow.

For this purpose the German confederates frequented Varus' summer headquarters where the Roman general conducted himself with all the arrogant security of the governor of a perfectly submissive

province. When September came and it was time for Varus to move
to his winter quarters, Arminius secretly directed certain of the tribes
near the Weser and the Ems to take up arms in open revolt against
the Romans. This was represented to Varus as an occasion that required his prompt attendance at the spot, but he was kept in ignorance
of its being part of a concerted national rising. Although again warned
by Segestes, he still looked on Arminius as his submissive vassal who
would aid him against the rebels. He therefore set his army in motion
and marched southeastward, with Arminius and his men escorting the
long column of troops. For some distance the route lay along a level
plain, but near the sources of the Ems River the country assumes a
very different character, and it was here that Arminius had fixed the
scene of his enterprise.

It was a vast hilly region, intersected by rapid streams flowing in
deep valleys through narrow defiles with precipitous sides, covered
with dense forests and known as the Teutoburger Wald, from whence
the battle derives its name. This is the district toward which Varus
is supposed to have marched, and it was in this region that the bones
of his legions were later discovered. We do not know the exact location
of the battle area but many of the localities in that region bear names
indicating that a great battle had been fought there at some time in
the distant past.

When the long array quitted the firm, level ground and began to
wind its way among the woods, the marshes, and the ravines, the
difficulties of the march, even without the intervention of an armed
foe, became fearfully apparent. In many places the soil, sodden with
rain, was impracticable for cavalry and even for infantry until trees
had been felled and a rude causeway constructed. In addition, contrary to the usual strict principles of Roman discipline, Varus had
permitted his army to be accompanied and impeded by an immense
train of baggage wagons, and the camp followers, who should have
been sent back ahead of time to the Rhine, were allowed to mingle
with the column. Then, while the army was trying to hack its way
through, a violent rainstorm burst upon them, and Arminius, together
with his followers, disappeared.

The duties of the engineer were familiar to all who served in the
Roman armies. But the crowding and confusion of the columns hin-
dered the working parties of the soldiers, and in the midst of their
toil the word was suddenly passed through their ranks that the rear
guard had been attacked by the barbarians. Varus resolved on pressing

forward, but a heavy discharge of missiles from the woods on either flank showed how serious was the peril. He saw his best men falling around him without the opportunity to retaliate. Many of his light-armed auxiliaries who were of Germanic race now rapidly deserted, and it was impossible to deploy the legionaries on such broken ground. Choosing a firm and open spot, the Romans forced their way to it, then halted for the night. Faithful to their national discipline and tactics, they formed their camp. Despite the harassing attacks of their thronging foes, they fortified it as they had been trained to do every time they halted for the night, with a ditch, a wall, and a palisade. The traces of these camps, built according to a systematic, carefully laid-out plan and requiring an immense amount of arduous labor, are impressed permanently on the soil of Europe, attesting the presence in the olden times of the imperial eagles.

On the morrow the Romans renewed their march, the veteran officers under Varus now probably directing the operations, and hoping to find the Germans drawn up to meet them, in which case they relied on their own superior discipline and tactics for a victory that would re-assure the supremacy of Rome. But Arminius was far too sage a commander to lead his followers, with their unwieldy broadswords and inefficient defensive armor, against the fully equipped Roman legionaries. Instead he permitted the Romans to march out from their camp, to form first in line for action and in column for marching, without opposition. For some distance Varus was allowed to move on, harassed only by slight skirmishes, but struggling with difficulty over the broken ground, the distress of his men being aggravated by heavy torrents of rain that burst upon the devoted legions as if the angry gods of Germany were pouring out the vials of their wrath upon the invaders.

After some little time their van approached a ridge of high wooded ground. Arminius had caused barricades of hewn trees to be formed here so as to add to the natural difficulties of the passage. Fatigue and discouragement now began to betray themselves in the Roman ranks. Their line became less steady; baggage wagons were abandoned because it was impossible to force them along. As this happened, many soldiers left their ranks and crowded round the wagons to secure the most valuable portions of their property; each was busy about his own affairs and slow to hear the word of command from his officers.

Arminius now gave the signal for a general attack. The fierce shouts

of the Germans pealed through the gloom of the forest as the thronging hordes assailed the flanks of the column, pouring in clouds of
darts on the encumbered legionaries as they struggled up the glens
or floundered in the morasses. Arminius, with a chosen band of personal retainers around him, cheered on his countrymen by voice and
example. He and his men aimed their weapons particularly at the
horses of the Roman cavalry. The wounded animals, slipping about in
the mire and their own blood, threw their riders and plunged among
the ranks of the legions, disordering all around them. The Roman
officer who commanded the cavalry rode off with his squadrons in
the vain hope of escaping by thus abandoning his comrades. Unable
to keep together, or to force their way through the woods and swamps,
the horsemen were overpowered in detail and slaughtered to the last
man.

The Roman infantry still held together and resisted, but more
through the instinct of discipline and through bravery than from any
hope of success or escape. Varus, after being severely wounded in a
charge of the Germans against his part of the column, committed
suicide to avoid falling into the hands of those whom he had exas-
perated by his oppressions. One of the lieutenant generals of the army
fell fighting; the other surrendered to the enemy. But mercy to a fallen
foe had never been a Roman virtue, and those among her legions who
now laid down their arms in hope of quarter drank deep of the cup
of suffering which Rome had held to the lips of many a brave but
unfortunate enemy. The infuriated Germans slaughtered their oppressors with deliberate ferocity, and those prisoners who were not hewn
to pieces on the spot were only preserved to perish by a more cruel
death.

The bulk of the Roman army fought steadily and stubbornly, frequently repelling the masses of their assailants, but gradually losing
the compactness of their array and becoming weaker and weaker
beneath the incessant shower of darts and the repeated assaults of
their enemy. At last, in a series of desperate attacks, the column was
pierced through and through. The Roman host that had marched forth
in such pride and might, now broken up into confused fragments,
either fell fighting beneath overpowering numbers or perished in the
swamps and woods in unavailing efforts at flight. Few, very few, ever
saw again the left bank of the Rhine. One body of brave veterans,
arraying themselves in a ring on a little mound, beat off every charge

of the Germans, and prolonged their resistance to the close of that dreadful day. The traces of a feeble attempt at forming a ditch and mound attested in afteryears the spot where the last of the Romans passed their night of suffering and despair. But on the morrow this remnant also, worn out with hunger, wounds, and toil, was charged by the victorious Germans and either massacred on the spot or offered up in fearful rites at the altars of the deities of the old mythology of the North.

A gorge in the mountain ridge, through which runs the road between Paderborn and Pyrmont, leads to the Extersteine, a cluster of bold and grotesque rocks of sandstone, near which is a small sheet of water, overshadowed by a grove of trees. According to local tradition this was one of the sacred groves of the ancient Germans, and it was here that the Roman captives were slain in sacrifice by the victorious warriors of Arminius.

Never was the liberation of an oppressed people more instantaneous and complete. Throughout Germany the Roman garrisons were assailed, cut off, and forced to fight their way out. Within a few weeks after Varus had fallen, the German soil was freed from the foot of an invader.

At Rome the tidings of the battle were received with an agony of terror. If the reports of the effect of the battle had not come to us from Roman historians, we would think them exaggerated. They tell us emphatically how great was the fear the Romans felt of the Germans, if their various tribes could be brought to unite for a common purpose. The Roman historian Cassius Dio says: "Then Augustus, when he heard the calamity of Varus, rent his garment, and was in great affliction for the troops he had lost, and for terror respecting the Germans and the Gauls. And his chief alarm was that he expected them to push on against Italy and Rome; and there remained no Roman youth fit for military duty that were worth speaking of, and the allied populations, that were not at all serviceable, had been wasted away. Yet he prepared for the emergency as well as his means allowed; and when none of the citizens of military age were willing to enlist, he made them cast lots, and punished by confiscation of goods and disfranchisement every fifth man among those under thirty-five, and every tenth man of those above that age. At last, when he found that not even thus could he make many come forward, he put some of them to death. So he made a conscription of discharged veterans and of emancipated slaves, and, collecting as large a force as he could, sent it, under Tiberius, with all speed into Germany."

Dio mentions also a number of terrifying portents that were believed to have occurred at the time, the narrative of which is not immaterial, as it shows the state of the public mind. The summits of the Alps were said to have fallen and columns of fire to have blazed up from them. In the Campus Martius the temple of the war god was struck by a thunderbolt. The nightly heavens glowed several times as if on fire. Many comets blazed forth together; and fiery meteors, shaped like spears, had shot from the northern quarter of the sky down into the Roman camps. It was said, too, that a statue of Victory, which had stood on the frontier pointing the way toward Germany, had of its own accord turned round, and now pointed to Italy. These and other prodigies were believed by the multitude to have accompanied the slaughter of Varus' legions, manifesting the anger of the gods against Rome. Augustus himself was not free from superstition, but on this occasion no supernatural terrors were needed to increase the alarm and grief that he felt. Months after the battle he would beat his head against the wall and exclaim, "Quintilius Varro, give me back my legions!" We learn this from his biographer Suetonius, and indeed every ancient writer who alludes to the overthrow of Varus attests the importance of the blow against the Roman power and the bitterness with which it was felt.

The Germans did not pursue their victory beyond their own territory; but that victory secured at once and forever the independence of the Teutonic race. Rome sent, indeed, her legions again into Germany, but all efforts at permanent conquest in that area were abandoned by Augustus and his successors. In later years they pushed forward and seized other regions, but the shortening of the frontier to the Elbe-Danube line was never accomplished. If this had been done, not only would the existence of the Roman Empire have been greatly prolonged, with a much easier frontier to defend, but also the inhabitants of Germany would have become latinized as were those of Gaul and Spain, and the subsequent history of culture and conflict in Europe would have been materially altered.

The blow that Arminius struck, as well as the loss of three legions, was not an overwhelming catastrophe to the Roman power at that time, but it was a great moral victory which never was forgotten. The Rhine became for all practical purposes the acknowledged boundary until the fifth century of our era, when the Roman Empire was sufficiently weakened and the Germans became the assailants, and carved with their conquering swords the provinces of imperial Rome into the kingdoms of modern Europe.

Synopsis of Events Between Arminius' Victory over Varus, A.D. 9, and the Battle of Châlons, A.D. 451

43. The Romans commence the conquest of Britain, Claudius being then Emperor of Rome.

64. A great part of Rome is destroyed by fire. Nero blames the Christians and orders the first mass persecution of the adherents of the Christian faith.

68–70. Civil wars disrupt the Roman world. The emperors Nero, Galba, Otho, and Vitellius are cut off successively by violent deaths. Vespasian becomes emperor.

70. Jerusalem is destroyed by the Romans under Titus.

79. A great eruption of Mount Vesuvius buries the cities of Pompeii and Herculaneum.

98–117. Trajan is Emperor of Rome. Under his rule the empire acquires its greatest territorial extent, including Dacia (modern Rumania, a portion of Russia and a part of Hungary), Armenia, Mesopotamia and Assyria. His successor, Hadrian, decides to halt all conquests, and abandons the greater portion of Trajan's newly acquired provinces in the East.

161–180. Marcus Aurelius is emperor. During the last fifteen years of his reign he is involved in wars with the barbarians who cross the Danube and threaten northern Italy. From this date onward the tide begins to turn; Rome is on the defensive.

193–211. After a series of civil wars, Septimius Severus is hailed as emperor. He succeeds in quelling the disorders.

212. Caracalla extends Roman citizenship to all free men in the empire.

222–235. Alexander, the last of the Severus line, succeeds to the throne. During his reign he wages an inconclusive war against Ardashir (Artaxerxes), a Persian who had, in 227, overthrown the Parthian Empire.

235–268. During this period the Roman Empire almost disintegrates in a series of civil wars and insurrections. The Alemanni and the

Franks invade Gaul and northern Italy; the Goths cross the Danube and attack Greece; the Persians threaten to overrun all the provinces of Asia Minor.

268–283.   The emperors Claudius II, Aurelian, Tacitus, Probus, and Carus defeat the enemies of Rome and restore order in the Roman state, although Dacia is abandoned.

284–305.   Diocletian, in order to establish a more efficient government, thoroughly reorganizes and divides the administration of the empire, then, after ruling for twenty years, abdicates.

312.   Constantine the Great wins the Battle of the Milvian Bridge and enters Rome.

313.   The Edict of Milan is published, proclaiming the principle of religious liberty, making Christianity a legal religion.

324–337.   After winning the Battle of Adrianople, Constantine reunites the empire. In the following year (325) he summons and presides over the first general council of the Christian Church at Nicaea. In 330 he dedicates Constantinople, built on the site of Byzantium, as his capital. Just before his death Constantine is baptized as a Christian.

357.   Julian defeats the Alemanni in the Battle of Strasbourg and drives them back across the Rhine.

364.   The empire is again divided, Valentinian becoming Emperor of the West and Valens of the East.

376–378.   Under pressure from the Huns, the Visigoths (West Goths) implore the protection of the Roman Emperor of the East. They are allowed to pass the Danube and settle in the Roman provinces, but are mistreated and rise in revolt. At the Battle of Adrianople (378) the Romans are defeated and Valens is slain. This battle marks the beginning of the downfall of the Roman legion and of the increasing importance of cavalry over infantry. (For a thousand years thereafter, the rapidly moving, armored cavalryman retained his superiority over the foot soldier.)

379–395.   After a campaign lasting two years, the Visigoths are subdued by Theodosius, and induced to settle in the country as military allies. Christianity is established as the sole official religion of the state.

395–406.   The Roman Empire is divided between the two sons of Theodosius; the division into East and West becomes permanent. The Visigoths under Alaric ravage Greece then are driven into Illyricum by Stilicho, a Vandal who had become a Roman general. Stilicho then frustrates Alaric's efforts to enter Italy. At about this time a varied host of Vandals, Franks, Burgundians, and other barbarians cross the Rhine and invade Gaul. A portion of these who attempted to invade Italy are defeated by Stilicho near Florence.

407. The Romans evacuate Britain.

410. Upon the death of Stilicho in 408, Alaric again enters Italy; in the year 410 he sacks Rome.

412–415. Under the leadership of Ataulf, Alaric's brother, the Visigoths move into southern Gaul and Spain.

429. Gaiseric leads the Vandals from Spain into North Africa; ten years later they seize Carthage.

441. The first of a long series of Anglo-Saxon invaders from the Continent attacks Britain's shores.

6

The Battle of Châlons, A.D. 451

A BROAD EXPANSE of plains, the Campi Catalaunici of the ancients, spreads far and wide around the city of Châlons in the northeast of France. The long rows of poplars through which the river Marne winds its way, and a few thinly scattered villages are almost the only objects that vary the monotonous aspect of the greater part of this region. But about five miles from Châlons the ground is indented and heaped up in ranges of grassy mounds and trenches which attest the work of man's hand in ages past. This ancient entrenchment encloses a large area of sixty acres; perhaps it was the site of a Roman camp or Gallic town, but local tradition gives to these ancient earthworks the name of Attila's Camp. Here then it may have been that, over fifteen hundred years ago, the most powerful heathen king who ever ruled in Europe mustered the remnants of his vast army which had striven against the Christian soldiery of Toulouse and Rome. For the Battle of Châlons, which derives its name from the principal Roman city on the Catalaunian Plains, was fought not far to the south, near Troyes, probably near the village of Méry-sur-Seine on the Mauriac Plain.

The pressure of the Huns upon Europe had first been felt in the latter part of the fourth century of our era. They had long been

94

formidable to the Chinese Empire but had then been driven, or migrated, westward. They crossed into Europe and rapidly reduced the Ostrogoths (East Goths) and other tribes living north and west of the Black Sea. The Visigoths (West Goths) were driven to the Danube where they implored the protection of the Roman Empire. These bold and hardy warriors were appalled at the number, the ferocity, the ghastly appearance and the lightning-like rapidity of the Huns.

Tribe after tribe, city after city fell before them. Then came a pause in their career of conquest, caused probably by dissensions among their chiefs. However, when in A.D. 433, Attila and his brother Bleda became their rulers, the torrent burst forth anew. In the first eight years of their reign they directed their attention to wars against other nations, and by 441 they had made themselves virtually supreme in central Europe, without a rival from the Caspian almost to the Rhine. In that year they conducted a gigantic raid across the Danube. When Theodosius II, Emperor of the East, refused to meet their terms, they continued their campaign of devastation. The soldiers of the Roman armies who attempted to oppose them were as struck by fear as had been the barbarians before them; the armies of the emperor that tried to check their progress were cut to pieces. Theodosius hastily sued for peace, agreeing to every one of Attila's demands.

In the meantime, by the middle of the fifth century, many of the Germanic nations had relocated themselves in some of the fairest regions of the Roman Empire. They had imposed their yoke on the provincials but had undergone, to a considerable extent, that moral conquest which the arts and refinements of the vanquished have so often achieved over the rough victors. The Visigoths, after crossing the Danube, had defeated the Romans in the Battle of Adrianople in A.D. 378; then, after passing through Italy and sacking Rome in 410, they now held land in the north of Spain and in Gaul south of the Loire. Franks and Burgundians had established themselves in other Gallic provinces. The Suevi were masters of a portion of the Spanish peninsula. A king of the Vandals reigned in North Africa. Many of these had by now become members of the Christian faith. But it had become an open question whether they or the Huns, who were following behind them, would reign over the former lands of Rome.

The victory the Roman general Aëtius, with his Gothic allies, gained over the Huns was the last victory of imperial Rome. But among the long roll of her triumphs, few can be found that, for the importance and ultimate benefit to mankind, are comparable with this expiring effort of her arms. It did not, indeed, open to her any career of conquest—it did not consolidate the relics of her power—it did not turn the rapid ebb of her fortunes. The mission of imperial Rome was, in truth, already accomplished. She had received and transmitted through her once ample dominion the civilization of Greece. She had broken up the barriers of narrow nationalities among the various states and tribes that dwelt around the coasts of the Mediterranean. She had fused these and many other races into one organized empire, bound together by a community of laws, of government, and institutions. The Christian faith had arisen on the earth, and during the years of Rome's decline it had been nourished to maturity; protected by her power it had spread over all the provinces that obeyed her sway. For no beneficial purpose to mankind could the dominion of the seven-hilled city have been restored or prolonged.

But it was all-important to mankind what nations should divide among them Rome's rich inheritance of empire: whether the Germanic and Gothic warriors should form states and kingdoms out of the fragments of her dominions and become the free members of the commonwealth of Christian Europe—or whether pagan savages from the wilds of central Asia should crush the relics of classic civilization and the early institutions of Christianized Germans in one hopeless chaos of barbaric conquest. When the Christian Visigoths of King Theodoric fought and triumphed at Châlons, side by side with the legions of Aëtius, their joint victory over the Hunnish host assured the preservation of the Germanic element in the civilization of modern Europe.

But what manner of man was this who led the Huns in their triumphal march across Europe? Attila's fame has not come down to us through the partial and suspicious medium of chroniclers and poets of his own race. It is not from Hunnish authorities that we learn the extent of his might. It is from his enemies, from the literature and the legends of the nations whom he afflicted with his arms, that we draw the unquestionable evidence of his greatness. Besides the express narratives of Byzantine, Latin, and Gothic writers, we have the strongest proof of the stern reality of Attila's conquests in the extent to which he and his Huns have been the themes of the earliest Germanic and Scandinavian lays. Wild as many of these legends are, they bear concurrent and certain testimony to the awe with which the memory of Attila was regarded by the bold warriors who composed and delighted in them. Attila's exploits repeatedly occur in the sagas of Norway and Iceland; the celebrated *Nibelungenlied* is full of them. Etzel, or Attila, is in many respects the hero of the latter part of this remarkable poem, and it is at his capital city, which evidently was near Buda (the half of Budapest which is on the right bank of the Danube), that much of the action takes place.

When we turn from the legendary to the historic Attila, we see clearly that he was not one of the vulgar herd of barbaric conquerors. Consummate military skill may be traced in his campaigns; and he relied far less on the brute force of armies than on his unbounded influence over the affections of friends and the fears his name inspired in his foes. He was conspicuous among a nation of warriors for hardihood, strength, and skill in every martial exercise—grave and deliberate in counsel, but rapid and remorseless in execution. He gave safety and security to all who were under his dominion, while he waged a warfare of extermination against all who opposed or sought to escape from it. He watched the national passions, the prejudices, the creeds, and the superstitions of the varied nations over which he ruled, and of those which he sought to reduce beneath his sway. All these feelings he had the skill to turn to his own account. His own warriors believed him to be the inspired favorite of their deities, and followed him with fanatic zeal. His enemies looked on him as the preappointed minister of heaven's wrath against themselves. They came to call him "The Scourge of God" and, though they did not believe in his creed, their own made them tremble before him.

In one of his early campaigns he appeared before his troops with an ancient iron sword in his grasp, which he told them was the god of war whom their ancestors had worshiped. It seems certain that the nomadic tribes of Asia, whom Herodotus described under the name of Scythians, had worshiped as their god a bare sword. That sword-god was supposed, in Attila's time, to have disappeared from earth, but the Hunnish king now claimed to have received it by special revelation. It was said that a herdsman, who was tracking a wounded heifer in the desert, found the mysterious sword standing fixed in the ground, as if it had darted down from heaven. The herdsman brought it to Attila, who henceforth was believed by the Huns to wield the Spirit of Death in battle, and their seers prophesied that the sword was to destroy the world. Among other titles, Attila designated himself as "By the Grace of God, King of the Huns, the Goths, the Danes and the Medes."

The "Huns" and the "Goths" are obvious enough, and it is not difficult to see why he added the "Medes" and the "Danes." His armies had been engaged in warfare against the Persian kingdom, and some of the northern provinces of that kingdom, which included the Medes, had been compelled to pay tribute. For similar reasons he included the "Danes," as his power may well have extended northward as far as the nearest Scandinavian nations. This mention of Medes and Danes as his subjects would serve at once to indicate the extent of his dominion. The immense territory north of the Rhine, the Danube, and the Black Sea, and eastward of the Caucasus, over which Attila ruled, first in conjunction with his brother Bleda, and afterward alone, cannot be very accurately defined. But it must have comprised within it, besides the Huns, many nations of Slavic, Gothic, Teutonic and Finnish origin.

Such was the empire of the Huns in A.D. 445, when Attila ridded himself of his brother by a crime which may have been prompted not only by selfish ambition but also by a desire to turn to his own purposes the legends and forebodings which then were universally spread throughout the Roman Empire, and must have been well known to the watchful and ruthless Hun.

The year 445 was only one year short of completing the twelfth century from the traditional date of the founding of Rome. It had always been believed by the Romans that the twelve vultures, which were said to have appeared to Romulus when he founded the city, signified the time during which the Roman power should endure. The twelve vultures denoted twelve centuries. This interpretation of the vision of the birds of destiny was current among the Romans even when there were yet many of the twelve centuries to run, and while the imperial city was at the zenith of its power. As the allotted time drew nearer and nearer to its conclusion, and as Rome grew weaker and weaker beneath the blows of barbaric invaders, the terrible omen was more and more talked and thought of. In Attila's time men watched for the momentary extinction of the Roman state with the last beat of the last vulture's wing. Moreover, among the numerous legends connected with the foundation of the city and the death of Remus, there was one most terrible one which told that Romulus did not put his brother to death in accident or in hasty quarrel, but deliberately and in compliance with the wishes of supernatural powers. The shedding of a brother's blood was thus the price paid to destiny by the founder of Rome for twelve centuries of existence.

We may imagine, therefore, with what forebodings the inhabitants of the Roman Empire must have heard the tidings that the royal brethren, Attila and Breda, had founded a new capital on the Danube, which was designed to rule over the ancient capital on the Tiber. And that Attila, like Romulus, had consecrated the foundations of his new city by murdering his brother. For the new cycle of centuries about to commence, dominion had been bought from the gloomy spirits of destiny in favor of the Hun by a sacrifice of equal awe and value with that which had formerly obtained it for the Roman.

It is to be remembered that not only the pagans, but also many of the Christians of that age of religious transition, knew and believed in these legends and omens, however they might differ as to the nature of the superhuman agency by which such mysteries had been made known to mankind. In this connection, Herbert's observation on the fulfillment of this augury is of interest, "if to the twelve centuries denoted by the twelve vultures that appeared to Romulus, we add for the six birds that appeared to Remus six lustra, or periods of five years each, by which the Romans were wont to number their time, it brings us precisely to the year 476, in which the Roman empire was finally extinguished by Odoacer."

Two years after Bleda's murder, Attila again invaded the Eastern Empire. His hordes advanced as far south as Thermopylae in Greece and up to the very walls of Constantinople. Peace was finally purchased by the payment of a large indemnity and by increasing the yearly tribute to the Huns. Attila then turned his eyes toward the Roman lands in Western Europe.

A strange invitation from a Roman princess gave him a pretext for the war. Some years before, Honoria, sister of Valentinian III, Emperor of the West, finding herself disgraced and placed in severe restraint because of an amorous adventure, had sent her ring to Attila, asking him to deliver her. This had been discovered by the Romans, and Honoria had been promptly imprisoned. Now Attila, interpreting the sending of the ring as a proposal of marriage, pretended to take up arms in her behalf.

Two sons of a Frankish king, whose tribe was then settled on the

Lower Rhine, upon the death of their father quarreled over the succession. One appealed to the Romans for aid; the other invoked the assistance and protection of the Huns. Attila thus obtained an ally whose cooperation secured for him the passage of the Rhine. Having crossed the river in the spring of the year 451, he divided his vast forces into three columns. His right wing Attila sent toward Arras, while the left wing drove toward Metz. The main force, in the center, marched in the direction of Orléans, where he intended to cross the Loire. The three columns moved forward, laying waste the land with fire and sword, destroying city after city as they advanced, with terrible slaughter. Arras and Metz were sacked and burned; Attila began the siege of Orléans.

While this campaign was under way the Roman general Aëtius, the commander in Gaul and the dominant personality in Rome's Western Empire, had been making strenuous efforts to collect and organize an army fit to face the Huns in the field. He enlisted every subject of the Roman Empire whom patriotism, courage or compulsion could collect beneath the standards. Around these troops, which assumed the once proud title of the legions of Rome, he arrayed all the barbaric forces that pay, persuasion, or the general hate and dread of the Huns brought to his camp. The most prominent of those whom he persuaded, and the one who brought the greatest number of men with him, was Theodoric, the powerful King of the Visigoths. They then hastened to the relief of the city of Orléans, where the defenders were resisting bravely but without much hope, arriving in the nick of time.

On the advance of the allies upon Orléans, Attila broke up the siege of that city and retreated toward the Marne. He did not choose to risk a decisive battle with only the central corps of his army against the combined power of his enemies. He therefore fell back to the Catalaunian Plains area, calling in his wings to concentrate in that region which would be favorable to the operations of his cavalry, the principal striking force of his army.

When the two armies at last met face to face, Attila appears to have lost a measure of his confidence, for perhaps the first time in his life. He delayed the opening of the battle until midafternoon while some preliminary skirmishing took place in which Aëtius had the advantage, securing possession of a sloping hill that would aid him in defending against an attack.

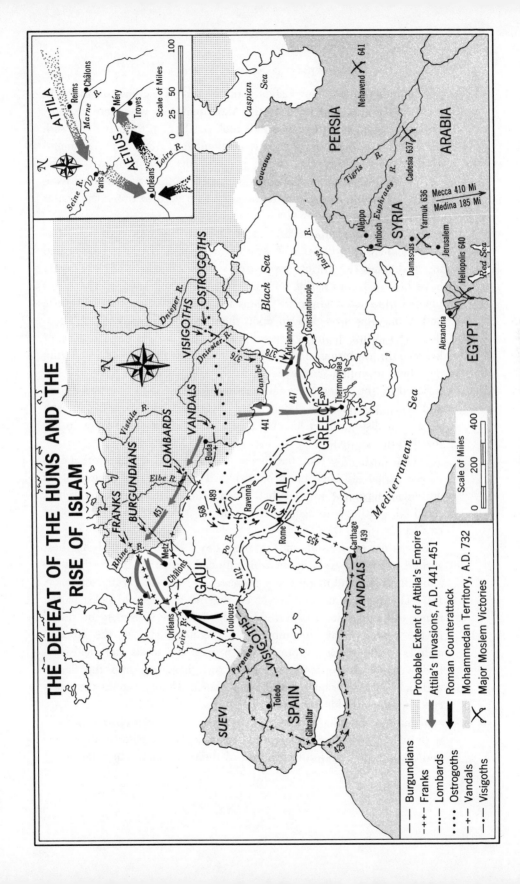

THE DEFEAT OF THE HUNS AND THE RISE OF ISLAM

Scale of Miles
0 25 50 100

ATTILA
Reims
Châlons
Marne R.
Méry
Troyes
AETIUS
Seine R.
Paris
Orléans
Loire R.
N

Caspian Sea
PERSIA
Nehavend ✕ 641
ARABIA
Tigris R.
Euphrates R.
Cadesia 637 ✕
Aleppo
Antioch
SYRIA
Mecca 410 Mi
Medina 185 Mi
Damascus ✕
Yarmuk 636
Jerusalem
Heliopolis 640 ✕
Red Sea
Caucasus
Halys R.
EGYPT
Alexandria

Black Sea

Dnieper R.
OSTROGOTHS
VISIGOTHS
Dniester R.
376
378
Adrianople
Constantinople
Danube
441
447
Thermopylae
GREECE
VANDALS
LOMBARDS
Buda
Elbe R.
489
Vistula R.
568
Ravenna
410
Po R.
Rome
455
ITALY
Carthage 439
VANDALS
Mediterranean Sea

Scale of Miles
0 200 400

BURGUNDIANS
FRANKS
Rhine R.
Metz
451
Châlons
Arras
GAUL
Orléans
Loire R.
Toulouse
412
VISIGOTHS
Pyrenees
SUEVI
Toledo
SPAIN
Gibraltar
429

N

Probable Extent of Attila's Empire
Attila's Invasions, A.D. 441-451
Roman Counterattack
Mohammedan Territory, A.D. 732
Major Moslem Victories ✕

——— Burgundians
—+—+— Franks
········· Lombards
•••••• Ostrogoths
—+—+ Vandals
—·—·— Visigoths

Aëtius then placed the Visigoths under King Theodoric on the right flank. In the center he lined up the Alan auxiliaries who were his most unreliable troops, while he himself took position on the left flank with the Romans. Upon observing this arrangement, Attila took command of the center of his line at the head of his own countrymen; the Ostrogoths, the Gepidae, and the other subject allies of the Huns were drawn up on the flanks. He then charged forward to break the center of the line.

Since the Huns' attack did not begin until the middle of the afternoon, and every witness who ever wrote of this battle has described in awed terms the terrific losses each side sustained, the fighting must have been extraordinarily furious, continuous and savage. The Huns pierced the center where the Alans fell back fighting, but Theodoric and Aëtius began to close in upon them from each flank. King Theodoric was struck down by a javelin as he rode forward at the head of his men. In the furious charge that followed, his own cavalry, charging over him, trampled him to death in the confusion. The Visigoths, infuriated by their monarch's fall, pressed forward with renewed efforts and nearly succeeded in slaying Attila, who had been exposing himself with utter disregard for his own safety, in an effort to drive his troops through to victory.

When Attila saw that the flanks of his central attack were being driven in, he fell back upon his camp. Then when the shelter of its entrenchments and wagons had been gained, the Hunnish archers repulsed, without difficulty, the charges of the vengeful Gothic cavalry.

Expecting an assault on the next day, Attila stationed his best archers in front of the wagons which he had drawn up as a fortification along his lines, and made every preparation for a desperate resistance. But "The Scourge of God" resolved that no man should boast of the honor of having either captured or slain him. He caused to be raised in the center of his encampment a huge pyramid of the wooden saddles of his cavalry; around it he heaped the spoils and wealth he had won; then prepared himself to rush headlong into the flames and balk the victorious foes of their choicest booty should they succeed in storming his defenses.

When the morning broke and revealed the extent of the carnage with which the plains were heaped for miles, the successful allies saw and respected the resolute attitude of their assailant. They dared not attack, nor did they attempt to besiege his camp to starve him into surrender. Attila was allowed to march back the remains of his army without molestation, and even with the semblance of success.

It is probable that the crafty Aëtius was unwilling to be too victorious. He dreaded the glory that his allies the Visigoths had acquired. Furthermore he feared the prestige that Prince Thorismund, who had acquitted himself nobly in the battle and been chosen on the field to succeed his father, might acquire if the victory were too complete. He persuaded the young king to return at once to his capital, and thus relieved himself at the same time of the presence of a dangerous friend, as well as of a formidable though beaten foe.

Attila's attacks on the Western Empire were renewed in Italy in the year 452, but his losses at the Battle of Châlons had been so great that he did not advance beyond the Po. Christian Europe had been saved by that battle, for in the year 453 Attila died, and the vast empire his genius had founded was soon dissolved, torn apart by the quarrels of his sons and by successful revolts of his subject nations. The name of the Huns ceased for some centuries to inspire terror in Western Europe, and their ascendancy passed away with the life of their great king.

Synopsis of Events Between the Battle of Châlons, A.D. 451, and the Battle of Tours, A.D. 732

455. The Vandals from North Africa, led by Gaiseric, enter Rome, plunder it thoroughly for two weeks, then return to North Africa.

476. The Roman Empire of the West is extinguished by Odoacer.

486–511. Under the leadership of Clovis, the Franks advance to the Loire. The Burgundians are defeated, and then the Visigoths are driven into Spain, retaining only a small foothold in southern Gaul. Clovis founds the Frankish monarchy.

489–493. Theodoric, the Ostrogoth, leads his countrymen into Italy, defeats Odoacer and establishes Ostrogothic rule.

533–554. Belisarius and Narses, the generals of Justinian, the Emperor of Constantinople, reconquer North Africa and Italy, annexing them to the Roman Empire of the East.

568–570. The Lombards overrun northern Italy.

540–630. For a period of ninety years the emperors of Constantinople and the kings of Persia are almost continuously engaged in wars against each other.

622. The Hegira. Mohammed is driven from Mecca and flees to Medina.

623–630. Mohammed conducts a series of campaigns against Mecca and finally captures the city.

632. Mohammed dies; his followers carry on his conquests.

633–637. The Moslems invade Syria. Khalid wins the decisive Battle of Yarmuk (636). Antioch and Aleppo soon fall; Jerusalem is captured in 637.

633–641. The Moslems invade Persia. Victories at Cadesia (637) and Nehavend (641) decide the fate of the Persian Empire.

639–642. Egypt is invaded. The Moslems win the Battle of Heliopolis (640); the city of Alexandria surrenders.

647–709. North Africa is brought under Moslem rule.

655. The Byzantine fleet is defeated and Constantinople attacked.

669. Constantinople is again attacked.

673–677. The Moslems blockade Constantinople.

711–725. Musa, the caliph's governor in northern Africa, sends his lieutenant Tarik across the Straits of Gibraltar into Spain. Tarik captures Gibraltar, which still bears his name (Geb el Tarik, the "Rock of Tarik") and occupies Toledo, the Visigothic capital. The following year (712) Musa crosses into Spain to complete its conquest. The Moslem advance continues across the Pyrenees.

717–718. The Moslems undertake another great siege of Constantinople but are defeated by the energetic efforts of the new emperor, known as Leo the Isaurian. This immensely important victory saves Eastern Europe from invasion for centuries.

7

The Battle of Tours, A.D. 732

The events that rescued our ancestors of Britain and our neighbors of Gaul from the civil and religious yoke of the Koran.

—GIBBON

THE BROAD TRACT of country between the cities of Tours and Poitiers is principally composed of a succession of rich pasture lands which are traversed and fertilized by the Cher, the Creuse, the Vienne, the Clain, and many other smaller tributaries of the Loire. Here and there the ground swells into picturesque eminences, and occasionally a belt of forestland, a brown heath, or a clustering series of vineyards breaks the monotony of the widespread meadows. But the general character of the land is that of a grassy plain, and it seems naturally adapted to the evolutions of large armies.

This region has been made famous by more than one memorable conflict. Of these the most interesting to the historian is the great victory won by Charles Martel over the Saracens in A.D. 732. This battle gave a decisive check to the career of Arab conquest, rescued Christendom from Islam, and preserved the relics of ancient, and the germs of modern, civilization in Western Europe. Gibbon devotes several pages of his great work to the Battle of Tours and to consideration of the probable results if Abd-ar-Rahman's enterprise had not been crushed by the Frankish chief. Schlegel speaks of this "mighty victory" in terms of fervent gratitude, and tells how "the arm of Charles Martel saved and delivered the Christian nations of the West from the deadly grasp of all-destroying Islam." Ranke points to this battle as "one of the most important epochs in the history of the world." Arnold ranks the victory of Charles Martel higher than the victory of Arminius, "among those signal deliverances which have affected for centuries the happiness of mankind."

In fact, the more we test its importance, the higher we shall be led to estimate it. Although authentic details of its circumstances and its heroes are meager, we can trace enough of its general character to cause us to watch with deep interest this encounter between the rival conquerors of the decaying Roman Empire. On the north the German, on the south the Arab, were rending away its provinces. At last the spoilers encountered one another, each striving for the full mastery of the prey. Their conflict brought back upon the memory of Gibbon the old Homeric simile, where the strife of Hector and Patroclus over the dead body of Cebriones is compared to the combat of two lions that in their hate and hunger fight together on the mountaintops over the carcass of a slaughtered stag. Then the reluctant yielding of the Saracen power to the superior might of the northern warriors might also recall those other lines of the same book of the *Iliad*, where the downfall of Patroclus beneath Hector is likened to the forced yielding of the panting and exhausted wild boar that had long and furiously fought with a superior beast of prey for the possession of the scanty fountain at which each burned to drink.

Although three centuries had passed away since the German conquerors of Rome had passed the Rhine, no settled system of institutions or government, no amalgamation of the various races into one people, no uniformity of language or habits had been established in the country where Charles Martel was called to repel the menacing tide of Moslem invasion from the south. Gaul was not yet France. There, as in other provinces of the Roman Empire of the West, the dominion of the Caesars had been shattered, and barbaric kingdoms and principalities had promptly arisen on the ruins of the Roman power. But few of these had any permanency, and none of them consolidated the rest, or any considerable number of the rest, into one coherent and organized civil and political society. The great bulk of the population still consisted of native Gauls who had long been under the dominion of the Caesars and who had acquired, together with an infusion of Roman blood, the language, the literature, the laws, and the civilization of Latium. Among these, and dominant over them, roved or dwelt the German victors. Some retained nearly all the rude independence of their primitive national character; others had become softened and disciplined by their contact with the manners and institutions of civilized life.

The Roman Empire in the West had not been crushed by a huge, sudden avalanche of barbaric invasion. The German conquerors had not crossed the Rhine in one enormous host, but in groups of several thousand warriors at a time. The conquest of a province was the result of a long series of invasions. The victorious warriors had either retired with their booty or fixed themselves in the invaded district, taking care to keep sufficiently concentrated for military purposes, ever ready for some fresh foray against a rival Teutonic band or another city of the provincials. Gradually, however, the conquerors acquired a desire for permanent landed possessions. They lost some of their restless thirst for novelty and adventure. They were converted to the Christian faith and lost some of the cruel ferocity fostered by their old mythology.

Although their conversion and other civilizing influences operated powerfully upon the Germans in Gaul, and although the Franks established a decisive superiority over the other conquerors of the province, the country long remained a chaos of uncombined and shifting elements. The early princes of the Merovingian dynasty, founded by Clovis, were generally occupied in wars against other princes of the same house, occasioned by the frequent subdivision of the kingdom, according to the Frankish custom, among the sons upon the death of the king. Thus there was no continued strong central government while, at the same time, the Merovingian dynasty gradually degenerated.

By contrast, the conquests the Moslems effected over the southern and eastern provinces of Rome were far more rapid than those achieved by the Germans in the north, and the new organization of society that they introduced was summarily and uniformly enforced. Exactly one hundred years passed between the death of Mohammed and the date of the Battle of Tours. During that century the followers of the Prophet, in addition to conquering Persia, had torn away half the Roman Empire; they had overrun Syria, Egypt, North Africa and Spain in an apparently irresistible career of victory.

Now, under one of their ablest and most renowned commanders, with an army of experienced soldiers, and with every apparent advantage of time, place and circumstance, the Saracens made their great effort at the conquest of Europe north of the Pyrenees. The victorious Moslem soldiery in Spain were eager for the plunder of more Christian cities and shrines, and were full of fanatic confidence in the invincibility of their arms.

The commander of the Moslem forces, Abd-ar-Rahman, is described by the Arab writers as a model of integrity and justice, an excellent administrator, and a careful military planner who made extensive preparations for his intended conquest in Gaul prior to launching the assault. In addition to the troops he collected from his province, he obtained from Africa a large body of chosen cavalry, officered by Arabs of proved skill and valor. In the year 732 he crossed the Pyrenees at the head of an army that some Arab writers rate at 80,000 strong; some of the Christian chroniclers claim that it numbered hundreds of thousands. The Arab account is undoubtedly far closer to the truth, and may be accepted as a fair approximation of the strength of the invading army.

Opposition to the advance was not organized by the Merovingian kings; they had long since sunk into absolute insignificance and had become mere puppets of royalty. As the central authority grew steadily weaker, the power of the bishops and the great nobles had grown; in fact, the feudal system had begun. Out of this confusion, and after a long struggle, there had arisen one strong man who had made himself the most powerful in the land. He was Pepin of Héristal, Mayor of the Palace of Austrasia and Neustria, the two major portions of the Frankish kingdom. He had not seen fit to rid himself of the king, but exercised in his name whatever paramount authority the turbulent rulers of districts and towns could be persuaded or compelled to acknowledge.

His son Charles had, upon the death of his father, been jailed by his stepmother but had escaped. He had then managed to have himself appointed Mayor of the Palace of Austrasia, waged a successful war against Neustria, extended his dominion over Burgundy, and forced Eudes, the Duke of Aquitaine, to recognize his authority. Therefore when the Moslem invasion came Duke Eudes attempted at first to meet it with only his own resources. He did not want to become further dependent upon Charles; the last thing he wished was to appeal to his former enemy for aid.

Abd-ar-Rahman crossed the Pyrenees at their western end and

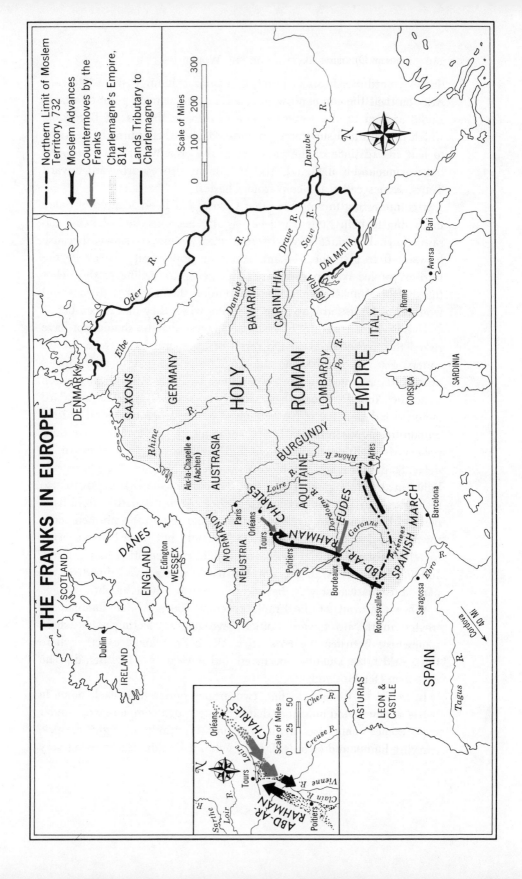

drove toward Bordeaux, sending a smaller column eastward toward Arles on the Rhône to confuse the enemy as to his main point of attack. Eudes arrived on the scene too late to prevent the loss of Bordeaux, which the Moslems captured, plundered and then burned. He tried to halt the advance of the Saracens at the crossing of the Dordogne but was decisively defeated. Abd-ar-Rahman drove northward toward Tours; Eudes called for help from Charles.

It is interesting to note here that Charles has been accused of delay in coming to help Eudes, and he has also been accused of being too rash. Some historians have asserted that he moved slowly because he wanted to give the Mohammedans an opportunity to ravage the territory of his rival Eudes. The more generous incline to the belief that he thought his enemies would burden themselves with loot and would thus be less able to cope with him when they met in combat.

Those who accuse him of rashness suggest that he should not have risked the fate of Gaul on the result of a general battle with the invaders. But Charles had no standing army. He had to make levies upon the Germanic tribes and equip them by using some of the Church treasures. And the Frankish warriors who fought under his standard were too independent to have followed him over a long period of time without engaging in battle. It was not in his power to adopt a cautious policy of watching the invaders and wearing out their strength by delay. So dreadful and so widespread were the ravages of the Saracenic light cavalry throughout Gaul, that it would have been impossible to restrain the Franks for any length of time. Even if Charles could have persuaded his men to look tamely on while the Arabs stormed more towns and desolated more districts, he could not have kept an army together when the usual period of a military expedition had expired. Judging from the Arab account, the battle was as well timed on the part of Charles as it was, beyond all question, well fought.

When the army of the Franks reached Tours, Abd-ar-Rahman retreated southward toward Poitiers, eventually selecting a battlefield somewhere between the two cities. We do not know exactly where this world-famous conflict occurred and have only a few details. The date was October, 732.

It would be difficult to find two armies opposed to each other in battle at any period in history that presented such completely dissimilar appearances. One was made up almost entirely of light cavalry, carrying lances and swords, largely without shields, and wearing very little armor. The other was almost entirely composed of foot soldiers, wearing mail and carrying shields. The Moslem tactics were not the same as those of the slow, heavy Western armies. The followers of the Prophet were highly mobile, fighting in a rapid series of flying attacks, retreating without hesitation, then returning to deliver another assault at the same or at a different point. Whereas the Franks stood firm, holding their ground, beating off a mounted charge of flying horsemen with javelin, sword and ax. In addition the Franks had an extremely important advantage over those armies that had been overwhelmed by the Arabs in Syria, Persia, Egypt, and North Africa. In the century since the death of the Prophet, the Mohammedans had lost some of their religious fervor. They were no longer so eager to die for Allah; their religious zeal had lessened to the point where they did not go into battle seeking death. They were probably actuated more by the thought of loot and spoils than by the religious appeal of being transported after death in battle to a land of everlasting bliss. In fact, we find that it was their fear of losing some of their plunder that proved to be a turning point in the Battle of Tours.

It is obvious that both armies had a healthy respect for their enemy, for they faced each other for seven days. Finally, on the seventh day, the Mohammedans' patience was exhausted; they began the battle with a furious cavalry charge, drew back to loose another, repeating their favorite tactics again and again. The monkish chroniclers, upon whom we are obliged to rely for some of the details of this memorable contest, describe fully the terror the Saracen invasion inspired and the agony of that great struggle. Then they conclude by saying that "the nations of the North standing firm as a wall, and impenetrable as a zone of ice, utterly slay the Arabs with the edge of the sword."

The Arab writers, as might be expected, have a somewhat different version: "Near the River Owar [the Loire], the two great hosts of the two languages and the two creeds were set in array against each other. The hearts of Abd-ar-Rahman, his captains, and his men were filled with wrath and pride, and they were the first to begin the fight. The Moslem horsemen dashed fierce and frequent forward against the battalions of the Franks, who resisted manfully, and many fell dead on either side, until the going down of the sun. Night parted the two armies; but in the gray of the morning the Moslems returned to the battle. Their cavaliers had soon hewn their way into the center of the Christian host."

As usual, the truth is somewhere between the accounts given by each side. Other evidence points to the fact that the battle lasted for only one day, but that it raged fiercely almost the entire day. It is most probable that the Moslem cavalry at first made no particular impression on the solid ranks of the Frankish infantry, but as the day wore on, late in the afternoon, the Mohammedan cavalry by repeated, violent attacks did break through the wall in a few places.

Then a rumor spread through the Mohammedan ranks. Here the Arab historians seem to have given a particularly candid description of their own defeat: "But many of the Moslems were fearful for the safety of the spoil which they had stored in their tents, and a false cry arose in their ranks that some of their enemy were plundering the camp; whereupon several squadrons of the Moslem horsemen rode off to protect their tents. But it seemed as if they fled; and all the host was troubled. And while Abd-ar-Rahman strove to check their tumult, and to lead them back to battle, the warriors of the Franks came around him, and he was pierced through with many spears, so that he died. Then all the host fled before the enemy and many died in the flight."

It would be difficult to obtain from an adversary, whose army had not surrendered, a more explicit confession of having been thoroughly vanquished than the Arabs here accord to the Europeans. The points on which their narrative differs from those of the Christians—as to how many days the conflict lasted, whether they penetrated the Frankish ranks or not—are unimportant compared with the admitted great fact that there was a decisive trial of strength between Frank and Saracen, in which the former conquered.

The European writers all concur in giving the death of Abd-ar-Rahman as one of the principal causes of the defeat of the Arabs. According to one writer, after finding that their leader was slain they dispersed in the night to the agreeable surprise of the Christians, who expected the next morning to see them issue from their tents and renew the combat. On that day the Franks sent scouts into the enemy camp who returned to report that the enemy had disappeared, taking with them as much of their loot as they could carry.

The casualties of the battle are obviously stated incorrectly by the writers of those days. One report puts the loss of the Arabs at 375,000 men (far more than they could possibly have had in their entire army), and gives the Christian loss as 1,500 men, a difference which the monkish chronicler attributes to divine aid. The second figure is certainly as inaccurate as the first; the losses of the Franks must have been very severe; otherwise Charles, who was an aggressive soldier, would have immediately pursued the Mohammedans to profit from his victory by extending the power and authority of his own dominion. Because he had broken and shattered his enemies in the battle, he did acquire a powerfully effective surname, undoubtedly derived from the favorite weapon of Thor, the war god of his forefathers' creed, a surname which served as a constant reminder to his enemies—Martel—"The Hammer."

The enduring importance of the Battle of Tours in the eyes of the Moslems is attested not only by their expressions of "the deadly battle" and "the disgraceful overthrow" which their writers constantly employ when referring to it, but also by the fact that no more serious attempts at conquest beyond the Pyrenees were made by the Saracens. Charles Martel, his son, and his grandson Charlemagne were left at leisure to consolidate and extend their power. The new Christian Roman Empire of the West, which the genius of Charlemagne founded, would never have existed if the Battle of Tours had been lost. It is true that the empire he organized and ruled did not retain its integrity after his death; fresh troubles came over Europe, but Christendom was safe. The progress of European civilization, and the development of the nationalities and governments of modern Europe, from that time forth went forward in a not uninterrupted, but ultimately certain, career.

Synopsis of Events Between the Battle of Tours, A.D. 732, and the Battle of Hastings, A.D. 1066

732–741.   Charles Martel enlarges the kingdom of the Franks at the expense of various barbaric tribes to the north and east of Gaul.

754–756.   Pepin the Short, King of the Franks, marches against the Lombards in Italy and gives some of their land to the Pope. This Donation of Pepin marks the beginning of the temporal power of the papacy, which was to endure for over eleven hundred years.

756.   Following a rebellion against the caliph and a slaughter of the Mohammedan princes, the Omayyad dynasty of Cordova is founded in Spain by one of the few survivors of the massacres. This kingdom of the Moors, independent of any central Mohammedan authority, included all Spain except the Christian kingdom of the Asturias in the northwestern part of the peninsula.

759. Pepin extends effective Frankish rule as far south as the Pyrenees.

768–814. The early death of his brother Carloman in 771 leaves Charlemagne as sole master of the dominion of the Franks.

By a succession of victorious wars Charlemagne vastly enlarged the kingdom until it included the major portion of Western Europe. The Lombards were first absorbed; Charlemagne took their iron crown and assumed the additional title of King of the Lombards. After re-affirming for the Pope the Donation of Pepin, he established his rule in Istria, Dalmatia, and Corsica.

On Christmas Day of the year 800, in St. Peter's in Rome, Pope Leo III solemnly crowned Charlemagne as Emperor of the Roman Empire of the West. However, being essentially a German monarch ruling over lands more German than Roman, Charlemagne established his main capital not at Rome but at Aix-la-Chapelle (Aachen).

Throughout his reign Charlemagne was almost continuously at war, enlarging his frontiers. In Spain, after an unsuccessful expedition against Saragossa, his rearguard under Roland was overcome at Roncesvalles, a defeat that has become legendary in song and story. Charlemagne then gradually reduced northeastern Spain, captured Barcelona, and established the Spanish March, a military province along, and south of, the Pyrenees to protect the southern border of his empire. His major conquests were to the east and to the north, where he overcame the previously uncivilized tribes. In the east he subdued and incorporated Carinthia and Bavaria, then exacted tribute from other, more distant tribes. The Saxons were his most obstinate antagonists; he conducted eighteen campaigns against them in a period lasting over thirty years.

Charlemagne has justly been termed the principal regenerator of Western Europe. Under his reign the greater part of Germany was civilized and converted from paganism to Christianity. Education was advanced and, throughout this vast assemblage of provinces, Charle-magne undertook to establish an organized and firm government. Although after his death the empire was repeatedly partitioned (ulti-mately the major elements corresponded roughly to France less

Burgundy, Germany and Italy), the major religious, intellectual, and social improvements effected during his reign were never lost.

789. The Vikings make their first raid on England. Six years later Ireland is attacked; in the next fifty years the Norsemen conquer about half of the island and settle there, founding the city of Dublin. Scotland is also raided frequently in the early period of Viking invasion.

825–829. Egbert, King of Wessex, acquires supremacy over the other Anglo-Saxon kings in England.

827. Sicily becomes a battleground for the Moslems of North Africa and the Christians.

835. The Viking storm breaks on Europe in all its fury. For the next hundred years fleet after fleet of sea rovers desolate all the western kingdoms of Europe and in many cases effect permanent conquests. They sail up the Elbe, harry the coasts of Germany, France and Spain, twice besiege Paris, enter the Mediterranean, and penetrate into Russia.

837. The Moslems attack southern Italy, seize Bari, and threaten Rome.

871–899. Alfred the Great, whose entire reign was spent in warfare against the Danes, saves England from being completely conquered by the invaders. His victory at Edington in 878 was the turning point in his favor.

911. The French king cedes a large tract of land to Hrolf the Northman. Hrolf (or Duke Rollo as he thenceforth is termed) and his army of Scandinavian warriors become the ruling class of the province that was later enlarged and called after them, Normandy.

962. The Pope crowns Otto of Germany Emperor of the Holy Roman Empire. (As constituted it consisted essentially of Germany and Italy, to which part of Burgundy was later added.)

987. The election of Hugh Capet marks the beginning of the Capetian line of French kings, which will last until 1328.

1017. Canute, King of Denmark, becomes King of England. On the death of the last of his sons, in 1042, the Saxon line is restored by calling Edward the Confessor (who had been raised in Normandy) to the throne.

1029. Norman adventurers settle in Aversa in southern Italy and begin the spread of their power in that region. In the year 1060 they undertake the conquest of Sicily, which is completed after a thirty-year struggle with the Saracens. The Normans retain control for two hundred years.

1035.   Duke Robert of Normandy dies on his return from a pilgrimage to the Holy Land and his son William succeeds him.

1037.   Ferdinand of Castile unites the two kingdoms of León and Castile in northwest Spain.

1066.   Edward the Confessor dies, ending the direct line of the Saxon kings.

The Battle of Hastings, A.D. 1066

ARLETTA'S PRETTY FEET twinkling in the brook made her the mother of William the Conqueror. Had she not thus fascinated Duke Robert of Normandy, Harold would not have fallen at Hastings, no Anglo-Norman dynasty could have arisen, no British Empire. The reflection is Sir Francis Palgrave's, and it is emphatically true. If anyone should write a history of "Decisive loves that have materially influenced the drama of the world," the daughter of the tanner of Falaise would deserve a conspicuous place in its pages. But it is her son, the victor of Hastings, who is now the object of our attention; and no one who appreciates the influence of England and her empire upon the destinies of the world will ever rank that victory as one of secondary importance.

It is true that some writers of eminence have mentioned the Norman Conquest in such terms that it might be supposed that it led to little more than the changing of some of the laws of the land, and the substitution of one family for another on the throne. But, at least since the appearance of the work of Augustin Thierry on the Norman Conquest, these fallacies have been exploded. Thierry made his readers keenly appreciate the magnitude of that political and social upheaval. He depicted in vivid colors the cruelties of the conquerors and the sweeping and enduring innovations that they wrought, involving the overthrow of the ancient constitution, as well as of the last of the Saxon rulers. In his pages we see new tribunals and tenures superseding the old ones, new divisions of race and class introduced, whole districts devastated at the command of the new tyrants. The greater part of the lands of the English are confiscated and divided among aliens; the very name of Englishman is turned into a reproach. The English language is regarded as barbarous, and all the high places in Church and State are filled exclusively by foreigners.

No less true than eloquent is Thierry's summing up of the social effects of the Norman Conquest on the generation that witnessed it, and on many of their successors. He tells his reader that to form a just idea of England conquered by William of Normandy he must picture—not a mere change of political rule—not the triumph of one candidate over another candidate—the man of one party over the man of another party—but the intrusion of one people into the bosom of another people. A new society was violently placed over another society, which it came to destroy. He must not picture to himself William, a king and a despot, versus his English subjects. He must instead imagine two nations, both *subject* to William; but the word has two quite different meanings, in one case it means *subordinate*—in the other case it means *subjugated*. There are two countries included in the same geographical circumference: that of the Normans, rich and free; that of the Saxons, poor and serving; the former full of spacious mansions, walled and moated castles; the latter filled with huts, piles of straw, and ruined hovels; the knights and nobles of the army and the court ruling over the farmers and the artisans; luxury and insolence opposed to misery and envy—not the envy of the poor, but the envy of the despoiled when in the presence of the despoilers.

Perhaps the effect of Thierry's work has been to cast into the shade the ultimate good effects on England of the Norman Conquest. Yet these are as undeniable as are the miseries that conquest inflicted on the Saxons. It was the Norman barons who compelled King John to sign the Great Charter at Runnymede; this alone should make England remember her obligations to the Norman Conquest, although it would be many ages before the general principles expressed therein were applied to the people of England.

It may sound paradoxical, but it is in reality no exaggeration, to say that England's liberties are due to her having been conquered by the Normans. It is true that the Saxon institutions were the primitive cradle of English liberty, but by their own intrinsic force they could never have founded the enduring free English Constitution. It was the Conquest that infused into them a new virtue, and the political liberties of England arose from the situation in which the Anglo-Saxon and the Anglo-Norman population and laws found themselves. The state of England under her last Anglo-Saxon kings closely resembled the state of France fifty years earlier; the Crown was feeble; the great nobles were strong and turbulent. Although the English local free institutions had more reality and energy than was the case on the Continent, still the chances are that the Saxon system, if left to itself, would have fallen into utter confusion. There would probably have arisen first an aristocratic hierarchy, like that which arose in France, next an absolute monarchy, and then a series of chaotic revolutions.

In spite of our sympathies with Harold and our aversion for the desolator of Yorkshire, we must acknowledge the superiority of the Normans. Of all the conquering races of the Gothic stock, they had an instinctive faculty for appreciating and adopting the superior civilizations they encountered. Thus Duke Rollo and his Scandinavian sea rovers, after they had acquired Normandy, readily embraced the creed, the language, the laws, and the arts that France had inherited from imperial Rome through Charlemagne. Their brilliant qualities were sullied by many darker traits of pride and cruelty, but their gradual blending with the Saxons softened these harsh and evil points of their national character. In return they fired the Saxon mass with a new spirit of animation and power.

Small had been the figure England made in the world before the coming of the Normans, and without them she never would have emerged from comparative insignificance. The authority of Gibbon may be taken when he pronounces that England was a gainer by the Conquest. Englishmen may proudly adopt the comment of the Frenchman Rapin de Thoyras who, writing of the Battle of Hastings, speaks of the revolution effected by it as "the first step by which England arrived at the height of grandeur and glory."

The interest of this eventful struggle by which William of Normandy became King of England is materially enhanced by the personalities of the competitors for the crown. They were three in number. One was a foreign prince from the north; one was a foreign prince from the south; and one was a native hero of the land. Harold Hardrada, the strongest and the most chivalric of the kings of Norway, was the first; Duke William of Normandy was the second; and the Saxon Harold, the son of Earl Godwin, was the third. Never was a nobler prize sought by nobler champions, or striven for more gallantly. The Saxon triumphed over the Norwegian, and the Norman triumphed over the Saxon; but Norse valor was never more conspicuous than when Harold Hardrada and his host fought and fell at Stamford Bridge; nor did Saxons ever face their foes more bravely than Harold and his men on the fatal day at Hastings.

During the reign of Edward the Confessor no one paid much attention to the claims of the Norwegian king to the crown, although Harold Hardrada's predecessor, King Magnus of Norway, had on one occasion asserted his right to rule. He claimed that he was entitled to the English throne by virtue of an agreement with the former king, Hardicanute, but he had made no effort to enforce his pretensions.

On the other hand the rivalry of the Saxon Harold and the Norman William was foreseen by the Confessor, who was believed to have predicted on his deathbed the calamities that would fall upon England. Some fifteen years before, Duke William had paid a visit to King Edward and had obtained some sort of a promise giving him a claim to the throne. With the passage of time Edward's ideas must have undergone a change. Harold was the head of the most important noble house in England; he was the bravest and most powerful chieftain in the land and had served Edward well for many years. Thus when the king died childless, he is supposed to have suggested Harold as his choice for the crown, setting aside his vague promise to William.

Two years before the death of King Edward, Harold had been on a fishing or inspection trip. His ship had been driven by a storm onto the French coast. There he had been seized by the local count and held for ransom. When Duke William learned that his vassal had Harold in his possession, he promptly obtained Harold's release and had him brought to the Norman Court. There a great friendship arose between the two. They even went together on an expedition into Brittany. William treated Harold with affection and courtesy, but never lost sight of his goal, the throne of England. Before William allowed Harold to return home, the ceremony of Harold's taking a solemn oath to renounce all claims to the throne and assist William to obtain it was enacted. The story of Harold's swearing upon holy relics that lay concealed under an altar or table, covered with a cloth, has been told many times, but not too often has it been emphasized that Harold must have felt the sanctity of this oath, even though his word was obtained by a trick. No matter how obtained, a swearing over relics in those days was a high and holy event. It must have been a weight on the spirit of the gallant Saxon, and also served to discourage others from adopting his cause.

When Edward the Confessor died and the Saxons proclaimed Harold as their king, Duke William made further use of the sacred oath. He submitted his claims to the Pope, who could not possibly side with Harold. He was forced to recognize William, since Harold could not deny the fact that he had taken his solemn oath, and the whole Christian feudal world was founded upon the sanctity of oaths. A banner was sent to William from the Holy See, which the Pope himself had consecrated and blessed for the invasion. The clergy throughout the Continent became energetic in praise of William's undertaking in the cause of God. All the adventurous spirits of Christendom flocked to the holy banner under which Duke William, the most renowned knight and sagest general of the age, promised to lead them to glory and wealth in the fair domains of England. His army was filled with the chivalry of Europe, all eager to demonstrate their valor in so great an enterprise, and eager also for pay and plunder. But of all these, the Normans were the flower of the army and William himself the strongest spirit.

Throughout the spring and summer of 1066 all the seaports of northern France rang with the busy sound of preparation. On the opposite side of the Channel, King Harold collected the army and the fleet with which he hoped to crush the invaders. But the winds were contrary; William could not sail, which was a great stroke of good fortune for the Normans. The English fleet after being at sea for nearly a month was forced to return to port to refit and obtain supplies. In the interim King Harold Hardrada of Norway launched his attack upon northern England. This expedition was large, imposing, and immediately successful. Sailing up the Humber, the Norwegians disembarked south of York and severely defeated the local levies, or fyrds as they were called, under the northern earls Edwin and Morcar. The gates of the city of York opened and all the country for many miles around submitted to King Hardrada who was now encamped near York at Stamford Bridge.

Faced with a double invasion, King Harold had no choice. He must defeat the northern one first and hope that he could accomplish this before King William and the Normans landed. His hopes of success were based on three factors: speed, Saxon fighting ability, and the direction of the winds from France. King Harold did not hesitate; it was his only chance, and he took it. Leaving London, he marched rapidly, covering 200 miles, and on the fifth day, September 25, 1066, attacked. His sudden arrival was a complete surprise; the battle that ensued was desperate and long doubtful. Unable to break the Norwegian line by force, Harold at length tempted them to quit their close, compact order by a pretended flight. Then, when the Norwegians were spread over the battlefield in hot pursuit, the English turned and, bursting upon the pursuing Norwegians, overwhelmed them. King Harold Hardrada and the flower of his nobility perished that day. The importance of this Battle of Stamford Bridge has naturally been eclipsed by the greater interest attached to the next battle, but it proved to be the last major effort ever made by a Scandinavian force to invade the British Isles.

Harold's victory was splendid but he had bought it dearly by the fall of many of his best officers and men, and still more dearly by the opportunity Duke William had gained of effecting an unopposed landing on the English coast. The whole of William's shipping had assembled as early as the middle of August, but for a long time they could not sail, and the army began to grow discouraged because the very elements seemed to be against them. They could not know that in reality the winds had been their best of friends, permitting the Norwegians to land first. Finally the wind veered. The Norman Armada left the French shores and steered for England. The invaders crossed an undefended sea and found an undefended coast. It was in Pevensey Bay, eleven miles west of Hastings, that the last conquerors of England landed on the 28th of September, 1066.

Harold was at York resettling the government of the counties Harold Hardrada had overrun when the news of the landing reached him, probably on October 1. He instantly hurried southward to meet this long-expected enemy, retracing his 200 mile march. In less than a week he was back in London. The old Roman roads must have been kept in good condition.

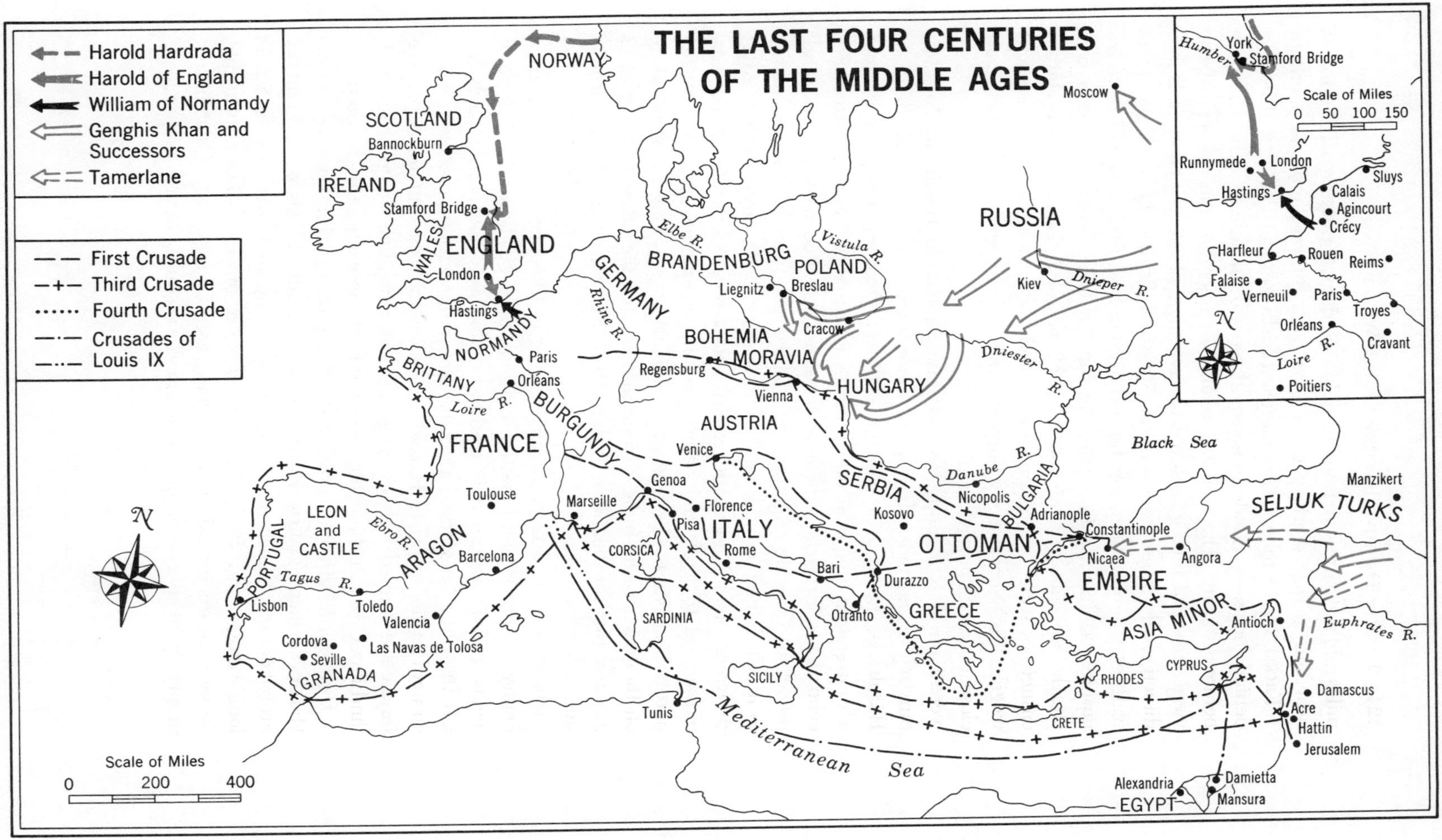
THE LAST FOUR CENTURIES
OF THE MIDDLE AGES
Harold Hardrada
Harold of England
William of Normandy
Genghis Khan and Successors
Tamerlane
First Crusade
Third Crusade
Fourth Crusade
Crusades of Louis IX
NORWAY
SCOTLAND
Bannockburn
IRELAND
Stamford Bridge
WALES
ENGLAND
London
Hastings
NORMANDY
Paris
BRITTANY
Orléans
Loire R.
FRANCE
BURGUNDY
Toulouse
LEON and CASTILE
PORTUGAL
Ebro R.
ARAGON
Barcelona
Tagus R.
Lisbon
Toledo
Valencia
Cordova
Seville
Las Navas de Tolosa
GRANADA
Marseille
Genoa
Florence
Pisa
ITALY
CORSICA
Rome
SARDINIA
SICILY
Tunis
Mediterranean Sea
Elbe R.
GERMANY
Rhine R.
BRANDENBURG
Vistula R.
POLAND
Liegnitz
Breslau
Cracow
BOHEMIA
MORAVIA
Regensburg
Vienna
HUNGARY
AUSTRIA
Venice
RUSSIA
Kiev
Dnieper R.
Dniester R.
Moscow
Black Sea
Danube R.
SERBIA
Nicopolis
BULGARIA
Kosovo
Adrianople
Constantinople
Nicaea
OTTOMAN EMPIRE
Bari
Durazzo
Otranto
GREECE
Angora
SELJUK TURKS
Manzikert
ASIA MINOR
Antioch
Euphrates R.
RHODES
CYPRUS
CRETE
Damascus
Acre
Hattin
Jerusalem
Alexandria
Damietta
Mansura
EGYPT
Scale of Miles
0 200 400
Humber
York
Stamford Bridge
Scale of Miles
0 50 100 150
Runnymede
London
Hastings
Sluys
Calais
Agincourt
Crécy
Harfleur
Rouen
Reims
Falaise
Verneuil
Paris
Troyes
Orléans
Cravant
Loire R.
Poitiers

Harold remained at London only five days, gathering all the forces he could in that short space of time from the midland and southern counties. On October 11 he marched forth to meet William. If he had waited longer in London he would have been able to collect a more numerous army. The trained, reliable housecarles, the soldiers of the king's personal bodyguard and the retainers of the principal earls and thanes, had suffered severely at Stamford Bridge. Given time, some of them who had been left behind at Stamford Bridge would have recovered sufficiently to rejoin. As for the local fyrds, five days was simply not enough time for them all to reach London. But Harold would not wait; he was impetuous, and eager to advance. He wanted to take the Normans by surprise and thus repeat his brilliant performance at Stamford Bridge.

William of Normandy was as brave as Harold Hardrada. In addition he was far more skillful and more wary. He was one of the great soldiers of his day, a capable engineer, and an ingenious planner who prepared long in advance for any eventuality that might arise. For example, he brought with him three prefabricated wooden castles, all ready for framing together, all shaped and pierced to receive the pins which had been brought cut and ready in large barrels. After the troops had landed and established a secure beachhead, the carpenters set to work and before evening completely finished erecting one of his castles. The next day William moved along the seashore to Hastings where he built a camp and erected the other two castles as part of the fortifications. Taking this Norman general by surprise would not be so easy.

Harold's army arrived in the evening of October 13 at the location of the present town of Battle, and took up a position on the slope of Senlac Hill across the main road to London sixty miles away. Early the next morning he learned that the Normans were approaching. There was to be no surprise. Harold was outnumbered and must prepare for defense immediately. Arranging his men in a line along the hill with the housecarles in the center and the fyrds on each flank, he prepared a hasty fortification of brushwood designed to offer some resistance to the Norman cavalry. Harold had no cavalry of his own. Many of his men used horses for transport, for those swift marches to Stamford Bridge and back, but they fought on foot. Their principal weapons were the spear, the sword, and a long-handled hatchet or ax. Those who could, or whose masters could, afford to purchase

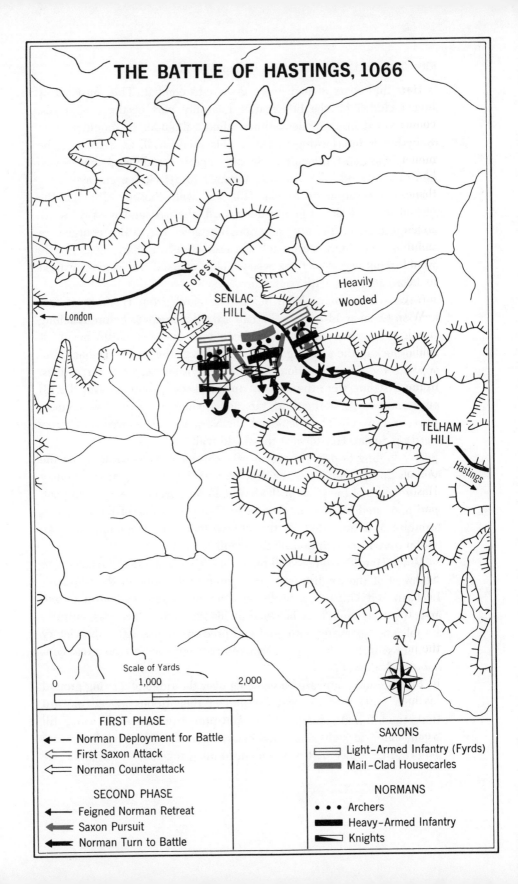

THE BATTLE OF HASTINGS, 1066

Forest

← London

SENLAC
HILL

Heavily
Wooded

TELHAM
HILL

Hastings

N

Scale of Yards

0   1,000   2,000

FIRST PHASE

←– – Norman Deployment for Battle
⇐ First Saxon Attack
⇐ Norman Counterattack

SECOND PHASE

← Feigned Norman Retreat
← Saxon Pursuit
← Norman Turn to Battle

SAXONS

▭ Light-Armed Infantry (Fyrds)
▬ Mail-Clad Housecarles

NORMANS

••• Archers
▬ Heavy-Armed Infantry
▭ Knights

helmets and coats of mail wore them into combat. This must surely have included all the housecarles but only part of the local fyrds. They formed in solid, dense lines, almost shoulder to shoulder, with their shields interlocking in front. This shield-wall, as it came to be known, was most difficult to break, superb for defense, but necessarily abandoned when moving forward to attack the enemy.

Harold's position on Senlac Hill was well chosen. Although the ground in front slopes gently downward, the east and west sides are both quite steep, presenting serious obstacles to cavalry charges. In addition the right, or west, flank was protected by a sharp ravine, while the left flank was near thick woods. Thus arrayed the Saxons awaited the Norman attack with confidence.

Duke William must have begun his march from Hastings at first light on October 14 because he had six miles to cover before reaching Harold's position, and we have been told that the battle began at nine o'clock in the morning. He deployed near the foot of Telham Hill, opposite the Saxon position, into three divisions, each of three lines. In the first line were the archers; in the second, footmen armed with pikes and swords; in the third, the mailed knights equipped with lance, mace, and swords. Thus deployed, the Norman army moved slowly forward up Senlac Hill toward the shield-wall.

By adopting in part the words of a chronicler who wrote while the feelings and prejudices of the time were still very much alive, we may capture more of the spirit of the battle. Robert Wace, the Norman poet, who presented his *Roman de Rou* to Henry II is one of the most picturesque and animated of the old writers, and from him we can obtain a vivid description of the conflict.

"When Harold had made all ready, and given his orders, he came into the midst of the English and dismounted by the side of the standard; Leofwin and Gurth, his brothers, were with him; and around him he had barons enough, as he stood by his standard, which was, in truth, a noble one, sparkling with gold and precious stones. After the victory William sent it to the Pope, to prove and commemorate his great conquest and glory.

"The Normans appeared advancing over the ridge of a rising ground [Telham Hill], and the first division of their troops moved onward along the hill and across a valley. And presently another division, still larger, came in sight, close following upon the first, and they were led toward another part of the field, forming together as the first body had done. And while Harold saw and examined them, and was pointing them out to Gurth, a fresh company came in sight, covering all the plain; and in the midst of them was raised that standard that came from Rome. Near it was the duke, and the best men and greatest strength of the army were there.

"The Normans brought on the three divisions of their army to attack at different places. They set out in three companies and in three companies did they fight. The first and scecond had come up, and then advanced the third, which was the greatest; with that came the duke with his own men, and all moved boldly forward.

"As soon as the two armies were in full view of each other, great noise and tumult arose. You might hear the sound of many trumpets, of bugles, and of horns; and then you might see men ranging themselves in line, lifting their shields, raising their lances, bending their bows, handling their arrows, ready for assault and defense."

The Norman army moved uphill to the attack. The archers opened fire as soon as they were within range, but since they had to shoot uphill most of their arrows must have either struck the shield-wall or passed harmlessly over the heads of the Saxons: "The Norman archers with their bows shot thickly upon the English; but they covered themselves with their shields, so that the arrows could not reach their bodies, nor do any mischief, how true soever was their aim, or however well they shot." When they had advanced close enough for the Saxon javelins, spears, and stones to become effective, there was a savage struggle; they were repulsed and withdrew. Then came the second line, the heavily armed infantry, who closed with their enemy and fought hand to hand. "The battle was up and down, this way and that, and no one knew who would conquer and win the land. Both sides stood so firm and fought so well, that no one could guess which would prevail."

The infantry of the left division of the Normans finally broke and ran from the hill, sweeping the knights down with them in their flight. Large bodies of Saxon footmen hurried in pursuit. Seeing this, Duke William wheeled his center division of horse to the left, charged, and cut them down. Those who succeeded in escaping ran back up to reform in the shield-wall.

Duke William then moved his infantry aside, brought up all his knights, and led them in a mounted assault upon the Saxons. In many places they dented the line, but the dense Saxon mass was not broken.

The battle raged for many hours; the Norman knights charged again and again; lances were shivered, knights cut down by the long axes of the defenders. Never before in their entire lives had these mailed knights seen such stubbornness; these Saxons simply did not know they were supposed to be overthrown and flee in terror before the attack of such a force as theirs. In years to come the stubbornness of British infantry in defense would become well known throughout the world, but it was a new and frightening experience to the Normans on that day.

"The Normans saw that the English defended themselves well, and were so strong in their position that they could do little against them. So they consulted together privily, and arranged to draw off, and pretend to flee, till the English should pursue and scatter themselves over the field; for they saw that if they could once get their enemies to break their ranks, they might be attacked and discomfited much more easily. As they had said, so they did. The Normans by little and little fled, the English following them. As the one fell back, the other pressed after; and when the Frenchmen retreated, the English thought and cried out that the men of France fled, and would never return.

"Thus they were deceived by the pretended flight, and great mischief thereby befell them; for if they had not moved from their position, it is not likely that they would have been conquered at all; but, like fools, they broke their lines and pursued."

Harold himself was probably not deceived by the stratagem and undoubtedly kept his housecarles under his control. It was, after all, the same trick that he had used to win against Harold Hardrada at Stamford Bridge. Control of the fyrds was a different matter. They were not well disciplined and in their eagerness rushed forward before Harold could stop them.

"The Normans were to be seen following up their stratagem, retreating slowly so as to draw the English farther on. As they still flee, the English pursue; they push out their lances and stretch forth their hatchets, following the Normans as they go rejoicing in the success of their scheme, and scattering themselves over the plain. And the English meantime jeered and insulted their foe with words. 'Cowards,' they cried, 'you came hither in an evil hour, wanting our lands, and seeking to seize our property, fools that ye were to come! Normandy is too far off, and you will not easily reach it. It is of little use to run back; unless you can cross the sea at a leap, or can drink it dry. Your sons and daughters are lost to you.'

"The Normans bore it all; but, in fact, they knew not what the English said; their language seemed like the baying of dogs, which they could not understand. At length they stopped and turned round, determined to recover their ranks; and the barons might be heard crying DEX AIE! for a halt. Then the Normans resumed their former position, turning their faces toward the enemy; and their men were to be seen facing round and rushing onward to a fresh *mêlée*, the one party assaulting the other; this man striking, another pressing onward."

Although the Saxons lost great numbers of men in the false pursuit, the remainder reformed beside the housecarles who maintained their discipline, standing fast in ranks on top of the hill. Repeated cavalry charges, interspersed with showers of arrows, gradually destroyed the Saxon troops until all that remained were the valiant housecarles who stood beside the standard. Harold's brothers had already been killed.

"And now might be heard the loud clang and cry of battle, and the clashing of lances. The English stood firm in their barricades, and shivered the lances.

"Then the Normans determined to shoot their arrows upward into the air, so that they might fall on their enemies' heads and strike their faces. The archers adopted this scheme, and shot up into the air toward the English; and the arrows, in falling, struck their heads and faces, and put out the eyes of many; and all feared to open their eyes, or leave their faces unguarded.

"The arrows now flew thicker than rain before the wind; fast sped the shafts that the English call 'wibetes.' Then it was that an arrow, that had been thus shot upward, struck Harold above his right eye, and put it out. In his agony he drew the arrow and threw it away, breaking it with his hands; and the pain to his head was so great that he leaned upon his shield.

"Duke William pressed close upon the English with his lance, striving hard to reach the standard with the great troop he led, and seeking earnestly for Harold, on whose account the whole war was. The Normans follow their lord, and press around him, they ply their blows upon the English; and these defend themselves stoutly, striving hard with their enemies, returning blow for blow.

"The standard was beaten down, the golden standard was taken, and Harold and the best of his friends were slain.

"The English were in great trouble at having lost their king, and at the duke's having conquered and beat down the standard; but they still fought on, and defended themselves long, and in fact till the day drew to a close. Then it clearly appeared to all that the standard was lost, and the news had spread throughout the army that Harold, for certain, was dead; and all saw that there was no longer any hope, so they left the field, and those fled who could."

Such is a Norman account of the Battle of Hastings which does full justice to the valor of the Saxons as well as to the bravery and skill of the victors. One other event deserves to be mentioned. When the Saxons withdrew into the forest, the Normans pursued but were immediately stopped. There was a ravine on the other side of Senlac Hill into which a group of Norman horsemen plunged headlong and were slaughtered. There is a possibility that if Harold, or either of his brothers, had survived, the remnants of the Saxon army might then have formed again in the woods, effected an orderly withdrawal and prolonged the war. But both brothers and all the bravest thanes of southern England lay dead on Senlac Hill, around their fallen king and the fallen standard of their country.

After the battle Harold's mother sought the victorious Norman and begged the dead body of her son. But William at first answered in his wrath that "Harold mounted guard on the coast while he was alive, he may continue his guard now he is dead." The taunt was an unintentional eulogy. A grave washed by the spray of the Sussex waves would have been the noblest burial place for the martyr of Saxon freedom. But Harold's mother was urgent in her pleas; the Conqueror relented; like Achilles, he gave up the dead body of his fallen foe to a parent's supplications, and the remains of King Harold were deposited in Waltham Abbey.

On Christmas Day in the same year, William the Conqueror was crowned at London, King of England.

Notes on the Battle of Hastings

This battle, the most decisive ever fought on English soil, has been the subject of a great deal of controversy. Over the years it acquired an alternate name, the Battle of Senlac or Senlac Hill, but it has now been proved that this name was a later invention. At the time of the battle the hill had no name at all. However, Senlac Hill is used on the map and in the text because it is helpful in describing the progress of the battle.

For many years it was thought that Harold's men might have erected a stout wall of timbers in front of their position. We now know that this was not done, but the Saxons certainly had time to strengthen their position with a hastily constructed brushwood fence to offer some resistance to the Norman cavalry. This fence is mentioned in Robert Wace's *Roman de Rou,* and it would be reasonable to assume that, if the Saxons had time to do anything at all, they would have prepared such a fence from materials readily available. In this connection the quotations used here from the *Roman de Rou* have been rearranged to conform to the sequence of events as developed by more recent research.

There is still a dispute about the numbers engaged. We may be certain that the Saxons were somewhat outnumbered, but many writers in the past have given Duke William's forces as 50,000 or higher. This many soldiers could not possibly have been brought to England by the Norman fleet. Major General J. F. C. Fuller has computed the Norman strength as probably exceeding 5,000 men, with a grand total, including boatmen, carpenters, and others, of possibly 8,000. He gives King Harold's army as about 5,000, probably a little less. These figures, supported by his computations, seem very reasonable.

Synopsis of Events Between the Battle of Hastings, A.D. 1066, and Joan of Arc's Victory at Orléans, A.D. 1429

1071. Following a period of expansion in the latter part of the tenth and the early years of the eleventh centuries, the Byzantine Empire enters a period of decline. In 1071 the Seljuk Turks win the Battle of Manzikert. As a result of this defeat the Asiatic provinces of the empire are lost. By 1081 the Byzantines retain none of their former extensive territory in Asia Minor, except a few places on the seacoast.

1075–1122. The rivalry between the emperors and the popes results in a long struggle over the question of lay investiture.

1085. Alfonso VI of Castile captures Toledo from the Moors.

1096–1099. The First Crusade, led by Peter the Hermit and others, begins. A large, irregular swarm of individuals moves in four groups down the Danube toward Constantinople. Only two groups reach Constantinople; the others are destroyed by starvation or by the Hungarians. The first two groups are then destroyed by the Turks near Nicaea in Asia Minor. (This strange mass movement was so ineffective that it is not shown on the map.)

The real crusading armies, led by Godfrey of Bouillon, Count Raymond of Toulouse, Bohemund of Otranto, and Robert of Normandy, then pass through Constantinople, capture Nicaea, and attack Antioch which falls after a long siege. They are in turn besieged by the Turks but win the Battle of Antioch in 1098 and assault Jerusalem in 1099. The Christian Kingdom of Jerusalem survives for nearly one hundred years.

1125. The great struggle begins between the Welf and Waiblingen families in Germany (the Guelphs and the Ghibellines in Italy).

1143–1147. Alfonso I is proclaimed King of Portugal; Lisbon is captured from the Moors.

1147–1149. The Second Crusade, led by Conrad III of Germany and Louis VII of France, collapses at the siege of Damascus. (Since this crusade was a complete failure, it is not included on the map.)

1154–1189 When Henry II becomes King of England, he establishes one of the most powerful monarchies in Europe. As a result of his own personal inheritance and his marriage to Eleanor of Aquitaine, he rules half of France, as well as England and Normandy. In addition, during his reign part of Ireland comes under his control.

1189–1192. At the Battle of Hattin, in 1187, Saladin, the most famous, romantic Saracen of the age, inflicts a crushing defeat on the Christians, then retakes Jerusalem. Three great armies are raised in Europe to undertake the Third Crusade. The Germans led by Frederick Barbarossa march overland while Richard the Lion-Hearted of England and Philip Augustus of France travel almost entirely by water. The taking of Acre in 1191 is the only tangible result.

1202–1204. The Fourth Crusade, originally designed as an attack upon Egypt, is diverted by the Venetians into an attack against Constantinople which is captured in 1203. Following a revolt within the city, the crusaders return and take it a second time. Venice profits commercially from this enterprise for sixty years, until the return of the Byzantine forces.

1203–1204. Philip Augustus of France succeeds in wresting Normandy and other portions of France from King John of England.

1206–1227. Genghis Khan is proclaimed supreme ruler of all the Mongols. In just twenty-one years he and his "conquering hordes" (actually well organized, trained, disciplined armies) overwhelm more than half of Asia and part of southern Russia. Upon his death the Mongol invasions of Europe ceased temporarily.

1212. The victory of Las Navas de Tolosa assures the predominance of the Christian cause in Spain.

1212–1229. Several crusading expeditions (not indicated on the map) take place in this period, including: the Children's Crusade in 1212, which may be the origin of the story of the Pied Piper of Hamelin; an attack against Damietta in Egypt which takes that city then loses it; and the crusade of Frederick II of Germany, who gains Jerusalem by a treaty with the Sultan of Egypt. (Fifteen years later it was recovered by the Moslems. The next leader of an army composed primarily of Christians to enter Jerusalem was General Allenby in World War I.)

1215. The barons force King John to accept the Magna Carta, which established the principle that English law is above even the king.

1236–1248. The Spanish obtain possession of Cordova, Valencia and Seville, thus completing the reconquest of Spain except for the Moorish Kingdom of Granada.

1237–1241. The Mongols subdue central Russia as far as Moscow, capture Kiev, and overrun southern Russia. Led by Sabutai, one of Genghis Khan's ablest generals, they conquer Hungary; the force covering the northern flank of this lightning campaign swept through Cracow and Breslau, then defeated a large German-Polish army at Liegnitz.

1248–1254. In his first crusade Louis IX of France captures Damietta, then surrenders his army near Mansura.

1259–1294. During the reign of Kublai Khan the Mongol Empire reaches its greatest extent, including most of Asia, the Near East, and a large portion of eastern Europe.

1270. The second crusade of Louis IX is diverted to Tunis where he and a great part of his army die of the plague. The Mohemmedans gradually reconquer the Holy Land, capturing Acre in 1291, almost exactly two hundred years after the start of the First Crusade.

1273. Rudolf of Hapsburg is elected as the German king and as Emperor of the Holy Roman Empire. He agrees not to interfere in Italy. After his election he forces the King of Bohemia to cede Austria to him.

1282–1283. Edward I conquers Wales. His son, later Edward II, born in Wales in 1284 is the first heir to the English throne to be given the title Prince of Wales.

1290–1326. The power of the Seljuk Turks, weakened by the crusades, had been destroyed by the Mongols. Into this vacuum step the Ottoman

Turks. Osman (Othman) I is the traditional founder of the Ottoman dynasty.

1295–1314. When Edward I asserts his claim to overlordship of Scotland, the Scots, led by John Balliol, rebel and ally themselves with
France. This alliance is to endure intermittently for three centuries.
Edward marches into Scotland, annexes the kingdom and crushes
William Wallace's uprising. Then Robert Bruce's defeat of Edward II
at Bannockburn in 1314 leads to eventual recognition of the Kingdom
of Scotland.

1328. Philip VI becomes King of France, the first of the Valois line.

1337. The Hundred Years' War between England and France begins.

1340. Edward III wins the naval Battle of Sluys which gives the
English the mastery of the English Channel.

1346. Edward III wins the Battle of Crécy. The longbow conclusively
proves its superiority over the crossbow. The English yeomen decisively
defeat the French armored knights. (Artillery may have been used
in this battle.)

1346–1347. Calais is invested and surrenders after a long siege in
which artillery is employed.

1347–1349. The Black Death sweeps over Europe.

1354. The Ottoman Turks obtain their first foothold in Europe.

1356. The Black Prince decisively defeats a far larger French army at
the Battle of Poitiers.

1371. Robert II, the first of the Stuart line, becomes King of Scotland.

1380–1399. Tamerlane conquers Persia and Mesopotamia and invades
India.

1389–1396. The Ottoman Turks crush the medieval Serbian Empire at
the First Battle of Kosovo, then defeat a large Christian army composed
primarily of Hungarians at Nicopolis. As a result Serbia, Bulgaria, and
the mainland of Greece come under Turkish rule.

1402. Tamerlane completely routs the Ottoman Turks at Angora
(modern Ankara), then devastates Asia Minor. He dies before he can
undertake his project of invading China.

1415. The Hohenzollern dynasty is established in Brandenburg.

1415. Henry V actively renews the Hundred Years' War, invades
France, takes Harfleur, and wins the great Battle of Agincourt.

1417–1419. Henry conquers Normandy. Supporters of the dauphin,
later Charles VII of France, assassinate the Duke of Burgundy, the most

powerful of the French nobles. His successor becomes the active ally of the English.

1420.   The Treaty of Troyes is concluded between Henry V of England, Charles VI of France, and Philip, Duke of Burgundy. The treaty disinherits the dauphin, recognizes Henry's claim to the French throne, but leaves Charles in nominal possession of the title until his death.

1420.   In Bohemia and Moravia followers of the reformer John Huss revolt against the Church. The Hussite Wars last until 1436, when a compromise is reached between the Church and the moderate reformers.

1421–1423.   Henry V drives the French forces who refuse to acknowledge the Treaty of Troyes southward across the Loire. Henry and Charles VI of France die. The infant Henry VI is proclaimed King of England and France. The followers of the dauphin proclaim him Charles VII, King of France, but, since Reims is in English possession, he cannot be formally crowned. The Duke of Bedford, the capable English regent in France, defeats the army of the dauphin at Cravant.

1424.   The Duke of Bedford gains another victory at Verneuil.

1428.   The English begin the Siege of Orléans.

Joan of Arc's Victory over the English at Orléans, A.D. 1429

The eyes of all Europe were turned toward this scene, where it was reasonably supposed the French were to make their last stand for maintaining the independence of their monarchy and the rights of their sovereign.

—HUME

WHEN, after their victory at Salamis, the generals of the various Greek states voted the prizes for distinguished individual merit, each assigned the first place of excellence to himself, but all concurred in giving their second votes to Themistocles. This was looked on as decisive proof that Themistocles ought to be ranked first of all. If we were to endeavor by a similar test to ascertain which European nation had contributed the most to the progress of European civilization, we should find Italy, Germany, England, and Spain each claiming first place, but each also naming France as clearly next in merit. It is impossible to deny her paramount importance in history. Even if we were to discount the formidable part that she has played in the history of European warfare, her influence over the arts, the literature, the manners, and the feelings of mankind have been such as to make the crisis of her earlier fortunes a topic of worldwide interest. It may be asserted, without exaggeration, that the future career of almost every nation in the world was involved in the struggle by which the heroine of France rescued her country from the English.

Seldom has the extinction of a nation's independence appeared more inevitable than was the case in France in 1428 when the English invaders began the Siege of Orléans. A series of dreadful defeats had

136

thinned the chivalry of France and blunted the spirits of her soldiers. Foreign armies of the bravest veterans, led by the ablest captains, occupied half her territory. Worse to her than the fierceness and strength of her foes were the vices and the crimes of her own children. Her native prince was a dissolute trifler whose supporters had, in his presence, assassinated the most powerful noble in the land. The successor to the murdered Duke of Burgundy, in revenge, had actively joined the enemy. Many more of her nobility, many of her prelates, her magistrates and rulers had sworn fealty to the English king. The condition of the peasantry amid the general anarchy was wretched.

In the autumn of 1428 the English, who were already masters of most of France north of the Loire, prepared their forces for the conquest of the southern provinces that still adhered to the French cause. The city of Orléans on the Loire was looked upon as the last stronghold. If the English could obtain possession of it, there appeared to be nothing to prevent them from undertaking a victorious march through the remainder of the kingdom. Accordingly the Earl of Salisbury, one of the bravest and most experienced of the English generals, who had been trained under Henry V, marched to the attack of the all-important city.

Orléans was on the north side of the Loire. It was heavily fortified with thick walls, a deep moat, and numerous cannon and catapults. It was correctly considered to be one of the strongest fortresses in France.

A strong masonry bridge crossed the Loire from the city to a small island close to the south bank. This bridge is particularly interesting because it had at its southern end twin towers called Les Tourelles. These were actually a part of the bridge which ended here. The connecting link between the towers at the south end of the bridge and the bank was provided by a drawbridge that spanned a moat with flowing water. Close to the water's edge the French had built a fort. Taken together, Les Tourelles, the drawbridge, and the fort on the south bank formed a strongpoint, capable of containing a garrison of considerable strength.

When Salisbury appeared south of the Loire below Orléans on October 12, 1428, he saw at a glance that the bridge and its defenses were the keys to the city; their capture would cut Orléans off from the friendly southern provinces. Accordingly he directed his principal operations against this position and, after a severe repulse, took Les

Tourelles by storm on the 24th of October. But the French had broken down an arch of the bridge. The English could not now make a direct assault upon the city from the south, but they did place a battery of cannon at Les Tourelles that fired down the main streets.

This is the first siege in which any important use appears to have been made of artillery. Yet even at Orléans both besiegers and besieged seem to have employed their cannon merely as instruments of destruction against their enemy's men, not for battering down walls. The use of artillery to breach solid masonry was taught Europe by the Turks a few years afterward at the memorable Siege of Constantinople. In the Hundred Years' War famine was looked upon as the surest weapon to compel the submission of a well-walled town, and the great object of besiegers was to effect a complete investment of the defenders.

In the case of Orléans this was not a simple matter. The English had only a few thousand men; the city was large; and the river not only split the besiegers' forces in two but also provided an additional way for supplies to reach the defenders. Nevertheless Lord Suffolk, who succeeded to the command after Salisbury was mortally wounded, carried on the necessary work. Strongly fortified posts called bastilles were constructed to block the approaches to the city. These were to be connected by numerous smaller forts until a complete investment was achieved. During the winter little progress was made, but when the spring of 1429 came, the English actively resumed their work. Gradually the communications between the city and the country were blocked until only the eastern side was open, and even on that side it was dangerous to attempt to break through. The people of the city were slowly approaching starvation.

In an attempt to obtain food a French force attacked a large wagon train carrying herring and other supplies to the English at Orléans. The resultant Battle of Rouvray, also called the "Battle of the Herrings," fought on February 12, 1429, was easily won by the English bowmen against odds of at least four to one. There seemed to be no possible way for the French to defeat these invaders, no matter how great a force was brought to bear against them. The English were confident, sure of victory, and completely unimpressed by the knowledge that Frenchmen would be glad to be rid of them if only they could be shown the way.

The Orléanais now, in their distress, offered to surrender the city to the Duke of Burgundy who, though the ally of the English, was yet one of their native princes. The English regent in France, the Duke of Bedford, was a capable, practical soldier. He saw no reason to agree to such a proposal because the city seemed certain to fall in a very few weeks. The Dauphin Charles despaired of continuing the struggle any longer; resistance seemed hopeless; no human skill could have predicted how rescue was to come to Orléans and to France.

In the village of Domrémy on the borders of Lorraine there was a farmer named Jacques d'Arc, respected in his station in life, who had reared a family in virtuous habits and in the practice of the strictest devotion. A daughter named by her parents Jeannette was called Jeanne by the French, which was Latinized into Johanna and Anglicized into Joan.

At the time when Joan first attracted widespread attention she was just seventeen years of age. She was naturally of a susceptible disposition, which diligent attention to the legends of saints, aided by the dreamy loneliness of her life tending her father's herds, had made peculiarly prone to enthusiastic fervor. At the same time she was noted for piety and purity of soul, and for compassionate gentleness to the sick and the distressed.

The district where she lived had escaped most of the ravages of war, but the approach of roving bands of Burgundian or English troops frequently spread terror through Domrémy. Once the village had been plundered by some of these marauders. Joan and her family had been driven from their home and forced to seek refuge for a time at nearby Neufchâteau. The people of Domrémy were principally in sympathy with the dauphin, and blamed the English and their allies the Burgundians for all the miseries which France endured.

Thus from infancy to girlhood, Joan had heard continually of the woes of the war and had herself witnessed some of the wretchedness that it caused. A feeling of intense patriotism grew in her. The deliverance of France from the English was the subject of her reveries by day and her dreams by night. Blended with these aspirations were recollections of the miraculous interpositions of Heaven in favor of the oppressed that she had learned from the legends of her Church. Her faith was unswerving and at length she believed herself to have received the supernatural inspiration she sought.

According to her own story, told by her to her merciless inquisitors during her captivity and with her death approaching, she was thirteen years old when her revelations began. She was in her father's garden when she heard a voice from God for the first time. Afterward Saint Michael and Saint Margaret and Saint Catherine appeared to her. They were always in a halo of glory; she could see that their heads were crowned with jewels; she did not distinguish their arms or limbs but she clearly heard their voices, which were tender and mild. She heard them more frequently than she saw them, and the usual time she heard them was when the church bells were sounding for prayer. When she heard the Heavenly Voices drawing near, she knelt down and prayed. Their presence gladdened her to tears, and after they departed she wept because they had not taken her back with them to Paradise. They always spoke soothingly to her. They told her that France would be saved and that she was to save it. Such were the visions and the voices that moved the spirit of the girl of thirteen. During the next four years they became more frequent and more clear.

At last the tidings of the Siege of Orléans reached Domrémy. Joan heard her parents and neighbors talk of the sufferings of its population, of the ruin its capture would bring, and of the distress of the dauphin and his court. Joan's heart was sorely troubled at the thought of the fate of Orléans. Her Voices now ordered her to leave her home, and told her that she was the instrument chosen by Heaven to drive the English away from that city, and to take the dauphin to be crowned king at Reims. At length she informed her parents of her divine mission, and said that she must go to the Sire de Baudricourt who commanded at Vaucouleurs and who was the appointed person to bring her into the presence of the king whom she was to save. Neither the anger nor the grief of her parents, who said they would rather see her drowned than exposed to the contamination of the camp, could move her from her purpose. When she arrived at Vaucouleurs the commandant Robert de Baudricourt at first thought her insane, but by degrees was led to believe, if not in her inspiration at least in her enthusiasm, and in its possible usefulness to the dauphin's cause.

The inhabitants of Vaucouleurs were completely won over to her side by the piety and devoutness she displayed, and by her firm belief in the reality of her mission. Baudricourt sent her to Chinon, where the Dauphin Charles was staying with his remnant of a court. Upon arrival she was after some delay admitted into the presence of the dauphin. Charles had dressed himself far less richly than many of his courtiers and mingled with them, to see if she would speak to the wrong person. She instantly singled him out and, kneeling before him, said, "Most noble Dauphin, the King of Heaven announces to you by me that you shall be anointed and crowned king in the city of Reims, and you shall be His viceregent in France." His features may have been seen by her in portraits, or have been described to her by others; but she herself believed that her Voices inspired her when she addressed the king. The report soon circulated that she had found him by a miracle. The fame of "The Maid," as she was termed, the renown of her holiness and of her mission spread far and wide through the land.

The state of public feeling in France was now favorable to an enthusiastic belief in a divine intervention in favor of the party that had been unsuccessful and oppressed. The humiliations that had befallen the French royal family and nobility were regarded as the just judgments of God upon them for their vice and impiety. The misfortunes that had come upon France as a nation were believed to have been the results of national sins. The English, who had been the instruments of Heaven's wrath against France, seemed now, by their pride and cruelty, to be fitting objects of it themselves. France in that age was a profoundly religious country. There was ignorance, there was superstition, there was bigotry; but there was Faith—a faith that itself worked miracles.

At this time also, one of those devotional movements began among the clergy in France. Numberless friars and priests traveled the rural districts and towns preaching to the people that they must seek from Heaven a deliverance from the pillaging of the soldiery and the insolence of the foreign oppressors. The idea of a Providence that works by general laws was alien to the feeling of the age. Every political event, as well as every natural phenomenon, was believed to be the result of a mandate from God. This led to the belief that His holy angels and saints were constantly employed in executing His commands and mingling in the affairs of men. The Church encouraged these feelings and at the same time sanctioned the concurrent popular belief that hosts of evil spirits were also actively interposing in the current of earthly events.

Thus all things favored the influence Joan obtained over both friends and foes. The French people, as well as the English and Burgundians, agreed that superhuman beings inspired her. The only question was whether these beings were good or evil angels. This question seemed to her countrymen to be settled decisively in her favor by the austere holiness of her life and by her exemplary attention to all the services and rites of the Church. The dauphin at first feared the injury that might be done to his cause if he laid himself open to the charge of having leagued himself with a sorceress. Every imaginable test, therefore, was resorted to in order to set Joan's orthodoxy and purity beyond suspicion. At last Charles and his advisers felt safe in accepting her services as a true and virtuous Christian daughter of the Holy Church.

It is indeed probable that Charles himself and some of his counselors may have suspected Joan of being a mere enthusiast, and it is certain that the celebrated Jean Dunois, commonly called the Bastard of Orléans, who was entrusted with the defense of that city, and others of the French generals, took considerable latitude in obeying or deviating from the military orders that she gave. But her influence over the mass of the people and the soldiers was unbounded. While Charles and his doctors of theology and court ladies had been deliberating as to recognizing or dismissing the Maid, a considerable period had passed, during which a small army had been assembled. It was resolved to send Joan with this force and a convoy of provisions to Orléans.

Joan appeared at the camp clad in a new suit of brilliant white armor, mounted on a stately black war-horse, wearing at her side a small battle-ax and the consecrated sword marked with five crosses that had at her bidding been brought to her from the shrine of Sainte-Catherine de Fierbois. Her banner was of white satin, strewn with fleurs-de-lis; on it was a representation of the Saviour and the words "JHESUS MARIA."

Thus accoutered she came to lead the troops of France who looked with admiration upon her, upon the skill with which she managed her war-horse, and the easy grace with which she handled her weapons. Her military education had been short but she had made the most if it. On the evening of April 28, 1429, they approached the city of Orléans. Joan's Voices had told her to enter the city from the north but her generals, knowing that this was the most dangerous approach of all, had directed the march to the south bank of the Loire. When Joan discovered this, she insisted that they cross the river. On the following night, under cover of rain and darkness, the army entered the

city from the north, with no trouble at all. Apparently the English
were so certain that the city was about to fall that they kept a very
careless watch. The fact that she and her army had entered Orléans
by the most dangerous road with such ease added greatly to her
reputation and to the general belief that her actions were divinely
inspired.

When the English learned that the Maid was in Orléans their minds
were not less occupied about her than were the minds of those in the
city—but in a very different way. The English believed in her supernatural powers as firmly as the French; but they thought her a sorceress
who had come to overthrow them. An old prophecy, which told that
a damsel from Lorraine was to save France, had long been current,
and it was known and applied to Joan by foreigners as well as by the
natives. The tales of miracles she was said to have wrought had been
listened to by the rough yeomen of the English camp with anxious
curiosity and secret awe.

It was known in the English camp that before Joan had marched
for Orléans she had sent a herald to their leaders to tell them, in the
name of the Most High, to surrender to the Maid, who was sent by
Heaven, the keys of the French cities they had taken. It was also known
that the herald had solemnly warned all in the English camp to leave,
or be visited by the judgment of God. Then the day after arrival in
Orléans Joan had sent another, similar message, only to receive an
insulting reply. She determined to make a last attempt to avoid bloodshed, by repeating the warning with her own voice. Accordingly she
came close enough to be within hearing distance of Les Tourelles,
spoke to the English, and urged them to depart, otherwise they would
meet with shame and woe. Sir William Gladsdale, who commanded at
Les Tourelles, and another English officer told her to go home and
mind her cows, then made other more insulting suggestions that
brought tears of shame and indignation to her eyes. But though the
English leaders taunted her, the effect on the soldiers was far different. Their morale, which had been so incomparably high, was shaken;
succeeding events did nothing to improve it.

Thus far she had succeeded in bringing relief to Orléans without
striking a blow, but the time had now come to test her courage in
battle. On May 4 she joined in an attack on the largest bastille east
of the city. After a severe struggle in which she led the final assault,
waving her banner and cheering the men forward to the walls, the

bastille was stormed. The French had gained their first victory since the beginning of the siege. The road to Jargeau was opened.

The next day was Ascension Day and it was passed by Joan in prayer. On the following morning the French crossed the river in boats to attack the strongly fortified positions on the south bank. Again, in this action, Joan distinguished herself. By nightfall all the bastilles on that side of the Loire had been cleared of the enemy, except Les Tourelles, the fort on the south bank, and the drawbridge between the two. By now Joan had become not only the guiding spirit of the soldiers but also the actual commander of the army on the battlefield. When the French generals decided that Les Tourelles was too formidable to assault and told her that they would prefer to reduce it by a siege, she promptly overruled them. She insisted, and rightly so, that they must strike immediately. They were finally forced to agree that the assault should be launched while the enthusiasm which her presence and heroic valor had created was at its height.

Early in the morning of the 7th of May some two thousand French soldiers assailed the fort on the south bank. It and Les Tourelles were defended by Gladsdale and five hundred of the best archers and men-at-arms in the English army. The Maid planted her banner on the edge of the moat and then springing down into the ditch began to mount a ladder. An arrow pierced her armor, wounding her severely between the neck and the shoulder. She fell bleeding from the ladder; the English leaped down from the walls to capture her, but her followers succeeded in rescuing her. Carried to the rear, she sat up and with her own hands drew the arrow out, had her wound dressed, and returned to the charge.

Meanwhile the English had repulsed the oft-renewed efforts of the French to scale the wall. Dunois, who commanded the attacking force, was at last discouraged and suggested abandoning the effort until the next day. Joan urged him not to despair. "By my God," she said, "you shall soon enter in there. Do not doubt it. When you see my banner wave again up to the wall, to your arms again." The faintness caused by her wound had now passed off, and she led the French in another rush against the fort. The English, who had thought her dead, were alarmed at her reappearance, while the French pressed furiously and fanatically forward. The soldier carrying Joan's banner let it touch the wall. She had told the troops that when her banner reached the wall, they should enter. Seeing the banner against the fort, all the French host swarmed madly up the ladders.

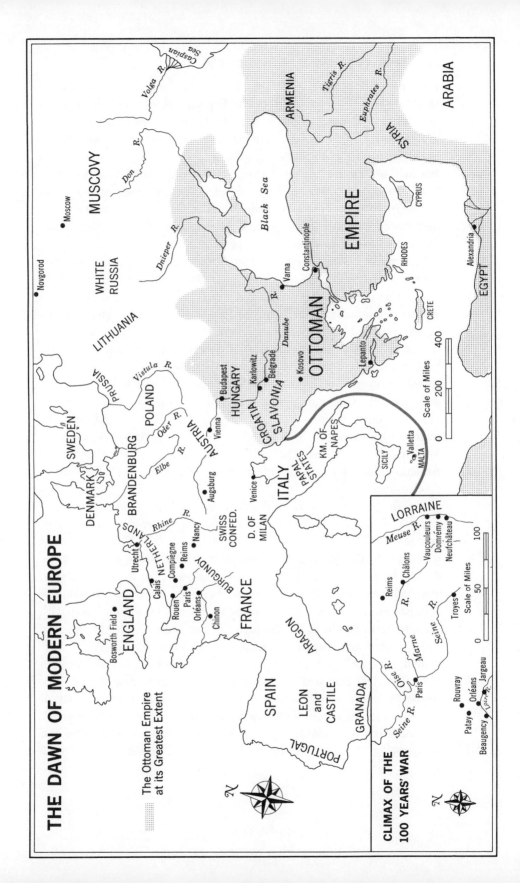

THE DAWN OF MODERN EUROPE

The Ottoman Empire at its Greatest Extent

ARABIA

ARMENIA

Tigris R.

Euphrates R.

SYRIA

MUSCOVY

Moscow

Volga R.

Caspian Sea

Don R.

CYPRUS

WHITE RUSSIA

Novgorod

Dnieper R.

Black Sea

EMPIRE

Alexandria

EGYPT

RHODES

LITHUANIA

OTTOMAN

Constantinople

Varna

CRETE

Lepanto

PRUSSIA

Vistula R.

POLAND

Budapest

HUNGARY

Karlowitz

Belgrade

Danube

Kosovo

Scale of Miles

0   200   400

SWEDEN

BRANDENBURG

Oder R.

AUSTRIA

Vienna

CROATIA

SLAVONIA

KM. OF NAPLES

Valletta

MALTA

DENMARK

Elbe R.

Augsburg

Venice

ITALY

PAPAL STATES

SICILY

NETHERLANDS

Utrecht

Rhine R.

SWISS CONFED.

D. OF MILAN

Calais

Compiègne

Reims

Nancy

BURGUNDY

Bosworth Field

ENGLAND

Rouen

Paris

Orléans

Chinon

FRANCE

ARAGON

SPAIN

LEON and CASTILE

PORTUGAL

GRANADA

N

CLIMAX OF THE 100 YEARS' WAR

LORRAINE

Meuse R.

Vaucouleurs

Domrémy

Neufchâteau

Reims

Châlons

Marne R.

Aisne R.

Seine R.

Troyes

Scale of Miles

0   50   100

Oise R.

Seine R.

Paris

Rouvray

Patay

Orléans

Jargeau

Loire R.

Beaugency

N

At this crisis the efforts of the English garrison were distracted by an attack from another quarter. The French troops who had been left in Orléans had made some hasty repairs to the broken arch of the bridge and at this critical moment were advancing to assault Les Tourelles from the northern side. Gladsdale saw that his only chance was to abandon the fort on the south bank and concentrate his whole force in the twin towers of Les Tourelles. He was crossing the drawbridge when it collapsed; he and several others perished in the water that flowed beneath. After his fall the remnant of the English abandoned all further resistance.

Joan made her triumphal reentry from Les Tourelles into the city over the bridge that had so long been closed. Every church bell in Orléans rang out; bonfires blazed; and throughout the night the sounds of rejoicing echoed. In the forts and bastilles which the besiegers retained on the northern shore there was despondent gloom. Never in history has morale played a more important part in warfare; never in a single campaign has there been such a sudden and complete reversal of morale. The English, who had been invincible, and knew it, were now sullen and full of helpless rage, while the French, who just ten days before had been desperate and ready to surrender, were now full of confidence, and eager to follow wherever Joan might lead them. The next morning the English burned their remaining bastilles and marched away, withdrawing slowly but in good order.

Within three months from the time of her first interview with the dauphin, Joan had fulfilled the first part of her promise: the raising of the Siege of Orléans. Within three months more she fulfilled the second part also. In the interval she took Jargeau and Beaugency by siege, decisively defeated and destroyed the prestige of the English at Patay, marched into Troyes and Châlons, and entered Reims in triumph; the enthusiasm of her countrymen knew no bounds. She then stood with her banner in her hand by the high altar at Reims while the dauphin was anointed and crowned as King Charles VII of France.

Joan now believed that her mission was accomplished. And, in truth, the deliverance of France from the English, though not completed for many years afterward, was then ensured. The ceremony of a royal coronation and anointment was not in those days regarded as a mere costly formality. It was believed to confer the sanction and the grace of Heaven upon the prince, who had previously ruled with only human authority. Thenceforth he was the Lord's Anointed. Those who had previously questioned his right to the throne now thought that Heaven itself had declared in favor of Charles. With this strong tide of national feeling in his favor, with victorious generals and soldiers around him, and a dispirited and divided enemy before him, he could not fail to conquer, though his own imprudence and misconduct and the stubborn valor the English still from time to time displayed, prolonged the war in France until the Wars of the Roses broke out in England, leaving France to peace and repose.

Joan knelt before the French king in the cathedral at Reims and shed tears of joy. She said that she had then fulfilled the work which the Lord had commanded her. The young girl now asked for her dismissal. She wished to return to her home, to tend her parents' herds again, to live in her native village. She had always believed that her career would be a short one. But Charles and his captains were reluctant to let her leave. They finally persuaded her for the sake of her beloved country to stay with the army. She still showed the same bravery and zeal for the cause of France. She still was as fervent as before in her prayers, and as exemplary in all religious duties, but she now no longer thought herself appointed by Heaven to lead her countrymen to further victories. Our admiration for her courage and patriotism ought to be increased a hundredfold by her conduct through the latter part of her career, when she no longer believed herself to be under divine protection. Indeed, she believed herself doomed to perish in a very short time, but she fought on as resolutely, if not as exultingly, as ever.

There is no need to retrace here the well-known fate of the Maid of Orléans, her severe wounding during an assault on Paris, her capture at Compiègne by the Burgundians, her sale to the English, and her burning at the stake in the marketplace at Rouen. Charles VII lifted not one finger to save her, but an English soldier who was there cried out: "We are lost. We have burnt a saint!" This proved to be the truth. The worthiest patriot of France became the most beloved of her saints; she was the inspiration and the spirit that not only saved the diverse groups of people who lived in France from domination by the English, but brought them together as a nation, the French nation, now ready to step forward and take its place in history.

Synopsis of Events Between Joan of Arc's Victory at Orléans, A.D 1429, and the Defeat of the Spanish Armada, A.D. 1588

1438. After the election of Albert, Duke of Austria, the imperial crown becomes for all practical purposes a hereditary possession of the house of Hapsburg.

1444–1448. The Hungarians lead another crusade against the Ottoman Turks. It ends in disaster. Murad II decisively defeats the Christian allies at Varna (1444) and at the Second Battle of Kosovo (1448).

1453. The Hundred Years' War ends when the English are driven from French soil, retaining only a small bridgehead at Calais.

1453. The Turkish Sultan Mohammed II takes Constantinople, bringing to an end the empire that had lasted over 1,100 years, and terrifying the Christian world.

1455–1485. During the reigns of Henry VI, Edward IV, and Richard III the houses of York (white rose) and Lancaster (red rose) fight for the English crown. The celebrated Wars of the Roses finally end with Richard III's defeat at Bosworth Field. Henry Tudor becomes Henry VII of England.

1462–1505. During the reign of Ivan III, Moscow throws off its allegiance to the Mongols. Ivan conquers the ancient trading republic of Novgorod, seizes a large portion of White Russia, and claims to be the rightful heir to the Byzantine emperors. His grandson, Ivan IV, the Terrible, formally adopts the title of Czar.

1469–1479. As a result of the marriage in 1469 of Isabella, who succeeded to the throne of Castile in 1474, and Ferdinand, who succeeded to the throne of Aragon in 1479, the Spanish kingdoms are united.

1477. The long struggle between the king and the feudal lords of France culminates in the Battle of Nancy. Charles the Bold of Burgundy is killed; Louis XI adds a large share of the Burgundian domains to the French crown. But Charles' daughter Mary marries Maximilian of Austria, thereby preventing Louis from acquiring the Netherlands, and thus also beginning a long rivalry between France and Austria.

1492. Ferdinand and Isabella complete the conquest of Granada.

1492. Columbus discovers the New World.

1495–1559. Charles VIII of France seizes Naples. A long series of wars ensues, involving France, Spain, Austria, England, and the Swiss. The two major opponents in the Italian Wars were Francis I of France and Charles I of Spain. The latter had inherited from his father the possessions of Austria, and from his mother the Kingdom of Spain. In 1519 he was elected Emperor Charles V. The Italian Wars, which were not confined solely to Italy, ended with Spain in possession of southern Italy, Sicily, and the Duchy of Milan. The English lost Calais, their last foothold in France from the Hundred Years' War.

1497. John Cabot, sailing for the English, reaches North America.

1497–1499. Vasco da Gama rounds the Cape of Good Hope, reaches India, and returns to Portugal.

1499. After a series of victories the Swiss Confederation is granted virtual independence from Austria. Independence is not formally acknowledged until 1648, at the end of the Thirty Years' War. By this time Swiss pikemen had established a tremendous prestige on the battlefield and were much sought after by other powers for employment as mercenaries.

1513. Balboa crosses the Isthmus of Panama and discovers the Pacific Ocean.

1514–1517. Under Selim I the Ottoman Turks defeat the Persians, conquer Armenia, Syria, and Egypt, then secure control of Arabia.

1517. The Reformation begins with Martin Luther's public protest against the misuse of indulgences.

1519–1521. Cortez conquers Mexico.

1519–1522. Magellan discovers the Straits that bear his name, crosses the Pacific to the Philippines where he is killed by the natives. One of his ships completes the circumnavigation of the globe.

1520–1566. During the reign of Suleiman the Magnificent, the Ottoman Empire reaches its zenith. In Asia it stretches to the Persian Gulf and the Caspian Sea; in Europe it includes Belgrade and Budapest and reaches almost to Vienna.

1521–1523. The Swedes revolt against Denmark; Gustavus Vasa is crowned as King Gustavus I.

1525. The domain of the Teutonic Knights becomes the Duchy of Prussia under Polish suzerainty but ruled by a branch of the Hohenzollern dynasty of Brandenburg.

1532. Pizarro begins the conquest of Peru.

1534. Cartier, the French navigator, reaches North America.

1534. Henry VIII renounces papal supremacy; Parliament passes the Act of Supremacy.

1541. De Soto discovers the Mississippi River.

1546–1555. Charles V attacks the Protestant League. He is at first successful; then, after France intervenes, defeated. The Peace of Augsburg, allowing each prince and free city to choose between Catholicism and Lutheranism, provides a temporary settlement, but the Calvinists are ignored.

1558. Elizabeth becomes Queen of England.

1568. Revolt flares in the Netherlands against the rule of Spain. William the Silent, Prince of Orange, becomes the leader of the revolt.

1571. Turkish naval prestige in the Mediterranean is shattered. Don Juan of Austria, in command of a combined naval force, furnished primarily by Spain and Venice but including a few ships of the Papacy, completely defeats the Turks in the famous naval Battle of Lepanto, the last great battle of oar-driven ships.

1572. A large number of Protestants in France are massacred on St. Bartholomew's Day.

1577–1580. Francis Drake sails through the Straits of Magellan, takes possession of California for England, then completes circumnavigation of the globe.

1579. The northern and southern provinces of the Netherlands separate. By the Union of Utrecht the Calvinist Protestant states of the north form a permanent confederation. In 1581 they proclaim their independence from Spain.

1580. The Spaniards invade Portugal; Philip II of Spain is crowned King of Portugal.

1584. William, Prince of Orange, is mortally wounded by a Spanish agent.

1586–1587. Mary, Queen of Scots, is tried and executed.

10

The Defeat of the Spanish
Armada, A.D. 1588

ON THE AFTERNOON of the 19th of July, 1588, a group of English captains was collected at the Bowling Green on the Hoe at Plymouth. And a more unusual group of restless adventurers, daring explorers, and valiant sailors has never since been gathered together on the eve of such a great event. There was the Vice-Admiral, Sir Francis Drake, the first Englishman to circumnavigate the globe, the terror of every Spanish coast in the Old World and the New. There was John Hawkins, the rough veteran who was primarily responsible for the improvements in design of the new English ships, rebuilding the old, and reorganizing the navy. There was Martin Frobisher, one of the earliest of those explorers who dared to venture into the unknown Arctic seas in search of the Northwest Passage. And there was the High Admiral of England, Charles Lord Howard of Effingham, who, although feeling the responsibility of his mission of protecting England from invasion, was as courageous, enthusiastic, and eager for combat as any of his subordinates.

In the harbor lay the English fleet, awaiting news of Spain's Invincible Armada. Drake and other high officers were playing bowls when a small armed vessel was seen running before the wind into Plymouth harbor with all sails set. Her commander landed in haste

151

and eagerly sought the place where the English lord-admiral and his captains were standing. His name was Thomas Fleming, and he was the captain of one of the smaller ships stationed to watch the approaches from Spain to the English Channel. He promptly reported that he had in the morning seen the Spanish Armada off the Cornish coast. At this exciting news the captains started to hurry down to the water, but Drake coolly checked his comrades. He insisted that the match be finished, "There is time to finish the game and beat the Spaniards too." With this touch of humor the tension was relieved, the game resumed, and of course Drake was correct. He had simply been the first to realize that no one was going anywhere with the wind blowing against them; the fleet could not leave the harbor until the incoming tide changed in their favor. Indeed, it was not until late that night that the English ships began to hoist their sails and beat to windward toward the enemy.

Great changes had taken place in Europe in the 159 years since Joan of Arc had raised the Siege of Orléans. The Hundred Years' War had finally come to an end in 1453 with the driving of the English from French soil; England had been left with only a small bridgehead at Calais. In that same year the Ottoman Turks had besieged and captured Constantinople. The final downfall of the Byzantine Empire after over eleven hundred years of existence not only brought fear to the other peoples of Eastern Europe and the Mediterranean who were not already under Moslem domination, but also completed the closing of the Mediterranean trade routes to the East. The European states had by this time begun a search for other ways of reaching the Far East, but the fall of Constantinople forced them to redouble their efforts, and ushered in the great age of discovery.

Actually, some forty more years were to pass before the great discoveries were made. These were years of importance to the growth of three European powers, England, France and Spain. In England the dreary thirty-year civil war known as the Wars of the Roses broke the power of the feudal barons. Half of the nobility were killed, and those who survived were ruined. The Tudor dynasty was established. In France the long struggle between the royal power and the feudal lords ended with the kings obtaining control over most of the territory of present-day France. In the process, however, that portion of land belonging to the House of Burgundy and known as the Netherlands had been acquired by the Hapsburgs of Austria. This failure on the part of France to obtain control of the Netherlands, which then included both Holland and Belgium, was to result in a long rivalry between France and Austria, and the Netherlands themselves were to play a great part in the history of Europe.

Almost unnoticed, a new power was arising. In 1492 the Spanish, who for centuries had been slowly advancing their frontiers southward, completed their conquest of Granada. After a period of almost eight hundred years, Mohammedan rule in Spain had ended. This victory tended somewhat to counterbalance in the Mediterranean the loss to the Christian world of Constantinople, and in that same year Christopher Columbus, sailing for Spain, discovered the New World. Five years later Vasco da Gama, sailing for Portugal, rounded the Cape of Good Hope and discovered the true route to India.

The rise of the power of Spain after 1492 was phenomenal. When Charles I came to the throne in 1516, he found himself the most influential monarch in Christendom. By a series of matrimonial alliances he had inherited the Kingdom of Spain, which by this time had acquired control over Naples, Sicily, and Sardinia, and the possessions of Austria, which included the Netherlands. Three years later he was elected Emperor Charles V. This, together with the amazing progress Spain had made in developing the New World, completely upset the balance of power in Europe. There were no great kingdoms in Germany or Italy, only a collection of miscellaneous small states. The only other powerful kingdom on the Continent was France, which now found itself almost completely surrounded by the Spanish-Austrian dominions. The natural result was a long series of wars, with France fighting for its existence as a national power against the might of Spain.

Into the middle of this struggle came the Protestant Reformation. In 1517 Martin Luther had made his public protest against the misuse of indulgences. While Cortez was conquering Mexico, while Magellan was sailing his ships around the world, while Francis I of France and Charles V were struggling for power in Italy and elsewhere, the Protestants in Germany were approaching a state of open revolt.

The passage of fifty more years brings us to the year 1571 when Spain won the great Battle of Lepanto, shattering Turkish naval prestige in the Mediterranean. Philip II is now King of Spain, and had been for fifteen years the strongest monarch in Europe. When his father Charles V abdicated in 1556, Philip had become absolute master of an empire so superior to the other states of Europe that he might look over the whole Continent without finding a single antagonist of whom he need stand in awe, except the Ottoman Turks, and now his fleet had checked their westward advance.

Of his other achievements Philip could also be proud. His father had been forced to sign the Peace of Augsburg by which the princes and free cities of Germany were permitted to choose between Catholicism and Lutheranism, but the Catholic Counter-Reformation was achieving a large measure of success in winning back some of the Protestant territories. Philip had triumphantly concluded the Italian Wars and had gained from them southern Italy, Sicily, and the Duchy of Milan, while his archenemy France gained only Calais, at the expense of the English. And simultaneously throughout this period his overseas possessions had continued to expand, bringing untold wealth to Spain, particularly from Mexico and Peru.

There were only two clouds on the Spanish horizon. The Netherlands were in revolt, and Elizabeth was queen of an England that had become the major stronghold of the Protestants in Europe and whose sailors were beginning to prey upon Spanish commerce with irritating frequency. Yet in the year of the triumph at Lepanto, Philip II could not have viewed either of these clouds on his horizon with alarm.

Upon her accession to the throne of England in 1558, Queen Elizabeth had found an encumbered revenue, a divided people, and an unsuccessful foreign war in which Calais, the last remnant of the English possessions in France, had been lost. She had also a formidable pretender to her crown, Mary, Queen of Scots, whose interests were favored by all the Roman Catholic powers. Even some of her own subjects were inclined toward the belief that Elizabeth was a usurper. As the years passed, she revived the commercial prosperity, the national spirit and the national loyalty of England, but her resources to cope with the colossal power of Philip II still seemed most scanty. There was not a single foreign ally except the Dutch, who were themselves struggling hard, and apparently hopelessly, to maintain their revolt against Spain.

In 1579 the northern and southern provinces of the Netherlands separated. By the Union of Utrecht the seven Calvinist Protestant states of the north formed a confederation and two years later these seven provinces, the forerunners of the Dutch Republic, defiantly proclaimed their independence from Spain. Elizabeth was able to provide a small amount of military assistance to these valiant people, but meanwhile the predominantly Catholic provinces of the southern Netherlands were being brought back under Spanish control. The Spanish governor general of the Netherlands who effected the reconquest of the southern half was Alexander Farnese, Duke of Parma. From all accounts he was a most capable, formidable enemy, and the army he commanded was an army of veterans. At this time the Spanish infantry was justly renowned throughout the world; Spanish soldiers had confidence in themselves and their commanders. If Philip II decided to invade England, and could land this general and these soldiers on English soil, the result could not long have been in doubt.

As the fateful year 1588 approached, there could not have been much question as to Philip's plans. In 1580 he had acquired dominion over Portugal, and with it all the fruits of the maritime enterprises of the Portuguese had fallen into his hands. The Portuguese colonies in America, Africa and the Indies acknowledged the sovereignty of the King of Spain, who thus almost doubled his overseas empire, and also increased the size of his navy.

One nation only had been Philip's active enemy, his persevering and his successful foe. England had encouraged his subjects in the Netherlands in their revolt against him and given them aid in men and money. English ships had plundered his colonies and defied his supremacy in the New World as well as in the Old. They had defeated his squadrons; they had captured his cities and burned his arsenals. The English had made Philip himself the object of personal insult. He was held up to ridicule in their stage plays and masks, and these scoffs at the man had (as is not unusual in such cases) excited the anger of the absolute king even more than the attacks upon his power. Personal as well as political revenge urged him to attack England. Were she once subdued, the Dutch must submit; France could not cope with him, and the empire would not oppose him; universal dominion seemed sure to be the result of the conquest of that hated island.

There was yet another and a stronger feeling that armed King Philip against England. He was one of the sincerest and one of the sternest Catholics of his age. He believed himself the appointed champion to stamp out heresy and reestablish the papal power. He was well aware of the fact that the Protestants throughout Europe looked to England as their protector and their refuge. The conquest of England would deal a mortal blow to the Protestant power. The Pope earnestly ex-horted Philip to this enterprise and when the tidings reached Italy and Spain that the Protestant Queen of England had found it necessary to put her rival Mary, Queen of Scots, to death, to stop the plots against the throne, the fury of the Vatican and Catholic Spain knew no bounds. Philip began the tremendous task of preparing an armada to sail against England. Although various pretexts were given out to account for the vast amount of work that was being undertaken in Spain and the Netherlands, it was quite obvious that an invasion of England was being readied, and the plan for the invasion was also quite apparent. The main fleet assembled on the coast of Spain and Portugal would secure command of the English Channel. Then the veteran Spanish army in the Netherlands under the Duke of Parma would cross to England, its passage protected by the Armada.

In the seaports of the Mediterranean and along the Atlantic coast the work was urged forward with all the earnestness of religious zeal as well as of angry ambition, when the whole project received a tremendous setback. In April, 1587, Sir Francis Drake raided the port of Cádiz. In this "singeing of the King of Spain's beard" a large quantity of ships and stores was destroyed and burned; the expedition was delayed for a year. Nevertheless, in May, 1588, the Armada was ready to sail, and the Pope had agreed to contribute a million gold ducats to defray the cost on the day that the first Spanish soldier was landed in England.

It was most fortunate for England that Drake's raid had been under-taken and had given the country an extra year in which to prepare for defense. As Ranke, the German historian of the Popes, wrote: "But whenever any principle or power, be what it may, aims at unlimited supremacy in Europe, some vigorous resistance to it, having its origin in the deepest springs of human nature, invariably arises. Philip II had to encounter newly-awakened powers, braced by the vigor of youth, and elevated by a sense of their future destiny. The intrepid corsairs, who had rendered every sea insecure, now clustered round the coasts of their native land. The Protestants in a body—even the Puritans, although they had been subjected to as severe oppressions as the Catholics—rallied round their queen, who now gave admirable proof of her masculine courage, and her princely talent of winning the affections, and leading the minds, and preserving the allegiance of men."

Ranke should have added that the English Catholics at this crisis proved themselves as loyal to their queen and true to their country as were the most vehement anti-Catholic zealots in the island. Some few traitors there were; but as a body the Englishmen who held the ancient faith stood the trial of their patriotism nobly. The lord-admiral himself was a Catholic, and (to adopt the words of Hallam), "Then it was that the Catholics in every county repaired to the standard of the lord lieutenant, imploring that they might not be suspected of bartering the national independence for their religion itself." The Spaniard found no partisans in the country he assailed.

An army was assembled at Tilbury, and while the Armada was still off the coasts of England and its fate uncertain, the lion-hearted Elizabeth rode through the ranks, encouraging her captains and her soldiers by her presence and her words. One of the speeches she addressed to them during this crisis has been preserved and, though often quoted, it must not be omitted here:

"My loving people," she said, "we have been persuaded by some that are careful of our safety to take heed how we commit ourselves to armed multitudes, for fear of treachery. But I assure you I do not desire to live to distrust my faithful and loving people. Let tyrants fear! I have always so behaved myself, that, under God, I have placed my chiefest strength and safeguard in the loyal hearts and good will of my subjects; and therefore I am come among you as you see at this time, not for my recreation and disport, but being resolved, in the midst and heat of the battle, to live or die among you all, to lay down for my God, for my kingdom, and for my people, my honor and my blood even in the dust. I know I have the body but of a weak and feeble woman, but I have the heart and stomach of a king, and of a King of England too, and think it foul scorn that Parma, or Spain, or any prince of Europe should dare to invade the borders of my realm; to which rather than any dishonor shall grow by me, I myself will take up arms, I myself will be your general, judge and rewarder of every one of your virtues in the field. I know already, for your forwardness, you have deserved rewards and crowns; and we do assure you, on the word of a prince, they shall be duly paid you."

Some of Elizabeth's advisers recommended that the principal care and resources of the government should be devoted to the raising and equipping of armies to meet the enemy when he attempted to land. But the wiser counsels of others, who saw that England's best defense

was her fleet, prevailed. They urged the importance of the fleet en-
countering the Spaniards at sea and, if possible, preventing them from
approaching the land at all.

The ships of the Royal Navy, the Queen's ships, amounted to only
thirty-four, but the most serviceable merchant vessels were collected
from all the ports of the country. The citizens of London, Bristol,
and the other great commercial cities showed as great a zeal in equipping and manning vessels as the nobility and gentry displayed in
mustering land forces. The total number of men who came forward
to sail in the English fleet has been estimated at about 17,000. We
do know that there were a total of 197 ships, but as many as half of
these were too small to be helpful in the actual fighting, although they
certainly aided by carrying messages, in scouting and reconnaissance
work, and in supplying the fleet. The battles were fought almost entirely between the big ships of the two fleets.

We have very complete information on the ships and armament
of the Spanish fleet, but a listing of the various squadrons, their commanders' names, and the types of ships, with their old-fashioned
nomenclature, would be more confusing than helpful, although certainly impressive. There were a total of 130 ships, including dispatch
ships and supply ships, which is 67 less than the English fleet; but a
far greater proportion were large fighting ships. The force embarked
consisted of nearly 19,000 soldiers, over 8,000 sailors and some slaves;
the total was about 30,000 men.

The comparison of 30,000 Spaniards versus 17,000 Englishmen brings
us immediately to a consideration of the tactics, the ships and the
armament on each side. The basic large Spanish and Portuguese fighting ships for Atlantic waters were called galleons. They had high castles
at the bow and at the stern, and were armed with heavy, short-range
cannon. In addition to these ships there were a number of galleys that
usually cruised under sail but could use oars to drive them forward
in battle. They were equipped with a large heavy prow for ramming
the enemy, and carried soldiers for boarding and seizing their opponents' ships in hand-to-hand fighting. This was the Mediterranean
style of fighting that had won the famous Naval Battle of Lepanto
against the Turks just seventeen years before. This conception explains
the high proportion of soldiers, over two to one, to sailors on the
Spanish ships.

The fighting ships of the Royal Navy, the Queen's ships, were different than the Spanish galleons. The man primarily responsible for

these differences was John Hawkins. For the past several years he had been building new ships and rebuilding old fighting ships for the queen. He had carefully considered the changes that had occurred in naval tactics as a result of the introduction of guns and gunpowder. There were basically three types of guns. The first to be introduced were small, and were used primarily against enemy soldiers and sailors; their use had led to the introduction of the castles with the guns mounted high up on the ship for greater range and to sweep the decks. Then came the powerful, shipsmashing guns of two general types, the cannon and the culverin. The cannon threw a heavy, iron shot at short or medium ranges. These guns obviously could not be mounted on the castles but must be mounted along the sides of the ship. The Spanish galleons were well equipped with these weapons of destruction.

John Hawkins, however, concentrated on the culverin, which threw a smaller shot at longer range. For this he needed faster, more maneuverable ships. The castles were cut down, though not eliminated. The ships were lengthened and their beams narrowed, their keels deepened. They were therefore faster than the Spanish ships, more seaworthy, less liable to drift in a strong wind, and could carry more guns along their greater length. The result when we compare the Armada with the English fleet is that, although the heaviest ships on each side were of about the same tonnage, the Spanish were slower, more heavily armed with more powerful guns; while the faster English ships had long-range weapons, suitable for battering their enemy at a range beyond his ability to fire back.

The commander of the Spanish Armada was to have been the famous Don Alvaro de Bazán, Marquis of Santa Cruz, but, unfortunately for Spain, he died early in the year. The new commander appointed to take his place was Don Alonzo Pérez de Guzmán, Duke of Medina Sidonia, undoubtedly a man of fine reputation but not too well acquainted with the sea. For this reason, when the duke asked that someone else be assigned the task, he was given a competent naval adviser to act as his chief of staff, but was told to go ahead with the assigned duty. He was also given very explicit orders to sail up the Channel and not to seek battle until he joined the Duke of Parma. His union with Parma was all-important; then he was to help transport the troops from the Netherlands to England; at that time he could seek a battle at his own discretion.

This brings us to the other two forces involved. The first was the

Duke of Parma's invading force and the second was the Dutch blockading force. In describing the defeat of the Spanish Armada, the tendency is to concentrate on the spectacular phases of the battles between the large fighting ships and overlook the part played by the Dutch. Their warships were mostly coastal sailing vessels, designed for shallow waters, but entirely adequate for pinning down in their harbors the flat-bottomed barges and other craft assembled for the invasion. They eagerly undertook this task and did it in a thoroughly capable manner. In addition they were reinforced by a squadron of English ships, including some Queen's ships, under the command of Lord Henry Seymour. The queen took no chances.

On May 18, 1588, the Armada set sail; two days later all ships were at sea, heading north, but very slowly, since their overall speed was regulated by the speed of the slowest ships. Then severe gales forced them to put in to Corunna to refit. They did not sail again until July 12.

Meanwhile a long discussion had been taking place between the queen and her admirals. Sir Francis Drake and other intrepid souls wanted to put to sea, to meet the Armada off the Spanish coast, attack it in its ports, and force it to fight in defense of its coastline. The queen and her advisers were nervous about even having the main battle fleet as far west as Plymouth, with only one squadron keeping watch with the Dutch over the Duke of Parma's force. This argument as to the proper employment of the English fleet at that time will probably go on as long as the Armada is discussed. It is certainly true that in later days the navy was employed as Sir Francis Drake would have wished, but in those early days the various problems of supplying the fleet at a great distance had never been studied; and, as it developed, the problem of food supply and ammunition was to prove critical even when in home waters.

In any event, Lord Howard finally received permission to sail against Spain and the English fleet cleared from Plymouth. Unfortunately, the same storms that forced the Spanish into Corunna struck the English and drove them back to Plymouth. Another attempt in June ended in the same unhappy way. Thereupon a screen of light-armed ships was left to watch the approaches from Spain, and it was one of these, commanded by Captain Thomas Fleming, that brought the news of the Armada's approach on the afternoon of the 19th of July.

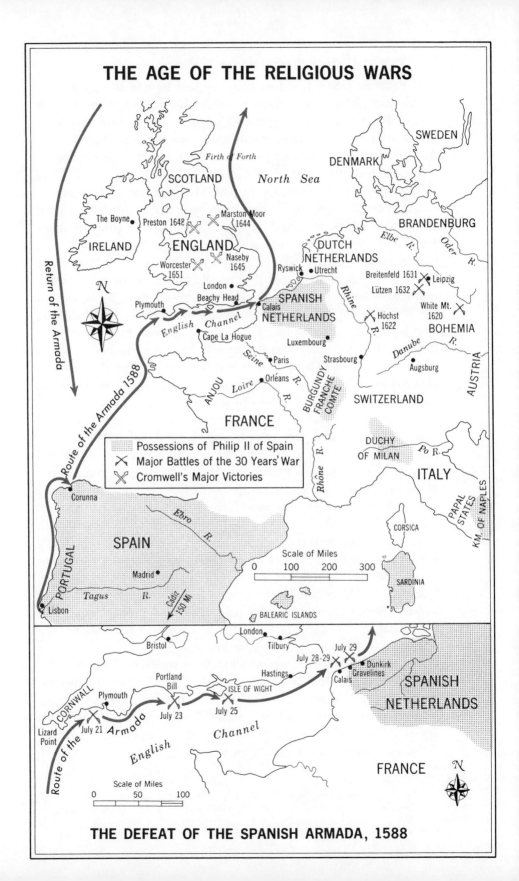

THE AGE OF THE RELIGIOUS WARS

SWEDEN

DENMARK

Firth of Forth

SCOTLAND *North Sea*

BRANDENBURG

Elbe R. *Oder R.*

The Boyne Preston 1648 Marston Moor 1644

IRELAND ENGLAND DUTCH NETHERLANDS

Ryswick Utrecht Breitenfeld 1631 Leipzig

Worcester 1651 Naseby 1645 Lützen 1632

London White Mt. 1620

Plymouth Beachy Head SPANISH NETHERLANDS Höchst 1622

Calais BOHEMIA

English Channel Cape La Hogue

Luxembourg *Rhine*

Seine Paris Strasbourg *Danube R.* AUSTRIA

Return of the Armada

ANJOU *Loire* Orléans Augsburg

R. BURGUNDY FRANCHE COMTE SWITZERLAND

FRANCE DUCHY OF MILAN *Po R.*

Possessions of Philip II of Spain ITALY

✕ Major Battles of the 30 Years' War *Rhône R.*

Cromwell's Major Victories PAPAL STATES KM. OF NAPLES

Route of the Armada 1588 CORSICA

Corunna *Ebro R.*

SPAIN Scale of Miles
0   100   200   300

PORTUGAL SARDINIA

Madrid BALEARIC ISLANDS

Tagus R. Cádiz 150 Mi.

Lisbon

London

Bristol Tilbury July 29

July 28-29 Dunkirk

Portland Bill Hastings Gravelines

Plymouth ISLE OF WIGHT Calais SPANISH NETHERLANDS

CORNWALL

Lizard Point July 21 *Armada* July 23 July 25

Route of the *English Channel*

Scale of Miles FRANCE
0   50   100

N

THE DEFEAT OF THE SPANISH ARMADA, 1588

The stirring events that followed may best be told by dividing the action into phases. First there was the meeting engagement, July 19–21; then the long run up the Channel to Calais, July 22–27; the Battle at Calais on the night of July 28–29; the Battle at Gravelines on the 29th; and finally the long homeward voyage of the Spanish fleet.

Beginning on the night of July 19 the English began to sail out of Plymouth against the wind. On July 20, Medina Sidonia, following his orders, proceeded up the Channel, thereby probably missing his great chance for victory. He should at least have made an effort to attack the English while they were still trying to get into the open sea. Orders or no orders, Drake or Nelson and possibly the Marquis of Santa Cruz would have seized this golden opportunity. The result might have been a tremendous defeat for the English. By evening of the 20th the English had the weather gauge, and on the following morning sailed in to attack. This actually proved to be a difficult task, for the Spanish fleet was sailing with its rear formed in the shape of a huge crescent. The English could not consider entering into the crescent to be shot at by several ships at once, but were forced to confine their attacks to the horns of the crescent.

The attacking ships took care not to close with their antagonists but availed themselves of their superior speed, and suffered little comparative loss. Raleigh justly praises the English admiral for his skillful tactics, using long-range gunfire and not attempting to grapple and board the enemy's vessels: "The Spaniards had an army aboard them and he had none; they had more [large] ships than he had, and of higher building and charging; so that, had he entangled himself with those great and powerful vessels, he had greatly endangered this kingdom of England. For twenty men upon the defenses are equal to a hundred that board and enter; whereas then, contrariwise, the Spaniards had a hundred, for twenty of ours, to defend themselves withal. But our admiral knew his advantage, and held it; which had he not done, he had not been worthy to have held his head up."

The result of this first day's action was greatly to increase the morale of the English sailors, who had been somewhat in awe of the huge force confronting them. They entered eagerly upon the pursuit up the Channel. When on July 23 off Portland Bill a sudden change of wind occurred, followed by a calm during which the Spaniards attempted a counterstroke with oardriven ships, and were beaten off, the English morale must have risen even higher.

The next engagement came on July 25 off the Isle of Wight. Although the fighting lasted for several hours the result was never in doubt. The Spaniards were driven to Calais Roads where they cast anchor on July 27. By this time the Spanish were very short of ammunition and their only hope of obtaining more was to reach the Netherlands. The Duke of Medina Sidonia sent a message to the Duke of Parma asking him for ammunition and requesting him to put to sea, which was of course impossible so long as he was blockaded by the Dutch fleet. By this time the English, who had also begun to run short of ammunition, had been able partially to refill their magazines. Furthermore, Sir Henry Seymour had joined with his full squadron and his own supplies of ammunition.

The crisis of the whole series of battles was reached on the night of July 28–29 when the English sent eight fire ships into the midst of the Spanish fleet. Confusion reigned as the Spanish captains cut their cables and put to sea. One of the largest ships ran aground; several collisions occurred. The fleet straggled up the coast toward Gravelines.

When the morning of July 29 broke, it was with difficulty and delay that the Spanish ships were again assembled near Gravelines. Led by Sir Francis Drake, the English closed in to attack at short range. With the Spanish ammunition almost gone they could afford to take this risk. Yet, in spite of the fierceness of the attack upon them, witnesses have agreed that the Spaniards bravely maintained their discipline and good order. Eventually they were forced past Dunkirk and far away from the Prince of Parma. This action is perhaps best described in the words of Hakluyt, the contemporary historian:

"The English ships using their prerogative of nimble steerage, whereby they could turn and wield themselves upon the wind, came often times very near upon the Spaniards, and charged them so sore, that now and then they were but a pike's length asunder. So continually giving them one broadside after another, they discharged all their shot, both great and small, upon them, spending one whole day, from morning till night in that violent kind of conflict, until such time as powder and bullets failed them."

It is customary at this point to blame Queen Elizabeth for the shortage of ammunition, but it is not appropriate. It is certainly quite true that she was parsimonious and pinched pennies at the expense of the navy as well as the army in many ways—but who had ever expected an almost continuous nine-day battle! The Spanish fleet, which had been preparing for this action for well over a year, also ran out of ammunition. In addition no one had ever had any real experience in this sort of a battle. The ship captains on both sides were undoubtedly overanxious and enthusiastic, trying to get as many hits as possible with guns that were by nature erratic. Nor would it be the last time in history that ammunition would be shot at a great rate— with far more accurate guns. Witness the terrific expenditures by some of the ships of the United States Navy, firing by radar spottings at targets at night, in the Solomons in World War II.

Although only about a dozen ships had been lost, the Armada was badly battered, without ammunition and also short of provisions. Medina Sidonia sailed into the North Sea. Lord Howard followed only far enough to be sure that no attempt would be made to land; off the Firth of Forth he abandoned the pursuit.

The English did not lose a single ship and only about 100 men died in battle, whereas the greatest Spanish losses were yet to come. The sufferings the unhappy Armada sustained in the flight around Scotland and Ireland are well known. Somewhat over half of the ships managed to land in Spanish ports, but many of them were so badly battered by gunfire or by storms that they were unfit for service. That more were not lost can only be attributed to the excellent qualities of the Spanish officers and sailors.

Synopsis of Events Between the Defeat of the Spanish Armada, A.D. 1588, and the Battle of Bleinheim, A.D. 1704

1589.   Henry of Navarre becomes Henry IV of France, the first of the Bourbon kings. In 1593 he conforms to the Roman Catholic Church and ends the religious civil wars that had long desolated France.

1603.   Queen Elizabeth dies; James VI of Scotland, the son of Mary Stuart, Queen of Scots, comes to the throne as James I of England.

1607.   The first successful English colony in North America is founded at Jamestown, Virginia.

1608.   Champlain founds the French settlement of Quebec in Canada.

1609.   The signing of a truce with Spain puts an end to fighting in the Netherlands, whose independence is thus virtually recognized, although not formally acknowledged by Spain until 1648 at the end of the Thirty Years' War.

1618.   The Thirty Years' War begins with a Protestant revolt in

Bohemia. (This war, the last great armed struggle between the Protestants and the Catholics in Europe, consisted of four wars and gradually involved almost all the states of Europe. The first two wars, the Bohemian and Danish wars, were predominantly religious, in which the Protestants resisted the influence of the Catholic German emperor. The second two developed into political wars in which Sweden and France fought the Hapsburgs on German soil.)

1620. The Pilgrims land at Plymouth in what later became a part of the Massachusetts Bay Colony.

1624–1629. Cardinal Richelieu, as chief minister of France in complete control of the government, breaks the power of the nobility and destroys the political power of the Huguenots. He establishes the absolute authority of Louis XIII in France.

1625. Following the defeats of Protestant forces by the Count of Tilly at the White Mountain (1620) and at Höchst (1622), King Christian IV of Denmark enters the Thirty Years' War.

1629. Defeated by the Catholic armies led by Tilly and by Albert Wallenstein, Duke of Friedland, the Danish king makes peace and withdraws from the struggle.

1630. The Puritans begin the settlement of the Massachusetts Bay Colony.

1630. Gustavus Adolphus, King of Sweden, lands in Germany to aid the Protestants who by this time are leaderless and almost ruined. Gustavus, "the Lion of the North," who may justly be termed the founder of modern tactics and warfare and one of the great captains of history, defeats Tilly near Leipzig at the Battle of Breitenfeld in 1631, then in 1632 wins the Battle of Lützen against Wallenstein. (If Gustavus had not met his death on this battlefield, the war might have been brought to an end. His intervention did prevent the overthrow of the Protestants in Germany.)

1635–1648. The last fifteen years of the Thirty Years' War are generally known as the Swedish-French Period. Cardinal Richelieu, unwilling to see the war end until Austria is thoroughly humbled, brings France into the war. The armies of Austria and Spain are defeated by the armies of Sweden, led by Torstenson and Wrangel, and by the French armies of Marshal Turenne and the Great Condé. The Treaty of Westphalia finally brings peace to a depopulated Germany. By its terms France and Sweden gain additional territory; Brandenburg is enlarged; the independence of the United Provinces of the Netherlands, and of Switzerland, is formally recognized; but it has been estimated that Germany itself was set back a century in progress and welfare.

1642.   The Civil War between Parliament and Charles I begins in England.

1644–1649.   The Fairfaxes and Cromwell win the Battle of Marston Moor in 1644. The New Model Army led by Sir Thomas Fairfax and Cromwell defeats the Royalists at Naseby in 1645. In the Second Civil War the Scots are defeated by Cromwell in 1648 at Preston. Charles I is tried and executed.

1649–1651.   Cromwell subdues Ireland and Scotland, then stops Charles II's attempt at invasion at the Battle of Worcester.

1653.   Oliver Cromwell is proclaimed Lord Protector.

1660.   The Stuarts are restored to the English throne.

1660.   Frederick William of Brandenburg, the Great Elector, obtains recognition of his sovereignty over East Prussia.

1661.   Louis XIV takes the administration of France into his own hands.

1664.   The English seize New Amsterdam (New York City).

1667–1678.   Louis XIV attacks the Spanish Netherlands (1667–1668) and the Dutch (1672–1678). As a result of these wars involving half the states of Europe, he adds territory to his kingdom to the north and along the Rhine.

1681–1683.   Louis XIV, now at the height of his power, marches into Strasbourg, Luxembourg, and other frontier cities. Nothing but verbal protests follow.

1682.   La Salle claims possession of the Mississippi Valley for France.

1683.   The Turks besiege Vienna, then are routed by an army of Poles and Germans led by John Sobieski, John III of Poland.

1685.   Louis XIV commences a merciless persecution of his Huguenot subjects, driving thousands from his kingdom.

1686.   William organizes a strong confederacy known as the League of Augsburg to oppose Louis XIV.

1688–1690.   The Glorious Revolution of 1688 brings William and Mary to the throne of England in 1689; the sovereignty of Parliament is permanently affirmed. James II's efforts to regain the throne, aided and abetted by Louis XIV, collapse at the Battle of the Boyne in Ireland.

1688–1697.   Claiming land in the Palatinate, Louis XIV begins his third war, sending armies into the territory. William III of England forms the Grand Alliance against him. (The war that resulted is known by three different names, the War of the Palatinate, the War of the League of Augsburg, and the War of the Grand Alliance. It was fought primarily in the Netherlands, without any startling success on either side on land. At sea the allied fleets were defeated at Beachy Head in 1690, then two years later countered with the famous naval victory off Cape La Hogue, which gave them naval supremacy. Both sides grew weary of the conflict, and peace was concluded by the Treaty of Ryswick, which everyone understood was merely a truce. Louis gave up Luxembourg but retained Strasbourg.)

1696. Peter the Great becomes sole Czar of Russia.

1697. Charles XII becomes King of Sweden.

1699. By the Treaty of Karlowitz the Turks cede most of Hungary, Croatia and Slavonia to Austria.

1700–1702. Russia, Poland and Denmark combine against Sweden. Charles XII forces Denmark to sue for peace and defeats the Russian forces of Peter the Great at Narva (1700). He then turns to relieve Riga, which had been under siege, and invades Poland, taking Warsaw and Cracow.

1700–1702. Charles II of Spain dies, having bequeathed his dominions to Philip of Anjou, Louis XIV's grandson. William III of England forms a Second Grand Alliance against France. Upon his death Queen Anne adheres to the Grand Alliance and the great War of the Spanish Succession begins.

1701. Frederick III, son of the Great Elector, assumes the title of King of Prussia.

1704. The English capture Gibraltar.

11

The Battle of Blenheim,
A.D. 1704

The decisive blow struck at Blenheim resounded through every part of Europe. It at once destroyed the vast fabric of power which it had taken Louis XIV, aided by the talents of Turenne and the genius of Vauban, so long to construct.

—ALISON

THOUGH MORE SLOWLY MOLDED and less imposingly vast than the Empire of Napoleon, the power Louis XIV had acquired and was acquiring at the commencement of the eighteenth century was almost equally menacing to the general liberties of Europe. If tested by the amount of territory that each procured *permanently* for France, the ambition of the royal Bourbon was more successful than were the enterprises of the imperial Corsican. At the end of all the devastating wars of the Consulate and the Empire, France was left with virtually the same boundaries as at the beginning of the French Revolution. But today she still possesses the territories that Louis XIV gave her.

When Louis took the reins of his government into his own hands, there was a union of ability with opportunity such as France had not seen since the days of Charlemagne. Moreover Louis' career was no brief one. For over forty years, for a period equal to the duration of Charlemagne's reign, Louis steadily followed an aggressive and a generally successful policy. He passed a long youth and manhood of triumph before the military genius of Marlborough made him acquainted with humiliation and defeat. The great Bourbon lived too long. Had he died when his great antagonist William III died in 1702, just before the opening of the War of the Spanish Succession,

168

his reign would be cited as unequaled in French annals. But he lived on to see his armies beaten, his cities captured, and his kingdom wasted by disastrous war.

Still, Louis XIV had forty years of success, and from the permanence of their fruits we may judge what the results would have been if the last fifteen years of his reign had been equally fortunate. Had it not been for Blenheim, the greater part of Europe might have come under French domination, with England perhaps standing alone, protected by her navy, somewhat as in the later days of Napoleon, but with different allies. It would be hazardous to attempt to predict the ultimate result of such a situation; it is enough to classify this battle as of tremendous importance, and decisive in its effects upon the course of history.

When Louis XIV began to exercise personal control over the affairs of his kingdom, he found all the materials for a strong central government at hand. Richelieu had completely tamed the turbulent spirit of the French nobility and destroyed the political power of the Huguenots. The assemblies of the States-General were obsolete. The royal authority alone remained. When he said, "L'Etat c'est moi," it was a simple statement of fact. He was the state; he knew it and fearlessly played the part.

Not only was his government a strong one, but the country which he governed was strong—strong in its geographical position, in the compactness of its territory, in the number and martial spirit of its inhabitants, and in their complete and undivided nationality. Furthermore, there were an extraordinary number of talented men in France eager to serve their king. One of the surest proofs of Louis' own genius was his skill in discovering genius in others and his promptness in calling it into action. Under him, minister of war Louvois organized, and Turenne, Condé, Villars, and Berwick led, the armies of France; and Vauban, the greatest fortification engineer of all time, designed her defenses. Throughout his reign French diplomacy was marked by skillfulness and activity. Great strides were made in the internal administration of the government, the building of roads, and in the provision of public services.

François Guizot, in his lectures on *The History of Civilization in Europe*, admiringly says that "the government of Louis XIV was the first that presented itself to the eyes of Europe as a power acting upon sure grounds, which had not to dispute its existence with inward enemies, but was at ease as to its territory and its people, and solely occupied with the task of administering government, properly so called. All the European governments had been previously thrown into incessant wars, which deprived them of all security as well as of all leisure, or so pestered by internal parties or antagonists that their time was passed in fighting for existence. The government of Louis XIV was the first to appear as a busy, thriving administration of affairs, as a power at once definitive and progressive, which was not afraid to innovate, because it could reckon securely on the future. There have been in fact very few governments equally innovating. Compare it with a government of the same nature, the unmixed monarchy of Philip II of Spain; it was more absolute than that of Louis XIV and yet it was far less regular and tranquil. How did Philip II succeed in establishing absolute power in Spain? By stifling all activity in the country, opposing himself to every species of amelioriation, and rendering the state of Spain completely stagnant. The government of Louis XIV on the contrary exhibited alacrity for all sorts of innovations, and showed itself favorable to the progress of letters, arts, wealth—in short, of civilization. This was the veritable cause of its preponderance in Europe, which arose to such a pitch, that it became the type of a government, not only to sovereigns, but also to nations, during the seventeenth century."

While France was thus strong and united, and ruled by a martial, an ambitious, and (with all his faults) an enlightened and high-spirited sovereign, what European power was there fit to cope with her or keep her in check?

Both Spain and Austria had been humbled during the Thirty Years' War. Cardinal Richelieu had made sure that his country would be more powerful than they. Also, on several occasions the French king was able to acquire allies among the numerous princes of the empire.

As for the northern countries at the beginning of the eighteenth century, when the last of Louis' wars began, Russia, Poland and Denmark were fully occupied in the Great Northern War, trying to curb the power of Sweden.

If we turn to the two remaining European powers of importance in this era, to England and to Holland, we find the position of England, from 1660 to 1688, most painful to contemplate. Bolingbroke rightly says that during these twenty-eight years prior to the Glorious Revolution of 1688 which brought William of Orange to the throne of England, the very period in which Louis XIV was acquiring such great power, the Stuarts' conduct of foreign policy was unworthy. England was either an idle spectator of what happened on the Continent, or a faint and uncertain ally against France, or a warm and sure ally on her side, or a partial mediator between her and the powers attempting to defend themselves against her. But the crime was not national; the people of England objected strongly to the policies of their Stuart kings.

The Dutch Netherlands, alone of all the European powers, opposed from the very beginning a steady and uniform resistance to the ambition and strength of the French king. It was against Holland that the fiercest attacks of France were made and, though often apparently on the eve of complete success, they were always ultimately baffled by the stubborn bravery of the Dutch and the heroism of their great leader, William of Orange. When he became King of England, the contest became less unequal, although France retained her general superiority.

This is not the place for any narrative of the first three wars of Louis XIV which resulted in his adding to his kingdom territory to the north, and along the Rhine. He thus conquered and annexed valuable lands and people who would increase his strength. However, throughout this period from 1667 to 1697, he had always in mind the possibility of a far greater expansion of his kingdom to the south, that is, to acquire for the House of Bourbon the empire of Spain.

As time passed and the prospect of Charles II of Spain dying without lineal heirs became more and more certain, the claims of the House of Bourbon to the Spanish crown after his death became matters of urgent international concern. At length when Charles died in 1700 he named Philip of Anjou, Louis XIV's grandson, to succeed him. Louis well knew that a general European war would follow if he accepted for his house the crown thus bequeathed, but he had been preparing for this crisis throughout his reign. When he announced that his grandson would go to Spain as King Philip V, the Spanish ambassador coined the memorable words, "There are no longer any Pyrenees."

The empire, which now received the grandson of Louis XIV, comprised, besides Spain itself, part of the Netherlands, Sardinia, Sicily, the Kingdom of Naples, the Duchy of Milan; the Philippine Islands in Asia; and in the New World, lower California, Mexico, Florida, Central America, and a large part of South America.

Loud was the wrath of Austria whose prince, the Archduke Charles, was the rival claimant for the empire of Spain. The wrath is understandable, but of far greater importance were the alarm and fear that swept through Europe. It was evident that Louis aimed at consolidating France and the Spanish dominions into one huge empire. The peril that menaced England, Holland, Austria, and the other powers is well summed up by Alison: "Spain had threatened the liberties of Europe in the end of the sixteenth century. France had all but overthrown them in the close of the seventeenth. What hope was there of their being able to make head against them both, united under such a monarch as Louis XIV?"

William III began to form a Grand Alliance against the House of Bourbon. It included England, Holland, Austria, and some of the Germanic princes. At this point Louis, who professed to desire peace, took a step forward that made war inevitable. The treaty concluding the last war had stipulated that the principal Spanish fortresses along the northern frontier of France would be garrisoned by Dutch troops as a barrier against French invasion. Under pretense of securing these barrier fortresses for the young King of Spain, Louis sent his troops to occupy them. The result was that all the famous strongpoints in what is now southern Belgium became Louis' property without a struggle. It seemed as if everything the allies had striven for in the last war was gone and that Louis was stronger than ever.

Then William, the guiding light of the allied league, died on March 8, 1702; but England's new queen took prompt action. Queen Anne immediately declared her intention to adhere to the Grand Alliance and to support the measures planned by her predecessor. The man primarily responsible for the rapidity of this decision and for the conduct of the war that followed was John Churchill, soon to become famous in history as the Duke of Marlborough. Many have attempted to cast a blot upon his reputation. It has been claimed that his advancement was due *primarily* to court intrigue, and it has been pointed out that he was once accused of treason. However it must be remembered that the latter charge, during those perplexing times of shifting allegiances, could be applied with equal ease to many prominent figures of the day. Furthermore, if his advancement was due *partially* to court intrigue it was indeed fortunate for England that this occurred. The fact is that without some influence at court it was almost impossible in that day and age to reach a high position.

It is, however, only in his military career that we must now consider him. There are few generals of ancient or modern times, possibly only one other English general, the Duke of Wellington, whose campaigns will bear comparison with those of Marlborough. He had served in his earlier years under Turenne and had obtained the praise of that great tactician. It would be difficult to name a single quality a general ought to have, with which Marlborough was not eminently gifted. What principally attracted the attention of contemporaries was the imperturbable evenness of his spirit. Voltaire says of him: "He had, to a degree above all other generals of his time, that calm courage in the midst of tumult, that serenity of soul in danger, which the English call *a cool head* (que les Anglais appellent *cold head, tête froide*), and it was perhaps this quality, the greatest gift of nature for command, which formerly gave the English so many advantages over the French in the plains of Crécy, Poitiers and Agincourt."

In his last illness King William recommended Marlborough, whom he had appointed commander in chief of the English forces in Holland, to his successor Queen Anne as the fittest person to command her armies. Since William knew how highly Marlborough already stood in her favor, because of his ability and because his wife was the queen's favorite companion and confidante, this recommendation was not at all necessary. It simply shows how thoroughly the two men, previously estranged by that unproved charge of treason, had become reconciled, and how anxious William was that no one but Marlborough be given the task of leading the armies in the coming crisis.

He was not only made captain-general of the English forces at home and abroad but also, upon his arrival on the Continent, he made such a good impression that the Dutch made him commanding general of their armies, and so did many of the Germanic princes. Unfortunately, however, in addition to commanding the armies, he had to deal with the civilian governments and try to reconcile their conflicting interests, jealousies, and disagreements. He was never permitted to carry out his plans without obtaining approval from the various states whose troops he supposedly commanded. This required all the tact and persuasiveness for which he became justly famous. At one point at the beginning of the Blenheim campaign, as we shall see, he found it necessary actually to conceal his true plans from all but a few selected persons in authority. Had it not been for his enduring patience, his intuitive ability to judge which persons could be thoroughly trusted, his resourcefulness, and his unrivaled diplomatic skill as a courtier and statesman, he would never have led the allied armies to victory on the Danube. His great political adversary, Bolingbroke, does him ample justice here. After referring to the loss that King William's death seemed to inflict on the allied cause, Bolingbroke observes that: "By his death the Duke of Marlborough was raised to the head of the army and, indeed, of the confederacy; where he, a new, a private man, a subject, acquired by merit and by management a more deciding influence than high birth, confirmed authority, and even the crown of Great Britain had given to King William. Not only all the parts of that vast machine, the Grand Alliance, were kept more compact and entire, but a more rapid and vigorous motion was given to the whole. Instead of languishing and disastrous campaigns, we saw every scene of the war full of action. All those wherein he appeared, and many of those wherein he was not then an actor, but abettor, however, of their action, were crowned with the most triumphant success.

"I take with pleasure this opportunity of doing justice to that great man, whose faults I knew, whose virtues I admired; and whose memory, as the greatest general and the greatest minister that our country, or perhaps any other, has produced, I honor."

War was formally declared by the allies against France in May, 1702. In that year the principal scenes of operation were along the Dutch border and in north Italy. Marlborough headed the allied troops in Holland and succeeded in conquering several fortresses along the Meuse; for these victories he was created a duke by the queen. In Italy Prince Eugène, although outnumbered by the French, was able to hold his own. But in September the Elector of Bavaria decided to join the French. Louis XIV was quick to seize the opportunity thus presented of aiming a blow at Austria through the territory of his new ally. By the end of the year 1703 the French and Bavarian armies had seized a number of vital points on the line of communications through the allied territory of Baden, joined forces, and were threatening Vienna. Because of political pressure Marlborough had been forced to confine his activities to northern France, the Meuse, and the area around Cologne on the Rhine.

Louis XIV's plan for the 1704 campaign would have done credit to Napoleon himself. On the extreme left of his line, in the west, the French armies in the Netherlands were to act on the defensive. The fortresses still in French hands were so many and so strong that it seemed unlikely that the allies could make any serious impression upon them in one campaign. The French king was thus making proper use of fortifications, to hold a line with fewer men while he massed his strength for decisive blows against the enemy in another region. Austria was his target; he could eliminate her from the war while remaining on the defensive opposite the Netherlands.

Large detachments were therefore to be made from troops holding the line on the left. They were to be led by Marshal Villeroy to the Rhine. The French army already in that region, commanded by Marshal Tallard, was to march through the Black Forest to join the Elector of Bavaria and the French troops of Marshal Marsin near Ulm. The French grand army of the Danube was then to march upon Vienna. High military genius was shown in the formation of this plan, but it was met and baffled by a genius higher still.

Marlborough had watched with the deepest anxiety the progress of French arms on the Rhine and in Bavaria. He saw the futility of carrying on a war of posts and sieges in the Netherlands while death-blows were being dealt on the Danube. Unlike most of the generals of his day, he believed not in the strength of the defensive but in the power of the attack with the bayonet. He taught his cavalry to rely on shock action, to charge with drawn weapons at a full trot. His belief in offensive tactics naturally led to the offensive in strategy. He resolved, therefore, to let the war in the west languish for a year, while he moved with all the forces he could collect to the central scene of decisive operations. Thus, unknown to each other, Louis XIV and Marlborough were both planning decisive victories in the same region.

In one important respect the French king had a tremendous advantage over the English general. Louis' word was law; when he ordered his armies to march there was no one to question his decision or obstruct his plans. Marlborough, on the other hand, had to overcome the objections of his own countrymen and of the Dutch, whose frontier he proposed to weaken. Fortunately he had a staunch ally, Anton Heinsius, the Chief Minister of Holland, who had been the cordial supporter of King William, and who now supported Marlborough in the council of the allies. To him, and a few others, the duke communicated his plan; but to the general councils of his allies he disclosed only part of his scheme. His proposal to them was that he should march to the Moselle with the English troops and part of the foreign auxiliaries, and commence vigorous operations in that region, while a defensive war was maintained in the Netherlands. Having with difficulty obtained the consent of the Dutch to this portion of his project, he exercised the same diplomatic zeal with the same success, in urging the other princes of the empire to increase the number of troops they supplied, and to post them in places convenient for his own intended movements.

Crossing the Meuse, Marlborough marched toward Koblenz on the Rhine. On May 23 he reached Bonn and learned that Marshal Villeroy was moving east. Louis XIV was also putting his plan of movement toward the Danube into effect, but Marlborough had moved first. When he reached Koblenz everyone, friend and foe, expected him to turn south and follow the Moselle. We have noted the advantage the French king had over Marlborough, of being able to dictate his orders without having to consult anyone else. Here we find Marlborough with the tremendous advantage of surprise on his side. The French could not believe that he had obtained permission from the Dutch to move any farther east than the Moselle. Therefore when he continued toward Mainz they were greatly puzzled until they learned that bridges were being built across the Rhine at Philippsburg. Believing that he had now divined his enemy's true purpose, Marshal Tallard made preparations to resist an advance from that direction.

Therefore when Marlborough reached Weisloch and turned southeast toward the Danube, revealing unmistakably his destination, he had already accomplished a great deal. He was between Marshal Tallard's army and his target, the armies of Marshal Marsin and the Elector of Bavaria. Marshal Tallard could do nothing but follow and hope he would arrive in time. Marshal Villeroy was left far behind.

Crossing the Neckar River, Marlborough met for the first time Prince Eugène, the famous general of Austria's forces, who had been called back from Italy to defend Vienna. There began a lasting friendship that grew into a feeling of mutual trust and confidence; the partnership of these two brilliant leaders would bring victory on many a famous battlefield.

Continuing toward Ulm, Marlborough was joined by the army of Louis of Baden and other reinforcements. Then while Prince Eugène undertook to delay, with a small force, the approach of Marshal Tallard from the Rhine, Marlborough marched eastward down the Danube. On July 2 he stormed the heights of the Schellenberg at Donauwörth

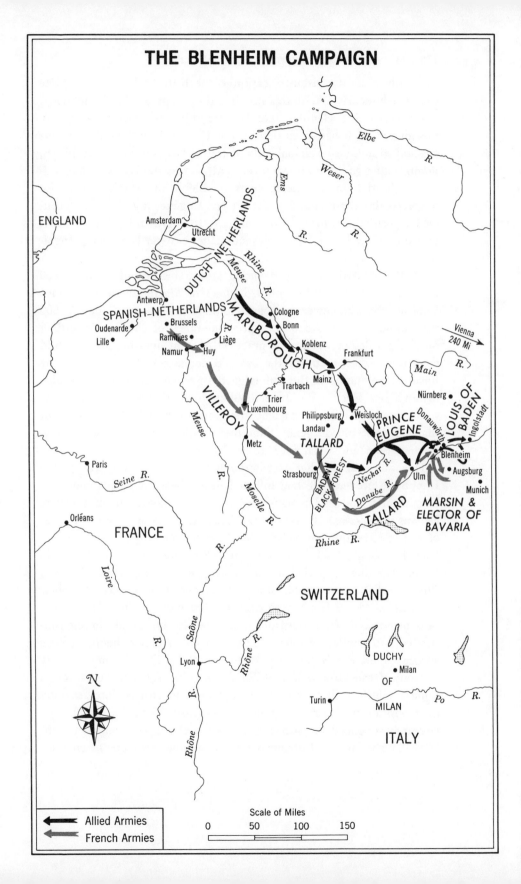

THE BLENHEIM CAMPAIGN

ENGLAND

Elbe

Weser

Ems

Amsterdam
Utrecht

DUTCH NETHERLANDS

Rhine

Meuse

R.

R.

Antwerp

SPANISH-NETHERLANDS

Brussels

MARLBOROUGH

Cologne
Bonn

Oudenarde
Lille

Ramillies
Namur Huy

Liège

Koblenz

Frankfurt

Main

R.

Vienna
240 Mi

VILLEROY

Meuse

Trarbach

Trier
Luxembourg

Mainz

Nürnberg

LOUIS OF BADEN

Ingolstadt

Paris

Metz

Philippsburg
Landau

TALLARD

Weisloch

PRINCE
EUGENE

Donauwörth

Blenheim

Seine R.

R.

Moselle R.

Strasbourg

BADEN
BLACK FOREST

Neckar R.

Ulm

Augsburg

Munich

Orléans

FRANCE

R.

Danube R.

TALLARD

MARSIN &
ELECTOR OF
BAVARIA

Rhine R.

Loire

Saône

SWITZERLAND

Rhône R.

DUCHY

Milan

R.

Lyon

OF

N

Turin

MILAN

Po R.

ITALY

Scale of Miles

0   50   100   150

Allied Armies
French Armies

and, after a stout resistance, captured the fortress. This was a prize well worth securing. With this stronghold in his possession, he marched south, across the Danube, into Bavaria. But the elector's army, although part of it had been defeated at Donauwörth, was still numerous and strong; also Marshal Tallard was at last coming to join forces. When these two united they moved north across the Danube and fortified a position on the north bank at Blenheim. Marlborough also recrossed the Danube and joined Prince Eugène; together they occupied a position downriver a few miles to the east, facing their enemy. Prince Louis of Baden had been sent farther eastward to besiege Ingolstadt.

At this point the French-Bavarian army consisted of about 60,000 men, outnumbering the combined forces of Marlborough and Prince Eugène who had fewer guns and could count no more than 56,000 men, although they did have a preponderance of cavalry. According to all the rules of warfare as practiced in that age, the allies should therefore retreat; certainly they should not attack. For the first time since the beginning of the campaign the French felt confident of ultimate victory. Eventually Marshal Villeroy would arrive with his army, which would give them sufficient strength to overwhelm the force under Marlborough and Eugène; then they could carry out King Louis' original plan and push forward to Vienna.

This was exactly what Marlborough had come all the way to the Danube to prevent. He had inflicted heavy losses upon his enemy at Donauwörth and had maneuvered Marshal Villeroy out of position. He was an exponent of offensive warfare and had no intention whatever of either retreating or waiting for Marshal Villeroy.

On August 12, 1704, he rode out to reconnoiter the enemy lines. He found that they occupied a very strong position facing to the east. The French-Bavarian right (south) flank rested on the Danube; their left was protected from assault by wooded high ground. They could be attacked only from the front, but here also he found himself confronted with serious obstacles. The enemy was posted behind a little stream called the Nebel, which runs into the Danube immediately in front of the little village of Blenheim. The Nebel flowed through a marshy little valley which he would have to cross before reaching their position on the rising ground to the west. Blenheim, which they were now engaged in fortifying, formed a strongpoint on their right flank. The village of Lutzingen formed another strongpoint on their left flank, while near the center of the line a third strongpoint was being constructed around the hamlet of Oberglau.

The average general would have decided that an attack upon such a position could have little chance of success, but Marlborough needed a victory. The fatal consequences if he were to retreat were obvious. His prestige would be lowered; the morale of the allied forces would decrease as the enemy increased in strength; and ultimately he might be defeated in battle far from his homeland, with little chance of returning safely. The allied confederacy, the Grand Alliance, would fall apart and Louis XIV's fondest hopes would be realized.

Marlborough and Eugène were well aware of the consequences of defeat, but they made their plans with victory in mind, and they counted heavily on two factors—surprise and maintaining the initiative by offensive action. The first element, surprise, they attained by beginning their march at 2:00 A.M., August 13. As they approached the enemy Marlborough's troops formed the left and center, while Eugène's forces were on the right. A thick haze covered the ground that morning, and it was not until the allied left and center had advanced nearly within cannon-shot that Tallard on the French right was aware of their approach. He made his preparations with haste, and about eight o'clock opened a heavy fire of artillery on Marlborough's advancing left wing.

With so little time to form, Tallard had done the best he could under the circumstances, but the result was that he formed as a separate army would form, with his main infantry force near the strongpoint of Blenheim and his cavalry on each side of his infantry. The army of Marsin and the Elector of Bavaria did the same thing, with their infantry near Oberglau, and their cavalry on each side. The result, for all practical purposes, was a formation of two separate armies in line beside each other. The gap between the strongpoint of Blenheim (held by Tallard's infantry) and Oberglau (held by Marsin's infantry, with the elector's infantry alongside them) was therefore held by cavalry. Later both Tallard and Marsin made an effort to strengthen the center of their combined line, but essentially it remained Tallard's left-wing cavalry and Marsin's right-wing cavalry.

The ground Eugène's column had to traverse was peculiarly difficult, especially for the artillery. It was noon before he could get his troops into line. Marlborough waited therefore until all was ready before launching his attack at 12:30. First he sent Lord Cutts with a strong brigade of infantry to assault the village of Blenheim. The attack was gallantly made and as valiantly repulsed. A second assault met the same result; the losses on both sides were severe. Marlborough made no further efforts to carry the village but turned his energies to effecting a crossing of the Nebel in the center of the allied line.

Meanwhile, farther to the north, a crisis was developing opposite Oberglau. The attack of the Prince of Holstein-Beck on that little hamlet had been driven back by the Irish brigade which held that village. The Irish were pressing forward in pursuit when Marlborough came up in person to restore order. With help from some of Prince Eugène's men, this was accomplished. Thus the fighting had centered around two strongpoints in the French line, neither of which had been captured. But both had been continuously exerting that power of attraction which is so common on any battlefield. The defending forces, including a large portion of the French reserves, had been gradually drawn to these two points.

Marlborough's next move, to keep the initiative in his own hands, was to press forward between Blenheim and Oberglau. Temporary bridges had already been prepared, and planks and fascines collected. With the aid of these he had already succeeded in getting troops across the Nebel. The French artillery had not been idle, nor had the French cavalry, but by degrees the allies had struggled forward across the bloodstained marshy streams and were now lined up on the enemy side of the river. Though the French saw the attack coming, there was little they could do to alter their situation. Very few reserves were available; they had been permitted to be drawn into the struggles at Blenheim and Oberglau. Nor were any available from their left flank. Prince Eugène's attacks had made little progress in that area, but here also the defenders had permitted their reserves to be drawn into the battle. The only commander on the field able to make an attack at this point was Marlborough.

The allied cavalry, strengthened and supported by foot and guns, advanced up the slope to where the French cavalry awaited them. On riding up the summit, the allies were received with so hot a fire from artillery and small arms that at first the cavalry recoiled, but without abandoning the high ground. The guns and the infantry they had brought with them maintained the contest with spirit and effect. The French fire seemed to slacken. The duke instantly ordered a charge all along the line. The allied cavalry, with the duke himself

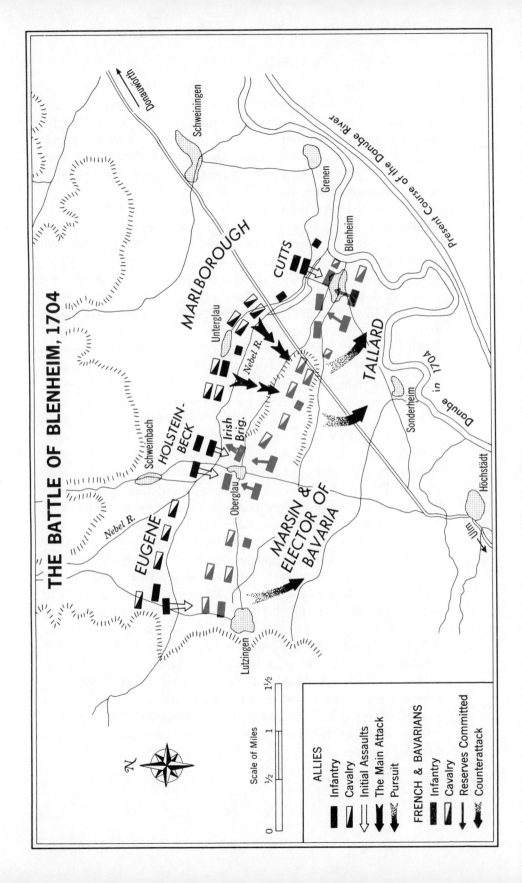

THE BATTLE OF BLENHEIM, 1704

Donauwörth

Schweiningen

Grenen

Present Course of the Danube River

Blenheim

CUTTS

MARLBOROUGH

Unterglau

Nebel R.

TALLARD

Danube in 1704

Schweinbach

HOLSTEIN-BECK

Irish Brig.

Oberglau

Sonderheim

Höchstädt

Nebel R.

EUGENE

MARSIN & ELECTOR OF BAVARIA

Ulm

Lutzingen

N

Scale of Miles

0   ½   1   1½

ALLIES
- Infantry
- Cavalry
- Initial Assaults
- The Main Attack
- Pursuit

FRENCH & BAVARIANS
- Infantry
- Cavalry
- Reserves Committed
- Counterattack

leading the charge, went forward in long, sweeping lines. It was of course impossible for the defending cavalry to wait halted, and meet the shock of a mounted charge. They wheeled and spurred from the field. The few infantry left alone were ridden down by the torrent of allied horsemen. By never losing the initiative, by pinning down the enemy's reserves near their strongpoints, and then charging through between them, the battle had been won.

Tallard and Marsin, severed from each other, thought only of retreat. Tallard drew up his remaining squadrons in a line extended toward Blenheim, and sent orders to the infantry in that village to join him without delay. But long before his orders could be obeyed, the conquering squadrons of Marlborough had wheeled to their left and thundered down on the array of the French marshal. Part of Tallard's force was driven into the Danube. Part fled with their general to the village of Sonderheim where they were soon surrounded and compelled to surrender. Meanwhile, Eugène had renewed his attack and was enveloping the Bavarian left; Marsin, finding his colleague routed and his own right flank uncovered, beat a retreat. Though he and the elector succeeded in withdrawing a portion of their troops, the large body of French remaining in Blenheim were left to certain destruction. Marlborough speedily occupied all the outlets of the village; then, collecting his artillery around it, he methodically began a cannonade that would have destroyed Blenheim and all who were in it. After several gallant but unsuccessful attempts to cut their way through, the French in Blenheim were compelled to surrender. Twenty-four battalions and twelve squadrons laid down their arms.

In the Battle of Blenheim the allies lost 4,500 killed and 7,500 wounded out of a total of 56,000 engaged. The French and Bavarian losses have never been accurately computed. Their army totaled 60,000 men; of these no more than 20,000 were ever reassembled. This means a loss of about 40,000 killed, wounded, captured, or missing. Almost all the artillery and almost all the supplies were captured. The army had not just suffered a defeat; it had been practically destroyed.

Before the year ended, Ulm, Landau, Trarbach, and Trier had surrendered. Bavaria submitted to the emperor. Germany was completely delivered from France. The military ascendancy of allied arms was established; throughout the rest of the war Louis XIV fought only in defense. Blenheim had dissipated forever his once-proud visions of universal conquest.

Synopsis of Events Between the Battle of Blenheim, A.D. 1704,
and the Battle of Poltava, A.D. 1709

1705.   The Archduke Charles lands in Spain with a small English army and takes Barcelona.

1706.   Marlborough wins the Battle of Ramillies.

1706.   Prince Eugène's victory at Turin practically ends the war in northern Italy.

1707.   England and Scotland unite to form Great Britain.

1708.   Marlborough and Eugène win the Battle of Oudenarde then besiege and capture Lille.

12

The Battle of Poltava, A.D. 1709

> Dread Pultowa's day,
> When fortune left the royal Swede,
> Around a slaughtered army lay,
> No more to combat and to bleed,
> The power and fortune of the war,
> Had passed to the triumphant Czar.
>
> —BYRON

THERE IS no need today to expound upon the strength and power of Russia. In fact, it seems strange to recall that just over two hundred and fifty years ago she was not one of the Great Powers of Europe. The actors who played the principal parts on the stage of history at the beginning of the eighteenth century (at the time of the Battles of Blenheim and Poltava), were aware of the existence of the Muscovite Empire, but were far more interested in the affairs of the real power in the North—Sweden.

If anyone has occasion to doubt the effect of a battle upon the course of history, he need not delve far back into ancient times. He need only compare Sweden and Russia prior to the Campaign of Poltava with the position that each occupies in the world today.

The history of Sweden as a separate country began in 1521 when, led by their national hero Gustavus Vasa, later crowned as Gustavus I, the Swedes revolted against Denmark and secured their independence. Slightly more than one hundred years later, in 1630, Gustavus Adolphus, Sweden's greatest king, intervened in the Thirty Years' War to rescue the failing cause of Protestantism. As a result of that struggle Sweden emerged as the dominant Protestant power of continental Europe. By the end of the seventeenth century when Charles XII became king, Sweden was one of the great nations of Europe. The Baltic

184

was practically a Swedish lake. Included in the kingdom were present-day Sweden, Finland, Karelia to the east, Ingria which includes the site on which the Russians built St. Petersburg (Leningrad), Estonia, a portion of Latvia, the western part of Pomerania, Wismar and Bremen.

From this proud preeminence Sweden was hurled down, at once and forever, by the defeat of Charles XII at Poltava. Russia gained all of Sweden's possessions along the eastern Baltic coast, and the fortress of Viborg in Finland. With the downfall of Sweden there disappeared from the scene the only power in the Baltic that could have opposed the growing strength of Russia. The decisive battle at Poltava was therefore all-important to the world, because of what it overthrew as well as what it established. It is the more interesting because it was not merely the crisis of a struggle between two states; it was also a trial of strength between two great ethnic groups, the Slavic and the Germanic. In the long and varied conflicts between the Slavic and Germanic nations, the Germanic had, before Poltava, almost always maintained a superiority. With the single but important exception of Poland, no Slavic state had cut any considerable figure in history before the time when Charles XII invaded the Muscovite Empire.

It is a singular fact that Russia owes her very name to a band of Swedish invaders who established a settlement in the land about twelve hundred years ago. They were soon absorbed in the Slavic population, and every trace of the Swedish character had disappeared several centuries before the arrival of Charles XII. Russia was long the victim and the slave of the Mongols; many Mongolian traits are Russian characteristics today. Then for some centuries the Poles and the Lithuanians held large areas of her land. Indeed, the history of Russia as a nation before the time of Peter the Great is one long tale of humiliation at the hands of other powers.

But, whatever may have been the amount of national injuries that she sustained from the Mongols or from others in the ages of her weakness, she has certainly retaliated tenfold during the two centuries and a half of her strength. Her rapid transition from being the prey of every conqueror to being the conqueror of all with whom she comes into contact, from being the oppressed to being the oppressor, is almost without a parallel in the history of nations. It was the work of a single ruler who, himself without education, promoted science and literature among barbaric millions. He gave them fleets, commerce, arts, and arms; and at Poltava demonstrated that victory in battle could bring Russia dominion over other nations.

The career of Philip of Macedon resembles most nearly that of the great Muscovite Czar, but there is one important difference. Philip had, while young, received in southern Greece the best education in all matters of peace and war that the ablest philosophers and generals of the age could bestow. Peter was brought up in a partially civilized society in a backward country. He strove to remedy this by seeking instruction abroad. For a year after he had become the sole Czar of Russia, he went as an ordinary workman to Germany, Holland, and England, that he might return and teach his subjects. There is a degree of heroism here superior to anything that we know of in the Macedonian king. But Philip's consolidation of the long-dis-united Macedonian kingdom; his raising of a people whom he found the scorn of their civilized southern neighbors to be their dread; his organization of a brave and well-disciplined army to take the place of a disorderly militia; his creation of a maritime force, and his systematic skill in acquiring and improving seaports and arsenals; his patient tenacity of purpose under reverses; his personal bravery, and even his proneness to coarse amusements and pleasures, all mark him out as the prototype of the imperial founder of the Russian power. In justice, however, to the ancient hero, it ought to be added that we find in the history of Philip no examples of the savage cruelty that deforms so grievously the character of Peter the Great.

In considering the effects of the overthrow the Swedish arms sustained at Poltava, and in speculating on the probable consequences if the invaders had been successful, we must bear in mind the wretched state in which Peter found Russia. We must also remember the fact that at the time Poltava was fought, many of his reforms had not yet been initiated, others were incomplete, and his new institutions were immature. He was still breaking up the Old Russia, and the New Russia which he was creating was still in embryo. Had Peter been defeated at Poltava, his immense labors would have been buried with him because they had barely begun, and Russia would have fallen back again into chaos. It is this fact that makes the repulse of Charles XII the critical point in the fortunes of Russia. The danger she incurred a century afterward from her invasion by Napoleon was in reality far less than her peril when Charles attacked her, though the French emperor, as a military genius, was infinitely superior to the Swedish king, and led a host against her compared with which the armies of Charles seem insignificant. For the difference between the Russia of 1709 and the Russia of 1812 was greater than the disparity between the power of Charles and the might of Napoleon.

Alison described the state of the Muscovite Empire when revolutionary and imperial France encountered it: "This immense empire, comprehending nearly half of Europe and Asia within its dominions, . . . inhabited by a patient and indomitable race, . . . was daily becoming more formidable to the liberties of Europe. . . . The Russian infantry had long been celebrated for its immovable firmness. . . . Her immense population, amounting in Europe alone to nearly thirty-five millions, afforded an inexhaustible supply of men. . . . Her soldiers, inured to heat and cold from their infancy, and actuated by a blind devotion to their Czar, united the steady valor of the English to the impetuous energy of the French troops." This description of the fighting qualities of Russian soldiers, supposedly exhibiting the finest characteristics of both the English and the French, is exaggerated, but they were certainly noted for their physical stamina and for their stolid acceptance of the hardships and misfortunes of war.

The Russia of 1709 had no such forces to oppose an assailant. They were in awe of their opponents and had not yet acquired any military spirit or tradition. There was no national feeling, nor was there any loyal attachment to their ruler. In numerous encounters with the Swedes, Peter's soldiers had run like sheep. Great discontent also had been excited among all classes of the community by the arbitrary changes their Czar had introduced, many of which clashed with the prejudices of his subjects. No victories had yet raised Peter above that discontent, nor had superstitious obedience to the Czar yet become a characteristic of the Russian mind. A great victory by Charles XII would have undoubtedly led to uprisings within this unsettled nation. Peter would have been forced to make peace, and Sweden would have remained the great power in the Baltic.

The military ability of Charles XII will always be a favorite topic for discussion: Was he a genius or simply an unusually bold, headstrong warrior? Certainly at the beginning of his career the consensus was that he deserved the name of genius, but his last campaign ending at Poltava makes us wonder.

When he came to the throne in 1697, he was just reaching his fifteenth birthday. His Baltic neighbors seized upon this opportunity to form a coalition against Sweden. They had long resented the rising power of that nation and sought to take advantage of the young king's age and inexperience. The three rulers concerned, Peter of Russia, Frederick IV of Denmark, and Augustus the Strong, Elector of Saxony and King of Poland, received an ugly surprise. When the Great Northern War begain in 1700, the young eighteen-year-old king struck first at Denmark. He made a surprise landing near Copenhagen and so frightened Frederick IV that he readily agreed to a peace treaty. Charles then turned on Russia. At this time Peter was besieging the citadel of Narva in Estonia with 40,000 Russians. With only 8,000 Swedish soldiers, Charles attacked in a snowstorm and routed his opponents, who fled in terror from the battlefield.

Having eliminated one of his foes, and driven another back into Russia, Charles turned on the third, who in the meantime had invaded Latvia and begun a siege of Riga. His operations against Poland in 1701 were as vigorous and the results were as spectacular as those of the previous year. The siege of Riga was raised in June; Latvia was recovered from the enemy, and the Polish province of Courland was overrun. In 1702 Charles captured Warsaw, defeated a combined Polish and Saxon army at Klissow, and entered Cracow. His principal military operation for the following year was a long but successful siege of Thorn.

While the Swedish king was thus occupied in Poland, his Russian adversary came back into Swedish territory and in May, 1703 founded St. Petersburg in Charles' province of Ingria. Then in 1704 Peter again besieged and this time captured Narva. Paying little attention to his Russian opponent, Charles continued his operations in Poland. He dethroned Augustus and obtained the election of his own candidate. This did not mean that Augustus agreed to the arrangement; it had yet to be forced upon him. A complete defeat of the Polish and Saxon forces, and the turning back of a Russian army which Peter sent to help Augustus, naturally took considerable time. In September, 1706, Charles dictated peace to Augustus in Altranstädt near Leipzig in Saxony. Augustus abdicated the throne of Poland, recognized Charles' elected candidate, and took Saxony out of the war.

Charles XII was now at the height of his career. He had forced Denmark to sue for peace; his candidate was installed on the Polish throne; the former king, the Elector of Saxony, had now withdrawn from the war. Charles' prestige was so great that the allies then engaged in their war with Louis XIV were fearful that he might enter their war. They sent the Duke of Marlborough, then in the full career of his victories, to Charles' camp to persuade the Swedes not to intervene in favor of the French king. But Charles at that time was solely bent on defeating Russia, and all Europe fully believed that he would entirely crush the Czar and dictate peace in the Kremlin.

If Charles XII had stopped here and concluded peace with Russia, which from all accounts Peter would have been willing to do on a reasonable basis, he would have saved Sweden from defeat, limited Russia's westward expansion, and undoubtedly be classified today as a military genius. No one would now be contending that he was simply an extremely brave and intrepid soldier—yet that is the conclusion that Napoleon and many others have reached after a study of his last campaign.

When Charles undertook his invasion of Russia, he looked on success as a matter of certainty. It is certainly true that he had many elements in his favor. His army consisted of 44,000 men, the largest he had ever commanded. The renown of Swedish arms was great. His men were veterans, accustomed to victory, and not at all in awe of the greater number of Russians they would have to encounter. Under the leadership of their great king they had always been victorious, even against odds as great as five to one, as at Narva in 1700. They had no way of knowing in advance that their leader in the coming campaign would violate all the rules of the art of war. They believed in him, trusted him and followed him with incredible devotion in a campaign that lasted for a year and a half, that brought many victories, frightful suffering, and one defeat nearly 1000 miles from home.

On New Year's Day in 1708 the Swedish army of 24,000 cavalry and 20,000 infantry crossed the Vistula on the road to Moscow. At first all went well. The army forced a crossing of the Niemen at Grodno, advanced to the vicinity of Minsk, and defeated a Russian army attempting to bar their way at a small river near the village of Holowczyn. The next move was to Mogilev on the Dnieper. It was now midsummer; well over half the distance to Moscow had been covered, but here the fatal wrong decisions were made.

Charles discovered that Peter was conducting a scorched-earth policy, burning Russian villages, farms, and fields so that the invaders would have to carry all their supplies with them. At this time the

Swedish General Adam Lewenhaupt had been ordered to move from Riga to join him with 11,000 men, a large supply column, artillery, and an ammunition train. Lewenhaupt was now moving to meet Charles and was not far distant. But then a messenger arrived from the hetman of the Cossacks of the Ukraine, Ivan Mazeppa, promising a rising of his followers in Charles' favor. Because of the abundance of supplies he knew to be available in the Ukraine, Charles, after some delay, decided to move to the southeast and join forces with Mazeppa. Charles did not wait for Lewenhaupt, but directed that the supply column follow. He thus exposed both his own troops, and those of Lewenhaupt separately, to the dangers of an extremely long flank march in the face of the enemy. His generals protested both the decision to move so far from their natural supply line and the decision to leave Lewenhaupt to his own resources, but to no avail. The possibility of ultimate defeat never seems to have occurred to the Swedish king.

The Czar had meanwhile collected a large army and, though the Swedes had been successful in every encounter, the Russian troops were gradually acquiring discipline. When Lewenhaupt in late September of 1708 was striving to join Charles in the Ukraine, he was suddenly attacked by an overwhelming force at Liesna. Lewenhaupt fought bravely against fourfold odds for two days, then buried his artillery and burned his supplies to prevent them from falling into enemy hands. He succeeded in cutting his way through to Charles' army with about half of his 11,000 men.

Learning of this catastrophe the Cossacks were slow to respond to Mazeppa's call. Peter then destroyed Mazeppa's capital at Baturin and suppressed the insurrection. The total number of Cossacks who came to Charles' camp cannot have numbered more than two thousand. Charles was compelled to remain in the Ukraine for the winter which was one of the most severe that men could remember. Without proper food or clothing the army suffered intensely yet never seems to have lost faith in their fearless leader who was still supremely confident. The fact that the effective strength of his total force dropped below 20,000 did not perturb him at all. When spring came and his generals tried to persuade him to return, he could see no reason to entertain such an idea. The army was still full of courageous, brave men and the Russians had never yet stood and fought against him.

At the beginning of May, Charles undertook a siege of the town of

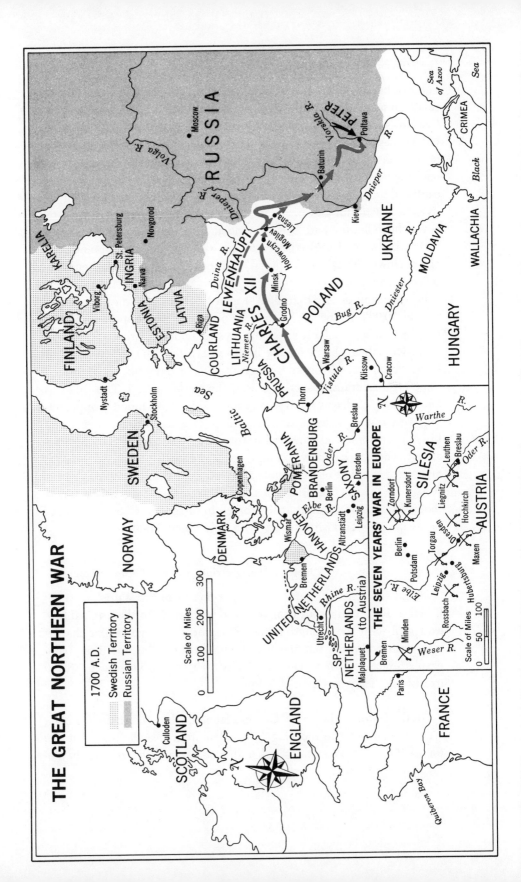

THE GREAT NORTHERN WAR

1700 A.D.

Swedish Territory
Russian Territory

Scale of Miles
0   100   200   300

THE SEVEN YEARS' WAR IN EUROPE

Scale of Miles
0   50   100

Poltava, but by this time he had very few artillery pieces and only a small amount of powder. The siege therefore dragged on, and the Czar was able to bring an army of about 60,000 men to its relief, but he hesitated to give battle. There had been a number of revolts in Russia; Peter was well aware of the fact that a severe defeat might cause other, more serious revolutions. Therefore he approached cautiously along the eastern shore of the Vorskla River, keeping the river between him and his enemy. However, when Peter received the news that Charles had been wounded in a skirmish he decided to accept battle, and crossed over to the western shore to a point north of the town. There he built an entrenched camp strengthened by several redoubts.

For an army of less than 20,000 men to attack an army of approximately 50,000 (some 10,000 had been left on the opposite shore of the river) seems foolhardy. Yet the Swedes undertook the task; Charles came with them, borne to the battle in a litter. The Swedish assault launched on June 27 broke through the line of redoubts; then, through some error in transmission of orders, the troops halted. The Russians, almost ready to flee as usual when they saw Swedish infantry approaching, were rallied. Peter ordered his troops to issue forth from his camp, brought up some 100 guns and awaited the next assault. The Swedish attack when it came was simply overwhelmed by massed artillery fire. What was left of that noble army attempted to cut its way out of Russia by way of the Black Sea. For three fearful days they fought their way southward until finally forced to surrender. Charles managed to escape into Turkish territory with only about 1,500 men.

A Note on the Description of the Battle of Poltava

Sir Edward Creasy's *Fifteen Decisive Battles of the World* was published in 1851. Numerous changes have been made in the original text, as described at some length in the "Foreword." This particular chapter was greatly altered, but the temptation to leave the last three paragraphs exactly as they were originally written 113 years ago proved irresistible. They are quoted below:

"In the joy of his heart the Czar exclaimed, when the strife was over, 'That the sun of the morning had fallen from heaven, and that the foundation of St. Petersburg at length stood firm.' Even on that battlefield, near the Ukraine, the Russian emperor's first thoughts were of conquests and aggrandizement on the Baltic. The peace of Nystadt, which transferred the fairest provinces of Sweden to Russia, ratified the judgment of battle which was pronounced at Pultowa. Attacks on Turkey and Persia by Russia commenced almost directly after that victory. And though the Czar failed in his first attempts against the sultan, the successors of Peter have, one and all, carried on a uniformly aggressive and uniformly successive system of policy against Turkey, and against every other state, Asiatic as well as European, which has had the misfortune of having Russia for a neighbor.

"Orators and authors, who have discussed the progress of Russia, have often alluded to the similitude between the modern extension of the Muscovite empire and the extension of the Roman dominions in ancient times. But attention has scarcely been drawn to the closeness of the parallel between conquering Russia and conquering Rome, not only in the extent of conquests, but in the means of effecting conquest. The history of Rome during the century and a half which followed the close of the second Punic war, and during which her largest acquisitions of territory were made, should be minutely compared with the history of Russia for the last one hundred and fifty years. The main points of similitude can only be indicated in these pages; but they deserve the fullest consideration. Above all, the sixth chapter of Montesquieu's great treatise on Rome, 'De la conduite que les Romains tinrent pour soumettre les peuples,' should be carefully studied by every one who watches the career and policy of Russia. The classic scholar will remember the state-craft of the Roman senate, which took care in every foreign war to appear in the character of a *Protector*. Thus Rome *protected* the Aetolians and the Greek cities against Macedon; she *protected* Bithynia and other small Asiatic states against the Syrian kings; she protected Numidia against Carthage; and in numerous other instances assumed the same specious character. But 'woe to the people whose liberty depends on the continued forbearance of an overmighty protector.' Every state which Rome protected was ultimately subjugated and absorbed by her. And Russia has been the protector of Poland—the protector of the Crimea—the protector of Courland—the protector of Georgia, Immeritia, Mingrelia, the Tcherkessian and Caucasian tribes, etc. She has first protected, and then appropriated them all. She protects Moldavia and Wallachia. A few years ago she became the protector of Turkey from Mehemet

Ali; and since the summer of 1849, she has made herself the protector of Austria.

"When the partisans of Russia speak of the disinterestedness with which she withdrew her protecting troops from Constantinople and from Hungary, let us here also mark the ominous exactness of the parallel between her and Rome. While the ancient world yet contained a number of independent states, which might have made a formidable league against Rome if she had alarmed them by openly avowing her ambitious schemes, Rome's favorite policy was seeming disinterestedness and moderation. After her first war against Philip, after that against Antiochus, and many others, victorious Rome promptly withdrew her troops from the territories which they occupied. She affected to employ her arms only for the good of others. But, when the favorable moment came, she always found a pretext for marching her legions back into each coveted district, and making it a Roman province. Fear, not moderation, is the only effective check on the ambition of such powers as ancient Rome and modern Russia. The amount of that fear depends on the amount of timely vigilance and energy which other states choose to employ against the common enemy of their freedom and national independence."

Synopsis of Events Between the Battle of Poltava, A.D., 1709, and the Defeat of Burgoyne at Saratoga, A.D. 1777

1709. The Duke of Marlborough and Prince Eugène win the Battle of Malplaquet.

1713–1714. The Treaties of Utrecht (1713) and Rastadt (1714) end the War of the Spanish Succession. (In America it was known as Queen Anne's War.) Philip V remains King of Spain on condition that the French and Spanish crowns should never be united. England retains possession of Gibraltar, and in North America acquires Newfoundland and Acadia (Nova Scotia and eastern New Brunswick), which had been taken from France during the war. A frontier barrier of forts is established to protect the Dutch. Austria's major gains were the Spanish Netherlands and the Duchy of Milan.

1714. Queen Anne dies; the Elector of Hanover becomes King George I of England. A subsequent rebellion in favor of the Stuarts is suppressed.

1718–1721. Upon the death of Charles XII a series of treaties are signed ending the Great Northern War. In addition to losing territory in Germany to Hanover and Prussia, Sweden concedes to Russia all her possessions along the eastern Baltic coast and the fortress of Viborg in Finland.

1740–1748. When the Austrian Emperor Charles VI dies, his daughter Maria Theresa succeeds him. Knowing that others will contest the inheritance, Frederick II of Prussia offers military aid to Maria Theresa —on condition that he occupy Silesia. When she refuses his offer, he marches into Silesia. Almost all the powers of Europe engage in the war that follows, known as the War of the Austrian Succession. Prussia is involved only during the years 1740–1742 and 1744–1745; these periods of Prussian participation are called the First and Second Silesian Wars. In America the conflict was named King George's War, and was limited to the years 1744–1748. The Treaty of Aix-la-Chapelle ends the struggles. The only power to gain anything of consequence was Prussia, who retained most of Silesia.

1745–1746. The last rebellion in favor of the Stuarts is crushed at the Battle of Culloden in Scotland.

1754–1755. The French and Indian War breaks out in North America. The French win the first round by ambushing an English force under General Braddock.

1756–1763. Determined to recover Silesia, Empress Maria Theresa forms a coalition of Austria, France, Russia, Sweden, and Saxony to crush the growing power of Prussia. The Seven Years' War, also known as the Third Silesian War, further develops into a struggle for colonial empire between England and France.

Successive Prussian victories over the French at Rossbach and the Austrians at Leuthen in 1757, and over the Russians at Zorndorf in 1758, quickly teach the combined powers that Frederick the Great is one of the outstanding military leaders in the history of the world. But Frederick is fighting enormous odds; he is defeated at Hochkirch in 1758, sustains a severe loss at Kunersdorf in 1759, and a Prussian army is captured at Maxen.

During these years the British under the leadership of William Pitt, Earl of Chatham, take an active part in the war. Lord Clive wins the Battle of Plassey in India in 1757; the English and Hanoverians defeat the French at Minden in 1759; in the same year Wolfe defeats Montcalm on the Plains of Abraham at Quebec; and Sir Edward Hawke wins a great naval victory over the French in Quiberon Bay.

Although Frederick wins the Battles of Liegnitz and Torgau in 1760 he is in a desperate situation, from which he is saved by the death of his enemy, Elizabeth of Russia. The war is concluded by the treaties of Paris and Hubertsburg.

Great Britain emerges as the greatest colonial power in the world. She acquires Canada from France, and her dominant position in India is recognized by France. Great Britain also obtains Florida from Spain, who in return receives Louisiana from France.

1765. Passage of the Stamp Act causes the American colonists to raise the cry of "Taxation [of the colonies] without representation [in the British Parliament]."

1768–1779. During this period Captain James Cook conducts his famous explorations along the coasts of New Zealand and Australia, into the South Pacific, and also in the Antarctic, meeting his death in Hawaii in 1779.

1768–1774. In her first war with the Turks, Catherine the Great of Russia secures control of strategic areas in the Crimea and north of the Black Sea.

1770. In Massachusetts ill feeling between the colonists and British soldiers culminates in the "Boston Massacre."

1772. Russia, Prussia and Austria take part in the first partition of Poland.

1773–1774. The "Boston Tea Party" results in the passage by Parliament of the "Intolerable Acts," which include the closing of the port of Boston.

1775. The American Revolution begins at Lexington and Concord. The Continental Congress appoints George Washington commander in chief of the army. British forces drive the colonists from Bunker Hill overlooking Boston. The American invasion of Canada is stopped at Quebec.

1776. The British evacuate Boston. The Americans are driven out of Canada. A British attack on Charleston, South Carolina is repulsed. The Declaration of Independence is signed.

General Howe drives Washington from New York City, then across New Jersey into Pennsylvania. The British advance from Canada down Lake Champlain is turned back. Washington counterattacks at Trenton.

1777. Washington wins the Battle of Princeton.

13

Saratoga, A.D. 1777

THE HISTORICAL IMPORTANCE of a battle cannot be judged by the number of men engaged or by the number of casualties. The two battles that saved the American Revolution were both comparatively small. They were not even the largest that occurred in that war; there were several others involving a greater number of men on each side, although none were more hotly contested. Yet these two marked the turning point. When the news of Burgoyne's surrender reached Europe, France entered the war. Spain followed France, and before long England was also at war with Holland. The end result nearly six years later was the recognition of the independence of the United States of America.

These are the positive results that flowed from the American victory. If, on the other hand, the British campaign of 1777 had been successful, it is difficult to see how even the indomitable Washington could have upheld the patriot cause through another winter.

When the American Revolution began at Lexington early in the morning of April 19, 1775, there was no general wish for independence from Great Britain. The majority simply wanted to be given the rights they thought British subjects should have, particularly the right to govern themselves by means of their own elected legislative assemblies.

197

After a year of war there was still no unanimity of opinion. The sentiment varied greatly between colonies, and it was only after long delay that the Declaration of Independence was finally signed on July 4, 1776. This still did not mean that the mass of the people of the thirteen colonies fought for independence. It has been estimated that only about one-half of the population were actively in favor of the war; the remainder were either indifferent or fought for the king.

When Burgoyne began his march from Canada in June, 1777, the war had already lasted over two years, and neither the colonies nor the mother country could truthfully claim to be winning. The first major action had been the Battle of Bunker Hill in June, 1775. British troops from Boston had driven the colonists from their positions, but only at heavy cost to themselves. The defeat did more to raise the morale of the Americans than that of the victors. Then the American invasion of Canada had failed at Quebec; by July, 1776, a very sadly depleted army had straggled back to Fort Ticonderoga. In March of that same year General Washington had forced the British to evacuate Boston. A poorly planned attack on Charleston, South Carolina had resulted in an ignominious British repulse.

At that period of the war the colonists had reason to feel confident. The only significant defeat they had suffered had been far away in Canada. There were no British soldiers on American soil; the king's soldiers had been forced out of Boston and driven away from Charleston, but the pendulum was about to swing in the other direction.

At the outbreak of the Revolution, England had not been prepared for war, nor had the king or his ministers thought it necessary to send a large force to America to quell the revolt. By midsummer of 1776, however, an army of 32,000 men had been transported to New York, escorted by an extremely large fleet. This was by far the most impressive force that had ever been assembled on the North American continent, and was a clear indication that King George had no intention whatever of letting his colonies obtain their freedom. It had not been an easy matter for England to gather together such a large body of troops to send to America, but by now it was obvious that halfway measures would not suffice. The population of the thirteen colonies came to about 2,500,000 people, over one-fourth of the population of the British Isles, and occupied an area one-half again larger than that of the Austrian Empire. This was an extremely large region to subdue, even if only one-half of the people were in rebellion; and the 3,000 miles of water that must be crossed presented a formidable obstacle. Furthermore, England had to provide garrisons for many other far-flung parts of her empire from Gibraltar to Africa and India. Also her ancient enemies, France and Spain, were only waiting for a chance to take revenge for their recent defeat in the Seven Years' War.

The British strategic plan for the summer and fall of 1776, the year before Burgoyne's campaign, had been threefold. Three attacks were planned, two in the North and one in the South. That in the South had already failed at Charleston, but it had never been more than a secondary effort designed to seize some of the major cities and, with the aid of the loyalist supporters of the king, begin to recover that region.

The main effort was to be in the North, and it was here that the British had expected to crush the rebellion. King George III considered the four New England colonies of New Hampshire, Massachusetts, Rhode Island, and Connecticut to be the strongholds of the insurrection. His wrath was particularly directed against Massachusetts and Boston, where the "Massacre" and the "Tea Party" had occurred, the city from which Washington had recently evicted his troops.

If New England could be separated from the rest of the colonies, the king felt sure that the revolution would end, and he was probably correct. With the loss of such a large segment of the population, the colonists would certainly have become disheartened, and it would be almost impossible to persuade any foreign country to intervene to back a losing cause, no matter how eager that power might be to strike a blow at England.

Furthermore nature had provided an obvious way to divide the colonies into two parts. At the back of the New England colonies a long, almost uninterrupted waterway stretches from New York City up the Hudson and then, by way of Lake George and Lake Champlain, to Canada. The 1776 plan was that the main British army would land at New York City while another pushed south from Canada. In August and September the troops commanded by General Sir William Howe had made themselves masters of New York City. By October, Howe had pushed northward along the Hudson, and the British under General Guy Carleton were moving southward from Canada.

For several reasons the plan had not been carried to completion. General Howe, commanding in New York City, had been very slow to advance and hesitant in pursuit, letting time slip away from him. As a result Washington's army had managed to escape again and again when they should have been cut off and captured or destroyed. On the other hand, Howe was faced with a peculiar problem. He and his elder brother Admiral Richard Howe, who commanded the fleet, were both members of the Whig party which had for years opposed the king and the Tory party, then in power in England. The Whigs were favorably inclined toward, and sympathetic to, the colonial cause if a satisfactory solution to the problem could be reached. In addition, King George had given the Howes authority to pardon the colonists. They therefore hesitated to shatter completely the forces under Washington. They seemed to think that a show of force or a partial victory on their part would be a better way to induce the patriots to stop fighting. This method would cause less hard feeling in the future when the colonists again became loyal subjects of the crown. It is difficult to explain in any other way the long intervals that occurred between battles and the absence of effective pursuit when a battle had been won, for General Howe was a trained soldier. He had failed to grasp the essential fact that the only effective method of winning any war, particularly a civil war, which is essentially what the revolution was in the colonies, is to wield the sword first, then extend the olive branch.

In this fashion the best season of the year had been wasted. At the end of October, Howe was no farther north than White Plains, where he had again defeated Washington's army on October 28. Howe considered it too late in the year to attempt an advance to meet the forces from Canada. He turned back, captured a large American garrison that had been left to guard the lower Hudson, and began a campaign through New Jersey.

In the meantime the advance of General Carleton from Canada had also been halted—by a naval battle. To guard against a British move the Americans had built a fleet on Lake Champlain. Since no large army could advance through the almost trackless forests in Canada and upper New York, the British had been forced to build a larger fleet to win control of the lake. A great part of the summer and fall had been consumed in this way. The two leaders concerned, General Benedict Arnold in charge of the construction of the American fleet, and General Carleton of the British fleet, had shown unusual energy, ingenuity, and resourcefulness in this contest. The fleets had finally met

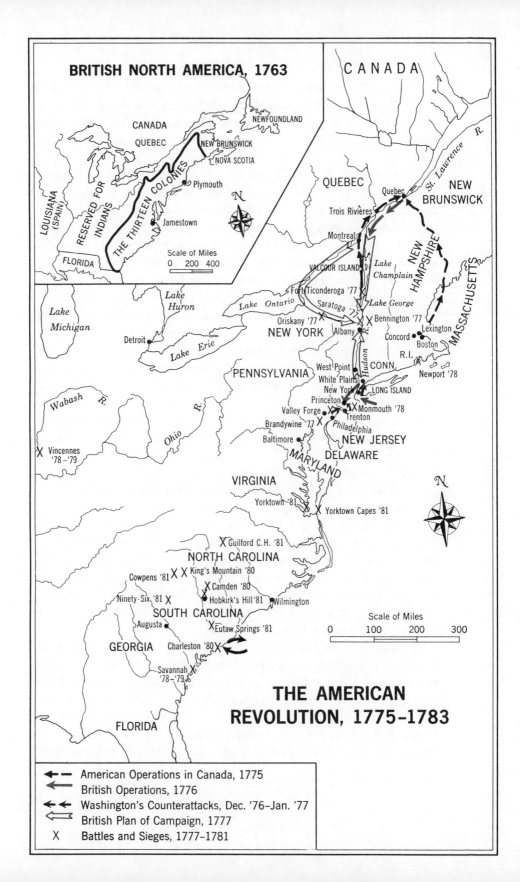

BRITISH NORTH AMERICA, 1763

CANADA

NEWFOUNDLAND

QUEBEC

NEW BRUNSWICK

NOVA SCOTIA

Plymouth

THE THIRTEEN COLONIES

Jamestown

LOUISIANA (SPAIN)

RESERVED FOR INDIANS

FLORIDA

N

Scale of Miles
0   200   400

CANADA

Lake Huron

Lake Michigan

Detroit

Lake Erie

Wabash R.

Ohio R.

Vincennes '78–'79

QUEBEC

Quebec

St. Lawrence R.

NEW BRUNSWICK

Trois Rivières

Montreal

NEW HAMPSHIRE

MASSACHUSETTS

VALCOUR ISLAND

Lake Champlain

Fort Ticonderoga '77

Lake Ontario

Saratoga '77

Lake George

Oriskany '77

NEW YORK

Albany

Bennington '77

Concord

Lexington

Boston

R.I.

West Point

Hudson R.

CONN.

PENNSYLVANIA

White Plains

New York

LONG ISLAND

Newport '78

Princeton

Valley Forge

Monmouth '78

Trenton

Brandywine '77

Philadelphia

Baltimore

NEW JERSEY

DELAWARE

MARYLAND

VIRGINIA

Yorktown '81

Yorktown Capes '81

N

Guilford C.H. '81

NORTH CAROLINA

Cowpens '81   King's Mountain '80

Ninety-Six '81   Camden '80

Hobkirk's Hill '81   Wilmington

SOUTH CAROLINA

Augusta

Eutaw Springs '81

GEORGIA   Charleston '80

Savannah '78–'79

FLORIDA

Scale of Miles
0   100   200   300

THE AMERICAN
REVOLUTION, 1775–1783

American Operations in Canada, 1775
British Operations, 1776
Washington's Counterattacks, Dec. '76–Jan. '77
British Plan of Campaign, 1777
X   Battles and Sieges, 1777–1781

on October 11 at Valcour Island. After a two-day battle the American fleet had been utterly destroyed, but the season was so far advanced that Carleton had decided to retreat into Canada. The British plan for dividing the colonies into two parts would have to wait for another year.

Any feeling of elation the colonists might have felt at their naval defeat which had turned back the invaders was soon overshadowed by the loss of New Jersey. By mid-December the remnants of Washington's little army were in Pennsylvania. General Howe concluded that the campaign had ended, and indeed it appeared to be. Washington's command had rapidly melted away; the militia were deserting in droves; on the 31st of December the enlistments of the one-year soldiers would expire. On the day after Christmas, Washington struck back, overwhelming the Hessians posted at Trenton. The cause that had seemed hopelessly lost was given new life. Another small victory at Princeton, New Jersey followed. The patriots recovered most of New Jersey but during the winter the enlistments expired, and the army almost disintegrated. Somehow Washington managed to build a new army.

This was the situation in the colonies when General John Burgoyne returned to England. He had been Carleton's second in command in Canada and had a plan for victory to submit to the king. The objective was the same as that of the previous year, the isolation of New England from the other colonies. But this time there would be three separate offensives converging on Albany, not just two. As before, the main army under General Howe was to move north from New York City. Burgoyne was to move south from Canada via Lake Champlain, but this time he would start soon enough to be able to reach his destination before the approach of winter. A third force was to move to Albany by way of Lake Ontario and the Mohawk Valley. Lieutenant Colonel Barry St. Leger was designated to command this force with the temporary rank of brigadier general.

The army in Canada was increased so that by mid-June General Burgoyne was able to assemble a force of about 7,850 men near the northern end of Lake Champlain. He had several very able and experienced officers under his command, among whom were Major General William Phillips, the second in command; Major General Friedrich Adolf, Baron von Riedesel, commanding the Germans; and Brigadier General Simon Fraser. His regular troops amounted to about

7,200 men, of whom 3,100 were German. He had also an auxiliary force of 250 Canadians and Tories and about 400 Indians. Much eloquence was poured forth both in America and in England denouncing the use of these savage auxiliaries. Yet Burgoyne seems to have done no more than Montcalm, Wolfe, and other French, American, and English generals had done before him. Actually, the lawless ferocity of the Indians and the utter impossibility of bringing them under any discipline made their services of little or no value at critical periods, while the indignation which their outrages inspired went far toward arousing the people of the invaded districts into active hostility against Burgoyne's army.

The army proceeded by water to Fort Ticonderoga, landing a little north of that place. Ticonderoga commanded the passage along the lakes and was supposed to be the key to the route Burgoyne wished to follow. The English had been repulsed in an attack upon it in 1758 during the French and Indian War with severe loss. Burgoyne's operations against it were conducted with great skill and General Arthur St. Clair, who had only an ill-equipped army of about 3,000 men, evacuated it on the night of 5–6 July. Burgoyne's troops, under Generals Fraser and von Riedesel, rapidly pursued the retiring Americans.

The king hailed the capture of Fort Ticonderoga with delight; its fall was a great shock to the Americans. Many people predicted a quick ending to the revolution. Then General Burgoyne made a serious mistake. There were two routes by which he could reach the Hudson. One was to continue overland from Lake Champlain for a distance of twenty-three miles through a wilderness of tall trees and deep ravines. The other was by way of Fort Ticonderoga, up Lake George, and thence across country to the Hudson. The second route would require a portage over to Lake George because of falls and rapids in the waterway connecting the two lakes, but from Lake George to the Hudson was a distance of only ten miles, and there was a road already in existence. He made the surprising decision to push straight ahead through the forest, yet sent his boats and his artillery over the other route. The Americans obstructed his route through the wilderness in every conceivable way, so that it took him three weeks to reach the Hudson, an average rate of advance of one mile a day.

Burgoyne's employment of Indians now produced the worst possible effects. Though he labored hard to check the atrocities which they were accustomed to commit, he could not prevent the occurrence of many barbarous outrages, repugnant both to the feelings of humanity and to the laws of civilized warfare. The most tragic affair occurred on July 27, two days before the army reached the Hudson. A party of marauding Indians had taken two women prisoners and, on their return trip, had shot and scalped one of them, a Miss Jane McCrea, a young lady who was engaged to marry an officer in Burgoyne's army. Apparently even the friends of the royal cause were liable to be victims of the indiscriminate savages. The American patriots took care that the reports of such tragedies should be circulated far and wide, well knowing the effect they would have upon the people of New England and New York; volunteers poured into the American camps.

On August 3, Burgoyne received the shocking news that General Howe was not on his way to join forces at Albany but had started for the capital at Philadelphia. This meant that the major British force, the main effort on which Burgoyne had counted most heavily, had disappeared from the campaign. There is no doubt that the planners in London had never intended this to happen. Explicit orders for Howe to cooperate with Burgoyne had been prepared for the signature of Lord George Germain, the colonial secretary, but through careless-ness had never been dispatched. At a later date he approved Howe's plan with the expressed hope that he might return to march up the Hudson. A force of about 7,000 men had been left in New York to move northward if necessary, but it started too late to be of any assistance to Burgoyne.

During the entire month of August and part of September, Burgoyne was occupied with the problem of supply. Too much time had been consumed hacking his way through the forest. Burgoyne decided to send a large force on a raid into New England to obtain horses and supplies. Colonel Baum's detachment of 650 men, and the relief ex-pedition sent to aid him, met with disaster at the Battle of Bennington on August 16. Shortly afterward the British general received word of another failure. St. Leger's force of 1,800 whites and Indians had left Oswego late in July, had fought a savage battle at Oriskany on August 6, then had given up the siege of Fort Stanwix on August 22 and was returning to Canada.

Burgoyne was now beginning to have very serious doubts of the success of his campaign. Howe had failed him; St. Leger had failed

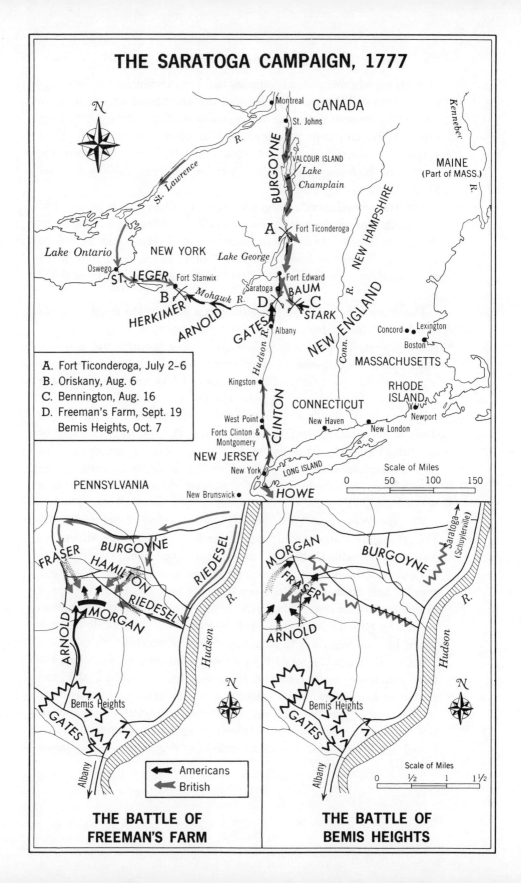

THE SARATOGA CAMPAIGN, 1777

CANADA

Montreal

St. Johns

Kennebec R.

VALCOUR ISLAND

Lake Champlain

BURGOYNE

MAINE
(Part of MASS.)

St. Lawrence R.

A Fort Ticonderoga

R.

Lake Ontario

NEW YORK

Lake George

Oswego

ST. LEGER

Fort Stanwix

B

HERKIMER

Mohawk R.

ARNOLD

Fort Edward

Saratoga

BAUM

D

C

GATES

STARK

NEW HAMPSHIRE

Conn. R.

NEW ENGLAND

Albany

Hudson R.

Concord · · Lexington

Boston

MASSACHUSETTS

A. Fort Ticonderoga, July 2–6
B. Oriskany, Aug. 6
C. Bennington, Aug. 16
D. Freeman's Farm, Sept. 19
    Bemis Heights, Oct. 7

Kingston

CLINTON

West Point

Forts Clinton &
Montgomery

NEW JERSEY

New York

CONNECTICUT

New Haven

RHODE
ISLAND

Newport

New London

LONG ISLAND

Scale of Miles

0   50   100   150

PENNSYLVANIA

New Brunswick ·

HOWE

FRASER

BURGOYNE

HAMILTON

RIEDESEL

RIEDESEL

ARNOLD

MORGAN

Hudson R.

Bemis Heights

GATES

Albany

N

Americans
British

THE BATTLE OF
FREEMAN'S FARM

MORGAN

FRASER

BURGOYNE

Saratoga
(Schuylerville)

ARNOLD

Hudson R.

Bemis Heights

GATES

Albany

N

Scale of Miles

0   ½   1   1½

THE BATTLE OF
BEMIS HEIGHTS

him; his expedition to obtain supplies had been annihilated at Bennington; he was still short of supplies, and the American forces were daily gaining in strength. Ever-increasing numbers of patriots were flocking to the American camp. Washington, although outnumbered and hard pressed by General Howe in Pennsylvania, had sent reinforcements northward, including some of his best regular troops under Colonel Daniel Morgan.

Nevertheless General Burgoyne moved resolutely forward. His only chance of success lay in the possibility of defeating his enemy in battle. He crossed to the west bank of the Hudson and moved to attack the American lines. General Horatio Gates, in command of the defending army, had about 7,000 men. Burgoyne had some 6,000 troops.

The Americans occupied a position on a bluff called Bemis Heights which rose steeply from near the water's edge to a height of over a hundred feet. They had strongly fortified this position, but across a small ravine to the west of their entrenchments the land rose even higher, reaching a height of three hundred feet or more above the river. This higher ground, which was not occupied, dominated the American lines, and it was toward this high ground that the British directed their attack. In fact, this area was the ultimate objective of the British in both of the Battles of Saratoga, but in neither case did they succeed in advancing that far to the south. Both battles were fought about one mile north of the main American position in a heavily wooded region containing only a few small clearings.

The Battle of Freeman's Farm: On the morning of September 19, 1777, General Burgoyne moved his army southward to attack the American position. Of his total strength of 6,000 men, he planned to use only 4,200, retaining a force of 1,800 men to guard his boats and supplies and act as a reserve. Since he never used this force to attempt to influence the course of the battle in any way, it is difficult to understand why he held out such a large reserve. This was a battle he must win if his campaign was to have any chance of success.

Logically, Burgoyne made the column on his right or west flank the strongest. It was commanded by Brigadier General Simon Fraser, and contained some 2,000 men; his mission was to seize the unoccupied high ground west of the American position, then turn east and drive toward the river. The center column, which Burgoyne accompanied, contained 1,100 men, and was commanded by Brigadier General James

Hamilton. The left column, on the east, nearest the river, also contained 1,100 men. It was commanded by Baron von Riedesel; General Phillips, the second in command, marched with this column.

General Gates wanted to wait for the British to attack his fortified lines, but the fiery General Benedict Arnold urged that they meet the British in front of the lines in the woods. He saw clearly the advantages that the Americans would have if they caught their enemy in the forest and around the small clearings. This area was well suited to the American frontier style of fighting. There the British and Germans would be unable to advance in close ranks, firing by volleys. Their favorite method of assault, a direct mass attack with the bayonet, could not be executed. Finally Gates yielded to Arnold's pleas and sent Morgan and his riflemen forward.

The battle that followed, centering around a little clearing called Freeman's Farm, was long and desperate. Arnold came forward, bringing more men with him, and strove to break through a gap between the British right and center columns. The struggling battle lines surged back and forth across the clearing. Arnold believed that, if given a few more men, he could break through, but Gates refused to help with reinforcements. Finally General von Riedesel broke the deadlock. He appeared with a regiment from his column, attacked Arnold's forces on their right flank and forced the Americans to withdraw. The British and Germans remained masters of the field but their losses had been heavy—about 600 men killed, wounded, and captured out of some 3,000 engaged. The Americans, who also had about 3,000 engaged, suffered a loss of some 300 men. The battle in the clearing around Freeman's Farm had lasted only a few hours, but it had been furious and bitter; one British regiment lost over three-quarters of its men.

The outstanding leaders in this battle were Baron von Riedesel, who had won it for the British, and Arnold and Morgan on the American side. Gates had proven to be utterly incompetent; he had remained idle throughout the entire day, holding 4,000 men away from the battle behind his fortified lines.

The Battle of Bemis Heights: The second battle did not occur until nearly three weeks had passed. Burgoyne had planned another assault to take place on the 21st, but that morning received a message from General Sir Henry Clinton, who had been left in command of the British troops in New York. The note was to the effect that Clinton would soon be on his way up the Hudson to attack the American forts that barred the passage up that river to Albany. Burgoyne, in reply, asked that the promised cooperation be speedy and decisive because he could not wait long. He then canceled his projected attack on Bemis Heights. This decision led inevitably to the surrender, for Clinton's diversion started too late and was conducted with only 4,000 men, a force far too small to have broken through to Burgoyne at Saratoga.

While waiting, both armies fortified their positions, but while Burgoyne's British forces went on short rations and his effective strength dwindled, Gates' American army grew larger. By early October, Burgoyne could count no more than 5,000 men fit for duty; Gates by then had at least 11,000 men.

Finally, on October 7, Burgoyne sent a force of 1,700 men out beyond his right flank to try to find a place where an attack might profitably be made upon the American line. This was a serious mistake; such a large detachment invited attack, but it was not large enough to repel a concentrated assault.

As in the previous battle, Gates sent Morgan forward to meet the British. At first Arnold did not appear. He and Gates had quarreled, and Arnold was confined to his tent; but when he heard the noise of battle Arnold could not restrain himself. Ignoring his orders he dashed into the conflict; Gates remained in his tent. Together Arnold and Morgan led the Americans in a spirited charge. The outnumbered British and German soldiers held their ground until their leader, General Fraser, fell mortally wounded, then fell slowly back upon their entrenchments.

Burgoyne's reconnaissance in force had been driven back, but the action was not yet over. The English had scarcely reached the shelter of their fortifications when the Americans, pursuing their success, assaulted their works. The struggle was obstinate and the outcome doubtful until Arnold led a final charge and entered the works with some of the most fearless of his followers. In that critical moment he received a painful wound in the same leg that had already been injured in the assault upon Quebec. Darkness brought an end to the battle, but the Americans were now in a position where they could turn the right flank of the British and gain their rear. Burgoyne skillfully withdrew his army in good order to some heights near the river, a little northward of the former camp. In this second battle the

British suffered a loss of about 600 men, while the Americans had 150 casualties. The campaign was at an end; the defeated army withdrew northward to Saratoga where on October 17, 1777, a total of over 5,700 officers and men surrendered.

During the winter General Washington and the gallant few who stayed with him still had to endure the misery, cold, and starvation of Valley Forge because Howe had captured the capital of Philadelphia. The losses sustained that winter from disease were appalling; the name Valley Forge has become synonymous in American history with suffering, cold, and hunger. It is almost impossible to visualize the men enduring that winter if Burgoyne's campaign had succeeded and New England had been lost; and, if at the same time, they had not been sustained by the knowledge that France would be on their side.

Actually, effective French help would be long in coming. Rochambeau's army was not actively employed until 1781 in the Yorktown Campaign. Dark days were still ahead. The year 1780 would be particularly gloomy. In that year Charleston had surrendered to a British army in May. Congress made the mistake of sending General Gates to fight Cornwallis; at Camden in August the American Army suffered the worst defeat ever inflicted upon it in its history, and the whole South seemed lost. One of their favorite leaders, Benedict Arnold, turned traitor in September. Eventually came Yorktown in 1781, and peace two years later.

Synopsis of Events Between the Defeat of Burgoyne at Saratoga, A.D. 1777, and the Battle of Valmy, A.D. 1792

1779–1783. The Spanish, aided by the French, conduct an intensive but ultimately unsuccessful siege of Gibraltar.

1781. Cornwallis surrenders at Yorktown.

1782. At the Sea Battle of the Saints in the West Indies, Admiral Comte de Grasse, whose French fleet had made possible the surrender at Yorktown, is defeated by Admiral Sir George Rodney.

1783. At the Treaty of Paris the independence of the United States of America is formally acknowledged. Great Britain returns Florida to Spain.

1783. Russia annexes the Crimea.

1787–1789. The Constitution of the United States is prepared and submitted to the states; it is ratified by the required number, and Washington is elected as the first President.

1787–1792. In her second war with Turkey, Catherine the Great of Russia gains additional land along the northern shore of the Black Sea.

1789. The States-General convenes in France; the National Assembly is formed. The French Revolution begins with the storming of the Bastille on July 14.

1791. Louis XVI and Marie Antoinette flee from Paris; they are arrested at Varennes.

1792. War is declared in April. In August the Paris mob storms the Tuileries and massacres the Swiss guards.

14

The Battle of Valmy, A.D. 1792

A little fire is quickly trodden out,
Which, being suffered, rivers cannot quench.
—SHAKESPEARE

A FEW MILES DISTANT from the little town of Ste. Menehould in the northeast of France are the village and hill of Valmy, and near the crest of that hill a simple monument marks the site of a battle that was a turning point in the history of warfare. At one and the same time it was the last battle of the old regular army of the Kingdom of France, the first successful battle of the new mass levies of republican France, the end of old-fashioned war and the beginning of total war.

The monument honors the memory of a soldier who himself was a symbol of that transition, François Christophe Kellermann (father of the officer who led the famous cavalry charge at Marengo) a general in King Louis XVI's army, general of the French Republic, and future honorary Marshal of the Empire. When Napoleon decided further to honor the elder Kellermann, he recognized the paramount importance of this battle, and chose the title Duke of Valmy. That the emperor should thus over the years continue to show his appreciation is significant, for if the French had not won the Battle of Valmy the French Revolution would have been crushed and there would have been no empire.

It is indicative also of those turbulent times that there is no monument to the other French general who contributed so largely to the

211

victory. Charles François Dumouriez had also been a general in the king's army, then an ardent revolutionary, and at the time of the battle was senior to Kellermann. After Valmy he conducted a successful invasion of Belgium, but in the next year made the mistake of losing a battle. The usual punishment during the Reign of Terror for such a mistake was the guillotine, "pour encourager les autres." Therefore when Dumouriez was charged with treason and his army refused to follow him in a revolt, he fled to the enemy's camp, leaving Kellermann in full possession of all the honors to be bestowed by France and its rulers for the victory at Valmy.

The French Army in 1792 was a curious mixture of the old and the new. When the French Revolution began with the storming of the Bastille on July 14, 1789, the French nobility began gradually to leave the country. Since almost all the officers of high rank and the majority of the junior officers were members of the nobility, the French Army gradually lost most of its trained leaders. Fortunately for France the army contained a number of qualified noncommissioned officers to take their places, but enlistments in the new National Guard, where the pay was higher, the discipline not so strict, and promotion much more rapid, were far more popular. The old army slowly began to disappear.

When war was declared in April, 1792, the forces of France contained both old and new, but a high percentage of the artillerymen were former members of the old army. At Valmy this would prove to be most fortunate for the future of the French Republic. The artillery of France had become famous throughout Europe for its efficiency and skill, due primarily to the reforms and reorganization of the great French artilleryman Gribeauval, who may accurately be called the father of modern field artillery.

After the fierce leaders of the revolutionary assembly declared the country in danger, volunteers flocked readily to the colors. They were full of zeal and courage, but utterly undisciplined and impatient of superior authority or systematic control. Many had taken part in the riots in Paris and were preeminent for misconduct before the enemy and for savage insubordination against their own officers. On one occasion eight battalions of these, intoxicated with massacre and sedition, joined the forces under Dumouriez and soon threatened to destroy all discipline. Their leaders said openly that the old officers were traitors and should be purged, as they had purged Paris of its aristocrats. According to the noted French author Alphonse Lamartine,

General Dumouriez called them out for a review, placed a strong force of cavalry behind them, and trained artillery on the ends of their lines. Then, surrounded by his staff and an escort of a hundred hussars, addressed them. "Fellows," said he, "for I will not call you either citizens or soldiers, you see before you this artillery, behind you this cavalry; you are stained with crimes, and I do not tolerate here either assassins or executioners. I know that there are scoundrels among you charged to excite you to crime. Drive them from among you, or denounce them to me, for I shall hold you responsible for their conduct."

Thomas Carlyle, writing of this incident, added: "Patience, O Dumouriez! this uncertain heap of shriekers, mutineers, were they once drilled and inured, will become a phalanxed mass of fighters; and wheel and whirl to order swiftly, like the wind or the whirlwind; tanned mustachio-figures, often barefoot, even bare-backed, with sinews of iron, who require only bread and gunpowder; very sons of fire, the adroitest, hastiest, hottest ever seen, perhaps, since Attila's time."

France ran a fearful risk during the early years when she was forced to rely for her safety upon such mobs of armed men, and France's generals ran fearful risks when they adopted stern measures against them. Their ranks included many friends and spies of the political leaders in Paris. These men came to the army eager to denounce their generals and thus gain power and prestige for themselves. It was comparatively simple, in this mixed atmosphere of politics and war, to bring an unpopular general to trial as an enemy of the country; once accused the officer had little chance of survival.

The first events of the war were certainly disastrous and disgraceful to France. The first flash of an enemy saber or the first sound of an enemy gun was enough to unnerve these disorganized levies. Near Lille a large French force of about four thousand men came suddenly upon a small detachment of Austrians. Not a shot was fired, not a bayonet leveled. With one simultaneous cry of panic the French broke and ran headlong, then murdered their general and several other officers. Another large division saw a few Austrian skirmishers reconnoitering their position. The advanced posts had scarcely given and received a volley when the cry, "We are betrayed," arose, and the whole army rushed madly off the field. Similar panics or repulses occurred frequently when the earliest French generals brought their troops into the presence of the enemy.

France had declared war on Austria only, but she soon found she was facing a coalition of Austria, Prussia, and other powers. The allied sovereigns rightly regarded the French Revolution as a threat to their existence, and were determined to restore the French king to power. They gradually collected a veteran and finely disciplined army for the invasion of France. Their plan was simple; it was to strike directly at the heart of the country. The line of advance would be by way of Longwy, where they would cross the frontier, and Verdun, thence through the Argonne Forest to Châlons and Paris. The obstacles that lay in their path, the fortresses of Longwy and Verdun and the Argonne Forest, were serious but no worse than along other routes, and should be easily overcome as long as disorder continued to prevail in the ranks of the French armies. There was really nothing to prevent the invaders from making that "military promenade to Paris" that the French nobility, the émigrés, so gaily talked of accomplishing. Furthermore the émigrés assured the allies that the people would rise spontaneously in favor of the king as they advanced.

The allied army that approached the French frontier numbered over 80,000 men. Over half were Prussians, trained in the school of the Great Frederick, heirs of the glories of the Seven Years' War, and universally esteemed as the best troops in Europe. There were 30,000 Austrians, trained soldiers who had seen actual service in the wars of the empire. There was a strong body of about 5,000 Hessians and an equal number of the noblest and bravest sons of France. These émigrés looked on the road to Paris as the path to victory, to honor, to the rescue of their king, to reunion with their families, and to the restoration of their order.

The nominal commander of this imposing army was King Frederick William II of Prussia, but the actual commander was the Duke of Brunswick, one of the minor reigning princes of Germany, who had acquired a fine military reputation in the Seven Years' War that had been enhanced in a short campaign in afteryears in Holland. As the operations developed the two commanders were to clash frequently, and in almost every case the king would be right and the general wrong. The king was impetuous and eager to advance. Over the years the general had become slow, cautious, and methodical. He had absorbed the drill and the mechanics of the Great Frederick's army, but he had lost the spirit. The general put the king's wishes into orders to the troops, but executed them at his leisure, losing valuable time.

In the coming years the generals of that era were to relearn the value of time from the energetic, enthusiastic leaders of the French Revolution.

Moving majestically forward, with leisurely deliberation, that seemed to show the consciousness of superior strength, the allies appeared before Longwy. After a short bombardment the fortress capitulated on August 27. On September 2 Verdun surrendered after scarcely a shadow of resistance. The allied forces were now in a perfect position, directly between the two French field armies, that of General Dumouriez to the north at Sedan and that of General Kellermann to the south. Each of these French armies numbered only about 20,000 men, and it was in the power of the German general to crush either, or both in succession, or march on Paris between them. The king wanted to push rapidly straight ahead. The general agreed to follow his wishes, but nine days passed while he made his preparations and waited for the muddy roads to dry. He was more interested in consolidating his position and improving his supply situation than in a rapid advance; he preferred a methodical advance with everything properly taken care of before the next move was made.

During those nine days Dumouriez acted with energy and resolution. The Prussian seizure of Verdun had ruined any chance he might have had to defend the line of the Meuse. The next obstacle in the enemy's path was the Argonne Forest. This ridge of broken ground has now been partially cleared and drained, but in 1792 it was heavily wooded and cut by streams and marshes whose soft clay rapidly turned into mud. American troops of World War I can vouch for the natural difficulties the ground still presented 126 years later. This natural barrier could be crossed by an army, with its supply wagons and artillery, only by five roads, leading through defiles which an inferior force could easily fortify and defend.

Dumouriez at Sedan was close to the northern defile at Le Chesne, but the Austrians, who were preparing to cross the Meuse at Stenay, were closer to the two center defiles of Croix-aux-Bois and Grandpré, while the main Prussian army was opposite the two in the south at La Chalade and Les Islettes. The last-named, the southernmost, was on the direct road from Verdun to Châlons and Paris. It was therefore the most important one to hold, the closest to the Prussians, the closest to Kellermann's French army in the south, but also the farthest from his present position at Sedan. Knowing that General Kellermann had been ordered to march to his support, General Dumouriez moved directly across the front of his Austrian enemy at Stenay and seized the three southern defiles, but did not have enough men in his army to do more than post small detachments at the two northernmost points. Simultaneously he sent messengers to speed Kellermann on his way, and to the north and west to obtain reinforcements, which promptly began to move to his aid.

Having accomplished all this in the nine days that his enemy was making preparations and waiting for the mud to dry, Dumouriez fortified his positions pending the arrival of Kellermann and the other reinforcements. He even boasted of the passes which he held as Thermopylaes, but the simile was nearly rendered fatally complete for the defending forces. Finding the pass on the direct road to Châlons strongly held, the Duke of Brunswick left a large force to watch that point, then marched toward the center defile of Grandpré. But he also sent the Austrian General Clerfayt from Stenay through the forest toward Croix-aux-Bois.

On September 12, after some sharp fighting, Clerfayt drove the small French detachment away from Croix-aux-Bois. An attempt to recapture the pass failed. His left flank turned, Dumouriez refused to retreat; he knew full well how impossible it would be to rally his undisciplined new soldiers once they started to fall back into the interior of France. Instead he abandoned Grandpré also and concentrated his forces beside the main road from Verdun to Châlons, west of the Les Islettes defile, between the town of Ste. Menehould and the village of Valmy.

This failure of the French to retreat after their flank had been turned seems to have mystified the Duke of Brunswick. However he was not surprised when it was reported to him that his advance guard, moving through Grandpré, had caused a panic of several thousand French troops who had fled at their approach. This was exactly what he expected. The main body of the Prussians and Austrians moved leisurely forward, confidently expecting to find their enemy in full retreat after they had marched past Grandpré.

The news of the loss of the northern and central passes of the Argonne and of the panic flight of some of Dumouriez's troops spread rapidly throughout the country. Kellermann and others marching toward Ste. Menehould halted for fear of falling into the hands of the victorious Prussians. This delay might have proved fatal to the French, but the Duke of Brunswick was moving so slowly that there was time

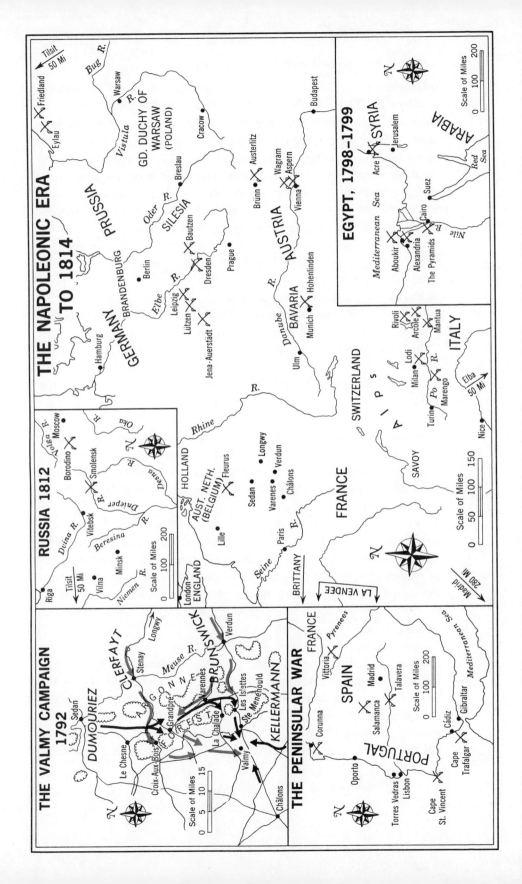

THE NAPOLEONIC ERA TO 1814

Tilsit 50 Mi

Bug R.

Warsaw

Vistula R.

Friedland

Eylau

Oder R.

GD. DUCHY OF WARSAW (POLAND)

Cracow

Breslau

Bautzen

SILESIA

PRUSSIA

Berlin

BRANDENBURG

Elbe R.

Leipzig

Lützen

Dresden

Prague

Hamburg

GERMANY

Jena-Auerstädt

Danube R.

Ulm

BAVARIA

Munich

Hohenlinden

Budapest

Brünn

Austerlitz

Wagram

Aspern

Vienna

AUSTRIA

Rhine R.

SWITZERLAND

A l p s

SAVOY

Turin

Marengo

Nice

Elba 50 Mi

ITALY

Rivoli

Arcole

Mantua

Milan

Lodi

Po R.

Scale of Miles
0   50   100   150

EGYPT, 1798–1799

Scale of Miles
0   100   200

SYRIA

Jerusalem

Acre

ARABIA

Mediterranean Sea

Aboukir

Alexandria

Cairo

The Pyramids

Nile R.

Suez

Red Sea

RUSSIA 1812

Tilsit 50 Mi

Volga R.

Moscow

Oka R.

Borodino

Smolensk

Vitebsk

Dvina R.

Beresina R.

Desna R.

Dnieper R.

Minsk

Riga

Vilna

Niemen R.

Scale of Miles
0   100   200

HOLLAND

AUST. NETH. (BELGIUM)

Fleurus

Lille

Sedan

Varenes

Verdun

Longwy

Châlons

Paris

Seine R.

BRITTANY

LA VENDÉE

FRANCE

London

ENGLAND

Madrid 280 Mi

THE VALMY CAMPAIGN 1792

CLERFAYT

Sedan

Stenay

Longwy

Verdun

Meuse R.

BRUNSWICK

DUMOURIEZ

Le Chesne

Croix-Aux-Bois

A R G O N N E   F O R E S T

Grandpré

Varennes

Les Islettes

Ste.-Menehould

La Chalade

KELLERMANN

Valmy

Châlons

Scale of Miles
0   5   10   15

THE PENINSULAR WAR

FRANCE

Pyrenees

Vittoria

SPAIN

Madrid

Talavera

Salamanca

Corunna

Cádiz

Gibraltar

PORTUGAL

Oporto

Torres Vedras

Lisbon

Cape St. Vincent

Cape Trafalgar

Mediterranean Sea

Scale of Miles
0   100   200

to reassure them. They resumed their march and joined Dumouriez.

When the Duke of Brunswick's forces issued from the defile at Grandpré and began marching toward the southwest they were as close to Paris as the French themselves. The King of Prussia advocated an instant attack south toward the Châlons road to cut the French off from retreat toward Paris. The result was that in the gray of the morning of the 20th of September the allies turned and, marching south, passed on the western side of Valmy, where Kellermann was concentrating his forces. An unexpected collision of some of the advanced cavalry warned each side of the nearness of the enemy, but a thick autumnal mist floated over the whole region, hiding the armies from each other's view.

The dense fog did not rise until late in the morning and, when the veil was lifted, the surprise was complete. The French found the major portion of the allied army drawn up in ranks facing eastward toward Valmy, between them and Paris. The allies, who had expected to see an army in precipitate retreat, discovered Kellermann's forces and part of Dumouriez's awaiting them in a long semicircular line on the hill of Valmy, with the remainder of the French in reserve behind them on the road toward Ste. Menehould.

The best and bravest of the French must have beheld this spectacle with secret apprehension and awe. However bold and resolute a man may be in the discharge of his duty, it is an anxious and fearful thing to be called on to encounter danger among comrades of whose steadiness you can feel no certainty. Each soldier of Kellermann's army, which stood closest to the foe, must have remembered the series of panic routs that had taken place on the French side during the war. He must have cast restless glances to right and left, looking for signs of wavering. He must have begun to calculate how long it would be before a general rush would either carry him to the rear in involuntary disgrace, or leave him alone and helpless to be cut down by the advancing enemy.

Contrary to the expectations of both friend and foe, the French infantry held their ground under the fire of the allied guns, while their own artillery thundered in reply. For perhaps two hours the cannonade continued. The noise was terrific, and observers report that the ground shook; but the fire was not very deadly. Thirteen hundred yards was a long range for the guns of that age, and the ground was still so wet that the cannonballs buried themselves when they struck.

The Duke of Brunswick saw that artillery fire alone would not shake the French. To cause them to flee before him, he must advance. At his command the Prussian infantry formed for the assault and moved forward toward Kellermann's position on the hill. That general had chosen to stand near the crest of the hill in the center of his line near a windmill where he could easily be seen by all; the monument stands there now. Encouraging his men to hold fast, he ordered his artillery to redouble their fire. At this critical moment the Prussian infantry halted.

There have been many attempts to explain why the attack was stopped, varying from the possibility of mud in the valley at Kellermann's feet to the terrible effectiveness of the redoubled French artillery fire. The logical explanation seems simple. The Duke of Brunswick had expected his enemy to flee panic-stricken at the sight of advancing infantry. He personally was in no hurry to reach Paris, and therefore saw no necessity for fighting a pitched battle to get there. When he saw that the attack would meet resistance and that casualties would result, he simply halted it so that he could turn his attention to consolidating the territory and fortresses he had already won—the completion of the war could wait until this had been accomplished, probably in the following year.

The remainder of the Battle or, as it is so frequently called, the Cannonade at Valmy, was an anticlimax. A Prussian artillery shell exploded some ammunition wagons behind the French lines. Some of the French began to turn and flee but, before the allies could take advantage of this break, Kellermann and his officers halted the troops and restored the lines. Thereupon the cannonade slowly ceased. A few days later the allies withdrew across the Meuse. Over 50,000 Frenchmen were present facing over 45,000 allies; the bulk of the remainder of the grand allied army had been left along the way to guard the captured fortresses or to watch the other (the eastern) end of the Les Islettes defile. The casualties could not have been over 300 on each side.

It never seems to have occurred to the Duke of Brunswick or to the majority of those present on the allied side that by failing to win the battle, they had lost it. On the very next day the National Convention met in Paris. With the news of the victory at Valmy ringing in their ears they voted to abolish the monarchy and establish a republic.

The old monarchy had no chance of support in the hall of the Convention, but had the Cannonade at Valmy resulted in an actual battle and been lost by the French, the history of France and of Europe could have been vastly different. There were at that time many leaders in the country who were in favor of an effective revival of the better part of the ancient institutions, and for substituting Reform for Revolution. Only a few weeks before, petitions had been presented to the king, signed by many of the representatives of the middle classes, expressing their horror of the anarchists, and their readiness to uphold the rights of the crown, as long as the liberties of his subjects were also taken into account. And, according to Alison, an armed resistance to the authority of the Convention, and in favor of the king, was in reality at this time being organized in La Vendée and in Brittany which "would have proved extremely formidable to the Convention, if the retreat of the Duke of Brunswick in September 1792 had not damped the whole of the west of France, then ready to break out into insurrection." The importance of this revolt, which did occur in the following year under much more disadvantageous circumstances, may be estimated by the fact that it was not wholly suppressed until 1796.

The Bourbon throne, if rescued in 1792, would have had a chance for stability, for it was not only among the zealots of the old monarchy that the cause of the king would have found friends. The atrocities of the early September massacres when people had been ruthlessly taken from the jails and summarily executed by the mob had just occurred. The reaction produced among thousands who had previously been active on the ultrademocratic side was fresh and powerful. Louis XVI was known to be just and humane, and deeply sensible of the necessity of a gradual extension of political rights among all his subjects. But the news of Valmy swept all before it.

It furnished the spark that electrified the spirit of the raw levies of France into an alert and self-confident power. They felt they had now stood up to the best armies in Europe. The fact that they had not done so, had not fought a real battle, was entirely overlooked and absolutely immaterial. The people acquired confidence in themselves and in each other; and that confidence soon grew into a spirit of unbounded audacity and ambition. France felt she possessed a giant's strength, and like a giant did she use it. War became no longer a matter for standing armies. France adopted universal conscription, the *levée en masse*, followed by total mobilization, the nation in arms.

The words of the German poet Goethe, who was present as an observer at Valmy, deserve quotation. On the evening of the battle he was asked for his opinion: *From this place and from this day forth commences a new era in the world's history, and you can all say that you were present at its birth.*

Synopsis of Events Between the Battle of Valmy, A.D. 1792 and the Battle of Waterloo, A.D. 1815

1792. The National Convention meets, abolishes the monarchy, declares France a republic, and pledges aid to all oppressed peoples who wish to overthrow their governments. French forces attack the Austrian Netherlands (Belgium).

1793. Louis XVI is executed in January. Russia and Prussia take part in the second partition of Poland. A royalist revolt breaks out in La Vendée; France is invaded by the allies. The Reign of Terror begins; France adopts universal conscription. Marie Antoinette is executed in October. By the end of the year the allies are driven from France, and the Vendéans have been defeated, although they are not completely pacified until 1796.

1794–1795. The gallant national uprising of the Polish people led by Thaddeus Kosciusko is followed by the third and final partition of Poland by Russia, Prussia and Austria.

After their victory at Fleurus the French overrun Belgium and Holland; the latter is then organized as the Batavian Republic. Following the execution of Robespierre, the Reign of Terror subsides. A new government consisting of a Directory and two assemblies or councils is formed; General Napoleon Bonaparte disperses a mob revolt with a "whiff of grapeshot."

1796–1797. Napoleon Bonaparte takes command of the French Army of Italy. In six short campaigns he startles the world: acquires Savoy and Nice for France; wins among other victories the Battles of Lodi and Arcole in 1796 and Rivoli in 1797; captures the fortress of Mantua; and approaches within a hundred miles of Vienna when a truce is declared. Only England, whose fleet had been victorious at Cape St. Vincent, remains at war.

1798. Napoleon embarks on his Egyptian expedition and wins the Battle of the Pyramids, but Admiral Horatio Nelson destroys his fleet at Aboukir Bay east of Alexandria. Angered and dismayed by France's establishment of republics in Rome, northern Italy and Switzerland, encouraged by Nelson's victory, a second coalition forms against France.

1799. Unsuccessful at the Siege of Acre, the city taken by Richard the Lion-Hearted in the Third Crusade, forced by the plague to return to Egypt, Bonaparte annihilates a Turkish force at Aboukir. He returns to find a France facing bankrutpcy, with her armies in Italy defeated. Napoleon overthrows the Directory, becomes First Consul, and begins the task of stabilizing the country's finances.

1800–1802. Napoleon makes his famous crossing of the Alps and wins the Battle of Marengo. Six months later Moreau gains a brilliant victory at Hohenlinden in Bavaria. Treaties of peace are signed with Austria in 1801 and with England in 1802. Napoleon becomes First Consul for life. During this period he begins his all-embracing legis- lative and administrative reforms, codifying the laws, reorganizing the tax structure, providing public services, building roads and bridges, constructing canals, and improving the seaports of the country.

1801. The legislative union of Great Britain and Ireland as the United Kingdom is accomplished.

1803. President Thomas Jefferson purchases Louisiana from Napoleon, thereby tremendously enlarging the territory of the United States.

1803–1805. England renews the war against France. Napoleon be- comes Emperor in 1804. In 1805 Napoleon, at war with a third coali- tion, captures an Austrian army at Ulm, but Lord Nelson destroys the combined French and Spanish fleets at the decisive Sea Battle of Cape Trafalgar where he loses his life but ends forever all hope of a French invasion of England. Napoleon goes on to capture Vienna and to win his great victory over the Austrians and Russians at Austerlitz.

1806. With Italy now thoroughly under his control, Napoleon con- verts Holland into a kingdom, forms the Confederation of the Rhine, and dissolves the old Holy Roman Empire. In a lightning-swift cam- paign Napoleon wins the Battle of Jena as Marshal Davout defeats the main Prussian army at Auerstädt. The French pursuit of the Prussians after Jena was a model of its kind. Shortly after his occupation of Berlin, Napoleon promulgated his famous decrees closing the Con- tinent to British trade.

1807. After an indecisive battle at Eylau, the Russians are thoroughly defeated at Friedland. At the Peace of Tilsit, Prussia loses half her territory, and the Grand Duchy of Warsaw is organized under

Napoleon's auspices; England is now Napoleon's sole remaining enemy.

1808. When Portugal had objected to the stopping of trade with England, a French army had occupied the country, but when Napoleon decides to install his brother on the throne of Spain a national uprising ensues. England sends troops to aid the Portuguese and Spanish.

1809–1810. Encouraged by the English and by Napoleon's difficulties in Spain, Austria again declares war. Napoleon is defeated at Aspern (or Essling) but is victorious at Wagram. The Austrians accept peace. In 1810 Napoleon marries Marie Louise, Archduchess of Austria. France annexes Holland and a large section of the coast of Germany. Napoleon's empire has now reached its greatest extent.

In Spain the British evacuate Corunna, then Sir Arthur Wellesley, later Duke of Wellington, defeats the French at Talavera but is forced to retire to the Torres Vedras lines near Lisbon, Portugal.

1812. Napoleon undertakes his great invasion of Russia, captures Smolensk, defeats the Russians at Borodino, and enters Moscow. After the Russians burn their capital, the disastrous retreat begins. In Spain, Wellesley wins the Battle of Salamanca. The United States declares war on England; then, because the country was completely unprepared for war, the Americans suffer a series of disgraceful defeats.

1813. Although victorious at Lützen, Bautzen, and Dresden, Napoleon is now facing almost all Europe in arms against him, and his enemies have learned from him how to wage war. Defeated at the great Battle of Leipzig (the Battle of the Nations), Napoleon retreats into France. In Spain, Wellesley defeats the French at Vittoria. Captain Perry wins the Battle of Lake Erie.

1814. Although greatly outnumbered, Napoleon's genius still wins victories, but his enemies are far too numerous. After their victorious entry into Paris, Napoleon abdicates and is sent to Elba. The Bourbons are restored.

In America the British enter Washington and burn the Capitol and the White House. Captain Macdonough wins the naval battle of Lake Champlain.

1815. General Andrew Jackson wins the Battle of New Orleans. Napoleon lands in southern France.

15

The Battle of Waterloo, A.D. 1815

WHEN IN APRIL, 1814, the Emperor Napoleon abdicated, all the war-weary people of Europe breathed a vast sigh of relief. The man whose genius and ambition had for so long disturbed the world was gone; twenty-two years of violence and tumult had come to an abrupt end. The world could breathe again; the people could return to peace.

The Bourbon kings of France were restored to the throne in the person of Louis XVIII, who promptly forgot that it was not Napoleon who had been responsible for the uprisings against his predecessor. It was the people of France who had initiated the revolution and the first ten years of war. The king almost immediately fell under the influence of the returned émigrés who were determined to recover their ancient properties and rights. The people whose motto had become *Liberté, Egalité, Fraternité* had seen their republic replaced by an empire. Were they now to be forced to return to nothing better than the original monarchy against which they had revolted? Were all the gains they had made toward freedom and social equality to be swept away by the dull, heavy hand of reaction? The years that stretched ahead seemed to hold little more than personal and national humiliation, coupled with persecution of those

224

who had fought for France and Napoleon. At least the years of the Empire had been active and splendid.

The allied sovereigns and their representatives who met in the brilliant international Congress of Vienna to decide the fate of Europe agreed that France could retain the frontiers she had possessed prior to the revolution. This decision was not based upon any feeling that these were the natural boundaries of the country, but only because it was thought it would strengthen the power of Louis XVIII in dealing with his turbulent people. Then the kings and emperors begain parceling out the remainder of Europe as if nothing had occurred in the intervening years, completely disregarding the tremendous social and political forces that had been let loose upon Europe, and promptly fell to quarreling among themselves.

After less than a year at Elba, Napoleon judged the time to be ripe to make a supreme effort to recover his crown. Landing with a thousand soldiers near Cannes in southern France, he moved northward by way of the French Alps, to avoid the larger military posts of the king's army. This precaution proved unnecessary. Everywhere he was received with acclaim. Marshal Ney, sent with a body of troops to arrest him, announced that he would bring Napoleon back to Paris in a cage. At the first sight of his emperor, Ney welcomed him with open arms. Napoleon's march through Lyon to Paris became a triumphal parade. King Louis fled; Paris welcomed its emperor with delight and joy.

Although Napoleon proclaimed his desire for peace, none of the allies trusted him. In fact they were stunned by his reappearance. A good way to determine the impact of the news upon the allied governments and people who were not sympathetic to Napoleon would be to quote the words of a celebrated English jurist and historian of the day who was not a member of the reactionary Tory government. Sir James Mackintosh, a statesman and leader of the Liberal party, said of the return from Elba: "Was it in the power of language to describe the evil? Wars which had raged for more than twenty years throughout Europe; which had spread blood and desolation from Cadiz to Moscow, and from Naples to Copenhagen; which had wasted the means of human enjoyment, and destroyed the instruments of social improvement; which threatened to diffuse among the European nations the dissolute and ferocious habits of a predatory soldiery—at length, by one of those vicissitudes which bid defiance to the foresight of man, had been brought to a close, upon the whole, happy, beyond any reasonable expectation, with no violent shock to national independence. . . . In the midst of this fair prospect and of these consolatory hopes, Napoleon Bonaparte escaped from Elba; three small vessels reached the coast of Provence; their hopes are instantly dispelled; the work of our toil and fortitude is undone; the blood of Europe is spilled in vain."

In this crisis the arguments between the allies were forgotten. Napoleon's return was the signal for all governments to turn against him. They took the unprecedented step of declaring him an outlaw; Prussia, Russia, Austria, and Great Britain formed an alliance against him and began to organize their armies for an invasion of France; almost all the other powers of Europe joined the alliance. Napoleon had no choice. There was nothing else for him to do but raise an army and take the field again; and never was his genius and activity more signally displayed than in the speed and skill with which he brought forward all the military resources of France. He had re-entered Paris on March 20. By early June, in addition to providing troops for defense of the frontiers and for suppressing an insurrection in La Vendée, he had prepared a striking force of 125,000 men.

At this time the allies had assembled two armies in Belgium: a Prussian army of 116,000 men under the command of Field Marshal Blücher; and a mixed force of British, Belgians, Dutch, and Germans numbering 93,000 commanded by the Duke of Wellington. These two armies were awaiting the arrival of their allies before moving into France. When the Austrians and Russians arrived, which could not be before July, the allies would then invade with over 600,000 men. Napoleon knew that if he waited he could collect more men to oppose the invasion, but the odds against him would be greater than if he acted immediately when he was outnumbered by slightly less than two to one. Delay could only result in a greater increase of his enemies than of his own force. He decided to attack his enemies in Belgium.

There is no doubt that Napoleon's decision to advance immediately was correct. Not only were the two armies opposing him in Belgium composed of different nationalities and therefore less likely to act effectively in coordination with each other, but also the Anglo-Dutch army of the Duke of Wellington contained many elements whose sympathies were inclined toward the French cause, particularly the

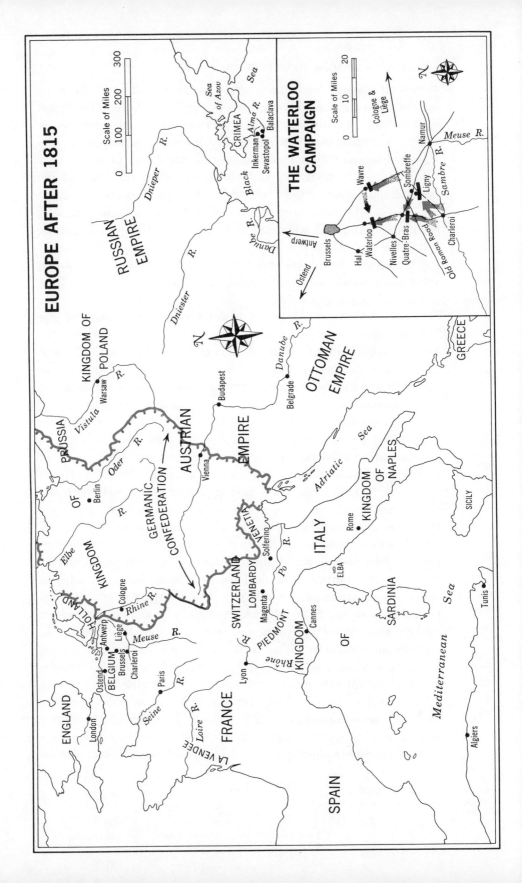

EUROPE AFTER 1815

Scale of Miles
0 100 200 300

RUSSIAN EMPIRE

Sea of Azov

CRIMEA

Inkerman Alma R.
Sevastopol   Balaclava

Black Sea

Dnieper R.

Dniester R.

KINGDOM OF POLAND

Warsaw
Vistula R.

PRUSSIA

Oder R.

KINGDOM OF

Berlin

Elbe R.

GERMANIC CONFEDERATION

AUSTRIAN EMPIRE

Vienna

Budapest

Danube R.

Belgrade

OTTOMAN EMPIRE

GREECE

Adriatic Sea

VENETIA

Solferino

Po R.

LOMBARDY

Magenta

SWITZERLAND

PIEDMONT

KINGDOM

Cannes

ITALY

Rome

KINGDOM OF NAPLES

SICILY

ELBA

SARDINIA

Mediterranean Sea

Tunis

Algiers

OF

SPAIN

FRANCE

LA VENDEE

Loire R.

Rhône R.

Lyon

Seine R.

Paris

ENGLAND

London

Ostend

BELGIUM

Brussels
Charleroi

Meuse R.

Liège

Antwerp

Cologne

Rhine R.

HOLLAND

KINGDOM

THE WATERLOO CAMPAIGN

Scale of Miles
0 10 20

N

Cologne & Liège

Meuse R.

Namur

Sombreffe

Wavre

Ligny

Sambre R.

Charleroi

Old Roman Road

Quatre-Bras

Nivelles

Waterloo

Hal

Brussels

Ostend

Antwerp

natives of Belgium. Napoleon believed that if he could drive his army in between the two opposing armies, he could then attack and defeat each in turn. In the campaign that followed he almost succeeded in doing so, and probably would have achieved a dramatic victory if he had chosen different subordinates to execute his plan.

He selected Marshal Ney and Marshal Grouchy to command the left and right wings respectively of his army, each of whom had to act independently at one time or another during the campaign, and each of whom failed when operating alone. If Ney, a courageous, fearless leader whom Napoleon called "the bravest of the brave," and Grouchy had been kept under the emperor's own personal supervision, they would have undoubtedly performed good service. Then if Marshal Soult, who acted as Napoleon's chief of staff in the campaign, and Marshal Davout had been given command of the left and right wings, events would have turned out quite differently. This is particularly certain in the case of Marshal Davout, who was undoubtedly the best of Napoleon's marshals, and had proved his exceptional ability in the Jena campaign when he had defeated the main Prussian army at Auerstädt while Napoleon was engaged at Jena. Davout was probably indispensable in his capacity as Minister of War, but he was sadly missed during the campaign.

Napoleon rapidly and secretly concentrated his army south of Charleroi preparatory to a drive toward Brussels. The Anglo-Dutch army occupied the area south and southwest of Brussels with the reserve at Brussels; its lines of communications stretched northwest to Ostend and north to Antwerp. The Prussian army was in the Charleroi-Liège area along the Sambre and the Meuse; its line of supplies stretched northeast through Liège and Cologne. Therefore when Napoleon struck he could hope that, when he drove between the two allied armies, they would retreat in diverging directions, each toward his own source of supplies. He could also hope that a sudden attack would catch his enemies unprepared. In this the emperor was not disappointed. The allied commanders had assumed that they would receive at least three days' warning of a French advance, which would give them sufficient time to concentrate.

There was a major highway running east and west between the forward areas occupied by the allied armies. It crossed the Charleroi-Brussels road at Quatre Bras, then crossed the Charleroi-Liège road at Sombreffe near a village named Ligny. Given sufficient time to prepare, the allies could seize these two points, only eight miles apart, and be connected by a major highway which they could use to mutually support each other. According to the map this was obviously the best place to await attack, but it would be dangerous to attempt to concentrate on a line so far forward, if there was not enough time for both allied armies to prepare their defenses. Yet this is exactly what Marshal Blücher attempted when he received warning of the French advance. Wellington, on the other hand, was worried about an attack by Napoleon upon his lines of communication. He expected a turning movement to the west, and concentrated his troops accordingly. Orders for assembly at Quatre Bras were issued only at the very last moment.

The French advance across the Sambre on June 15 did not proceed as rapidly as Napoleon had expected. The Prussian outposts resisted vigorously and both the right and left wings were slow to move. Yet by nightfall the French army was in excellent position, concentrated in a twelve-mile square, ready to launch a major attack against either the Anglo-Dutch army or the Prussians on the following day.

On June 16 two battles were fought eight miles apart along the east-west highway, one at Quatre Bras, the other at Ligny. Marshal Ney should have seized Quatre Bras when it was weakly held, but when Wellington arrived that morning he found everything quiet and rode over to Ligny to see Marshal Blücher. The general promised the field marshal that he would come to his aid, unless he himself were attacked. He fully expected to keep that promise, but when he returned he found his troops hotly engaged and maintaining their position with difficulty. With the help of reinforcements that reached the field in response to his hurried orders for concentration at this point, Wellington was able to hold his position. Wellington's losses were over 4,500 men killed, wounded, captured and missing; Ney's were somewhat less.

The major battle of the day had meanwhile begun at Ligny, where Napoleon personally took charge. Marshal Blücher's Prussian army, with only three of its four corps present on the battlefield, fought stubbornly but was driven from its position. The losses on both sides were very heavy. The French sustained about 10,000 casualties. The Prussian loss was much greater; their casualties numbered over 20,000, including prisoners and a large number who departed in the direction of Liège. Marshal Blücher himself was seriously injured, but fortunately for the allies he was able to resume command.

It is manifestly impossible in a work of this size to describe fully the Campaign and Battle of Waterloo when entire books have been written on the subject. Generations have argued and reargued every point and incident of these few days. Every possible error committed on either side has been magnified and discussed at length. Equal attention has been paid to the exploits of individual units and the leading characters in the drama. In a general description, however, certain points can be emphasized, and the main features of the campaign and battle can be described to advantage.

Napoleon had expected Marshal Ney on June 16 to seize Quatre Bras with comparative ease while it was held by only a small force. With this vital crossroads in French possession, the Prussians at Ligny could be attacked and overwhelmed by using all available forces. Ney's failure to do so had various repercussions. Blücher's army was defeated and driven from the field; but it was not routed or destroyed; it retreated in fairly good order. One French corps marching toward Quatre Bras was redirected to Ligny to take part in that battle; its orders were then countermanded; it turned back to Quatre Bras with the result that it spent its time in useless marching and was unable to take part in either battle. Therefore when the fighting ended on June 16, Napoleon had accomplished only part of what he had expected. The Prussians had been driven away but now another opportunity for positive action had developed. Wellington, instead of being forced backward, had held his position at Quatre Bras. Wellington could now, on the morning of June 17, be attacked at Quatre Bras while his Prussian ally was in full retreat. Both Napoleon and Ney were slow to act. The Duke of Wellington soon realized how dangerous it would be to remain in his present position, and began to retreat northward toward Waterloo. Ney simply let him march away. Napoleon sent Marshal Grouchy with 33,000 men to follow Blücher, then marched the remainder of his army to Quatre Bras, but too late to catch Wellington. The French pursued almost to Waterloo, where Napoleon prepared to attack the next morning, June 18. He felt sure that the Prussians would be unable to join the English in less than two or three days, which would give him ample time to destroy Wellington's army if the English general would only stand and fight.

Now we must turn back to follow Marshal Blücher after his defeat at Ligny. When his troops were driven from the field, where he had been personally severely injured, the seventy-two-year-old soldier was presented with two possible avenues of retreat. The most natural and certainly the safest course of action would be to retire toward his base at Liège. This was the route that Napoleon and Marshal Grouchy expected him to take. At this point the indomitable old field marshal knew that if Wellington retired along his line of communications their two lines of retreat would diverge and Napoleon would gain what he so greatly desired, the complete separation of the two allied armies. One of the two commanders would have to make the sacrifice; Marshal Blücher unhesitatingly chose to do so; he threw aside all other considerations and marched northward toward Wavre to be close to Wellington. If he had not made this decision, the Battle of Waterloo would never have been fought where it was. Wellington did not actually decide to defend the position he occupied until early in the morning of the day of the battle, when he received assurance from Blücher that a Prussian corps would start marching at daybreak and that other corps would follow.

When Wellington made his decision to stand at Waterloo, he could not have known how wholeheartedly his Prussian ally would support him. Not just one corps came to his aid. Before the battle was over, Blücher came himself with three corps, leaving the fourth to be overwhelmed by Marshal Grouchy at Wavre. "It is not at Wavre, but at Waterloo," said the field marshal, "that the campaign is to be decided." He risked the destruction of his last corps, and won the campaign accordingly.

It was in full reliance on Blücher's promise that the duke stood his ground and fought. Those who have ventured to criticize him for having been able to win only by the help of the Prussians overlook the fact that he won the battle by the very means on which he relied. The Prussians in fact constituted his general reserve; he would not have stayed to defend himself against Napoleon's attack without that general reserve. At the same time it is interesting to learn that the duke was still worried about his right flank. He left a large detachment of 17,000 men off to the west near Hal to watch for a turning movement in that direction. He thus stood at Waterloo with only 67,600 men and 156 guns, when many more could have been made available on the battlefield.

Napoleon came with 74,000 men and 246 guns which, after the losses at Ligny and Quatre Bras and the detachment of 33,000 under Grouchy to pursue the Prussians, was about all he could posibly have been expected to have brought to Waterloo. The infantry strength of the two armies was almost exactly equal; the French preponderance was in cavalry and artillery. Although the difference in numbers was slight, Napoleon fully expected to win the battle. As for Marshal Grouchy, the emperor never doubted that he was performing his mission of preventing the Prussians from joining Wellington. Here both Napoleon and Grouchy were at fault. Great recriminations passed afterward between the marshal and the emperor as to how this duty was performed. It may be sufficient to remark here that Grouchy was not sent in pursuit until late on the 17th and that Napoleon's orders to him were not clear. Grouchy also was very slow in moving. Furthermore, instead of placing his army between the Prussians and Wellington, he followed directly on his enemy's rear, thus converting his pursuit into a stern chase, following Blücher as the latter curved inward toward Wellington, thus failing in his mission. The action at Wavre late on the 18th, completed on the morning of the 19th, wherein Grouchy defeated the lone Prussian corps had no effect upon the action at Waterloo.

The battlefield can be pictured as a valley about two and a half miles long, generally not exceeding half a mile in width, running between two winding chains of low hills somewhat parallel with each other. The slope from each of these hills to the valley between is gentle but not uniform. The Anglo-Dutch army was posted on the northern, and the French army on the southern ridge. The village of Mont St. Jean is located a little behind the center of the northern chain of hills, and the village of La Belle Alliance is close behind the center of the southern ridge. The main road from Charleroi to Brussels runs through both these villages and bisects, therefore, both the English and the French positions. The line of this road was the line of Napoleon's intended advance on Brussels.

The strength of the British position did not consist merely in the occupation of a ridge of high ground. In front of the British right there stood an old-fashioned Flemish house called Hougoumont. With its farm buildings, surrounded by orchards and gardens, and enclosing walls it could easily be converted into a strong fortress. In front of the British center was a farmhouse called La Haye Sainte. Wellington prepared both of these as strong centers of resistance.

The night of the 17th was wet and stormy; and when dawn of the memorable 18th of June broke, the rain was still coming down. Between seven and eight o'clock the weather grew clearer, and each army was able to watch the position and arrangements of the other on the opposite side of the valley. Napoleon had planned to begin the battle at nine, but so much rain had fallen that it was difficult to move the guns through the mud; both artillery and cavalry needed a few hours of dry weather before they could maneuver rapidly and effectively. Since his preponderance of strength was in these two arms, and the mud favored troops on the defensive, Napoleon postponed action.

To meet the coming attack the Duke of Wellington drew up his infantry along the northern ridge, carefully placing each unit so that most were protected from hostile gunfire by the crest. A few had to be left exposed. In various places the lines were strengthened and supported by additional troops, particularly behind those units that were not so well trained as others, whose loyalty was questionable, or who had received heavy losses at Quatre Bras. The cavalry was stationed along the line in the rear, the largest bodies of horsemen being assembled near the center of the line.

At last, about eleven-thirty, Napoleon began his attack. His plan was to smash through the center of the English line; but first, as a diversion, he sent a division of Reille's corps to make an attack on Hougoumont to attract his enemy's attention to the right end of his line. The French assailed that post with fiery valor, which was met with the most determined bravery. In their eagerness to capture that stronghold the French committed additional units who won the copse around the house but did not succeed in entering. The men stationed there, reinforced by some British Guards, held the position the entire day against repeated attacks. This additional expenditure of French troops should not have been permitted; the diversion was allowed to develop into a full-fledged struggle, which cost the French more casualties than their opponents and diverted other units that should have been prepared to support the main attack on the center of the line. As a diversion to attract Wellington's attention to the right of his line it therefore failed completely, and actually had the opposite effect of drawing too many French troops away from the center of their own line.

The main attack of d'Erlon's corps was launched at one-thirty in the afternoon with its left along the main road aimed at La Haye

Sainte. Eighty guns had been brought forward to prepare the way. For over an hour they had been firing at the allies. The troops who were sheltered by the crest suffered comparatively little, but those in front sustained heavy casualties. When the attack came the defenders who had suffered the most from the artillery were easily routed. The French came confidently forward, but were checked by Picton's division of British infantry. Here neither side would give way; the struggle in which the brave Picton lost his life was bitter and prolonged. D'Erlon was supposed to have been supported on his left by Reille's corps and on his right by divisions of Lobau's corps, but was not. As the French began then to fall back, cavalry was loosed upon them. They retreated in disorder. The cavalry kept on to the artillery positions, but they in turn were driven back by the French cavalry.

The failure of part of Reille's corps to support d'Erlon has been explained; they had become too deeply involved in the attack on Hougoumont. The absence of Lobau's supporting divisions had been caused by the approach of Bülow's Prussian corps. Napoleon had been forced to send the bulk of Lobau's corps and two cavalry divisions to protect his right flank.

It was now about half past three o'clock. Marshal Ney, who had led the first charge against La Haye Sainte, now led another assault, which also failed. Although no part of the British position had been captured, Wellington's army had suffered severely from the unremitting cannonade, and Ney thought he detected signs of wavering. He decided to try a cavalry charge on the British west of the highway, but it was made without infantry support.

Shortly after four o'clock, squadron after squadron of the French cuirassiers accordingly ascended the slopes and rode forward with dauntless courage against the gun batteries. The artillerymen were driven from their guns; the cuirassiers cheered at their supposed triumph. But the duke had formed his infantry into squares, placed checkerwise. The cuirassiers charged in vain against the impenetrable hedges of bayonets, while the fire from the inner ranks of the squares told with terrible effect on the French squadrons. There are few troops of any nation who could have withstood such fierce, repeated cavalry attacks. Time after time the French rode gallantly forward with invariably the same result. As they receded from the attack the British artillerymen rushed forward from the centers of the squares

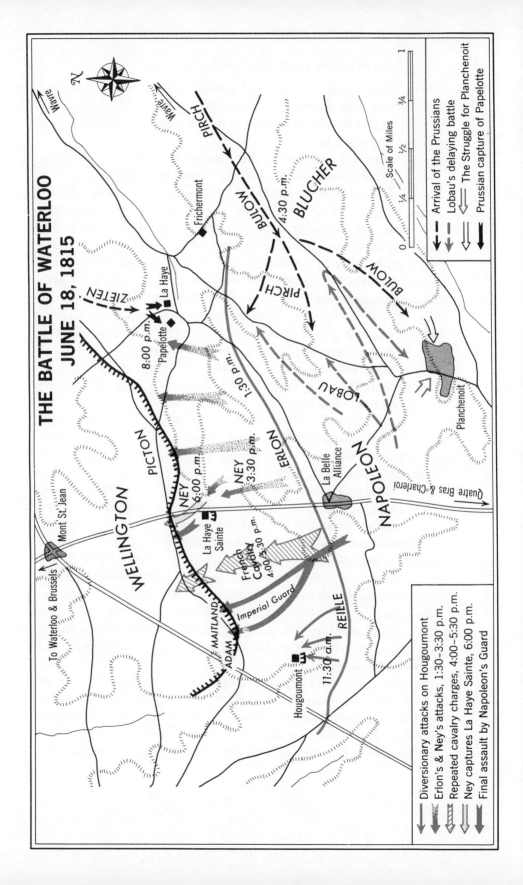

THE BATTLE OF WATERLOO
JUNE 18, 1815

N

Wavre

Wavre

PIRCH

BULOW

BLUCHER

4:30 p.m.

Frichermont

PIRCH

ZIETEN

La Haye

8:00 p.m.

Papelotte

LOBAU

BULOW

1:30 p.m.

PICTON

NEY
6:00 p.m.

NEY
3:30 p.m.

ERLON

WELLINGTON

Mont St. Jean

To Waterloo & Brussels

La Haye
Sainte

French
Cavalry
4:00–5:30 p.m.

NEY

Imperial Guard

MAITLAND

ADAM

La Belle
Alliance

NAPOLEON

Planchenoit

Quatre Bras & Charleroi

REILLE

Hougoumont

11:30 a.m.

Scale of Miles

0   1/4   1/2   3/4   1

- - ▶ Arrival of the Prussians
══▶ Lobau's delaying battle
⇨ The Struggle for Planchenoit
━▶ Prussian capture of Papelotte

↓ Diversionary attacks on Hougoumont
⇊ Erlon's & Ney's attacks, 1:30–3:30 p.m.
⇊ Repeated cavalry charges, 4:00–5:30 p.m.
⇊ Ney captures La Haye Sainte, 6:00 p.m.
⇊ Final assault by Napoleon's Guard

where they had taken refuge and poured gunfire upon the retiring horsemen. Nearly the whole of Napoleon's magnificent body of heavy cavalry was used in these brave but fruitless assaults on the British squares.

About 6:00 P.M. Ney led another assault. At Waterloo he had five horses shot under him, and his hat and clothes were riddled with bullets. In this charge he succeeded, with some of the men of d'Erlon's corps, in capturing La Haye Sainte and penetrating the enemy line. The means were now available for organizing another formidable attack on the British center. There was no time to be lost, but first Napoleon believed he should clear his right flank. Somewhat earlier in the afternoon Bülow's Prussians had managed to seize the village of Planchenoit. Napoleon had been obliged to send his Young Guard to retake that strongpoint, which they did with great gallantry. Then about the time Ney took La Haye Sainte the Prussians again captured Planchenoit. Napoleon now sent some battalions of the Old and Middle Guard into the battle; they took the village at the point of the bayonet. His right flank temporarily secure, Napoleon turned his attention to Wellington's army.

The really critical moment had actually passed. Right after Ney had captured La Haye Sainte was the time when Wellington's army had been in the greatest danger. Now there was actually small hope of driving through the British line.

The Iron Duke had taken advantage of the time consumed by Napoleon in retaking Planchenoit to reinforce his threatened center and to restore his line. With the Prussians now present on the field, the French were heavily outnumbered. Napoleon had the means of effecting a retreat; most of his Old Guard had taken no part in the action. Using it to cover his retirement, he could have withdrawn beyond the French frontier. If his Empire had not been at stake he undoubtedly would have done so, but he knew what the end result would surely be. A victory at Waterloo was his only alternative to utter ruin. He decided to use his Old Guard in one bold stroke to try to make that victory his own.

Between seven and eight o'clock eight battalions of the infantry of the Old and Middle Guard were formed into a huge column on the slope near La Belle Alliance. Ney was placed at their head. Napoleon himself rode forward to a spot by which his veterans were to pass. As they approached, he raised his arm and pointed to the position of the allies, as if to tell them that their path lay there. They answered with loud cries of "Vive l'Empereur!" and descended the hill from their own side into that "valley of the shadow of death" while their batteries thundered over their heads upon the allied line.

The march of the Guard was directed between Hougoumont and La Haye Sainte. As it advanced the column separated into two, of four battalions each, the Old Guard in front, the Middle Guard inclining slightly to the left, so that it appeared to present two columns advancing in echelon. At the same time the French infantry came forward from La Haye Sainte and commenced a fierce attack upon the center of the line just west of the highway. This part of the battle has drawn less attention than the celebrated attack of the Guard, but it formed a perilous crisis for the allied army. The French skirmishers who were posted in clouds in La Haye Sainte, and the sheltered spots near it, completely disabled the artillerymen of the English batteries near them. The French brought some fieldpieces up and began firing grape on the infantry of the allies at a distance of not more than two hundred paces. The allied infantry here consisted of some German brigades, who were formed in squares, as it was believed that there was cavalry behind La Haye Sainte, ready to charge if they did not remain in square formation. In this state the Germans stayed with heroic fortitude, though the grapeshot was tearing huge gaps in their ranks. The attack was so threatening and making such good progress that the duke himself had to gallop forward, leading reinforcements to reestablish order.

The partial success of this attack, accompanied by only the threat of cavalry being present, illustrates what might have occurred if cavalry had actually been used, as it should have been, to support the attack of the Guard. Throughout the day the French again and again failed to use infantry and cavalry together to aid each other. The great charge of the cavalry at four o'clock was unsupported by infantry; now the charge of the Guard was launched without even its own cavalry support. Yet, properly used together, French infantry and cavalry had achieved spectacular success on a hundred fields.

The British troops that the leading column of Napoleon's Guard assailed were Maitland's brigade of British Guards, with Adam's Light Brigade on their right. Maitland's men were lying down to avoid as much as possible the destructive effect of the French artillery. Meanwhile the British guns were not idle. Shot and shell plowed through the ranks of the stately veterans moving imposingly forward. Several of the French superior officers were at the head of the column. Ney's horse was shot under him, but he still led the way on foot, sword in hand. The front of the column, seventy men wide, was now on the crest of the ridge. To their surprise they saw no troops before them. The French advanced to within about fifty yards from where the British Guards were lying down. The Duke of Wellington himself is reputed to have given the order, "Up, Guards, and at 'em!" This story seems to be about on a par with other legends that inevitably arise after a famous battle, such as the French cavalry hurling themselves into a sunken lane and General Cambronne's ringing statement that, "The Old Guard dies; it does not surrender!"

The British started up, poured an instantaneous volley upon the head of the column, and charged with the bayonet. The élite corps of the French Army broke and fell back. Maitland's men pursued for only a short distance, then returned to take part in the repulse of the second column of the Imperial Guard. This column also advanced with great spirit and firmness under the cannonade. Passing by the eastern wall of Hougoumont, it diverged slightly to the right when it moved up the slope. As it advanced it was taken in flank by fire from regiments of Adam's brigade, encountered a steady cannonade from the British batteries, and was met by musketry fire from the British Guards. In such a position, all the bravery and skill of the French veterans were in vain. Although they deployed into line and offered a stout resistance, when additional regiments came into line against them and the British charged forward, they too broke and fell back. Seeing the Guard falling back caused the French at La Haye Sainte to waver. Simultaneously Marshal Blücher had brought a second Prussian corps onto the field. He sent it into the battle at Papelotte where the right of the French line curved toward the south. At this moment the Duke of Wellington seized the initiative and ordered a counterattack all along the line. The French army retired from the field in great confusion. Only a few battalions of the Guard and some soldiers in the village of Planchenoit stood fast and helped protect the flight of the remainder.

The battle was lost past all recovery. The British did not pursue beyond the heights which the enemy had occupied. When Wellington and Blücher met at La Belle Alliance, they agreed that the Prussians should continue the pursuit with their third corps, which had arrived on the field. Of the magnificent host which had that morning cheered their emperor in expectation of victory, only a portion were ever assembled again in arms. Their loss in killed and wounded has been computed to be about 25,000 plus some 8,000 prisoners, a total of 33,000 casualties.

The army under the Duke of Wellington lost over 15,000 men in killed and wounded on this day of battle at Waterloo. The loss of the Prussian army was nearly 7,000 men, which does not include the losses sustained at Wavre, where the remaining Prussian corps was defeated. At such a fearful price was the peace of Europe purchased.

Synopsis of Events Between the Battle of Waterloo, A.D. 1815, and the Vicksburg Campaign, A.D. 1863

1815. The allied powers sign a treaty in Paris, confirming most of the decisions already arrived at by the Congress of Vienna. Louis XVIII is restored to the throne. France is restricted to the approximate boundaries she had before the revolution and required to pay a large indemnity. Austria gains additional territory in northern Italy and along the eastern shore of the Adriatic Sea. The Kingdom of the Netherlands is established, comprising Holland and Belgium. Great Britain acquires Malta and other possessions, including important Dutch and French colonies. In Central Europe a Germanic Confederation is formed. The greater part of Poland becomes a subject kingdom of the Russian Empire, while Prussia gains additional land in central and western Germany.

1816–1825. During this period Mexico, Central America, and almost all the countries of South America achieve their independence from Spain and Portugal. The two most famous leaders in the Wars of Independence were Simón Bolívar and José de San Martín.

1819. Spain cedes Florida to the United States.

1820. (As the United States grew, new states were generally admitted into the Union in pairs, so that the balance of power between the North and the South was maintained.) By the Missouri Compromise of 1820 the division of slave and free states is extended across the Mississippi River. Missouri is to be admitted without restriction as to slavery, but slavery is to be forever prohibited in all the remaining portions of the Louisiana Purchase north of Missouri's southern boundary, 36° 30′ N. Lat.

1823. President James Monroe, in his message to Congress, proclaims the Monroe Doctrine.

1830. A French expeditionary force lands and takes Algiers, thus beginning the expansion of France into North Africa. Charles X's efforts to restore the monarchy to a more powerful position in France are abruptly ended by the July Revolution in Paris; Louis Philippe is proclaimed king.

1830–1831. The people of Belgium revolt and establish a kingdom separate from that of the Netherlands. (In 1839 the great powers recognized Belgium as an independent and perpetually neutral state. They further agreed to intervene if any party to the agreement violated that neutrality. This guarantee was the "scrap of paper" Germany chose to ignore in 1914.)

1832. Greece obtains recognition of its status as an independent kingdom.

1835–1836. Texas revolts against Mexico. General Santa Anna, with overwhelming numbers, captures the Alamo in March, 1836. He, in turn, is badly defeated at the Battle of San Jacinto in April by General Sam Houston. The independence of Texas is proclaimed.

1835–1837. (As a result of the Napoleonic Wars the British obtained possession of the Dutch colony at Capetown in South Africa.) To escape from British control the Dutch (Boer) settlers undertake their Great Trek northward.

1840. As a result of the Earl of Durham's report, Upper and Lower Canada are united into one government.

1845. The United States annexes Texas; the state is admitted to the Union.

1846. Despite the cries of ardent expansionists whose slogan was "Fifty-four Forty or Fight," the Oregon boundary dispute is settled by compromise at the 49th parallel.

1846–1848. In the Mexican War, General Zachary Taylor marches into Mexico, takes Monterey, and in February, 1847, defeats Santa Anna at Buena Vista. In March, General Winfield Scott begins the main campaign by landing on the Mexican coast and, after several American victories, enters Mexico City. (Meanwhile, Colonel Kearny had marched with a small force into California.) As a result of the war the United States receives large additional areas of land in the Southwest, later increased in 1854 by the Gadsden Purchase.

1848. Gold is discovered in California, beginning a rush of hopeful prospectors to the West.

1848–1852. A violent revolution in Paris sweeps Louis Philippe from the throne. Louis Napoleon Bonaparte is elected President of the French Republic. Four years later, after a successful *coup d'état*, he is proclaimed emperor as Napoleon III.

1848–1849. Fired with enthusiasm by the revolution in Paris, the Hungarians, led by Louis Kossuth, rise in revolt. They are overpowered by the Austrians aided by Russian troops.

1850. The five statutes commonly known as the Compromise of 1850 are passed by Congress, but are not effective in settling the growing differences between the North and the South.

1851. The discovery of gold in Australia brings a great tide of immigrants from all over the world to that continent.

1853–1854. Commodore Perry visits Japan and secures a treaty opening ports to Western trade.

1853–1856. Great Britain, France, and later Sardinia join Turkey in war against Russia. The allies invade the Crimea late in 1854 and undertake a siege of Sevastopol. The most famous battles that took place were at the Alma River; at Balaclava which Alfred Lord Tennyson immortalized in his poem "The Charge of the Light Brigade", and at Inkerman. Sevastopol, ably defended by the Russian general Todleben, was finally evacuated by the Russians after a siege lasting eleven months. Florence Nightingale was the heroine of the Crimean War, caring for the poorly attended sick and wounded of the British and their allies.

1854. The Kansas-Nebraska Act repeals the Missouri Compromise of 1820 and leaves the future of slavery in the territories to be decided by popular vote. The struggle that followed was characterized by violence and bloodshed.

1857. The decision of the Supreme Court in the Dred Scott case causes bitter criticism in the North.

1857–1858. The Great Sepoy or Indian Mutiny breaks out. As a result the East India Company is deprived of its governing powers, which are assumed by the British Crown.

1859. John Brown attempts to start a revolt among the slaves by seizing the United States Government arsenal at Harpers Ferry. He is tried, convicted, and hanged for treason.

1859–1861. (After the defeat of Napoleon in 1815, Austria acquired Lombardy and Venetia in northern Italy and undertook the task of

keeping all revolutionary movements in Italy suppressed. The King-
dom of Sardinia, which included Piedmont, became the hope of the
revolutionists who wished to unify Italy.) In the Austro-Sardinian
War, provoked by Count Cavour in an effort to expel Austria from
Italian soil, the Sardinians, aided by the French, win the Battles of
Magenta and Solferino and acquire a large part of northern Italy.
Then the adventurous daring of the patriot Garibaldi adds Sicily,
the Kingdom of Naples, and the greater part of central Italy to the
Sardinian Crown. Victor Emmanuel is proclaimed the first King of
Italy.

1860. Abraham Lincoln, the candidate of the Republican party, is
elected President of the United States. South Carolina secedes.

1861. Six other southern states follow South Carolina's lead. Jefferson
Davis is chosen President of the Confederate States of America. Fort
Sumter, in the harbor of Charleston, South Carolina is fired upon by
the Confederates. When called upon for volunteers to suppress the rebellion, four other states secede. Richmond, Virginia becomes the
capital of the Confederacy.

1861–1862. Wilhelm I becomes King of Prussia. He appoints Otto
von Bismarck minister-president and minister of foreign affairs.

1861–1863. France, Great Britain, and Spain undertake joint intervention in Mexico to force payment of foreign debts by that country.
Great Britain and Spain withdraw, when they realize that Napoleon
III is planning to take advantage of the fact that the United States
is engaged in a civil war, to establish an empire in America. A French
army occupies Mexico City in June, 1863.

16

The Vicksburg Campaign,
A.D. 1863

ONE HUNDRED years ago, for the only time in its history, the United States of America was engaged in a civil war. When people speak of the Great War today they are usually referring to World War I or World War II, yet the great war in American history was the Civil War, or War Between the States. Today, in a united country, it is sometimes difficult for us to realize the effect that this conflict had upon the people of the United States. A simple comparison should serve to impress us with the magnitude and complexity of this struggle. In 1860 the total population, both North and South, was about thirty-one and a half million. During World War II the nation numbered over 130,000,000 people. Yet the total cost in American lives in the Civil War was more than twice as great.

When the great American experiment in democracy was launched after the successful conclusion of the Revolution, the thirteen original states soon discovered that their Articles of Confederation were completely unsatisfactory. The prime ingredient lacking was a strong central government, but there was a great deal of disagreement as to what form this should take and how much power should be given to it. In fact, when the national convention was called, which eventually drafted the Constitution, most of its delegates arrived with the idea that they were simply meeting to amend the Articles of Confederation. They soon recognized, however, that the best way they could serve the people would be to prepare a written constitution providing for a national government.

The end product was naturally a compromise between the large and small states, between various sections of the country, and numerous other conflicting interests; so much of a compromise was it that it was very doubtful that a sufficient number of states would ever ratify it. Foreseeing the difficulties that lay ahead, the authors adopted the principle that the federal union would have certain powers given to it by the states, but specified that certain other powers would be retained by the states themselves. Where possible the Constitution was written in a general way so that it was subject to interpretation by later generations according to the conditions then prevailing. This has proved to be its saving grace, and it is a great tribute to the ability of the original authors that, although the Supreme Court has rendered many decisions interpreting the meaning of the Constitution, it has been amended only twenty-three times in a period of over 170 years.

Ten of these amendments came almost immediately. When the Constitution was submitted to the people of the individual states there was a great deal of criticism of the document because it did not contain a Bill of Rights. There was a widespread feeling that, in order to protect the rights of the people and of the states, it should contain a definite statement of fundamental rights. Therefore, when they ratified the Constitution, many northern and southern states recommended that a Bill of Rights be added. This was done by the First Congress and ratified by the states. It is indicative of the spirit of the times that these first ten amendments were designed to limit the power of the national government, not the power of the individual states. The necessity for a strong central government was recognized, but there was a definite fear that it could become so powerful that the rights of the people of the individual states would be trampled upon if that central government became too strong. The small states were worried about their large neighbors, and no section of the country wanted to be dominated by any other section.

To avoid either of these possibilities the framers of the Constitution created a Congress composed of a Senate and a House of Representatives. The Senate represented the states equally, while the House

represented the states according to their population. Thus in later
years when the arguments arose as to whether the Constitution was
established by all the people of the United States or by the people of
the several states, each side could point to the Constitution itself as
proof that they were correct. The stronger, more populous section of
the country could claim that it was a union of all the people of all the
states by referring to the House of Representatives. The section with
a fewer number of people but with an equal number of states proved
their argument by pointing to the Senate. In a way each was correct.
Certainly it is true that, in the beginning, the great majority of the
people of the thirteen original states felt a stronger allegiance to their
state than to the federal government.

In the beginning, also, the North and the South were approximately
equal in strength, but gradually the states in the northern part grew
stronger. They received the bulk of the foreign immigrants, and most
of the heavy industry became concentrated in the North, while the
South remained largely agricultural, with its economy based on the
slave system. One of the very first economic differences that arose
between the two sections was over the tariff, designed to protect the
growing industries of the North, to which the South, desiring free
trade, strongly objected. Then, as both North and South expanded
westward, new states were admitted into the Union, and equal representation in the Senate became extremely critical. Since each of the
new states allied itself with either the slave or the free states, it
became a contest between the two economic systems. With its faster-
growing population, the North became slowly and steadily more
powerful. The South could not hope to remain equal in the House of
Representatives; its only hope for economic survival lay in keeping
the number of northern and southern states balanced on equal terms
in the Senate.

In the years preceding the Civil War many compromises to admit
states by pairs were offered to try to maintain this equality. Concurrent with the discussions and arguments that grew apace as each
new compromise was proposed, an increasing number of people in
the North, feeling that slavery was morally wrong and must be
abolished, began to object to the admission of additional slave states
on moral grounds. Although many southerners realized that the slave
system must come to an end, the southern people resented the
"abolitionists" who were telling them how to run their affairs. They

felt that they were better able to solve their own problem in their own way. And, since the owning of slaves represented wealth, slavery was a very definite economic problem, which the "abolitionists" refused to consider pertinent. A deep hostility gradually developed between the two sections, until it often appeared as if two separate nations were battling each other in the halls of Congress and on the frontiers of the nation. With every passing year came new arguments, each more bitter, more violent than the last.

Under these circumstances the South began to talk about secession from the Union. Since the states had voluntarily entered the Union, they believed they had an equal right to secede. Their contention was that the powers granted to the central government were strictly limited and that, when the federal government began to dictate to the states, it was exceeding those powers. Furthermore, a citizen's allegiance must be first to his State, next to the Union.

Northern leaders asserted that the federal government must be supreme or the laws of Congress would be worthless. No state could, at any time it pleased, declare a federal law null and void. A central government whose laws could be ignored was no government at all. If the Union could be dissolved at will, the great American experiment in democracy would fail. Thus in 1861 the future of the country was at stake.

If the South had succeeded in its efforts to depart from the Union, the country would have been immediately split into two parts. Under the same principle and theory other sections could have broken away later, and the foreign powers of Europe would probably have been only too happy to intervene and aid them in their efforts to do so, in order to halt the growing strength of the United States. During the Civil War, Napoleon III, in violation of the Monroe Doctrine, took advantage of the involvement of the country in war to establish an empire in Mexico with French troops. With the country divided into two or more sections, other, probably more successful, efforts would have followed.

Although it may well be true, as many have contended, that eventually the South would have deemed it advisable to come back into the Union, this split into sections would have seriously retarded the development of the nation. The next half-century following the Civil War was the very period during which the United States began to emerge as a world power. A southern victory, even though it were to result in only a temporary division of the country, would certainly have delayed this important event and would have had an effect upon the history of the world as well as upon that of the United States.

World War I could have, and probably would have, ended somewhat differently. The mobilization of the United States after its entry into World War I was one of the most remarkable achievements of the world's military history. A regular army of slightly over 130,000 men had been increased by the end of that war to a force of over 3,500,000, and the initial elements had arrived in France in time to tip the scales in favor of the Allies. It is very doubtful if this magnificent achievement could have been accomplished by a country that had been for many years divided. The final German drives of 1918 might then have met with success, and a different sort of peace concluded. In like manner the Second World War, in whatever form it took, could have been won by the aggressors because they would have been fighting a far less powerful America. When we realize how close Germany and Japan came to winning that great conflict, we may well be thankful that the country had been united since 1865, had grown economically and politically to become the dominant industrial nation of the democracies. If the United States had not won its own Great War, it would not now be standing as strongly in its present position as the major bulwark of democracy opposed to the power of communism.

Today then, no matter how much we admire the heroic resistance the southern people opposed to the northern forces, and even though we accept the fact that their concept of states' rights more nearly agreed with the general feelings of those who were responsible for the creation of the Constitution, we must recognize that the correct decision was reached on the field of battle.

The Civil War began with the bombardment of Fort Sumter, South Carolina on April 12, 1861. The first large battle occurred at Manassas (Bull Run), Virginia in July, 1861, where the Union forces suffered a severe defeat. Immediately thereafter President Lincoln called Major General George B. McClellan to take command of the Union armies around Washington.

Major General Ulysses S. Grant began the major campaign in the West in February, 1862, by capturing Fort Henry and Fort Donelson in northern Tennessee. In April he fought the Battle of Shiloh, which ended in a Union victory. In this same month Union military and naval forces captured New Orleans, Louisiana.

Meanwhile General McClellan had been moving his Union Army of the Potomac by water from Washington to Fort Monroe, Virginia, which he used as a base for operations against Richmond. There, in June and July, he was defeated by the Confederate Army of Northern Virginia commanded by General Robert E. Lee. At the end of August, Lee won the Second Battle of Manassas and embarked on his first invasion of the North. This ended in September at the Battle of Antietam Creek in Maryland. A concurrent Confederate invasion of Kentucky also ended in failure.

The pendulum had swung twice this year. First, in April and May, when Grant had won the Battle of Shiloh and McClellan was knocking on the gates of Richmond, it had been in favor of the North. Then, in September, with the Confederates invading Maryland and Kentucky, the pendulum had swung back in favor of the South. Now it was again in the middle. It would seem as if neither side had gained anything by all its strenuous efforts. As the year drew to a close, the Union forces were severely defeated by Lee, this time at Fredericksburg, Virginia, and on the very last day of the year the Battle of Murfreesboro, Tennessee began.

As the eventful year of 1863 opened, several facts about the war had become clear. Both sides had confidently expected a quick and easy victory; both the North and the South now realized that this was going to be a long and bloody conflict. With a numerical superiority of twenty-two and a half million to nine million, the people of the North had assumed that they could win easily, especially since three and one half million of their enemy's population consisted of colored people, and the South would not employ colored troops. With odds of four to one against them, the South should be conquered easily, but the seizure and occupation of such a vast territory was presenting enormous problems. In actual fact the odds were only about three to one, because there was a very large peace party in the North that violently opposed the war, while the southern people were almost solidly in favor of the war.

On the other hand the people of the South had also received several very unpleasant surprises. They knew of the existence of the northern peace party and they had been initially led to believe that very few of the northern people would actually fight for the Union. The previous administration had been weak and vacillating; President Buchanan had done everything he could to evade the issue. After Lincoln became President and shooting had actually begun, they were shocked to discover how many northerners had responded quickly and eagerly to the call to arms. A great many southerners expected that the numerous defeats inflicted upon northern forces would quickly cool the ardor of their enemies. The South, after all, was asking only to be permitted to exist as a separate nation. They were not trying to conquer the North or to impose their will upon the northern people; surely, they argued, when the mass of the people of the North realized how difficult a task it would be to conquer the whole vast territory of the Confederacy on its own soil they would stop trying to beat the South into submission. Yet the northern people, in spite of numerous defeats, were continuing their prosecution of the war.

One other hope of the Confederacy was also rapidly fading. In the beginning she had expected early foreign recognition and intervention. This hope was primarily based on the expectation that a shortage of cotton would cause the shutdown of foreign cotton mills. The resultant hardship abroad, particularly in England, was expected to result in a demand by the people that their government recognize the Confederacy. In addition, southern agents had embarked on an extensive commercial campaign to purchase arms and other munitions of war abroad. It was known that the aristocratic and moneyed classes of England were favorably disposed toward the South; the British government was openly sympathetic, and France could be expected to follow its lead. With her armies winning great victories in the East, the Confederacy had expected that foreign intervention would soon occur. In fact, one of the main reasons for conducting the first invasion of the North had been to impress the European nations with the strength and power of the Confederacy.

Thus far, official northern policy had been that the war was being fought for the sole purpose of restoring the Union. Yet President Lincoln well knew that, if he could bring the suppression of slavery into the picture as a war aim, the working class of England, who were almost to a man against slavery, would never agree to recognition of the South. But the President needed a victory before he could issue such a proclamation; without a victory on the field of battle a statement of this nature would sound like a cry of despair asking for more aid. When the first invasion of the North came to an end at the Battle of Antietam, President Lincoln seized the opportunity presented by the Union victory to issue his preliminary announcement of the Emancipation Proclamation, to become effective on the 1st of January, 1863. Although it decreed the end of slavery only in those states that were in rebellion, and left slavery untouched in the loyal slave states, it was a powerful document that practically prohibited any foreign nation from intervening.

In the first two years of warfare neither side had gained any great strategic objective in the East. Indeed it was becoming quite clear that unless the Confederate Army of Northern Virginia was decisively defeated on the field of battle the war would not be decided in this theater. With General Robert E. Lee as its commander, it was very unlikely that such an event would occur. From the beginning it had been obvious that Virginia would be a major battleground. Washington, the Capital of the Union, was in a very vulnerable position; it was practically in the front lines. When Virginia seceded, the Confederacy had, for political reasons, moved its capital from Montgomery, Alabama to Richmond, thus voluntarily placing itself in the same unfortunate military position as had been forced upon the North— that of having its capital too close to the enemy. The straight-line distance between the two is less than one hundred miles. Thus for a period lasting as long as the war itself, this region automatically became a major theater of operations, with the South winning most of the major battles. However, the Confederate army was never strong enough to make a serious effort to reduce the extensive fortifications with which Washington was surrounded, or to accomplish its primary objective, the destruction of the larger Union army on the field of battle.

It was in the West that the war was to be decided. Here there were two main axes of advance into southern territory, by way of the Cumberland and Tennessee Rivers to Chattanooga, and along the line of the Mississippi. By early January, 1863, the northern forces had made some progress along both these axes. After the Battle of Murfreesboro, which ended on January 2, the Confederates had retreated southward; the Union army had then occupied the city. But it was in the all-important Mississippi Valley that the Union would make its most rapid advances; victory in this decisive region would split the Confederacy into two parts and turn the tide of the war

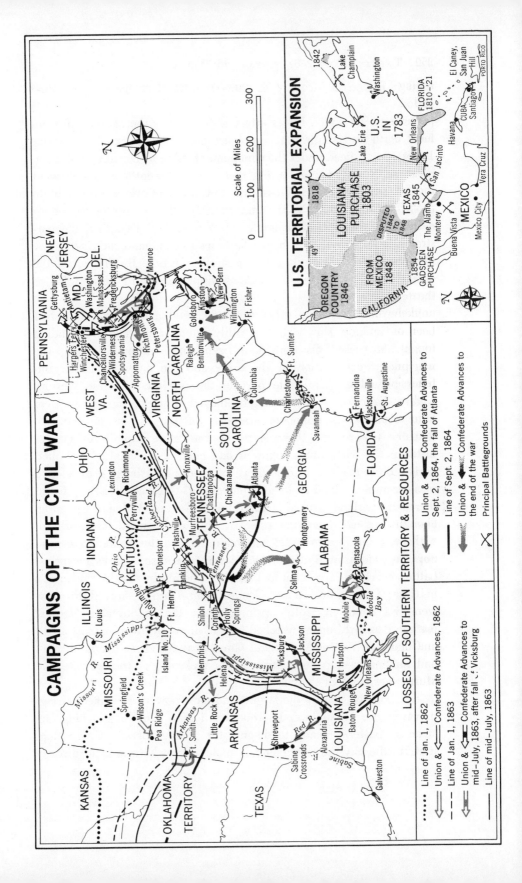

CAMPAIGNS OF THE CIVIL WAR

U.S. TERRITORIAL EXPANSION

U.S. IN 1783
LOUISIANA PURCHASE 1803
OREGON COUNTRY 1846
FROM MEXICO 1848
CALIFORNIA 1848
GADSDEN PURCHASE 1854
TEXAS 1845
DISPUTED 1845 TO 1846
FLORIDA 1810-21
MEXICO

Lake Champlain 1842
Washington
Lake Erie
New Orleans
El Caney, San Juan Hill
CUBA
Santiago
PORTO RICO
Havana
San Jacinto
The Alamo
Monterey
Buena Vista
Mexico City
Vera Cruz

Scale of Miles
0   100   200   300

KANSAS
MISSOURI
St. Louis
Springfield
Wilson's Creek
Pea Ridge
OKLAHOMA TERRITORY
Ft. Smith
TEXAS
Galveston
Sabine Crossroads
Shreveport
Alexandria
ARKANSAS
Little Rock
Helena
LOUISIANA
Baton Rouge
New Orleans
Port Hudson
MISSISSIPPI
Vicksburg
Jackson
Memphis
Island No. 10
Columbus
Corinth
Holly Springs
Shiloh
Mobile
Mobile Bay
Pensacola
ALABAMA
Montgomery
Selma
Franklin
Nashville
Ft. Henry
Ft. Donelson
KENTUCKY
TENNESSEE
Murfreesboro
Chattanooga
Chickamauga
Knoxville
Atlanta
GEORGIA
Savannah
Columbia
Charleston
Ft. Sumter
Fernandina
Jacksonville
St. Augustine
FLORIDA
SOUTH CAROLINA
Raleigh
Goldsboro
Bentonville
Kinston
New Bern
Ft. Fisher
Wilmington
NORTH CAROLINA
VIRGINIA
Richmond
Petersburg
Appomattox
Spotsylvania
Wilderness
Chancellorsville
Fredericksburg
Monroe
WEST VA.
Lexington
Richmond
Perryville
Winchester
Harper's Ferry
Antietam
Gettysburg
PENNSYLVANIA
MD.
Washington
DEL.
NEW JERSEY
OHIO
INDIANA
ILLINOIS

Missouri R.
Mississippi R.
Arkansas R.
Red R.
Sabine R.
Ohio R.
Cumberland R.
Tennessee R.

LOSSES OF SOUTHERN TERRITORY & RESOURCES

.... Line of Jan. 1, 1862

Union & Confederate Advances, 1862

- - - Line of Jan. 1, 1863

Union & Confederate Advances to mid-July, 1863, after fall of Vicksburg

Line of mid-July, 1863

Union & Confederate Advances to Sept. 2, 1864, the fall of Atlanta

Line of Sept. 2, 1864

Union & Confederate Advances to the end of the war

X Principal Battlegrounds

until it flowed as strongly as that majestic river itself to eventual victory.

During 1862 Union forces attacked the line of the Mississippi from both north and south. Late in April the navy struck at the lower Mississippi. A fleet, under the command of Admiral David G. Farragut, captured New Orleans. During the next two months he twice went up the river as far as Vicksburg, but these efforts served only to alert the Confederates to the importance of the defense of Vicksburg and the Mississippi. They immediately began to strengthen the garrison and provide it with heavy batteries to command the river. They also converted Port Hudson into a strong position. By the end of the year the Union controlled the Mississippi northward only as far as Baton Rouge.

Meanwhile, from the other direction, land and naval forces had been advancing slowly but steadily southward. The outstanding feature of these operations had been, and continued to be, the magnificent cooperation of the army and the navy. Ironclad gunboats played an invaluable part in the warfare on these western waters. Here the United States enjoyed a great superiority over their Confederate opponents because of the ability of northern industry to produce these ships of war more rapidly in greater numbers. By early June, Memphis had been occupied. In November, Union forces made their first effort to capture Vicksburg. It developed into a combined land-and-water movement. General Ulysses S. Grant marched overland while his subordinate General William Tecumseh Sherman moved down the river by ship and landed just north of Vicksburg. On December 29, Sherman attacked the Confederate positions on Chickasaw Bluffs but was severely repulsed. In the meantime Grant's overland expedition had also been halted by cavalry raids upon his line of communications. General Van Dorn destroyed his new advanced depot at Holly Springs, while the redoubtable General Nathan Bedford Forrest wrecked his rail lines northward almost as far as Columbus, Kentucky. General Grant abandoned his overland route and, moving by ship, concentrated near Vicksburg on the opposite side of the river north of the city.

Vicksburg was easily the largest and most powerful fortified strongpoint on the Mississippi. It stood on a high bluff overlooking the river, its batteries ready to dispute the passage of any Union ship. Right at the city the river channel made a great hairpin bend directly under the menacing guns of the defenders; there was no other way for ships to pass. During the American Revolution, Fort Ticonderoga was mistakenly referred to as the Gibraltar of the Lake Champlain–Hudson River region; Vicksburg was truly the Gibraltar of the Mississippi River.

Furthermore, the city was extremely difficult for an army to approach either from the north or from the west. The line of hills on which the fortifications stood comes up from the south, then, at Vicksburg, turns abruptly northeast, following the line of the Yazoo River. Between these hills and the Mississippi is a vast bottomland known as the Yazoo Delta, stretching northward for 175 miles. It is sixty miles wide in places, and covers an area of several thousand square miles. Most of this land is very soft and very low. If it were not for the levees along the Mississippi, it would be underwater a great part of the year. Crisscrossed with small streams, large bayous, and rivers, it presented an almost impassable obstacle to a large army with heavy guns and wagons. On the west side of the river opposite Vicksburg, the bottomland, though not so wide as the Yazoo Delta, extends for many miles north and south of the city.

Thus the problem confronting an army trying to capture Vicksburg was how to reach the high ground to the east or south of the city. The approach from either direction presented immense difficulties. The first involved a long overland march, swinging wide to the east, or a crossing of the Yazoo Delta. The alternative meant finding a way through the bottomland on the opposite bank, then crossing the Mississippi below Vicksburg to the eastern shore. Supply would be difficult along either route. General Grant's first effort to capture Vicksburg by a combined land-and-water movement in November and December of 1862 had been halted by the destruction of his supply depot at Holly Springs and the wrecking of his line of supply by Confederate cavalry. Supply across the Yazoo Delta would be extremely hazardous, and it might be impossible by the alternative method of following troops marching along the western shore, because the supply ships would have to run down past the Vicksburg batteries to reach the troops operating below the city. During the next four months the northern forces based on the west side of the river opposite but north of the city made four more unsuccessful attempts to reach Vicksburg before the fifth finally succeeded.

Before describing the various efforts of the Union forces to reach their objective, it would help to set the scene by outlining briefly the conditions under which the army was forced to operate. It was wintertime; and even in Mississippi this meant chilly, rainy weather, particularly in that low swampy country where it was almost impossible to find dry land. Everything—clothing, tents, bedding—was wet and stayed wet. Smallpox and malarial fever broke out, yet the work went on, and a great deal of it was just plain hard labor. This phase of the campaign was primarily an engineer's war of digging and construction rather than of combat.

This phase was not only an engineer's war; it was also a naval war. Every plan of approach to Vicksburg entailed movement over water, whether it was through a canal, by river, or through a bayou. In this campaign General Grant was particularly fortunate in having assigned to work with him an extremely capable and energetic naval officer, Admiral David D. Porter. In fact, the army's efforts to reach the Confederate stronghold of Vicksburg would have been absolutely impossible without the help of the navy.

The four unsuccessful efforts can be resolved into two attempts to bypass Vicksburg toward the south and two attempts to cross the Yazoo Delta to the north. At times, work on all four projects was carried on simultaneously. The first of these was the digging of a canal across the narrow neck of land enclosed by the hairpin bend in the river opposite the city. General Grant himself did not have much faith in this solution, but he knew the President was anxious that the effort be made. Therefore the work was pushed with vigor and determination, despite floods and other discouraging difficulties. Much of the digging was done by hand, although dredges were also used. When the levee at the north end of the canal broke, the water poured in and drowned the whole Vicksburg Neck; yet the dreary work went on until eventually Confederate artillery across the river, below the city, forced abandonment of the entire scheme.

The other attempt to bypass Vicksburg, known as the Lake Providence Route, was purely a construction project, and no Confederate opposition was ever encountered. The plan, in this instance, was to cut a canal westward from the Mississippi River into Lake Providence, then to pass through an intricate, winding labyrinth of bayous and rivers for a distance of two hundred miles—south to the Red River. Counting the return passage up the Mississippi, this would have meant a detour of nearly four hundred miles to reach Vicksburg

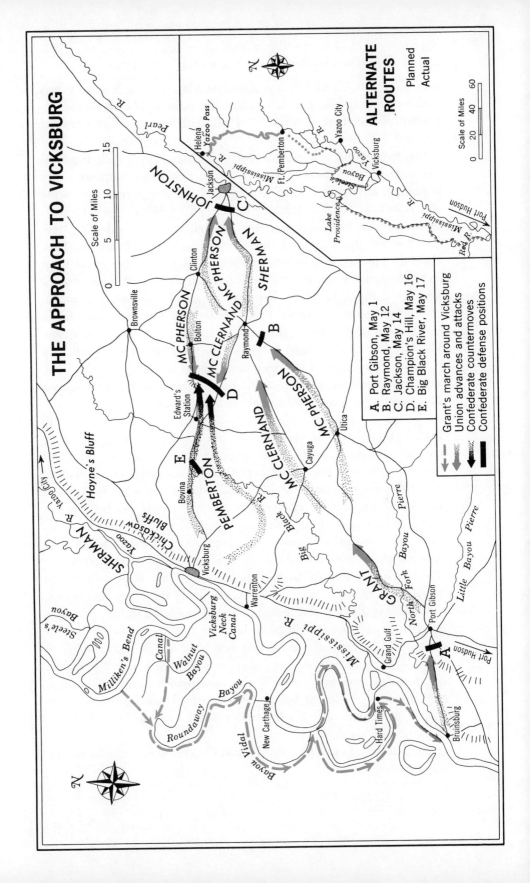

THE APPROACH TO VICKSBURG

Scale of Miles
0 5 10 15

ALTERNATE ROUTES
Planned
Actual

Scale of Miles
0 20 40 60

A. Port Gibson, May 1
B. Raymond, May 12
C. Jackson, May 14
D. Champion's Hill, May 16
E. Big Black River, May 17

Grant's march around Vicksburg
Union advances and attacks
Confederate countermoves
Confederate defense positions

from the south. This effort was abandoned late in March when it was found that a special type of underwater saw would be needed to remove obstructions. A great deal of hard work was also poured into this failure.

The two efforts to cross the delta provide a great deal more interest. The first of these, called the Yazoo Pass Route, appeared very promising, although it also was long and winding, stretching all the way from near Helena, Arkansas to Yazoo City, Mississippi. The Confederates, who had expected some such effort to be made, cut trees to fall across the water and clog the way for the gunboats and ironclads. It took nearly a month of strenuous labor for the naval ships and transports to thread their way through this treacherous swampland across the delta. There they were stopped by a newly constructed cotton-bale battery named Fort Pemberton, for the Confederate commander at Vicksburg, Lieutenant General John C. Pemberton. The fort was cleverly sited at a bend in the channel surrounded by bayous and swamps. The Union army could not move on the land, and the channel was so narrow that the gunboats could not maneuver. This expedition was forced to halt and turn back.

The story of the Steele's Bayou Route is the most intriguing of all. It was attempted as a diversion to help the forces struggling along the Yazoo Pass Route. Admiral Porter himself commanded the naval force of ironclads, boats, and tugs that led the way; General Sherman followed with parts of his corps. Almost immediately Admiral Porter ran into serious trouble. The passage, which had been represented to him as comparatively simple, was blocked by trees, some as large as three feet in diameter; no large ship had ever attempted to navigate these streams. With his ironclads Porter knocked down the trees, pulled others up by the roots, heaved his ships around the bends in a channel only slightly wider than the ships themselves, tore his way through bridges, but found himself making only four miles a day. Then the flagship became stuck in a dense bed of willows. It required the combined efforts of all the other ships to pull it out stern foremost. The Confederates closed in on all sides and began to fell trees in the rear of the ships, which could not possibly turn around but had to bump their way backward, surrounded by swarms of Confederate sharpshooters who kept anyone from daring to show himself on deck.

Admiral Porter's call for help reached General Sherman, who hastily dispatched all the troops he had at hand. Then, alone in a canoe, Sherman paddled through the black swampland to reach more Union soldiers and lead them forward through the dense canebrake by candlelight. He arrived just in time to save the Union fleet from capture by the Confederate army. It took four more days to disentangle the fleet. During the first three the ships were still backing out, looking for a place to turn around.

Every attempt to reach Vicksburg had failed. The northern press, forgetting Grant's many past victories and completely oblivious to the problems facing him, began to call for his removal. But in spite of the unfavorable criticism and the clamor, General Grant steadfastly refused to divulge his plans. To his eternal credit, President Lincoln stood behind his army commander, letting him work out his own problem in his own way.

At this moment Major General Ulysses S. Grant was certainly at the crossroads of his career. All those qualities for which he has been so long remembered: persistence, calm determination, quiet resolution, had availed him nothing. The memory of his later campaign in the East and the final, long Siege of Petersburg tend to make us think of those qualities alone and forget the daring and unorthodox way in which he finally solved the tremendous problem confronting him. Nor should we overlook the lightning campaign when in just eighteen days the Confederates were defeated in five separate battles, then bottled up in their fortifications around Vicksburg. These operations establish beyond any doubt Grant's place in history as an outstandingly skillful general and leader.

His final plan was hazardous both for his own army and for the naval force accompanying him. It was to move down the west bank of the Mississippi and, with the help of the fleet, cross the river below Vicksburg. Most of his supplies would have to be provided by the fleet, which would mean their undertaking the dangerous passage of the guns of the Vicksburg batteries. Only two corps were to be employed in this movement, those of Major General McClernand and Major General McPherson. The other corps, commanded by Sherman, was to be left temporarily near Vicksburg to demonstrate against the city and confuse the Confederates as to Grant's intentions. This second part of the plan was essential to Grant's scheme. He could not possibly expect to march his entire army at one time through the treacherous bottomland west of the river and arrive on the eastern shore in one concentrated force.

Therefore, since he must divide his army, he hoped to make his enemy do the same; Sherman must make a very convincing demonstration at the proper time at Vicksburg. Another essential part of the plan to confuse the Confederate leaders was to send simultaneously a force of cavalry down through Mississippi. Grant's army around Vicksburg numbered about 50,000 men, and he believed that at first he would be outnumbered if his diversions were not successful and if the enemy concentrated against him before he could get his first two corps in strength across the river.

As soon as General Grant divulged his plan to Admiral Porter, that officer enthusiastically agreed to do his part; but no one else liked the plan; even his trusted subordinate General Sherman argued that it was far too great a gamble. The movement began late in March. Using small boats and constructing roads that promptly turned into seas of mud as they advanced, the Union forces struggled through the bottomland opposite Vicksburg. On the night of April 16–17, 1863, occurred one of the truly dramatic events of the war, the passage of the first part of the Union fleet past the Vicksburg batteries. Admiral Porter made his preparations with great care; the sides of the transports were piled high with cotton, hay, and grain, and even the ironclads were strengthened with logs. But the Confederates were on the alert for such an attempt. As the ships drifted down with the current, the defenders of Vicksburg lit huge barrels of tar and set fire to buildings on the opposite shore to light the scene so their gunners could see their targets. For two and a half hours the vessels were subjected to intense shelling, but only one transport was sunk. Six nights later the remainder of the fleet successfully ran the batteries. Admiral Porter was now safely below the city and ready to assist Grant's army across the river.

On the 17th, also, Colonel Grierson began his cavalry raid from the Tennessee border southward through Mississippi. Because almost all the Confederate cavalry had been previously ordered away on other missions, the Confederates had no way of keeping in contact with him. Exaggerated reports of the size of his command caused the defenders to divert large infantry detachments to try to cut him off. With only one thousand horsemen Grierson cut through the entire state of Mississippi and joined the Union troops at Baton Rouge, Louisiana. The raid caused the greatest alarm and excitement, out of all proportion to the size of the force involved, diverting attention away from Grant's command at a most critical time, just when he was making preparations to cross the river. For that reason alone, this raid was one of the most successful cavalry operations of modern times.

On April 29, Sherman began vigorous demonstrations north of Vicksburg, and Porter bombarded Grand Gulf, but found the opposition too strong to land at that point. The following day the troops began to land downstream. By noon McClernand's corps and two brigades of McPherson's, a force of about 20,000 men, were ashore. General Grant says in his *Memoirs:* "When this was effected I felt a degree of relief scarcely ever equalled since. Vicksburg was not yet taken it is true, nor were its defenders demoralized by any of our previous moves. I was now in the enemy's country, with a vast river and the stronghold of Vicksburg between me and my base of supplies. But I was on dry ground on the same side of the river with the enemy. All the campaigns, labors, hardships and exposures from the month of December previous to this time that had been made and endured, were for the accomplishment of this one object."

Few men would have felt quite the sense of relief that Grant describes. It is true that his landing had been unopposed, and the remainder of McPherson's corps soon crossed, but Sherman's corps could not reach the scene for over a week. Furthermore, Grant believed that the enemy confronting him numbered about 60,000 men. It is very difficult to determine how many troops General Pemberton actually had in that region. They were not so numerous as Grant supposed; not counting the troops at Port Hudson guarding against an advance up the river from Baton Rouge, the Confederates seem to have had about 32,000 men in the region. There should have been more, and the greater part should have been immediately available to resist an advance inland.

General John C. Pemberton had been left to guard Vicksburg with an adequate number of infantry and artillery but with practically no cavalry; almost all of the latter had been set away to East Tennessee. Then, shortly before Grierson's raid, he had been ordered to send additional reinforcements to East Tennessee, if they could be spared. He had agreed and sent three infantry brigades. Then Grierson's operations had caused him to further spread his infantry over the state. Nevertheless he should have assembled as many troops as possible on his side of the river to counter a landing as soon as possible, wherever it might occur. When, on May 1, Grant's forces moved to Port Gibson, they were able easily to defeat the few Confederates assembled there. Grant then pushed forward to seize the ground to the east and there await the arrival of Sherman's corps, which reached the scene a week later.

These first days of May, 1863, were memorable in the annals of the Confederacy. It was then that Lee and Jackson won their greatest victory, defeating General Hooker at the Battle of Chancellorsville. For this victory, however, the South paid dearly with the loss of their beloved leader General Stonewall Jackson. These events received a great deal more attention at the time than the doings of General Grant and General Pemberton in the Mississippi, but it was at Vicksburg that the future of the Confederacy was at stake.

On May 2, Grant received word that General Banks, who was supposed to cooperate with him in an advance from Baton Rouge northward upon Port Hudson, would be delayed and that his strength would be much smaller than Grant had been led to believe. At this point Grant, who had promised the War Department that he would help Banks, made a momentous decision. To wait meant the loss of days, possibly weeks, while his enemy brought reinforcements to the scene, probably more than Banks could bring. Grant must retain the initiative. Unhesitatingly he reached his decision: to abandon his line of communications and, taking with him only supplies that could be carried, primarily ammunition, advance into enemy territory. If defeated, without any base to fall back upon, his army could be destroyed. He did not consult the War Department; he was certain they would not approve and would prohibit him from marching. He simply notified them of his action; by the time they could reply he would be on his way.

His opponent, General Pemberton, was also in an awkward position, but for entirely different reasons. His problem was due to conflicting orders from two commanders. On the one hand the senior general in the West, Joseph E. Johnston, was hurrying to his assistance with the few troops he could summon, and urging him to unite his army, abandon Vicksburg if necessary, and join forces. On the other hand President Jefferson Davis was telling him to hold Vicksburg and Port Hudson at all costs. Poor Pemberton was caught in the middle, and at the same time he had a personal problem of his own that severely restricted his freedom of action. He was a northerner from Pennsylvania who had come to fight for the South. If he followed Johnston's advice, which he knew to be wiser than that of Davis, and lost Vicksburg, even though he saved the army, his actions and motives would be severely criticized. In the end he tried to compromise. He sent some troops to meet Grant, but left two divisions idle at Vicksburg. Neither he nor President Davis believed that Grant could remain for long away from his base of supplies, although Union troops might attempt a raid to the east on the city of Jackson, the capital of Mississippi. Therefore when some reinforcements intended for his army reached Jackson, he left them to guard that area. In effect, he strung his forces out on a line all the way from Vicksburg to Jackson, far too large an area for his inferior numbers to hold.

Instead of moving north as General Pemberton expected him to do, General Grant turned northeast, depending entirely upon the country to provide his supplies. His object was to place his army between Jackson and Vicksburg. By so doing, he could cut the Confederate supply line into Vicksburg, stop reinforcements from reaching the city, and also stand squarely across Pemberton's probable line of retreat.

On May 12, the Union forces defeated a Confederate brigade at Raymond. The next day Joseph E. Johnston arrived at Jackson to take command, and found only two Confederate brigades present on the field. These were defeated the following day. General Grant then promptly turned toward Vicksburg. On May 16, he won a hard-fought fight at Champion's Hill, the decisive engagement of the campaign. The following day the Union army forced a crossing of the Big Black River. By evening of May 18 it reached the outskirts of Vicksburg.

The remainder of the story, though long and drawn out, can be briefly told. The gallant defenders repulsed two general assaults, then both sides settled down to a long, grim siege that lasted for over six weeks. There was no hope at all of relief. Grant's army was increased until it reached a strength of 70,000 men, while Johnston could never collect a sufficiently large number of troops to attack Grant's greatly reinforced army. The Confederates fought on bravely as ammunition ran low and food became practically nonexistent; the civilian inhabitants hid in caves dug into the hills. Finally, on the Fourth of July, Vicksburg capitulated. Concurrently Lee's second invasion of the North, which had been undertaken for various reasons, not the least of which had been the hope that it might relieve the pressure on Vicksburg, ended on July 1–3 at the Battle of Gettysburg. Port Hudson fell five days after Vicksburg.

The winning of the Mississippi meant the cutting of the Confederacy in two. The South could no longer draw men and supplies from the region west of the river. In the past she had won glorious victories against superior numbers. Now, with fewer men and the loss of a productive region, she was facing an enemy who was growing ever stronger. For since the South had failed to achieve victory in the early stages of the war, northern industry had been given the time needed to swing into war production. From now on the North would have more and better ships, and her armies would be supplied with better weapons and other munitions of war, whereas the South would suffer slow strangulation from the loss of the western region and the ever-tightening naval blockade. The South would yet win victories, but they would be dearly bought with men who could no longer be replaced.

In March, 1864, General Grant was assigned to command all the armies of the United States; then, for the first time since the beginning of the war, a concerted plan of action was evolved for all the Union forces. As the northern armies marched forward that year, the only hope of the southern soldier and sailor fighting for the lost cause was that the North might decide that the war was too costly and should be stopped. So long as there was any hope at all, the southern armies refused to admit defeat. When President Lincoln was reelected at the polls in November, 1864, that last hope was removed. The end finally came on Palm Sunday, 1865, at Appomattox.

Synopsis of Events Between the Vicksburg Campaign, A.D. 1863, and the Battle of Sadowa, A.D. 1866

1864. In an effort to settle the highly complicated Schleswig-Holstein question, Austria joins Prussia in an alliance against Denmark. In the ensuing war Denmark is easily defeated and surrenders the two duchies to the joint control of Austria and Prussia. (The disputes that then arose resulted in the Seven Weeks' War in 1866 between Prussia and Austria.)

1864–1866. With the support of French troops sent by Napoleon III, Archduke Maximilian of Austria is proclaimed Emperor of Mexico. At the close of the American Civil War, U.S. troops are dispatched toward the Mexican border; the United States demands withdrawal of the French.

1866. Bismarck concludes an alliance with Italy against Austria. The Seven Weeks' War begins.

17

The Battle of Sadowa,
A.D. 1866

The war of 1866 between Prussia and Austria was a necessity of the history of the world; it must have sooner or later broken out. The German nation could not forever exist in the political weakness into which it had sunk between the Latin West and the Slavic East.

THUS BEGINS the official history of *The Campaign of 1866 in Germany*, prepared by the military historians of the Prussian Staff. It sounds like Field Marshal Helmuth von Moltke; if he did not actually write it, he certainly approved it. These two sentences accurately represent the thought of the political and military leaders who consolidated the various kingdoms, free cities, and principalities of Germany into one united nation. Although the greater mass of the German people objected to some of the "blood and iron" methods employed in accomplishing this union, they were in full agreement with the necessity for ending the political weakness into which Germany had sunk. Every other state in western Europe with the exception of Italy, which was making great strides in that direction, had been able to form a national government.

To begin an account of the founding of the German nation with the French Revolution may seem strange at first, but one of the principal ideas or forces let loose upon Europe by that great unheaval in France was the spirit of nationalism. Furthermore, during the course of his brilliant career, Napoleon had in 1806 dissolved the old Holy Roman Empire, which had been in existence since A.D. 962. Originally the empire had consisted essentially of Germany and Italy, but when Rudolf of Hapsburg became emperor in 1273 he had been less interested in the empire than in the building of his family's fortune. He therefore renounced Italy and acquired Austria as a part of his personal domain. Beginning with the election of Albert in 1438, the imperial crown had become practically a hereditary possession of the House of Hapsburg.

In its place Napoleon had founded the Confederation of the Rhine under French auspices. In doing so, he ultimately reduced the more than three hundred states involved to about forty states. This was a great administrative accomplishment, but Napoleon began more than he knew. For at the Congress of Vienna and at the Treaty of Paris following his final defeat, the idea of a German league was preserved. The prime mover in this enterprise was Prince Metternich, the chancellor of Austria, whose main purposes were to make Austria supreme in Germany and to suppress the spirit of liberty aroused by the French Revolution. He believed that Austrian interests would best be served by continuing the existence of this loose confederation of German states, with Austria as President of the league. The Federal Diet composed of representatives of the several states was given no power; Austria was the dominant figure in his new Germanic Confederation of thirty-nine states.

By this time, however, the Hohenzollern dynasty of Prussia had risen to prominence. The family had come into possession of Brandenburg in 1415. Frederick William, the Great Elector, had increased his dominions as a result of the Thirty Years' War, and in 1660 obtained recognition of his sovereignty over East Prussia; his son assumed the title of king in 1701. Then, under Frederick the Great, Prussia had become a strong power, acquired Silesia, and shared in the first partition of Poland. The second and third partitions were followed by disastrous defeat at the hands of Napoleon in 1806; then his downfall had given Prussia additional lands in central and western Germany.

Thus, although Austria was the dominant figure in the Confederation, there was a second figure that might challenge that supremacy. The authors of the Constitution of the United States who found their Articles of Confederation unworkable for thirteen states would certainly have sympathized with the people of Germany divided into thirty-five heterogeneous states and four free cities, with the two most powerful countries extremely jealous of each other. Furthermore, each of these countries owned additional territory outside the boundaries of the Confederation. In this respect, however, Prussia had the advantage in her dealings with the other members of the league, for Prussia's population was essentially Germanic in character, whereas Austria's was not. Over half of that country's territory was outside the Confederation, and contained millions of non-Germans.

At first Prussia yielded precedence to Austria, but in the meantime she took certain steps to straighten out her complex administrative and financial structure, which in the long run led to great political changes within Germany. The Prussian territory, which was primarily within the boundaries of the Confederation, but partially outside it, was separated into two distinct pieces with an amazing frontier bordering over twenty states and surrounding others. Prussia reformed and greatly simplified her numerous customs laws and tariffs, removing or lowering the duties on many classes of goods. The advantages to be derived from free trade in such an organization as the Germanic Confederation were so apparent that within a comparatively short space of time almost all the states, with the significant exception of Austria, were united in a Customs Union, or *Zollverein*. Many people came to regard this as the first step toward nationalization and, since Prussia had begun the enterprise, they looked upon her as their natural leader.

Then in 1848 came the news of the revolution in Paris that swept away the reactionary kingdom of Louis Philippe. In France it resulted in the election of Louis Napoleon Bonaparte as President of the French Republic; four years later he was proclaimed Emperor Napoleon III. In Germany the reaction was twofold. The Liberals arose, demanded constitutional government, and wrung concessions from their rulers. Then, seeking to establish a unified nation, and turning to Prussia as their natural leader, they drew up a constitution and elected Frederick William IV of Prussia as emperor. The king, who was fundamentally a reactionary himself, refused to accept because the crown had been offered to him by the Liberals rather than by the reigning princes of the states. The real reason was that he and his advisers knew that acceptance would mean war with Austria, and Prussia was not prepared to fight. The country sank back into its second-place position in the Confederation until Wilhelm I came to power.

In 1858 King Frederick William, whose mind had become affected by a series of strokes, was adjudged unfit to rule. His brother Wilhelm was appointed; he became king three years later. From then on, Prussia began to prepare for war. The principal leaders responsible for preparation, all of whom had been personally selected for their positions by the king, were: Otto von Bismarck, who was given the positions of minister-president and minister of foreign affairs; General Albrecht von Roon, who was appointed minister of war; and General Helmuth von Moltke, who became chief of staff of the army.

These were the men who guided Prussia through three wars and ended by establishing the German Empire. Their ideas are well expressed by the official military history:

"During the centuries in which, with the exception of Italy, all the neighboring States consolidated themselves, broke the power of their vassals, and firmly knitted together the forces of often heterogeneous races, an independence of the different parts sprung up in Germany, which condemned the whole to a state of impotence. The experiment of installing some thirty sovereignties as the constituent members of a Confederation which should take its place as an European Power, was successful neither as regarded its internal or external relations. A deep inclination towards unity was current in the whole German nation, but for the sake of unity neither were the princes prepared to sacrifice their rights nor the people their peculiarities. The experience of fifty years had shown that the goal of unity was not to be attained by means of moral advancement, but that to achieve it a physical compulsion on the part of some German Power was necessary. The gradual development of events had now left only two great European Powers in Germany, each too strong to submit to the other; on the equal balance of power of both existed the minor States in the fatherland. Germany's importance in the European world, whenever Austria and Prussia followed a mutual external policy, has always been proved by the results obtained by their alliances, but in Germany itself their interests were irreconcileable. In Germany there was not room for both, one or the other must succumb. Austria had an existence foreign from Germany. Prussia could not give up her Germanic situation without being annihilated."

Many eminent writers, forgetting that the history of every country includes instances of wars being provoked intentionally, have severely criticized Germany for deliberately planning war. Yet it is undoubtedly true that Austria would never have permitted the unification of the German nation by peaceful means. Certainly, also, it would be extremely difficult to deny that the Germans had a right to form a national government and that Prussia's leadership represented progress.

Unfortunately, for the world, the future leaders of Germany drew two conclusions from these quick and comparatively easy victories, which in the twentieth century plunged millions of people into two fearful world wars. Some of Bismarck's unscrupulous tactics in provoking wars were to lead to the conviction that the end result justified the means employed. Probably the best example of the application of this conclusion was the German decision to invade neutral Belgium in 1914 in order to ensure a rapid victory over France. The second conclusion was that wars not only brought glory, success, power, and recognition but that they could be made financially profitable to a nation. Prominent leaders in Germany, after computing the loss of life in the war with France in 1870, balanced against the large indemnity extracted from France and the gain in territory and inhabitants, contended that a statesman who hesitated to go to war because of questions of right or justice was not worthy of the name. The decisive battle that led to the founding of this German nation, which then took such a leading part in the development of Europe, but kept the world in suspense for nearly eighty years, is surely as decisive as those that brought about the downfall of that empire.

The three wars that resulted in the establishment of Germany were the Danish War of 1864, the Seven Weeks' War of 1866, and the Franco-Prussian War of 1870–71. The first was but the prelude to the second, and the third the almost inevitable consequence of the winning of the second. At the conclusion of the Danish War, Austria and Prussia acquired joint possession of the duchies of Schleswig and Holstein. A long, involved dispute over their administration became the excuse for war between Austria and Prussia. A majority of the German states, including Bavaria, Saxony, and Hanover, sided with Austria, but Bismarck found a ready ally in Italy, who was anxious to rid her territory of Austrian troops and complete the unification of her own country. As a result the contestants appeared to be fairly evenly matched; in fact most military observers fully expected Austria to win the war, which would have meant the end of all hope of the unification of Germany for many long years. The later Franco-Prussian War, which created the German Empire and for which France was unprepared, was simply the logical aftermath of Prussia's victory over Austria. Furthermore by that time the North German Confederation of over half the states of Germany had been established and the unification of the greater part of the country had been assured, even if France had managed to win the war. Therefore the prime contest, and the one upon which the future of most of Germany depended, was the second war, the Campaign of 1866.

The Seven Weeks' War may be considered for all practical purposes as one campaign against one enemy—Austria. It is true that Prussia was faced by a group of German states in the northwest and by a second group in the south, while there was a third front in Italy. But the crucial test would occur and the ultimate decision would be reached by Prussia in Austria. General von Moltke, who was a serious student of the art of war, saw clearly that no matter who won elsewhere, if he defeated Austria the other German states would necessarily be forced to sue for peace. As for the war in Italy, this was simply a means of attracting Austrian troops away from the main battlefront; no final decision would be reached on any field there. Even if he suffered defeats in these other areas, they would not affect the final result. Von Moltke's predictions were accurate; this is precisely what occurred. He concentrated the bulk of the Prussian army against Austria, and there the major battle of the war was fought.

Despite the fact that Prussia's main effort was directed against Austria, the operations in Germany proceeded very satisfactorily from the Prussian point of view. Hanover was defeated in the first few days of the war, more rapidly than the Prussians had any right to expect. They were therefore freed of any worries in the northwest. Their opponents in southern Germany, consisting primarily of Bavaria, Württemberg and Baden, were unprepared for war and uncoordinated in their efforts, factors that von Moltke had already taken into consideration. Here also the Prussians were generally successful, although the operations could have dragged on for a long time if word of the armistice caused by the victory of Sadowa had not caused the cessation of hostilities.

Nine days before the Battle of Sadowa, the Austrians defeated a large Italian army. One month later the Austrians inflicted a severe defeat upon the Italian Navy. But both of these events were completely overshadowed by the great Prussian victory.

Before describing the main campaign it would be well to make a brief comparison of the two opponents and the military leaders. We have already mentioned that most observers expected Austria to emerge as the victor. Their opinions were based upon three factors. Austria's overall population was nearly twice that of Prussia; her regular army required a longer period of training; and she had been engaged more recently in actual warfare, whereas the Prussians had not, with the exception of the short war against Denmark, experienced any combat in fifty years. Napoleon III of France, who hoped to profit from this war between two of his enemies, expected it to be a long, exhausting contest, draining the resources of both nations, which would give him the chance to intervene as mediator, from which he could surely profit.

Those who forecast victory for Austria overlooked some very important considerations. The first was the Prussian General Staff System. The foundations for such a system as we understand it today had been laid down by the Prussians as early as the Napoleonic Wars, but had not been fully developed before those wars ended. In the long interval of peace the Prussian Army had continued to train its staff officers and improve upon its staff methods, while other armies were paying hardly any attention at all to the problem. General von Moltke was himself a product of the system and had made many improvements upon it. The result was that when the Prussian Army took the field in 1866, it was far better organized, more ably administered, and more efficiently led than its enemy. This was the first and foremost difference between the two opposing armies.

The second element that gave the Prussians superiority on the field of battle was a weapon, the new needle gun, with which most of the infantry soldiers were equipped. It was a breech-loading rifle whose range was less than that of the Austrian muzzle loader but had two tremendously significant advantages: a far more rapid rate of fire and the fact that it could be loaded from the lying-down position.

In other respects the two opposing armies were fairly evenly matched. Although there had been concluded, just a year before, a great war on the American continent, neither army appears to have paid much attention to it. The general opinion seemed to be that there was nothing to be learned from a war fought by masses of untrained people in a wilderness. The lessons learned by Americans in that war had to be learned all over again by the Austrians and Prussians in this war, under fire, the hard way. The tactics of both armies at the beginning were little different from those of the days of Napoleon; they failed to take into account the effectiveness of modern artillery and infantry fire. As a result of this campaign the Prussians made some changes before their war with France, so that when that conflict began the Prussians appeared to have learned some of the lessons of the American Civil War, while the French had learned none. We therefore find numerous examples of valiant but completely un-successful infantry and cavalry attacks that resulted in nothing more than tremendous loss of life.

Between the commanders of the two armies in the Seven Weeks' War there was a vast difference. General von Moltke was aggressive and believed firmly in the spirit of the offensive. He had thoroughly indoctrinated his commanders and staff with this same spirit. Indeed, to have failed to do so would have been equivalent to casting aside the greatest asset which he had developed in the Prussian Army, the ability of the staffs to plan and the troops to execute rapid movements efficiently.

On the other hand the Austrian commander, General Ludwig von Benedek, was one of those unfortunate people who find themselves propelled into positions of responsibility for which they do not feel qualified. Well aware of his limitations, he had protested to the emperor against the decision to place him in supreme command; then, when he found that he had no choice, he had loyally accepted the assigned position, fearful of the consequences to his beloved country. Under such conditions it was inevitable that he should act with hesitation and with caution. To make matters worse, when he arrived to take command he found himself blessed with an incompetent staff whose ideas were limited to suggestions for waging a defensive war; the combination proved fatal.

The differences between the two commanders were strikingly appar-ent from the very beginning. By early June the Prussians were lined up along the frontier ready to advance, waiting only for permission from the king. Here occurred a considerable delay. Neither King Wilhelm of Prussia nor Emperor Francis Joseph of Austria wished to appear in the eyes of the world as the aggressor. During this waiting period the Austrians completed their concentration around the fortress of Olmütz in Moravia, then began moving forward to Josephstadt in Bohemia.

Meanwhile the Prussians had formed into three armies: the Army of the Elbe, a small army of about 45,000 men, around Torgau, opposite Saxony; the First Army disposed along the frontier from Senftenberg to Gorlitz; and the Second Army concentrated in Silesia west of Neisse. Shortly before the Austrians began their move into Bohemia, von Moltke had received permission from King Wilhelm to invade

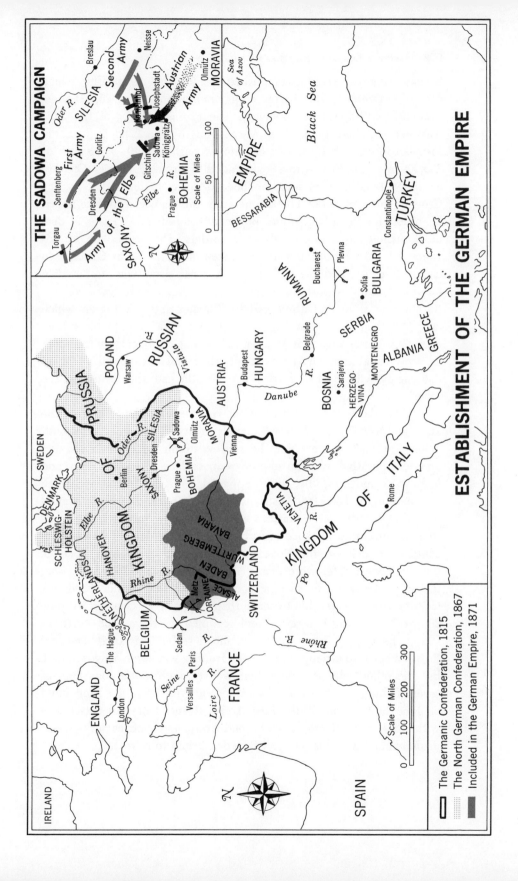

THE SADOWA CAMPAIGN

Second Army

Austrian Army

First Army

Army of the Elbe

Breslau
Neisse
SILESIA
Oder R.
MORAVIA
Olmütz
Josephstadt
Horsenmhof
Königgrätz
Sadowa
Gitschin
Görlitz
Senftenberg
BOHEMIA
Prague
Elbe R.
Dresden
SAXONY
Torgau

Scale of Miles
0   50   100

ESTABLISHMENT OF THE GERMAN EMPIRE

IRELAND

ENGLAND
London

SWEDEN

DENMARK

SCHLESWIG-HOLSTEIN

NETHERLANDS
The Hague

BELGIUM

HANOVER

KINGDOM OF PRUSSIA
Berlin
Elbe R.
Oder R.
SAXONY
Dresden
SILESIA
Sadowa
Olmütz
MORAVIA

POLAND
Warsaw

RUSSIAN
Vistula R.

FRANCE
Paris
Versailles
Seine R.
Loire R.
Sedan
Metz
LORRAINE
ALSACE
BADEN
WÜRTTEMBERG
BAVARIA
Rhine R.
SWITZERLAND

Prague
BOHEMIA
Vienna
AUSTRIA-HUNGARY
Budapest
Danube

VENETIA
Po R.

KINGDOM OF ITALY
Rome
Rhône R.

SPAIN

RUMANIA
Bucharest
Plevna
Sofia
BULGARIA
Constantinople
TURKEY

Belgrade
SERBIA
BOSNIA
HERZEGO-VINA
Sarajevo
MONTENEGRO
ALBANIA
GREECE

EMPIRE
BESSARABIA
Black Sea
Sea of Azov

Scale of Miles
0   100   200   300

☐ The Germanic Confederation, 1815
▦ The North German Confederation, 1867
▨ Included in the German Empire, 1871

Saxony. This was easily accomplished by the Army of the Elbe which occupied Dresden; the Saxon corps, numbering only 25,000 men, prudently withdrew into Bohemia. The Prussian Army of the Elbe was then attached to the First Army. Thus by the 22nd of June the Prussian forces had been formed into two armies with a strength of 255,000 men: the First Army, commanded by Prince Frederick Charles, of about 140,000 men, and the Second Army, commanded by the Crown Prince, of about 115,000 men. On this date von Moltke issued his orders for the advance into Bohemia. There has been a great deal of discussion, pro and con, about his orders. They called for an advance by both armies toward a concentration point at Gitschin in enemy territory, and the bulk of the Austrian army was supposed to be united near Josephstadt in between the two. This forward concentration, similar to that attempted by Blücher and Wellington which ended in their defeats at Ligny and Quatre Bras, would have been extremely dangerous against an able, daring opponent commanding an army capable of rapid movement. He could have simply held off one enemy with a small force while he attacked and destroyed the other.

Von Moltke was well aware of the risk he was taking, but he, the king, and von Bismarck were anxious to avoid, at almost any cost, a long, exhausting war. For the success of his venture he counted upon comparative Austrian unpreparedness, lack of coordination, and inability to move rapidly. As it happened, von Benedek's army which had a strength of 245,000 Austrians plus 25,000 Saxons, was not united near Josephstadt. Large portions were still strung out along the roads from Olmütz for a distance of forty miles. Strong detachments, which could have delayed the Prussian advance and given von Benedek time to concentrate, were facing the Prussians; but those opposing the First Army made such a poor showing that Prince Frederick Charles' troops were able to reach their objective of Gitschin by June 29, and by evening had seized and occupied the town. The Austrians facing the Crown Prince put up a much stiffer resistance. The first Prussian corps to attempt to cross the frontier was summarily repulsed, but the other columns drove their way through. After four days of severe fighting the Crown Prince's Second Army reached Königinhof on June 29. On June 30 the First Army advanced beyond Gitschin to within one day's march of the Second Army, and their cavalry patrols made contact. On this day von Benedek began to retreat.

The next event was, to say the least, extraordinary. The Prussian cavalry completely lost track of their enemy for a period of nearly forty-eight hours. In this war neither army made good use of its mounted troops, but of all the failures in reconnaissance work this was the most serious. Von Molkte was now forced to guess where his enemy had gone, and he was given no clues at all to solve the problem. If ever the fog of war enveloped a commander, this was the occasion. Placing himself in the shoes of his opponent, he assumed that the Austrians would make every effort to cross the Elbe, to avoid fighting with their back to that river, and issued his orders accordingly. In solving his problem von Moltke made one mistake; he gave his enemy greater credit for energy and resolution than he deserved. This appears to have been von Benedek's plan but, instead of pressing onward, he was resting his troops on the west side of the river.

Late on the night of the 2nd of July, King Wilhelm and his chief of staff were roused by news from Prince Frederick Charles that his First Army had made contact with the enemy near Sadowa. There was no indication whether it was the whole Austrian army or only a large portion of it, but in any event the prince planned to attack the next morning; he had asked the Crown Prince to cooperate. Realizing full well how fatal mere "cooperation" could be under such circumstances, and that if the prince was going to attack the whole Austrian army on the morrow he could easily suffer a drastic defeat, von Moltke reached a decision. The previous orders were canceled and the Crown Prince was told to march at once. The critical element here was time. The telegraph line to the Crown Prince was out; two mounted officers were sent at midnight by alternate routes to his headquarters twenty miles away; they arrived about 4:00 A.M. As the First Army advanced to the assault, the question in everyone's mind was, can the Second Army arrive in time? The commanders well knew that if the answer was Yes it could mean a complete victory; if not, it might result in the defeat of Prussia and the end of all hope for German unification, at least in this century. Having made their decision, the king and his advisers went resolutely forward to the battle.

In the Austrian camp von Benedek was in a very different frame of mind. Imbued with a sense of his own inadequacy, depressed by heavy losses in the engagements on the frontiers where the Austrians had suffered far more grievously than their opponents, primarily because of the effectiveness of the needle gun, he had telegraphed his emperor advocating peace at any price. The obvious but disconcerting reply had been, "Has a battle been fought?" Meanwhile von Benedek had dismissed his incompetent chief of staff and operations officer, but their successors had not had time to make their presence felt. Under these circumstances the Austrian commander was not expecting or searching for means of securing a victory. The position he had chosen between Sadowa and the fortress of Königgrätz was designed only to delay the Prussian advance so that he might escape across the Elbe to his rear. The position was difficult to attack frontally but was weak on both flanks.

The Austrian army on the ground now numbered some 205,000 men, and was drawn up in an arc about seven miles long on the east side of the Bistritz River overlooking the town of Sadowa, stretching to the right as far as the Trotina River. The cavalry, instead of being used to watch the flanks, was collected in rear of the infantry line. The terrain was hilly and wooded in places; the infantry had done some work toward constructing hasty field fortifications, while the artillery was well sited with good fields of fire. Both the Bistritz and the Trotina were small streams, easily waded by foot troops, but presenting serious problems to the passage of artillery. The principal hills and woods that were to become the scene of furious combat were the hill and village of Chlum, the Swiep Wald, and the woods near Sadowa.

Early in the morning of July 3, 1866, Prince Frederick Charles' troops reached the battlefield that is known to history as either Sadowa or Königgrätz. The Prussian plan was that the First Army of 85,000 men would keep the enemy fully occupied in the vicinity of Sadowa, without becoming too involved with the greatly superior Austrian army, while waiting for the arrival of the Prussian Second Army, which would then attack the enemy's north flank. Meanwhile the Army of the Elbe, 39,000 strong, would be sent on a turning movement against the south flank. The Austrians seem to have had no plan. Although the hills and folds in the ground made it impossible for General von Benedek to estimate accurately the number of troops against him, he should have known simply from their direction of advance that he was opposed only by the forces of Frederick Charles. But, as we have already noted, any idea of offensive action had long since been forgotten.

The Prussians deployed along the hills west of the Bistritz with one division, the 7th, north of the river. As the rain and mist, which had

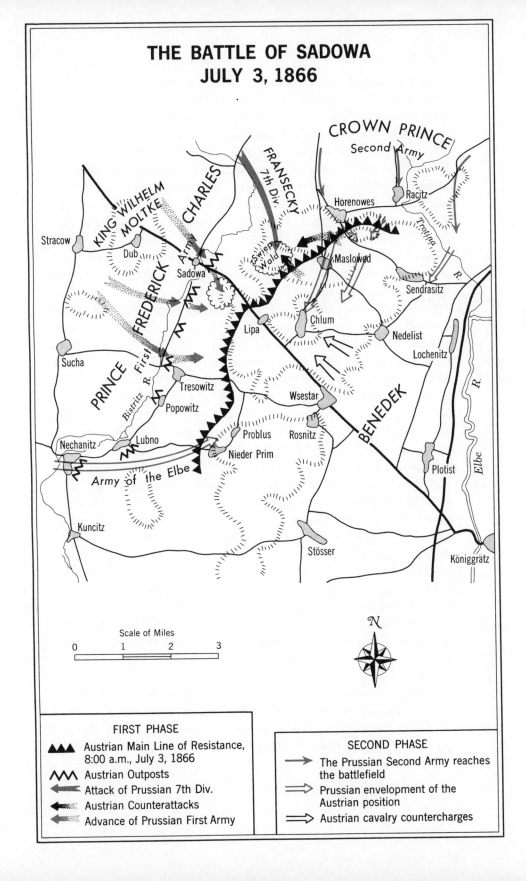

THE BATTLE OF SADOWA
JULY 3, 1866

CROWN PRINCE
Second Army

KING WILHELM

MOLTKE

CHARLES

FRANSECKY
7th Div.

Horenowes

Racitz

Stracow

Dub

Swiep
Wald

Maslowed

Trotina R.

Sadowa

FREDERICK

First Army

Sendrasitz

PRINCE

Sucha

Bistritz R.

Lipa

Chlum

Nedelist

Lochenitz

Tresowitz

Popowitz

Wsestar

BENEDEK

Elbe R.

Nechanitz

Lubno

Problus

Rosnitz

Nieder Prim

Plotist

Army of the Elbe

Kuncitz

Stösser

Königgrätz

Scale of Miles

0   1   2   3

N

FIRST PHASE

▲▲▲ Austrian Main Line of Resistance, 8:00 a.m., July 3, 1866

∧∧∧ Austrian Outposts

⬅ Attack of Prussian 7th Div.

⬅ Austrian Counterattacks

⬅ Advance of Prussian First Army

SECOND PHASE

➡ The Prussian Second Army reaches the battlefield

⇒ Prussian envelopment of the Austrian position

⇒ Austrian cavalry countercharges

persisted since dawn, began to clear, King Wilhelm and his staff appeared and took position on the hill at Dub where they could get a good view of the field of action. At the same time, shortly before eight o'clock, the Austrian artillery opened fire. Hearing the sound of the Prussian guns returning the fire, General von Fransecky, commanding the isolated 7th Division north of the Bistritz, advanced to the attack of the Swiep Wald. His aggressive action precipitated a far more serious battle than the Prussians had intended at this stage. Two Austrian corps counterattacked von Fransecky. To save him from destruction King Wilhelm ordered the First Army to move across the river. The town of Sadowa was captured, but the wood near it became the scene of a severe and bitter struggle. The Austrian infantry far outnumbered the Prussians; the Austrian artillery was firing with deadly effect upon the attacking troops who were having great difficulty getting their own guns across the river. At noon Frederick Charles was forced to commit his reserve. With the First Army locked in a desperate battle for existence, many long and anxious glances were directed toward the north where the army of the Crown Prince was supposed to appear.

Although it might have been difficult for some of those present to believe, and many may have wondered if orders had gone astray, the Second Army was moving with all possible speed. The leading brigade of the Guards, hearing the sound of the guns, had begun its march even before it received any orders. As they hurried forward at a rate that taxed the limits of human endurance, animated by the same spirit and resolution which brought Blücher to Waterloo, the similarity must have been recalled by many. Here also the Prussians arrived on time. Seizing the hill of Horenowes, they swept forward to catch the Austrians off balance, as they were retiring from the Swiep Wald to meet the flank assault. The attackers broke through and stormed the hill at Chlum, the key to the Austrian defense. Bravely the Austrians launched counterattacks again and again, but were thrown back. The Army of the Elbe, having seized Problus, was now advancing north, rolling up the Austrian left flank. King Wilhelm ordered an attack all along the line; by this time he had almost all his 220,000 men engaged.

To slow the advancing Prussians von Benedek loosed his cavalry in a series of desperate but valiant countercharges. Then, under cover of the fire of their artillery, whose steadiness and valor on that day won praise from friend and foe alike, the Austrians withdrew. Although the greater part of their army escaped, the Austrians and the Saxons lost 40,000 men, half of whom were prisoners. For their great victory the Prussians paid a price of over 9,000 men killed and wounded. Three weeks later an armistice was declared; the second and most critical step leading to the foundation of the German Empire had been successfully taken.

Synopsis of Events Between the Battle of Sadowa, A.D. 1866, and the First Battle of the Marne, A.D. 1914

1866. As a result of the Seven Weeks' War, Venetia is ceded by Austria to Italy.

1867. The North German Confederation is formed.

1867. In recognition of the growing demands of the Magyars for self-government, a dual monarchy is established for Austria-Hungary. However, the rights of other minorities are not recognized.

1867. Canada becomes the first of the self-governing British Dominions.

1867. The United States purchases Alaska from Russia.

1867. Napoleon III withdraws the French troops supporting the Archduke Maximilian in Mexico. The archduke is captured and executed by the Mexicans.

1869. The Suez Canal is officially opened.

1870–1871. The Franco-Prussian War begins. One French army is defeated and besieged in Metz; the other is defeated and, with Napoleon III, surrenders at Sedan. Paris is invested. In January, 1871, Wilhelm I is proclaimed Emperor of Germany in the famous Hall of Mirrors at Versailles. Paris capitulates. By the treaty of peace the French Republic is forced to cede Alsace and part of Lorraine, and to pay a large war indemnity.

1870. Upon the outbreak of the Franco-Prussian War, French troops are withdrawn from Rome. An Italian army enters Rome, which then becomes the capital of the now united Kingdom of Italy. This marks the end of the temporal power of the papacy, which had lasted over 1,100 years, since the Donation of Pepin in A.D. 756.

1877. Queen Victoria is proclaimed Empress of India.

1877–1878. Russia declares war on Turkey. Her march toward Constantinople is delayed by the memorable Siege of Plevna. After a further Russian advance, a preliminary treaty is concluded between

Russia and Turkey, then revised at the Berlin Congress. Turkey loses most of her European possessions. The full independence of Serbia, Montenegro, and Rumania is recognized; a portion of Bulgaria is granted partial independence. Russia receives southern Bessarabia, while Austria is given Bosnia and Herzegovina to administer. This settlement preserves general peace in the Balkans and in Europe for over thirty years.

1881–1896. Inspired by the reports of explorers of the "dark continent," of whom the most famous were David Livingstone and Henry M. Stanley, the nations of Europe turn their attention to Africa. During this fifteen-year period the greater part of Africa is divided among the European countries. The most outstanding leader in this movement was the Englishman Cecil Rhodes.

1894–1895. Japan easily defeats China in the Sino-Japanese War and acquires control over Formosa. (She would also have gained the Liaotung Peninsula, on which Port Arthur is situated, but Russia, France and Germany prevented it.)

1896–1898. General Sir Herbert Kitchener, Sirdar of the Egyptian Army, leads an expedition to reconquer the Sudan, and to avenge General Charles Gordon and those who had been massacred with him in the Mahdi Revolt in 1885. After a two-year campaign covering nearly a thousand miles, the army of the Khalifa is defeated at the Battle of Omdurman near Khartoum on the Upper Nile.

1898. The battleship *Maine* is sunk in the harbor of Havana, Cuba. In response to public sentiment, aroused by newspaper reports of Spain's inhumane treatment of Cuban revolutionaries, the United States declares war. On May 1, Commodore Dewey wins the Battle of Manila Bay; a military expedition attacks and captures the city in August.

Meanwhile, another Spanish fleet had crossed the Atlantic and entered the harbor of Santiago, Cuba. American troops were landed. On July 1, they won the Battles of El Caney and San Juan Hill; the latter was the action in which the "Rough Riders" participated. As a result of these Spanish defeats on land, Santiago became untenable. Admiral Cervera bravely sailed out of the harbor to fight against insurmountable odds; in the decisive engagement of the war his ships were sunk by the American fleet of Commodores Sampson and Schley. Porto Rico was invaded late in July.

At the treaty of peace signed in Paris, Spain surrendered all claim to Cuba, ceded Porto Rico and Guam to the United States as indemnity, and surrendered the Philippines for a payment of $20,000,000.

1898. The Hawaiian treaty of annexation is ratified by a joint resolution of the Congress of the United States.

1899. The First Hague Conference establishes the Permanent Court of International Arbitration, popularly known as the Hague Tribunal.

1899–1902. In the South African War the Boers initially win victories over the British. When large British reinforcements arrive, the tide slowly turns. After a valiant resistance the Boers accept British sovereignty with a large measure of local autonomy, and are given a grant to rebuild their homes and farms.

1901. Australia acquires dominion status.

1901. Queen Victoria dies after a reign of nearly sixty-four years.

1904–1905. To the surprise of the world, the Japanese administer a severe defeat to the Russians in the Russo-Japanese War. The army, commanded by Field Marshal Oyama, wins the ten-day Battle of Liaoyang in August and September, 1904, obtains the surrender of Port Arthur on January 2, 1905 after a long siege, and then is victorious in an eighteen-day battle south of Mukden in February and March. In May the Russian Baltic Fleet, after a seven-month voyage, is destroyed by Admiral Togo's Fleet at the Battle of Tsushima Straits. (Peace was brought about by the friendly offices of the United States. Japan obtained southern Sakhalin and rights in Port Arthur, and her paramount interest in Korea was recognized.)

1907. New Zealand becomes a British Dominion.

1908. Following the revolution of the Young Turks, Austria announces annexation of Bosnia-Herzegovina, and Bulgaria declares her complete independence of Turkey.

1910. The Union of South Africa acquires dominion status.

1910. Japan annexes Korea by treaty.

1912–1913. As a result of the Balkan Wars, all the Balkan countries gain territory from Turkey, which is then reduced to a small region around Constantinople. Albania is created as an independent country.

1914. The Archduke Francis Ferdinand is assassinated at Sarajevo.

1914. The Panama Canal, constructed under the supervision of Colonel, later Major General, George W. Goethals, is opened.

18

The First Battle of the Marne, A.D. 1914

NEVER BEFORE in the history of the world had so many nations been so fully prepared for war. To say that Europe was a vast armed camp would be merely to repeat what has been said many times before in attempting to describe the situation in the years preceding the World War. Furthermore, such a description is not really accurate, for it implies that the armies and navies were kept ready at all times for combat. No country could possibly afford to maintain its army at war strength; such a policy would ruin any nation's economy.

In days gone past, armies had made general plans to be put into operation upon a declaration of war. When the day came, the regular army would be made ready for action, and reserves would be called to the colors and organized into units. Eventually they would receive their marching orders. During this preliminary period, supplies of food, clothing, arms and ammunition would be assembled and issued to the troops. All this took time, and whoever was ready first certainly had the advantage over his enemy. Various means were devised to shorten the time required. The standard method was to mobilize in advance of a declaration of war; a partial mobilization of only a portion of the active army and reserves could be announced as a simple training exercise. In this respect a navy had a distinct advantage over an army as an inital striking force. After a period of preparation it could simply vanish over the horizon on a training voyage, to reappear on the prescribed day, firing at its target. In February, 1904, the Japanese had begun the Russo-Japanese War by a naval attack on the Russian fleet at Port Arthur, prior to a declaration of war.

On the other hand, a full or partial mobilization was also a very effective weapon of diplomacy, a threatening gesture, useful to overawe an enemy and force him to yield to demands, without resorting to war. Furthermore, this old-style method of mobilization could be halted at any time during the period of preparation, which might last for several days, weeks, or even months.

By 1914 all this had been changed radically. The Prussian victories over Austria and France in the preceding century had shown how much time might be saved if the mobilization plan included a definite plan of attack. No nation on the continent of Europe, which felt itself threatened by the growing power of Germany, could afford to ignore the warning. Confronted with the problem of how to have their armies ready in the shortest possible time, every nation arrived at approximately the same solution. In every case it was a compromise between safety and economy, resulting in the maintenance of the largest possible active army that the country's financial condition could stand. But this was only the first step. Universal conscription was adopted; every able-bodied man was required to serve for a period, usually of two years, with the colors, followed by a much longer period with the reserves, on call at any time. Thus the active army, in addition to its normal duties, trained the yearly quotas of reserves, maintained the equipment of the reserve units as well as its own, and held itself in instant readiness for expansion to war strength, and immediate movement in advance of the reserve units.

The greatest burden fell upon the general staffs who were responsible for the formulation of suitable war plans, the coordination of every unit with these plans, the scheduling, timing, and composition by number and type of railway car of every one of the thousands of troop and supply trains required. No detail that might interrupt this mass movement could be left to chance. The plans must be continuously checked. If the international situation required a change in plans, this meant a complete revision from top to bottom, from the order of march of the leading reconnaissance units along specific roads in the enemy's territory, to the stockpiling of supplies at different points in different quantities, and the resultant changes in the railway scheduling for the units and their supplies to the new concentration points.

Several years ago a prominent American politician said he could stamp his foot and a million men would spring to arms overnight. Applied to the United States, the statement was obviously preposterous. The men would not have known in which direction to "spring"; there would have been no one to receive them. They would have had no shelter upon arrival, no food, no uniforms or clothing. If each brought a rifle, the difficulties of supplying the different kinds of ammunition would be insuperable, and there would have been no other arms to give them. Above all, they would not have been trained; and there would have been no artillery, engineers, signal units, cavalry, or services of supply.

If the German Kaiser had made that statement, it would have been true. The standing army was fully prepared; every officer and soldier had specific orders. The reserves knew exactly when and where to report; their arms, equipment and supplies were ready for them. Every item had been foreseen. The exact number of trains to take the men and supplies to concentration points had been carefully computed and orders issued in advance. The entire railway system of Germany was prepared to move trains at exact intervals like a well-oiled machine, according to a fixed timetable. The amount of detailed work that had been accomplished to ensure the success of every element of the plan, which had been revised and kept up to date every year, was simply incredible. Everything was ready to move swiftly at a moment's notice. It was the proud boast of the General Staff that all that was needed was the initial order; then they could sit back with nothing more to do, while everything functioned smoothly according to plan.

Yet Germany was not the only country that had made such preparations. France was also ready; she knew that if she were not, she simply would be overwhelmed. To a lesser degree, so also were Russia, Austria-Hungary, and many smaller countries. Under these circumstances no nation could afford to let another mobilize without ordering its own forces to do likewise. For it was almost a certainty that such a mobilization would also mean that the enemy would be putting his war plan into effect. Once the wheels had been set in motion, the leading troops would be poised at the frontier, waiting to cross at the scheduled time. Gone were the days when a large "maneuver" close to the enemy's frontiers could be used as a diplomatic weapon. The nations of Europe were actually too well prepared for war. An order to mobilize was, for all practical purposes, an order to attack. Once the troops had been set in motion, rapid action indeed would have to be taken to prevent a war, because every major land power in Europe had planned to take the offensive.

In the years following the Franco-Prussian War of 1870, Europe had become divided into two groups. The Triple Alliance of Germany, Austria-Hungary, and Italy confronted the Triple Entente of France, Russia, and Great Britain. Neither was a solid bloc. Italy, the junior member of the Triple Alliance, was not so firmly bound to Germany as Austria-Hungary was; nor was Great Britain fully committed to the Triple Entente, which was basically an alliance between France and Russia.

The key to the whole situation was Germany and the belief of her leaders that aggressive war was profitable to a nation. Her large and efficient army was a menace to all her neighbors on land, and when she began to build a strong navy to protect her growing colonial empire, it brought her interests into conflict with those of Great Britain, whose existence depended upon command of the sea, at least in European waters. This threat upon the sea was sufficient to cause Great Britain's statesmen to establish more cordial relations with France, their traditional enemy, despite the centuries of friendship that had existed with Germany.

In like manner, the war plan of the German Empire was the major element that influenced the war plans of all the other Great Powers of Europe. For several years Germany had planned to stand on the defensive against a weaker France, while a vigorous offensive was launched, in conjunction with the Austrians, against Russia. But as the years passed and an embittered France arose from the ashes of her defeat, determined to revenge herself upon Germany and recover the lost provinces of Alsace and Lorraine, the German General Staff completely reversed its ideas.

Field Marshal Alfred von Schlieffen, the father of the new war plan, was an extremely intelligent, able soldier and an ardent disciple of the elder von Moltke who had won those rapid decisive victories that had established the German Empire in all its glory and power. Confronted with the possibility of a war simultaneously against France in the West and Russia in the East, von Schlieffen saw clearly that there was only one way to win quickly, which was essential to the German doctrine that war was financially profitable to the nation. Russia's territory was so vast that, even if her armies were defeated at the frontiers, Russia could prolong the contest by retiring slowly toward Moscow, hundreds of miles away. If, on the other hand, France were rapidly overrun, Russia would then be a much easier prey, and a negotiated peace to Germany's advantage could be obtained with comparative ease.

Could he afford to turn his back on Russia at the very beginning? To do so might mean the temporary loss of East Prussia, but it was a risk that von Schlieffen was prepared to accept, although it would be a horrible shock to the German people. He knew that, even though Russia was capable of invading East Prussia, it would take her several weeks to mass her full strength, simply because of the huge extent of her territory. If France could be rapidly defeated, the German Army, taking advantage of its central position and the country's excellent railway system, could be redeployed in time to halt and overwhelm the advancing Russians.

The basic idea was, like so many other great plans, simple, direct and bold; its success depended upon Germany's ability to overwhelm France rapidly and thoroughly. Here also von Schlieffen approached the problem with simple, direct logic. The French frontier from Switzerland to Luxembourg was short, easily defensible, and backed by a series of strong fortifications. To penetrate this line would be a long and costly process. Von Schlieffen therefore proposed that the German Army invade France through Belgium, which, north of the Ardennes, was smooth, level country, magnificently adapted to the movement of large armies and well provided with a splendid network of highways and railroads. The fact that all the Great Powers of Europe had, in 1839, guaranteed the neutrality of Belgium was considered from a military point of view. Violation of this neutrality might bring Great Britain into the war against Germany, but the British regular army, although excellent, was very small and could be safely ignored as a factor worthy of consideration. It is extremely interesting to note that Britain's failure to be adequately prepared for war in a world of Great Powers, all of whom were too ready to engage in a great armed conflict, was the very factor that brought her into that war. Three years later the United States, as the major neutral nation, found herself engaged in the same war for the same basic cause, a state of unpreparedness which Germany thought could be safely ignored in order to win that war by using submarines that violated international laws of neutrality.

When von Schlieffen's plan was approved by the rulers of Germany on the theory that ultimate victory would justify the means employed and that the invasion of Belgium was therefore essential, he proceeded, over the years, to perfect it. When he retired in 1906, he bequeathed to his successor, the nephew of the world-famous von Moltke, a highly practical plan. It provided for a tremendously strong right wing to advance through Belgium and northern France, turning the flank of the French armies, swinging wide on both sides of Paris. Everything else was secondary to the success of this great turning movement. Five armies were assigned to the great task. The other two armies on the Western Front were simply to hold the attention of the French and, if attacked, defend themselves while the main blow was delivered that would envelop and utterly destroy the enemy. As for East Prussia, only one army, the Eighth, was assigned to defend that region to the best of its ability.

The German strategists did not believe that little Belgium would have the temerity to resist invasion. They expected a protest, perhaps a token resistance, but not much more. However, to guard against delay for any reason, a special advance force was provided whose mission was to seize Liège, by force if necessary, and clear a wide path through Belgium while the German concentration was under way, thus ensuring the uninterrupted march of the main body when it started to move.

For over thirty years after the defeat of 1870–71, the French war plan was primarily defensive in nature. It contemplated surrendering large areas of France without a struggle. In the earlier versions even Paris was to be abandoned to the enemy. Then, some years after the alliance with Russia, the French began to think in terms of the offensive. Military leaders began preaching that the true warrior spirit of France could be found only when French troops were advancing in an assault upon the enemy, that the French soldier fought better in the attack than on the defensive. Many people came to believe that all training and all tactical doctrine must stress the offensive, that nothing else suited so well the French temperament. Naturally, then, Plan XVII, the war plan in effect in 1914, was a plan for attack, to seize the initiative from the Germans wherever they might be found, drive them back, and recover the lost provinces. The French General

Staff considered the possibility that the invaders might come through Belgium, but made their plans on the assumption that only the southern corner in the vicinity of the Ardennes would be violated. The major German effort was expected to come through Lorraine. There, in the vicinity of Metz, the major strength of France should be concentrated to drive the invaders back toward the Rhine. From this region an advance through southern Belgium could also be taken in flank. Simultaneously French troops to the south would press forward into Alsace, while their allies, the Russians, were advancing toward Berlin in the German rear. If Field Marshal von Schlieffen had been in command of the German armies in 1914, he would have welcomed this plan. It left his strong right wing free to continue its great envelopment, free to wheel like a huge steel scythe around the French northern flank. Therein lay the whole idea of his plan; everything else was subordinated to it. Let the French attack in Alsace and Lorraine, fall back before them if necessary, lose East Prussia also temporarily, then crush all before him with the great turning movement. This was the essence of his plan. His only fear was that his successor might not have the courage to carry it through, regardless of every other consideration and distracting influence. His dying words, in 1913, were an injunction and a plea to keep "the right wing strong."

The German defeat at the Marne, the German failure to bring the war to a rapid, profitable conclusion, and the ultimate loss of the war itself can be traced directly to failure to keep "the right wing strong." The changes which the younger General Helmuth von Moltke made in the Schlieffen Plan came gradually. He still believed in the idea of a great turning movement through Belgium, but worried over the comparative weakness of his left, and the fate of the lone German army facing the Russians. As a result, when the war began the Schlieffen Plan had been altered slightly to increase the left wing somewhat at the expense of the right. Having thus dared to make a change in the sacred plan, it became easier to make others.

It had long been feared that some incident in the Balkans would ignite the spark to set the world aflame, and such proved to be the case. It occurred in Bosnia, annexed six years before by Austria-Hungary over the protests of Russia and Serbia. There on June 28, 1914, at Sarajevo, the capital of the province, the Archduke Francis Ferdinand and his wife were assassinated. The crime was committed by a young Bosnian revolutionary, a member of a group whose weapons were supplied by a secret Serbian society known as the Black Hand; the Serbian government had no part in the plot.

The world was shocked by the murder and sympathized with the rulers of Austria in their grief. However Austria, after assuring herself of Germany's support, decided to take advantage of the crime to attack Serbia, whose independence had long been a source of irritation. On July 23, the Austrian government presented a completely unreasonable ultimatum to Serbia, demanding a reply within forty-eight hours. When Serbia's reply was received, it was pronounced unacceptable. Austria declared war on July 28 and bombarded Belgrade the following day. Russia could not stand aside and watch Austria overwhelm her smaller Slavic neighbor; this would mean German supremacy in the Balkans; therefore Russia mobilized on July 30. Nothing short of a miracle, and certainly not the halfhearted attempts of the rulers and various chiefs of state to avoid the onus of beginning the war being placed upon them, could stop the armies now. Every military leader felt the pressing necessity of setting his own army's machinery in motion before his enemy could steal a march upon him. Almost simultaneously on August 1, both Germany and France declared general mobilization. That evening, at 7:00 P.M., Germany declared war on Russia, and the leading detachment of German soldiers crossed the Luxembourg frontier.

Exactly twenty-four hours later, while Luxembourg was in the process of being completely overrun, the German ambassador in Brussels presented a note to the Belgian government demanding free passage across the country to attack France, and a reply within twelve hours. Faced with a terrible decision involving the ruin and destruction of his country, at the worst possible time when his small army was in the process of reorganization, Albert, King of the Belgians, never hesitated. He could not, with honor, accede to the request; his heroic reply, undoubtedly the most important document of the war, thrilled the world. As expected, Germany declared war on France on August 3 but in the eyes of the world Germany was now definitely established as the aggressor. Her reluctant ally, Italy, felt perfectly free, both legally and morally, to declare her neutrality. King Albert's refusal, followed by the news of German troops crossing the Belgian border early in the morning of August 4, brought Great Britain into the war that evening.

The special advance force of 60,000 men to clear the way through

Belgium began crossing the frontier at eight o'clock in the morning of August 4. By late afternoon the German army had reached the ring of forts surrounding Liège. It was absolutely vital to the plan that these forts be reduced promptly. For this purpose an assault force of six infantry brigades commanded by General von Emmich was allotted. The first infantry attack on August 5 was repulsed with heavy loss. But that night, when five columns of troops attempted to penetrate the intervals between the forts, one column managed to break through. Led by General Ludendorff, a staff officer who had attached himself to the brigade and whose name was soon to become famous throughout the world, this column entered the city of Liège on August 7, its arrival causing a great deal of confusion. The Belgian commander, General Leman, thereupon concentrated his forces upon the defense of the forts themselves, abandoning the intervals between them.

The heroic resistance of the outnumbered Belgians excited the admiration of the world, and it was not until the Germans brought forward huge new heavy siege cannon and battered the forts to pieces that the Belgians surrendered. When the Germans entered the last fort, General Leman was found unconscious, pinned under fallen beams. So much publicity was given to the stubborn resistance, which was not completely overcome for a period of almost two weeks, that the people of the world received the impression that the valiant defense of the little Belgian Army had delayed the advance of the mighty German forces for that length of time. Such was not at all the case. The special advance force, composed of regular troops of the active army held in readiness at all times, had been sent ahead for the express purpose of preventing this from happening. It is difficult to calculate accurately how much the Belgian defense interfered with the German plans. The march of the main body was delayed by possibly two days, rather than two weeks. The defense of the forts was generally excellent, but the loss of the intervals between them made the defense ineffective. The defenders held the forts themselves as long as it was possible for them to do so, but they failed to destroy the tunnels and bridges essential to the supply of the invading armies.

It was fear of sabotage of their lines of communication that was the primary cause of the German atrocities in Belgium. No army can permit the uninterrupted breaking of its railways and telegraph lines, nor the indiscriminate shooting of its soldiers by the local inhabitants.

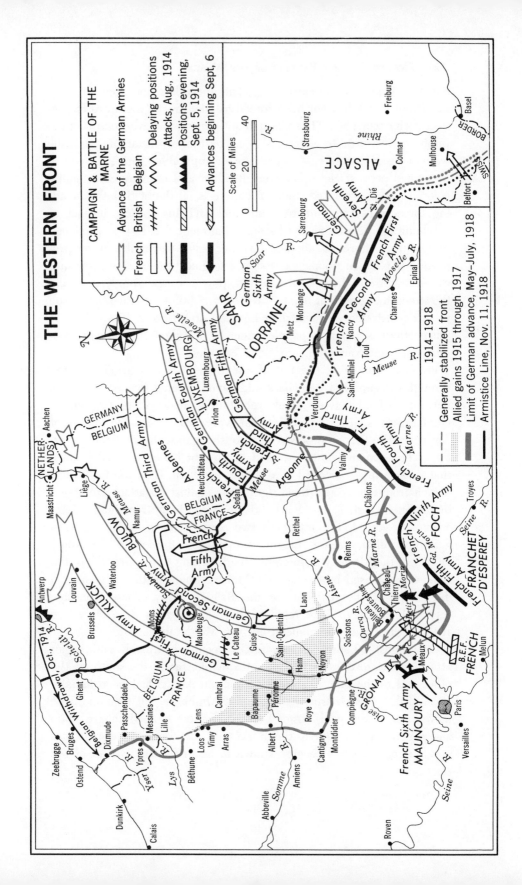

THE WESTERN FRONT

CAMPAIGN & BATTLE OF THE MARNE

Advance of the German Armies

	French	British	Belgian
Delaying positions			
Attacks, Aug., 1914			
Positions evening, Sept. 5, 1914			
Advances beginning Sept. 6			

1914–1918

Generally stabilized front
Allied gains 1915 through 1917
Limit of German advance, May–July, 1918
Armistice Line, Nov. 11, 1918

Scale of Miles
0   20   40

N

BORDER

SWISS

Basel
Freiburg
Strasbourg
Rhine R.
Colmar
Mulhouse
Belfort
ALSACE
St. Dié
German Seventh Army
French First Army
Sarrebourg
Moselle R.
Epinal
Charmes
Saar R.
German Sixth Army
Morhange
Metz
Nancy
French Second Army
Toul
Saint-Mihiel
Meuse R.
LORRAINE
SAAR
Moselle R.
Luxembourg
LUXEMBOURG
German Fifth Army
Arlon
Neufchâteau
Sedan
Ardennes
German Fourth Army
French Third Army
Verdun
Vaux
French Third Army
Meuse R.
GERMANY
BELGIUM
Aachen
NETHER-
LANDS
Maastricht
Liège
Meuse R.
Namur
Sambre R.
German Third Army
MONS
BELGIUM
FRANCE
Argonne
Valmy
Aisne R.
Rethel
Châlons
Marne R.
French Fourth Army
French Fifth Army
Troyes
Seine R.
FOCH
French Ninth Army
Gd. Morin
FRANCHET
D'ESPEREY
French Fifth Army
Reims
Laon
Soissons
Ourcq R.
Aisne R.
Petit Morin
Château-Thierry
Belleau
Bouresches
Marne R.
Montmirail
French
Fifth
Army
Guise
Saint-Quentin
Ham
Noyon
Compiègne
Oise R.
GRONAU IV
French Sixth Army
MAUNOURY
Meaux
B.E.F.
FRENCH
Melun
Versailles
Paris
Seine R.
Roven
Antwerp
Louvain
Waterloo
Brussels
Ghent
Belgian Withdrawal, Oct., 1914
Scheldt R.
German First Army
KLUCK
Maubeuge
Le Cateau
Mons
German Second Army
BELGIUM
FRANCE
Cambrai
Bapaume
Péronne
Roye
Montdidier
Cantigny
Albert
Somme R.
Amiens
Abbeville
Zeebrugge
Ostend
Bruges
Dixmude
Passchendaele
Messines
Ypres
Yser R.
Lys R.
Loos
Lens
Vimy
Arras
Lille
Béthune
Dunkirk
Calais

Severe punishments are necessary, and there has not been an army in history which has not been forced to take drastic measures to prevent such occurrences. The German authorities, however, carried their punitive measures to extremes. The best-known example was the wanton destruction of Louvain and its incomparable Library. Of course the Allied press seized upon every incident and in many cases highly colored and exaggerated them. Yet there is no doubt that the invading forces executed numerous innocent civilians, which, instead of subduing the people, caused keener resentment that in turn produced more daring efforts at sabotage. The net result was that a larger proportion of German troops was assigned to guard the lines of communications than had been contemplated, thus correspondingly reducing the strength of the right wing. The Germans' failure to learn this lesson was demonstrated again in their invasion of Russia in World War II when otherwise friendly people, eager to throw off the yoke of communism, were converted into bitter enemies.

Promptly following the fall of Liège the German armies poured through the gap. The Belgians could have retreated toward the south, but King Albert was extremely reluctant to leave all of Belgium in German hands. He ordered a retreat westward toward the fortress of Antwerp. The French protested vigorously against this apparent desertion. The Germans, however, tried to prevent his escape. They knew that if his army succeeded in reaching Antwerp, they would have to detach troops to secure their right flank against an attack from that direction. In fact, King Albert did escape with the remainder of his army, and von Moltke left nearly two corps facing Antwerp. Thus, in a purely military sense, Belgium's main contribution to the Allied victory at the Marne was therefore the lessening of the strength of the right wing, caused by the Germans' mistreatment of the Belgians and the escape of the remnants of the Belgian Army. These front-line troops should have been replaced by others drawn from elsewhere at the earliest possible moment, but von Moltke did not do so.

On August 20, the German forces occupied Brussels and began attacking the fortress of Namur. Meanwhile, far to the south, at the other end of the line, a French advance in Alsace had been initially successful; a French army had occupied Mulhouse, but then had been driven out. A renewed, larger French offensive took Mulhouse again and penetrated Lorraine to the outskirts of Sarrebourg. The stage was now set for what has become known to history as the Battles of the

Frontiers. These raged all along the line for a period of four days, from August 20 to August 24; each side fought with great determination and each sustained extremely heavy casualties. At the end the French armies were in retreat. The French War Plan XVII, designed to win by using the supposed superior French morale, dash, and offensive spirit had failed in the face of the firepower of modern defensive weapons. The little British Expeditionary Force, near the left of the line, after a valiant resistance at Mons, was also falling back. Then for a period of two weeks, day after day, the Allies withdrew, step by step, grimly giving ground when forced to do so, while General Joffre vainly sought a favorable opportunity to renew the offensive. The only bright spot in the ever-darkening picture was a counter-attack by the French Fifth Army at Guise on August 29, which succeeded in temporarily checking the enemy at that point. By this time the strength and power of the German right wing had become known to all. Fear for the safety of Paris was growing with the passing of every day, as the German armies moved ever closer.

If the weary Allied soldiers could have been permitted a look at the advancing German columns they might have been encouraged, for the invaders were becoming as exhausted as they themselves by the rigors of the relentless pursuit. But if their commanders could have learned what dreadful damage had been done to the Schlieffen Plan, they would have been overjoyed. The ambitious commanders of the German armies in the south, encouraged by their success against the first French attacks, had persuaded von Moltke to send them additional troops. Instead of following the Schlieffen Plan, the German commanders had begun to dream of a second, greater Cannae. Visions of a huge double envelopment of over a million French troops, a victory that would eclipse even the memory of Hannibal's great victory, which had obsessed the minds of so many leaders throughout the ages, danced before their eyes. Then suddenly into their dreams had come alarming news from East Prussia. General von Prittwitz, commanding the German Eighth Army, was reporting that East Prussia must be abandoned to the advancing Russians. General von Moltke made two decisions, a proper one, and another that was decidedly wrong. First he relieved von Prittwitz from command; General Paul von Hindenburg was called from retirement to take his place, and the hero of Liège, General Erich Ludendorff, was appointed his chief of staff. The second decision was to send two corps from the German

right wing to aid the Eighth Army. Before they could arrive on the
the scene, Hindenburg and Ludendorff had won (August 26–30) the
Battle of Tannenberg, and the two corps were to be sorely missed at
the Marne. As if this were not enough, additional troops had been
taken to besiege the fortress of Maubeuge, which was still holding out,
and these troops had not been replaced.

As von Moltke was thus destroying the Schlieffen Plan, Joffre was
strengthening his left. Two new armies were created: the French
Sixth near Paris, commanded by General Maunoury; and the French
Ninth under General Foch, in the line between Paris and Verdun. The
units to form these armies were taken from other parts of the line,
primarily from the armies on the right flank who were protected in
their defense by the large fortresses of Verdun, Toul, Epinal, and Belfort near the Swiss border. With disaster staring them in the face, the
retreating French armies were still prepared to turn about and fight if
their commander would only give them the word, but were beginning to wonder if the word would ever be given. At this point the
two commanders in chief present a remarkable contrast. The solid,
phlegmatic Joffre, unruffled by a continuous series of defeats, was
calmly discussing the possibilities of abandoning Paris and retreating
farther south. On the other hand, von Moltke, the representative of the
cold, calculating Prussian General Staff, was becoming ever more
worried; his headquarters in Luxembourg was too far from the front;
his communications were unreliable; he was losing contact with and
control over his armies; he felt that the situation was getting out of
hand. The French commander needed a spark to detonate him into
action; the German commander needed only an excuse to fall back,
regroup, and consolidate his position. Both were to be provided.

The spark was provided by a French general, Joseph Simon Gallieni,
the Military Governor of Paris, who for a brief period had been Joffre's
superior officer and in case of need had been selected as his successor. On September 3, the day after the French government evacuated Paris, Gallieni learned that the German First Army had turned
to the southeast and would pass northeast of Paris. The responsibility
for this change of direction has been the subject of heated debate and
furious argument. General von Kluck, commanding the First Army
on the extreme west flank, believed that he had defeated the French
near Paris, that the British were close to defeat, and that his proper
move was to attack the flank of the French Fifth Army which was

next in line. His neighbor, General von Bülow, commanding the German Second Army, had in fact previously called upon him for support. When von Moltke was consulted he agreed, because wide gaps were appearing between the armies of the right wing, gaps that would never have occurred if the right wing had been strong. It no longer had the strength and power to encircle Paris.

As the German First Army began sweeping by Paris, General Gallieni saw his chance. With the French Sixth Army he could attack the Germans in flank. Actually, the situation was more favorable than he knew. Von Kluck was an aggressive soldier. Once committed to the change in direction, he had pursued so rapidly that he was ahead of Bülow on his left. By September 4, only the IV Reserve Corps remained north of the Marne to cover the flank of the whole German army. And north of the Marne was exactly where Gallieni determined to launch his assault.

First he must obtain Joffre's approval. The cooperation of the British next in line must be assured. Then the French Fifth Army should also swing into the assault. Gallieni issued warning orders to Maunoury to prepare his Sixth Army for an advance. Next there began a telephone campaign to persuade Joffre to agree to the plan. Many have criticized the French commander in chief for his slowness in seeing the opportunity and making up his mind. Hindsight is easy, and those who have its benefit do not have the fate of a nation resting upon their shoulders at the moment of decision. Joffre was responsible not only for the defense of Paris but also for the future of France. Furthermore, he could not order the British commander, Sir John French, to advance; he could only do his best to persuade. At this moment Sir John French was worried, not so much about the ability of his army to counterattack, but of the future of that army committed to his care if it were left in the middle of a defeated country, far from the Channel ports. Visions of disaster haunted him. Twenty-six years later another British army, facing overwhelming, victorious German forces, was much closer than he to possible rescue at the beaches of Dunkirk. It should be no surprise to learn that both Joffre and French took time to reach their decisions, but of the two Joffre acted first. On the evening of September 4, he issued orders for the attack to begin two days later, then learned to his horror that his ally, whom he understood had already agreed, was still wavering. Without the British in their place in the line, the battle could surely not be won, and the orders to the French troops were already on their way. A personal appeal to the British commander finally had its effect. Sir John French assented but, as will be seen, moved forward with great caution and lost many of the possible fruits of victory.

The evening of September 4 was, curiously enough, the time when von Moltke also reacted and issued orders. Yet, even at this late date, his instructions to his two right-wing armies to face west toward Paris contained little information as to the reasons for the change. There was no warning of the possibility of serious attack from that direction. Communications were so poor that von Kluck could not, like Gallieni, talk to his commander by telephone. It was not until the next day when the leading French troops of Maunoury's Sixth Army, moving to their assault positions for attack on September 6, collided with the German IV Reserve Corps north of the Marne that von Kluck had the situation clarified for him.

Little attention has been paid in general narratives of the Battle of the Marne to General von Gronau, the commander of that corps. He proved to be a very able soldier; by his prompt, intelligent action he saved the German army from being completely surprised. Unlike many others he was not pressing forward, supremely confident that the enemy were thoroughly beaten. From the reports of his cavalry he decided that something worth a thorough investigation was developing from the direction of Paris. To find out, he turned toward the west, attacked and defeated the foremost French divisions. Although successful in this venture, he concluded from the actions of his opponents that his corps was far outnumbered. He wisely retreated to a strong defensive position and sent word to his army commander. Thus warned, von Kluck also reacted promptly. There was need for haste. Shortly after midnight he had turned one of his other corps around and had it marching to von Gronau's assistance. The development of the battle that began on the morning of September 6 is, from this point onward, almost predictable, so long as we do not attempt to follow events in detail. Von Kluck did a masterly job of defending simultaneously against both Maunoury's army from Paris and the left flank of the French Fifth Army, but was forced, corps by corps, to increase the strength on his right flank toward Paris. Here the Germans fought so furiously that Maunoury's army was halted. Gallieni had to rush reinforcements to his aid— the famous, dramatic ride of the "taxicab army."

However, by pulling troops back across the Marne to halt Maunoury's advance from Paris, von Kluck perforce opened a gap in the line. Into it marched the left flank of the French Fifth Army, followed more slowly by the little British Expeditionary Force, who, it must be admitted, had a greater distance to cover to regain contact. Their advance was skillfully delayed by German cavalry and a few infantry rear guards only. For the Allies, it was most unfortunate that this march was so cautious. No one has ever doubted the bravery or efficiency of the British, but Sir John French appears to have been afraid that he was walking into a gigantic ambush. As a result the Allies lost their chance of attacking von Kluck from the rear and destroying his army.

The climax of the battle came on September 8, in the form of a strange mission by a staff officer, and a surprise night attack. That morning von Moltke became greatly disturbed by reports of a gap between his First and Second Armies. Unable to obtain definite information because of the poor communication facilities, he sent Lieutenant Colonel Hentsch, Chief of the Intelligence Section, to investigate. He gave him authority to give orders for retreat if rear- ward movements had already begun. Strangely, he give him no written instructions, which caused controversy in later years, but there seems no reason to doubt his authority, nor did the com- manders concerned question it at the time. A court of inquiry officially declared that he acted entirely according to the spirit of his instructions.

In any event, when Colonel Hentsch visited the Fifth, Fourth and Third Armies that afternoon, he found the German situation quite satisfactory. Especially was this true at the Third Army, which was handling General Foch's Ninth Army very roughly. Although Foch's situation was critical, he was fighting desperately, attempting to counterattack. Refusing to admit defeat, Foch's men were respond- ing magnificently, but were being slowly pushed ever backward. The Germans had the upper hand here, and Colonel Hentsch so in- formed his commander.

That same night General Franchet d'Esperey, the new, energetic commander of the French Fifth Army, launched a surprise assault across the Petit-Morin against the right flank of the German Second

Army. Colonel Hentsch found von Bülow discouraged and ready to withdraw in front of Franchet d'Esperey's army. Although a retreat would greatly widen the gap between the Second and First German Armies, Hentsch could do nothing but acquiesce and go onward to meet General von Kluck. When, after a long delay caused by troop traffic clogging the roads, he reached First Army Headquarters the commander was not personally present. He and von Kluck's chief of staff agreed that as a result of the withdrawal of von Bülow, they must also turn back, before the British, now crossing the Marne, could assail them in their rear. When von Moltke learned of the situation he ordered a general withdrawal to the line of the Aisne.

Thus ended the German bid for a short, glorious war won by a rapid, decisive campaign. If they had won this battle, they could have dictated a profitable peace with France upon their own terms. As later events proved, von Schlieffen was correct in believing that Russia would then have been subdued. England, after the loss of her army in central France, and after Russia had been defeated, would probably have been willing to negotiate peace. (A treaty of peace with the Kaiser would have been a far different thing than a treaty with Hitler.) The continent of Europe would then have obeyed a single master.

The Battle of the Marne had extended from Paris to Switzerland, but the heaviest fighting had been along the front from Paris to beyond Verdun. It had begun at sunrise on the 6th of September and ended with the German retreat on the 9th, although some authorities prefer to extend the closing date to the 12th of September. Nearly two and a half million men were engaged: 1,125,000 Allies and 1,275,000 Germans. The casualties were not nearly so heavy as in many of the longer, more bitterly fought battles which occurred later in the war, because the Germans had seen fit to withdraw. The victory was a strategic victory rather than a tremendous tactical success. It had been a moral victory over the German High Command, and the narrow margin between defeat and victory had lain in the failure of von Moltke to carry out the plan conceived by his brilliant predecessor von Schlieffen. Fully cognizant of this fact, German leaders in later years convinced themselves that they should have won the Battle of the Marne and that short, profitable wars were still possible if properly conducted, as this campaign should have been. This strong belief, and the legend

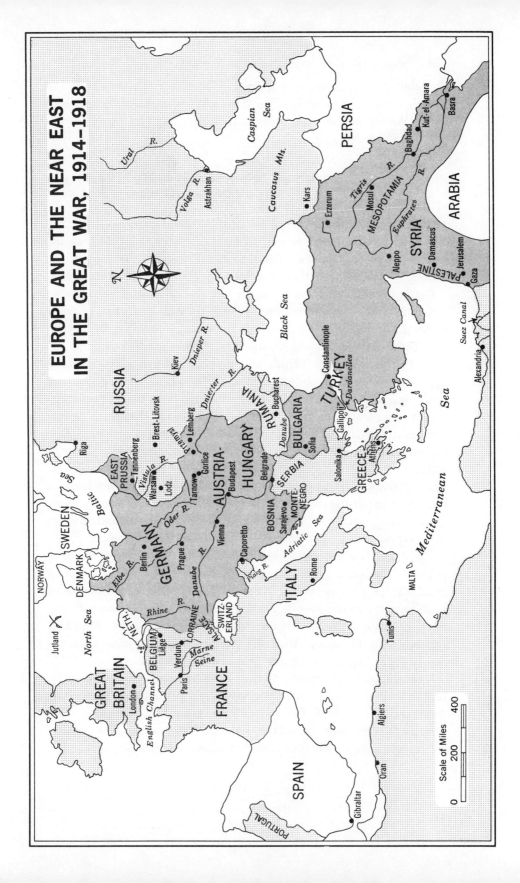

EUROPE AND THE NEAR EAST
IN THE GREAT WAR, 1914–1918

that the German Army was invincible, had in fact never been defeated, but had been "stabbed in the back," were major factors leading to the second German attempt to win the mastery of the world.

Synopsis of Events Between the First Battle of the Marne, A.D. 1914, and the Battle of Midway, A.D. 1942

1914. Following the Battle of the Marne, each side extends its lines westward in an attempt to outflank its opponent. This "Race to the Sea" ends when German efforts to break through are stopped at Ypres. Trench warfare then develops all along the Western Front.

Russia is initially successful in an invasion of Austria but German troops, after their victory at Tannenberg, are rushed to the assistance of Austria, where they aid in halting the Russian offensive. In November, Turkey enters the war on the side of the Central Powers.

On the high seas the British and French navies establish supremacy. A German fleet defeats a British squadron off the coast of Chile in November, but in December another British squadron almost completely destroys the German force at the Battle of the Falkland Islands, off southern Argentina. Keeping their main fleet in home waters, the Germans begin to concentrate upon submarine warfare.

1915. Trench warfare continues on the Western Front; neither side is able to break the deadlock. In May, German and Austrian forces launch a huge offensive, break through the Russian lines and advance over 200 miles beyond Warsaw. Italy joins the Allied Powers.

The Allies land on the Gallipoli Peninsula. After a vigorous campaign the troops are withdrawn in January, 1916, with a resultant great loss of prestige in the Near East. A British expedition from India invades Mesopotamia. By the end of the year a large British force is invested by the Turks; after a long siege it is forced to surrender the following April. In October, Bulgaria joins Germany and Austria; together their troops overwhelm Serbia.

Meanwhile, in February, Germany had announced a submarine blockade of the British Isles. In May the British transatlantic liner *Lusitania* is sunk with the loss of over a hundred American lives. Germany eventually gives the United States assurances against future occurrences, but continues her submarine campaign.

1916.   In an attempt to bring the war to a close, Germany launches a great offensive upon the fortress of Verdun on February 21. Furious fighting develops which lasts for months. In July the British, together with the French, begin an extended drive along the Somme River. Although it helps to relieve the pressure upon Verdun, enormous losses are sustained.

On the Eastern Front, in June, the Russians had attacked Austria in an effort to sustain the French at Verdun. Although the Austrians are badly defeated, the Russian drive is finally stopped with the aid of German troops. In August, Rumania joins the Allies, but the Central Powers combine against her; in December and January, 1917, almost all of the country is overrun.

At the end of May the great naval Battle of Jutland is fought. Although the German fleet inflicts greater losses upon the Royal Navy, the Germans return to port for the duration of the war. In response to a strong protest from the United States, Germany again promises greater care for neutrals in her submarine warfare. As a result her underseas campaign becomes less effective.

1917.   Hoping to win the war at sea by choking off supplies to the British Isles, Germany proclaims a policy of unrestricted submarine warfare. In March the Russian Revolution begins; Czar Nicholas II abdicates; the Provisional Government takes control. In April the United States declares war. Thus the Allies gain another Great Power but, before her influence can be felt, Russia is lost. A Russian offensive collapses; the revolution spreads to the army; the Germans and Austrians attack; the Bolsheviks led by Lenin seize control of the government in November and open negotiations for peace.

Meanwhile, in April and May the great French offensive on the Western Front, designed to achieve a major breakthrough, fails; the British are forced to continue the assaults to keep their enemy occupied while the French stand on the defensive. Then in October and November another major ally, Italy, is almost lost at the near disaster known as the Battle of Caporetto. But by the end of the year the British reputation in the Near East is restored when they advance northward through Palestine and General Allenby enters Jerusalem in December.

1918.   A continuation of the German advance on the Eastern Front forces the Bolshevik Government to sign the Treaty of Brest-Litovsk in March, on Germany's terms. Now free to concentrate on the

Western Front, von Hindenberg and Ludendorff launch their great peace offensives. From late March until early June the German drives achieve astounding successes. Faced with disaster the Allies are forced to accept unity of command; General Ferdinand Foch, soon to become a Marshal of France, is appointed general-in-chief.

In mid-June an Austrian advance against Italy is defeated at the Piave River. The final German offensive in France in July is halted. Foch seizes the opportunity to begin a great counteroffensive near Soissons in which American troops play the leading part; this Second Battle of the Marne marks the turning of the tide. From this point onward the French, British, and American armies, led by Pétain, Haig, and Pershing, progressively advance. Deserted by her Allies, Germany signs the Armistice on November 11.

1919–1920. The Paris Peace Conference opens in January, 1919, with President Woodrow Wilson of the United States, Prime Minister David Lloyd George of Great Britain, Premier Georges Clemenceau of France, and Prime Minister Vittorio Orlando of Italy as the outstanding figures in the negotiations. Germany is excluded from the discussions, and Russia is not represented.

The treaty with Germany providing for the establishment of the League of Nations, the most important of the five treaties terminating World War I, is signed in the famous Hall of Mirrors at Versailles on June 28, 1919. France regains Alsace-Lorraine. Germany cedes large sections of territory to Poland, who had proclaimed her independence at the close of the war. Included in the new Polish territory is a strip of land called the Polish Corridor, giving access to the Baltic Sea, thus separating East Prussia from the rest of Germany. The future of many other smaller parts of Germany's territory is to be determined by future plebiscites; Germany also loses her colonies. The United States fails to ratify the Treaty of Versailles, thereby imposing a handicap upon the operation of the League of Nations by not becoming a member.

By the terms of other treaties Italy's claims were partially met; Austria and Hungary became small, separate states; Czechoslovakia and Yugoslavia were created as independent countries; the boundaries of Rumania, Bulgaria, and Greece were altered. The end of the war brought about the downfall of the once mighty Ottoman Empire, which had lasted for over six centuries.

In 1918 Allied forces had landed in various parts of Russia and Siberia. Their presence tended further to confuse the already enormously complicated situation within Russia resulting from the civil wars between the White Russian forces, opposing the Bolsheviks, and the Red Army, organized by Trotsky. As a result of these wars Finland, Estonia, Latvia and Lithuania acquired their independence. Poland's eastern boundary was not settled until the year after Marshal Pilsudski's victory over the Russians at the Battle of Warsaw in August, 1920.

1920. The League of Nations creates the Permanent Court of International Justice, popularly named the World Court.

1921–1922. The Washington Conference results in the signing, among other treaties, of an agreement covering construction of capital ships over 10,000 tons. This Five-Power Treaty establishes for Great Britain, the United States, Japan, France, and Italy a ratio of 5-5-3-1.67-1.67.

1922. The Irish Free State comes into existence, with the status of a British dominion.

1922. Benito Mussolini organizes the Fascist "March on Rome." The king appoints him premier, which he gradually converts into a dictatorship.

1923. The Turkish Republic is proclaimed with Mustapha Kemal as President.

1924–1927. Upon the death of Lenin a struggle for power in Russia begins. Joseph Stalin emerges as dictator; Trotsky is expelled from the Communist party.

1931. The Statute of Westminster recognizes the changes already brought about in the organization of the empire henceforth to be known as the British Commonwealth of Nations.

1931–1932. Japan invades Manchuria, renaming it Manchukuo.

1933. In January, Adolf Hitler becomes Chancellor of Germany. In October, Germany withdraws from the League of Nations.

1933. When the League objects to Japan's operations against China, the Japanese announce their withdrawal from the League (to take effect in two years). Simultaneously they add the province of Jehol to Manchukuo.

1934. Upon President von Hindenburg's death, Hitler assumes the title of Führer, as dictator of Germany.

1935. At a plebiscite conducted by the League of Nations, 90 per-cent of the voters of the Saar favor reunion with Germany. Hitler denounces the military clauses of the Treaty of Versailles limiting German armament.

1935–1936. Upon Mussolini's orders Italian troops invade Ethiopia and rapidly overcome resistance.

1936. Hitler sends German troops into the demilitarized Rhine-land. (It was a tremendous gamble. The troops had orders to with-draw if the French opposed them. France could easily have crushed the small German army, but made no effort to do so.) The greatest chance to ruin Hitler is lost.

1936–1939. The Spanish Civil War provides an excellent oppor-tunity for Germany and Italy to test their weapons and tactics. They support the insurgent forces of Francisco Franco, while Com-munist Russia does the same in support of the Loyalist forces.

1937. To forestall Generalissimo Chiang Kai-shek's efforts to build an army to resist them, the Japanese launch a powerful offensive south-ward from Manchukuo on Tientsin and Peiping, then follow with a landing near Shanghai which they capture after a prolonged and bitter resistance. By the end of the year Japanese forces advancing south from Tientsin capture Tsinan; in central China they indulge in the infamous "Rape of Nanking."

1938. Despite stout Chinese resistance, the Japanese succeed in uniting their invading armies, capturing Suchow. Their initial efforts to take Hankow fail until, in October, their armies land near Hong Kong and take Canton; the fall of Hankow follows immediately there-after. Several ports along the coast west of Formosa, and the island of Hainan are also seized.

1938. German forces cross the Austrian frontier in March; Austria is joined to Germany. Hitler's demands that the Sudetenland, or Ger-man-speaking portion of Czechoslovakia, be given the right of self-determination, lead, six months later, to the Munich Pact where, in an ardent desire for peace, Britain and France reach the height of their appeasement policy. Germany occupies the Sudetenland; shortly thereafter Poland and Hungary obtain slices of Czechoslovakia.

1939. In March, Hitler seizes the remainder of Czechoslovakia, ex-cept for another slice given to Hungary, forces Lithuania to cede a small district along the Baltic, and presents to Poland demands for the reunion of Danzig with Germany and the right to construct a road and railway across the Polish Corridor. Poland refuses to be coerced and rejects the demands; Great Britain and France pledge their aid to Poland in the event of attack.

At this juncture Italy invaded and conquered Albania. But, far more startling to the world was the announcement, in August, of a non-aggression pact between Germany and Soviet Russia. It included, as many people suspected at the time, secret agreements to divide the Baltic States and Poland into spheres of influence. On September 1, 1939, ignoring the formality of a declaration of war, the German armies poured across the Polish frontier, as the German Air Force unleashed a surprise attack on Polish airfields. Two days later Great Britain and France declared war on Germany.

Within the first two days of combat the Polish Air Force was annihilated. The Polish Army fought valiantly against hopeless odds. Its spirited resistance excited worldwide admiration but it had no chance against the efficient German war machine. In five weeks the last organized resistance was overcome. Poland ceased to exist as a nation. Her downfall came about so quickly that a shocked world felt that some new kind of warfare must have been introduced. It was promptly labeled "Blitzkrieg" by the press, and most of the credit was given to the air and armored forces, whereas the greater part of the fighting had been done, as usual, by hard-marching, disciplined infantry supported by efficient artillery. It was the intelligent employment of all arms in accordance with a well-conceived plan prepared in advance, with the initial element of surprise, which had produced this lightning campaign.

The complete removal of Poland from the map of Europe was originally proposed, not by Nazi Germany, but by Communist Russia whose troops advanced into Poland from the east on September 17. Stalin soon also occupied bases in Estonia, Latvia and Lithuania, but Finland manfully rejected his demands for military and territorial concessions. On November 30, Stalin's forces attacked, without a formal declaration of war. The Finns, commanded by Field Marshal Mannerheim, courageously met the assault of their traditional enemy, and halted the invaders in their tracks. The Russians, counting purely on their tremendous numerical superiority, had made but scant preparations for winter warfare in this country of deep snow, lakes and forests. By year's end the Russian effort appeared to be a dismal failure.

1940. Tremendous artillery bombardments followed by wave after wave of Russian infantry, driven forward without regard to losses, on a narrow front, finally break the Finnish line. (With her world prestige at stake, Communist Russia was willing to accept losses of ten to one.) The exhausted defenders finally give way. Finland is forced to cede Viborg (Viipuri) and several other border territories to Russia.

To acquire naval and air bases which would be invaluable against the British blockade, German amphibious and airborne forces conducted a surprise attack in April upon Norway, simultaneously overrunning Denmark. Although great numbers of troops were not employed, the German sea, ground, and air forces were superbly handled and cooperated splendidly together, ensuring victory over surprised but stubbornly resisting Norwegian troops. Hastily assembled British and French forces coming to the aid of Norway could do little to halt the invasion. Within a month, except for a small section of northern Norway, the entire country was in German hands.

The next German target would obviously be France where practically nothing had occurred for months. On May 10, Hitler loosed his forces upon neutral Holland and Belgium, and upon France. That evening Winston Churchill became Prime Minister of Great Britain.

As the French and British hurried northward to aid Belgium and Holland, the main German effort came through the Ardennes behind them. Holland was overrun in five days. Six days later the swiftly moving Germans, spearheaded by air and massed armored forces, reached the English Channel. The Belgians, the British, and a French army were cut off from France. Then came the almost miraculous evacuation from Dunkirk. France fell soon thereafter. The British people, inspired by their great leader, who offered them nothing but "blood, sweat and tears," stood alone.

In July came the German Air Force to pave the way for a possible invasion of England. In this four-month struggle, known to the world as the Battle of Britain, the gallant Royal Air Force beat back the *Luftwaffe* and emerged victorious.

While Hitler was thus receiving his first major setback, Mussolini was widening the theater of war. In mid-September, Italian forces crossed the border from Libya into Egypt and, in late October, Mussolini hopefully sent his armies across the Albanian border into Greece. Both Italian efforts were thrown back. In addition, a large portion of the Italian fleet was damaged or destroyed by British naval aircraft, while it was riding at anchor in the harbor of Taranto.

Meanwhile, events in Europe had profoundly affected the balance of power in the Far East. With the Netherlands in German hands, France defeated, and Britain fighting for her life, the Dutch, French, and British possessions south of Japan seemed easy prey. The weakened French government was forced to agree to Japanese occupation of northern Indo-China. In September, Japanese troops moved to bases there, from which they could, and did, attack the Chinese.

1941. At a secret conference held in Washington beginning late in January, American and British planners agree that, in the event of a global war, the concentration of force should be against Germany first. This basic strategic decision was never altered.

General Wavell's offensive in North Africa, begun the preceding December, meets with complete success. By early February almost all of the Italian army in Libya is either destroyed or captured. British ground forces are then sent to aid Greece. The Royal Navy inflicts a severe defeat upon the Italian Navy at the Battle of Cape Matapan.

Irritated by the failures of his Italian ally and by unexpected political developments in Yugoslavia, Hitler determines to put an end to the conflict in the Balkans. In April, German troops again demonstrate their skill and efficiency, overrunning Yugoslavia in a week, and all of Greece in two more weeks. In April also, General Erwin Rommel, now in charge of German and Italian forces in North Africa, advances across Libya, invests Tobruk, and drives the British back into Egypt. In May, Crete is captured by an airborne assault.

By the passage of the Lend-Lease Act in March, giving the President power to aid nations whose defense he considered vital to that of the United States, the Congress takes a definite forward step in favor of the Allies versus their enemies. With the continued deterioration of Britain's position in the Mediterranean, and with German sinking of merchant ships far exceeding the capacity of British shipyards to replace them, President Franklin D. Roosevelt extends the limits of naval patrol operations in the Atlantic. Then in May he reinforces the Atlantic Fleet and proclaims an unlimited national emergency.

On June 22, 1941, Adolf Hitler sends his armies into Russia.

Although they had received advance warning, the Russians were caught completely by surprise. The swift progress of German arms was watched with increasing amazement. The destruction and capture of hundreds of thousands of Soviet troops seemed to promise complete success.

While the Germans were thus achieving such startling triumphs, Japanese forces occupied all of French Indo-China. President Roosevelt promptly froze all Japanese credits in the United States, thus bringing trade between the two countries to a halt. That August the two leaders of the Free World met at Argentia Bay, Newfoundland. The result of their secret meeting was the issuance of a joint declaration, called the Atlantic Charter, outlining the postwar aims of the two countries.

In September, President Roosevelt took the unprecedented step of ordering the Navy to attack any vessel threatening United States shipping or ships under United States escort, thus committing the country to a limited, undeclared war. One month later, in Japan, the militarists achieved complete control of the government; General Hideki Tojo became premier. From this time forward it was simply a question of when and where Japan would strike.

In November, British Commonwealth forces, now commanded by General Auchinleck, began an offensive in North Africa. After severe fighting Tobruk was relieved. Then, on December 7, 1941, the Japanese launched their surprise attack on Pearl Harbor.

The Battle of Midway,
A.D. 1942

The Japanese loss of four aircraft carriers and their complement of 250 aircraft with many first-line pilots completely reversed the strategic situation in the Pacific. This was their last great offensive against American territory. Thereafter the United States took the offensive and started the long advance toward the Japanese homeland and final victory.

THESE WORDS, inscribed upon the walls of the United States Government war memorials erected by the American Battle Monuments Commission at Honolulu and at Manila, accurately reflect the considered opinion of the Army, Navy, Air Force, and Marine Corps. For they, like all historical inscriptions prepared by the Commission, were submitted to the Armed Services before being engraved in place. It is not always a simple task to obtain complete agreement within any government, but in this case it was comparatively easy. There was no debate whatever as to the importance of the battle. The only problem was the exact choice of words to describe accurately the effect of the Battle of Midway upon the course of the war.

The Japanese strike at Pearl Harbor on December 7, 1941 had dealt the United States Navy a stunning blow. Four battleships, one

307

minelayer, and a target ship were sunk. Four battleships, three cruisers, three destroyers, and two other ships were damaged. One hundred and eighty-eight naval and army aircraft were destroyed and an additional one hundred and fifty-nine were damaged. American military and naval casualties numbered over thirty-six hundred men killed and wounded. The Japanese lost five midget submarines, twenty-eight aircraft and fewer than one hundred men. Fortunately, on that Sunday morning, the U. S. aircraft carriers were at sea.

On the same day, which was December 8 across the international date line, the Japanese bombed Hong Kong, Singapore, the Philippines, Guam, and Wake. Simultaneously their ground forces crossed the Hong Kong border, the Thailand frontier, and were landed at several places on the Malay Peninsula. Two days later landings were effected on Luzon; Guam was forced to surrender; and the British battleship *Prince of Wales* and the battle cruiser *Repulse* were sunk by air attack off Malaya. The week of December 21 brought additional Japanese advances and victories. After successfully repulsing one assault, Wake was forced to surrender on December 23. Hong Kong fell on Christmas Day. The main Japanese landings on Luzon were successful; Manila was declared an open city; United States and Philippine forces began a planned withdrawal toward the Bataan Peninsula.

On swept the Japanese down the Malay Peninsula toward Singapore, into the southern Philippines, thence to Borneo, Celebes, and southeastward to Rabaul. Pitting their limited means against overwhelming odds, the Allies resisted the successive assaults; but as resources diminished their defense was conducted with ever-increasing difficulty.

Swiftly, methodically, relentlessly the Japanese continued their advance. Singapore capitulated in mid-February. After a series of hard-fought naval battles, the Japanese landed on Sumatra, Java and Timor. Their aircraft bombarded Darwin, Australia, while to the southeast other Japanese forces landed on the eastern shore of New Guinea and on Bougainville in the northern Solomons. Meanwhile, on the continent of Asia, to secure their right flank and cut off supplies to their Chinese enemies, the Japanese crossed from Thailand to Burma and occupied Rangoon. Falling back before progressively mounting odds, the Allies were suffering heavy losses. The only bright spot in the allied picture was the admirable defense being conducted by General Douglas MacArthur's U. S. and Philippine troops on Bataan. There the Japanese attacks were contained; an amphibious envelopment of the peninsula

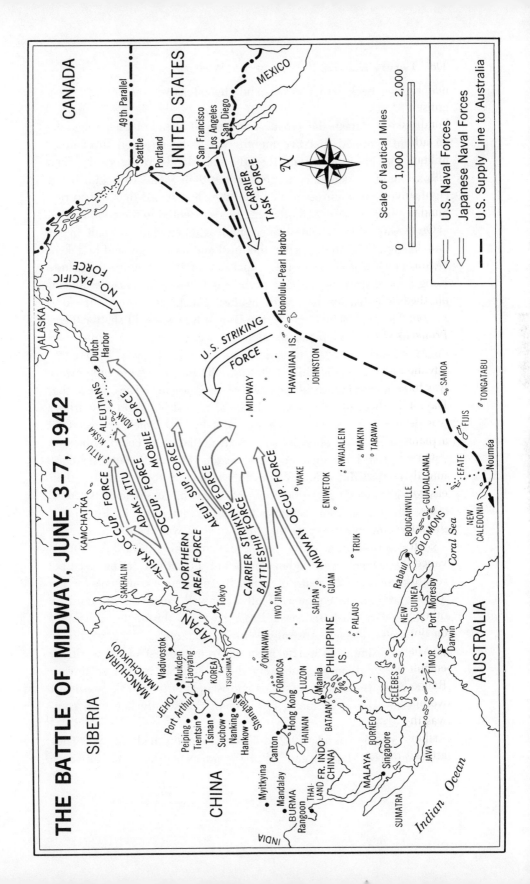

was thrown back into the sea, and the offensive was brought to a halt.

Except for Bataan the Japanese were well ahead of their schedule. They had assumed that five months would be required to conquer Malaya, the Philippines, and the adjacent islands to the south. Then a halt would be necessary to consolidate their gains, to begin to tap the vast natural resources of this land they had seized that was so rich in oil, rubber, tin, rice, and other materials essential to the continuation of their war effort. Their planners had assumed that the halt might last as long as six months. Then the third and final step could be taken. This would involve the further expansion of their empire to include the seizure of strategic outposts in the Pacific essential to the establishment of a defensive perimeter against which the counterattacking forces of their principal enemy, the United States, could shatter themselves in vain. The Japanese planners were realistic. Despite wild rumors prevalent in the United States early in the war, they never expected to invade the United States itself, and they were fully aware of the immense industrial capacity of their enemy. They knew that eventually the United States could build new fleets, train new armies and employ large masses of aircraft. But by that time they expected to have made their outposts so powerful that they could withstand attack. And if their own fleet was strong and their outposts close enough to the United States (possibly even including Hawaii), their carrier forces could make bombing raids on the American west coast. Under these conditions, and with Hitler victorious in Europe, it seemed reasonable to expect that their enemies would agree to a peace.

Such was the outline of the Japanese plan looking toward the United States, but there were other important objectives to be secured. Australia lay directly south of them. It was a huge continent, far too large to attempt to conquer. If all went well, some troops could be landed on the northern coast. From bases in this region air forces could bombard major Australian cities and targets. But it would be much easier simply to isolate Australia from the rest of the world by cutting the vital supply line from the United States. The seizure of New Guinea, the Solomon Islands and islands farther to the southeast would allow Japanese forces to interrupt this supply line with comparative ease.

Now, in early March, 1942, only three months had elapsed. They had conquered Malaya, and all of the adjacent islands to the south were in their grasp. They were two months ahead of schedule; losses had been far less than had been anticipated. Perhaps the whole time-table could be advanced. Why wait six months to consolidate their gains? Furthermore, in the process of further expansion, the U. S. Pacific Fleet might be induced to fight for the protection of a specific area. A decisive naval engagement would give Japan absolute mastery of the sea. With this highly desirable objective foremost in their thoughts, the conquerors set to work in their methodical way to re-appraise the situation. Their forces had already landed on the eastern shores of New Guinea and on Bougainville in the northern Solomons. A quick dash southward might secure for them the air bases around Port Moresby from which they could bomb northern Australia. The seizure of this strategic region, of the southern Solomons and of other islands beyond would permit them to cut the line from the United States to Australia. A bold advance in March or April, while the Allies were still off balance, might have succeeded. But the Japanese leaders felt they must secure their right flank in Burma and, for the sake of their own prestige in the Far East, eliminate the Americans still grimly defending the Bataan Peninsula.

Japanese victory in Burma proved to be a comparatively simple task. In March and April their troops drove northward from Rangoon; a strong naval force destroyed opposition in the Indian Ocean, and additional troops were landed. The outnumbered and outfought defenders were hustled out of Burma into India and back into China.

The elimination of the defenders of Bataan was a different story. By early February the Americans and Filipinos had completely halted the invaders and forced the Japanese commander to call for reinforcements. While these were being assembled, the American planners in Washington concluded that there was no possible way to reinforce the garrison in sufficient strength to sustain the defense. Accordingly, President Roosevelt ordered General MacArthur to leave for Australia to assume command of the Allied forces in the Southwest Pacific. Much against his expressed desire, General MacArthur was forced to leave in March, turning over the command of the doomed garrison to General Jonathan M. Wainwright. Until that time the troops had been confident that United States forces would come to their rescue, but from then on their hopes grew dimmer with every passing day. While they slowly wasted away for lack of food and medical supplies, they determined to resist as long as possible, hoping only that their sacrifice would not be in vain. Such proved to be the case; for as we have seen, in order to concentrate a large enough force to overcome their gallant defense, the Japanese had withheld troops from offensive operations against New Guinea and the Solomon Islands. Finally, on April 3, following a devastating air bombardment and artillery barrage, the Japanese launched an assault. Counterattacks failed to halt the onslaught. No longer able to inflict damage upon the enemy, the Bataan forces surrendered on April 9. The offshore island fortress of Corregidor was forced to capitulate on May 6.

The apparently irresistible Japanese advance in the Pacific had greatly alarmed Allied leaders and posed for them an extraordinarily complicated problem. The basic strategic decision to defeat Germany first had been taken early in 1941. They were determined that this decision would not be altered. Every effort would continue to be exerted to prepare a powerful offensive to be launched against Nazi Germany as soon as practicable but, in the process of doing so, they could not afford to lose too much in the Pacific. Not only were they losing vital regions, islands and outposts in the Pacific, the supply line from India to the Chinese forces was being cut, and, above all, Australia was being isolated. United States leaders felt they must give Australia and New Zealand all possible immediate aid, without sacrificing the basic plan against Germany. It was a most difficult, complex problem; Japan must be stopped before she advanced too far, became too strong in her conquered territories, and made the task of liberating those territories too difficult and costly. Furthermore, the United States, by agreement among the Allies, was now responsible for the defense of the Pacific including Australia. In Washington Admiral Ernest J. King and General George C. Marshall agreed that the Japanese must be contained. American troop strength in Australia and on the intervening islands along the route to that continent must be increased. Immediate action was essential before it was too late. A carrier task force had already been dispatched to the threatened region.

For command purposes the Pacific was divided into three regions: the Pacific Ocean Areas under Admiral Chester W. Nimitz; the Southwest Pacific Area under General Douglas MacArthur; and a minor Southeast Pacific Area, alongside the American continent south of Mexico. By mid-April both commanders were receiving reports that led them to believe that a new Japanese strike was impending. From radio intercepts and other indications they concluded that the new offensive would be aimed at Port Moresby. It was imperative that this operation be halted if at all possible, for Port Moresby was not only the key to the safety of northern Australia but also the point from which General MacArthur planned to start his return march, on the long road back to the Philippines.

The result was the Battle of the Coral Sea, the first naval battle in history in which all losses were inflicted by carrier-based aircraft, and no ship on either side sighted a surface enemy. Rear Admiral Frank Jack Fletcher began the battle on May 4 by attacking Tulagi, a small island in the Solomons just north of Guadalcanal, which the Japanese had occupied the preceding day. The carrier battle occurred on May 7 and 8. On the first day the Japanese sank a U. S. destroyer and so severely damaged an oiler that she was scuttled four days later. Aircraft from the carriers *Lexington* and *Yorktown* attacked and sank the light carrier *Shoho,* but the presence of United States and Australian ships had caused the Japanese commander to turn the Port Moresby Invasion Force back, until the Allied fleet could be defeated. On May 8 the Japanese more than evened the score. While their own aircraft carriers *Shokaku* and *Zuikaku* were under attack by United States planes, Japanese aircraft were engaged in an assault upon the American carriers *Yorktown* and *Lexington.* The latter was so severely damaged that she had to be abandoned and was sunk that evening.

Thus the Japanese could rightly claim a tactical victory. They had inflicted much greater losses than they had sustained; the sinking of the large carrier *Lexington* was a great blow to the U. S. Pacific Fleet. In warfare, however, losses alone are often not the true measure of success. The large Japanese carrier *Shokaku* was so heavily damaged that she was unable to return to active service for a period of two months, while the *Zuikaku* lost so many aircraft that she also was temporarily unfit for further combat. Furthermore, the Port Moresby Invasion Force did not return. The attack was postponed because the Japanese had no desire to face land-based aircraft in these waters without the protection of their naval carrier planes. Thus, for the first time in the war, a Japanese invasion thrust had been thwarted. The Allies could justly claim a strategic victory; and, occurring as it did, two days after the surrender of Corregidor, its moral value was immeasurable.

Both fleets left the Coral Sea to prepare for the larger battle yet to come. Here again Admiral Nimitz had received advance warning and had correctly interpreted his intelligence reports and the intercepted radio messages. He concluded that the main Japanese thrust would be aimed at Midway Island and made his preparations accordingly. By early May he also learned that the Japanese might attack the western Aleutians at the same time, but decided to concentrate his fleet for a major engagement near Midway, leaving only a portion of his force to try to protect Alaska. He did not have sufficient strength at his disposal to protect both, in fact it was very doubtful that the fleet would be strong enough to ward off a thrust at Midway alone. At this time there were only four U. S. aircraft carriers in the Pacific, and of these, two had been seriously damaged. The *Saratoga* had been hit by a torpedo in January and was still at San Diego on the west coast. She could not be made ready in time for the coming battle; in fact, she sailed from San Diego while the battle was in progress.

This left just three aircraft carriers, the *Enterprise,* the *Hornet,* and the *Yorktown,* damaged at the Battle of the Coral Sea. All three reached Pearl Harbor in the last days of May, just as the Japanese fleets were setting forth for the coming battle. To add to the anxiety of all concerned it was estimated that the *Yorktown* could not possibly be repaired in time. Nevertheless, the work was begun with a desperate urgency that took no account of daylight hours. The men engaged in the enormous task of repair, rebuilding, and new construction kept at the job until it was completed in just over two days, instead of two months which had been one of the gloomy estimates of the time required. Possibly never in history have those engaged in such tasks, which normally are rewarded with only general commendations and expressions of goodwill for work well done, seen their labors bear fruit so rapidly and so dramatically in battle. Although the ship was to be lost at Midway, if the United States Navy had been forced to engage with only two carriers instead of three the battle might have been won by the Japanese.

The importance of Midway cannot be judged by its size. It is one of the smaller of the atolls in the Pacific, measuring only about six miles in width. It contains only two small islands, barely large enough to hold airfields of reasonable size. In the years preceding World War II it had been gradually developed first as a coaling station, then as an airport, then as a naval base. When war came, reinforcements were rushed to the area. The naval and marine garrison was strengthened and additional aircraft were based there, including some long-range army bombers. By early June, 1942, it was the only strong American base in the Central Pacific Area west of Hawaii. Both sides were well aware of its importance. If the Japanese captured the atoll it would not be just another victory. Its seizure would mean the extension of their defensive perimeter for a distance of hundreds of miles eastward from Wake. And the Japanese were anxious to bring it under their control for another reason. In April a carrier task force had managed to slip through their defenses and send a flight of army bombers on a raid over Tokyo, which had been a surprise and a shock to the Japanese people. The capture of Midway should prevent a recurrence of such attacks. But, above all, an invasion should bring the United States Pacific Fleet out to battle to defend the atoll. A decisive naval victory would ensure Japanese command of the Pacific and permit them to continue their advance southward beyond New Guinea and the Solomons to isolate Australia.

Admiral Isoroku Yamamoto, the commander in chief of the Combined Fleet, knew little of his opponents' dispositions but was entirely confident of success. He knew that his fleets outnumbered his enemy's in every type of ship. Two of his large carriers had been put out of operation at the Coral Sea. One of them, the *Zuikaku*, would be able to put to sea soon, but he did not wait for its arrival. He had seven carriers (three light and four large carriers); surely these would be adequate to take care of any opposition that might be encountered.

Sending a large submarine force in advance of his fleets, Admiral Yamamoto sailed into the Central Pacific. The composition of the various Japanese forces is somewhat difficult to explain. There were three targets; in order of importance these were the U.S. Pacific Fleet, Midway, and the western Aleutians. Yamamoto chose to advance in four main groupings. First there was the Carrier Striking Force with the four large carriers and a suitable number of cruisers and destroyers. Next in importance was the Battleship Force under the admiral's personal command; it included a light carrier. Then came the Midway Occupation Force. Finally, there was the Northern Area Force, whose target was Alaska. This last was further subdivided into a Mobile Force including two light carriers, two Occupation Forces, and an Aleutian Support Force.

If this arrangement seems unduly complicated, the operation plan was even more so. First the Mobile Force of the Northern Area Force was to bombard Dutch Harbor to confuse the Americans as to the true destination of the Japanese. Then it would cover the landings of the Adak-Attu and Kiska Occupation Forces. While these operations were taking place, the main Carrier Striking Force would attack Midway and entice the United States fleet into battle. The Battleship Force would complete the action, and the Midway Occupation Force would seize that island. The function of the Aleutian Support Force was not at all clear. It apparently was to be stationed somewhere between Alaska and Midway, prepared to move in either direction as required. Thus the Japanese forces were spread over the Northern and Central Pacific Areas while the Americans were far more concentrated in the vicinity of Midway, with only a portion of their forces in the Alaskan area.

The Battle of Midway began on June 3, 1942, as planned by the Japanese, with an attack by the Mobile Force of the Northern Area Force on Dutch Harbor. It was renewed on the second day, but by that time the climactic carrier battle near Midway was well under way. It also began as planned with a carrier attack upon Midway, but here the Japanese pilots ran into more serious trouble. U.S. Marine antiaircraft batteries and land-based aircraft manned by Marine, Navy, and Army Air Forces pilots destroyed more than forty of the Japanese aircraft. The counterattack by Midway-based planes resulted in only slight damage to the Japanese and the loss of several American pilots and their aircraft, but may have contributed to a fatal decision by the Japanese admiral commanding the Carrier Striking Force.

Vice Admiral Nagumo had kept nearly one hundred of his planes standing by, ready for launching at any naval force that might appear, but there was no evidence of any American ships near Midway. He therefore decided to make a second strike at the atoll. This meant rearming of the planes that had been standing by, changing from torpedoes to bombs. While his four carriers were in the process of converting, beating off the Midway-based aircraft and recovering their own, American carrier planes were approaching to catch the Japanese at their most awkward moment.

Admiral Fletcher in tactical command of the United States Striking Force had, in compliance with Admiral Nimitz's orders, concentrated his ships well to the northeast of Midway. From this position he could hope that the enemy ships would be located first by the Midway planes before the enemy could find his own ships. As we have seen, this is exactly what had happened. While the four Japanese carriers were launching their first strike toward Midway, the three American carriers were preparing to send their aircraft against the Japanese. Admiral Fletcher's force was divided into two Task Forces, his own, which included the *Yorktown*, and another, commanded by Rear Admiral Raymond A. Spruance, which included the carriers *Enterprise* and *Hornet*. Admiral Spruance was the first to launch his planes; Fletcher sent his about two hours later. Some of them never found their targets; others located the Japanese ships but at varying intervals by flying different courses. The result was not one concentrated blow but a series of attacks, which greatly increased the danger to each squadron as it attempted to penetrate the screen of antiaircraft fire. Casualties among the torpedo-bombers were extremely heavy because, with their obsolescent torpedoes, they had to approach at slow speed, low over the water. As the Japanese ships took violent action and the defending aircraft dived upon them, these young pilots flew bravely, steadily forward through a hail of antiaircraft fire, heedless of losses. Not one torpedo hit its mark—but, by their sacrifice, they paved the way for their own dive-bombers to follow. The result of their attack was spectacular. The aircraft carriers *Akagi, Kaga,* and *Soryu* were all three hit; all three burst into flames and were abandoned.

This left the Japanese with only one aircraft carrier, the *Hiryu*, which sent two waves of planes to bomb the *Yorktown*. The Japanese pilots proved as brave as their American counterparts. In spite of heavy losses from the aircraft flying to intercept them and from the defensive antiaircraft fire surrounding the American carrier, they continued onward to strike the *Yorktown*. The first wave started fires aboard the ship and temporarily brought her to a stop; the second attack wave caused the crew to abandon her.

The last major action of the 4th of June came about five o'clock in the afternoon when a flight of American carrier aircraft, including planes from the disabled *Yorktown*, bombed the *Hiryu*. Four direct hits were recorded. During the night Admiral Yamamoto abandoned his invasion plans and decided to retire westward. Of his four large carriers the *Kaga* and the *Soryu* had already sunk; the *Akagi* and the *Hiryu* were sunk on the 5th of June by the departing Japanese. On the following day, in the pursuit phase, the Japanese cruiser *Mikuma* was also sunk. That same afternoon a submarine, searching for the damaged *Yorktown,* torpedoed the escorting U. S. destroyer *Hammann* and ended the career of the gallant carrier, which sank at dawn on the 7th.

Far to the north the Occupation Forces abandoned their plan to seize Adak and landed unopposed on the islands of Attu and Kiska on June 7, thus successfully accomplishing the least important of the Japanese objectives. Without Midway this northern extension of the defensive perimeter was of minor significance. Neither side had any intention of invading the other by this forbidding route.

The Battle of Midway "completely reversed the strategic situation in the Pacific." The Japanese never again attempted an invasion of American territory, and abandoned their most ambitious plans for the isolation of Australia by the seizure of islands along the supply route from the United States. They abandoned efforts to reach Port Moresby by sea but decided instead to attack overland across New Guinea. They were thus reduced to undertaking far more limited offensives, while the United States was now able for the first time to begin a limited offensive of her own, which, until the victory at Midway, had been entirely impractical.

Thus the battle fought on June 3–7 led to the landing on Guadacanal on August 7, 1942. The succession of hard-fought naval battles and grim struggles on land and in the air that followed marked the turning point of the Pacific War. In New Guinea, United States and Australian forces repulsed the Japanese thrust toward Port Moresby and advanced on the long road back to the Philippines. Final victory would not come until September 2, 1945, and in the interim thousands of Allied prisoners of war would die in harsh captivity, while untold numbers of men, women, and children in the conquered territories would suffer the same fate. It is heartwarming to record that after her defeat Japan renounced her former militaristic leaders and refused to plot vengeance upon her former enemies. Her islands are now one of the major strongholds in the struggle against communism.

20

The Battle of Stalingrad, A.D. 1942–1943

IN ALL THE DISCUSSIONS of the preceding battles and campaigns it has been easy to feel sympathetic toward one side or the other. We can share, at least in spirit, the triumph or the despair of the victor or the vanquished. But when we come to the campaigns fought in Russia during World War II, we can feel little sympathy for either side. Both the Nazi party and the Communist party were led by men who were aggressive, utterly ruthless, and entirely willing to sacrifice thousands of human lives to attain their ends. It was of little moment to them whether the human beings concerned were fighting for or against them. Prisoners were kept alive only so long as they were capable of working; then they died. The life of a soldier was expendable. The Germans were less likely than the Russians, however, to sacrifice their soldiers in wave after wave of attack against an almost impregnable position. The Nazi party could not afford to use men in this way because they had fewer soldiers, whereas the Russian supply of manpower was comparatively limitless. Furthermore, the German soldier was better trained and more highly educated than the average Russian. Therefore he was more valuable to the Nazis than the Russian soldier was to the Communists.

We can feel a great deal of sympathy for the individual Russian and

319

the individual German, including many of their military leaders, who had no choice but to fight on, hoping that they might survive and live to see a better day. We can also feel, from a professional point of view, admiration for the skill and efficiency of the German war machine, which Hitler utterly ruined in the snows of Russia.

The question as to whether or not Adolf Hitler was a military genius was freely debated in the early days of the war. At the beginning he seemed to be. His lightning conquests of Poland, in 1939, Norway and France, in 1940, and of the Balkans, in 1941, were remarkable indeed, and some of these triumphs were undoubtedly due in part to his own personal influence. This record of victory cannot be overlooked; and, if he had never sent his armies and air fleets into Russia, he might today be ranked high among the military leaders of history. The question of how much of Germany's success was due to his generals, the staff, the officers, and the ability and endurance of the trained German soldier would never have been firmly settled. Russia provided the answer.

In the field of politics and international relations, Hitler was undoubtedly a genius. Every patriotic German bitterly resented the military clauses of the Treaty of Versailles limiting German armament. It was Hitler who successfully denounced them in 1935; then, in the following year, he sent troops into the demilitarized Rhineland. Almost all the German generals were sure that France would mobilize and crush the little German army. The troops had orders to withdraw if the French moved to oppose them, but Hitler won his gamble. Then, in 1938, Austria had been seized with very little protest by the Allies, which led to the famous Munich Pact, in which Hitler acquired the Sudetenland from Czechoslovakia. It was not until he began to threaten Poland that he ran into serious opposition. His solution was to sign a nonaggression pact with Stalin and then seize Poland by force, thus beginning World War II.

At this point it should be noted that, although Hitler thus acquired most of Poland by fighting for it, Stalin obtained a large slice without going to war, and then quietly absorbed Estonia, Latvia and Lithuania without firing a shot. Stalin had to fight to obtain what he wanted from Finland, which cost him dearly, but he had not yet involved his country in the general world conflict. We cannot read the mind of a madman like Hitler, but it must have irked him greatly to discover that Stalin was playing the game with just as much success as he.

Therefore, after his victories in Poland, Norway, and France, he turned with longing eyes upon Russia, which had always been his primary target. Hitler had now proved to his own satisfaction that he was a military genius; Stalin's army had done very poorly in Finland. Now he could demonstrate to the world his military superiority over his principal rival. Here is illustrated one of the main differences between the two: Stalin could wait; Hitler would not, even though he was already at war with England. It would end with Stalin obtaining what he sought, while Hitler lost everything.

Yet when Hitler invaded Russia the odds were in his favor. First, he had the German Army, magnificently trained, superbly led, flushed with victory and confident of success. Next he had the *Luftwaffe,* which was superior man for man and plane for plane to the Russians. Both suffered from a shortage of transport and supply vehicles but, if this was a quick, decisive campaign as Hitler expected, this shortage would not matter too greatly. The Russians had initially a numerical superiority in tanks and planes, but Hitler expected to overcome this disadvantage in the first few battles; in this assumption he was correct.

He was also correct in assuming that he would have the advantage of surprise, although this is difficult to explain. The Russians had plenty of advance warning. Possibly Stalin and his advisers simply could not believe that Germany would attack them when she already had a war on her hands with Great Britain. It simply did not make sense for Hitler to enlarge the conflict so that he would be fighting on two fronts. We may feel sure that because Stalin knew that this was the type of mistake he would never make, he could not bring himself to believe that Hitler would actually be so foolish. Furthermore, an attack on Russia would make her an ally of England. Stalin could then probably call upon the British for supplies and assistance; also the Americans could be induced to furnish a large number of Lend-Lease materials.

Hitler had initially told his generals to be ready to attack Russia by the middle of May, 1941, but the continued failure of his Italian ally, Mussolini, to achieve success in the Balkans was proving very damaging to the prestige of the partnership. The Greeks had proved to be more than a match for the Italians. They had driven the invaders back well beyond their starting point in Albania and had repulsed a second Italian offensive with ease. Then, in March, a political coup in Belgrade had upset Hitler's plans for bringing Yugoslavia into the war on his side. Irritated by this upset and by Mussolini's failures, Hitler decided to send German troops into the Balkans to put an end to the conflict. In April, 1941, the German Army and Air Force again proved their power, skill and efficiency by overrunning Yugoslavia in one week and Greece in two weeks more, ejecting the British who had come to the aid of that unfortunate country. In May, they captured Crete by an airborne assault. German forces were also sent to Africa to aid Mussolini. There, in April also, General Erwin Rommel had taken the initiative, recaptured Libya, driven the British back into Egypt, and was besieging Tobruk. But the Balkan operation, although brilliantly successful, was a mistake. It delayed the opening of the war against Russia by about three weeks, and the loss of those three weeks would be keenly felt in the last days before Moscow as the Russian winter settled over the front.

The German attack on Russia was launched about three o'clock in the morning of June 22, 1941. As previously mentioned, it caught the Russians completely by surprise and made tremendously rapid progress. In a series of violent air battles the *Luftwaffe* beat down the Russian Air Force and gained almost complete air superiority. But before describing the campaign it would be well to mention a number of very important factors. First, the Germans had little accurate information as to Russian strength and capabilities. As it turned out, the opposing armies at the beginning had about equal numbers but the Russians later brought into the war, from Siberia and elsewhere, vast numbers of troops until they greatly outnumbered their opponents. The Germans also brought Hungarian, Rumanian, and Italian soldiers into the war, but their combat effectiveness was far below German standards and their numbers did not begin to compensate for the huge Russian forces that reached the front.

In the north, from the beginning, Finland fought on Germany's side, and German troops also were engaged in this sector. Finland, however, was never wholeheartedly in sympathy with the German aims and aspirations. Her primary objective was the recovery of the territory torn from her in the Soviet-Finnish War of 1939–40. Once this was accomplished, Finland halted her troops and was content to let the fighting languish in the extreme northern sector.

In 1939 and 1940 Russia had done very poorly indeed against the Finns. Lack of planning and preparation, inept leadership, inadequate equipment and improper training had resulted in the prompt repulse of every one of her initial assaults. Finally, after months of dismal failure, the Russians had succeeded in overcoming their courageous opponents by the sheer weight of numbers alone. The Russian victory, wherein they suffered casualties of ten to one, attacking in masses along a narrow front, was not calculated to impress the Germans with any awe of their opponents. Of course it could be assumed that after this fiasco Russia would make every effort to correct the deficiencies in her armed forces, but it takes time to rebuild and breathe new life into an army and an air force which have just gone through such a depressing experience. The German generals fully expected to find a better Russian Army than that which had fought so poorly in Finland, but were confident that they could defeat it with their own highly trained forces. Hitler, on the other hand, expected to meet little resistance. That is undoubtedly why he saw no harm in losing three weeks to clear out the Balkans before launching an attack on Russia.

In the interval between the end of the Finnish war in March, 1940, and the attack in June, 1941, the Russians had indeed made strenuous efforts to revitalize their armed forces, provide better equipment for them, and improve their training. But their dispositions to meet a possible German attack were peculiar, to say the least. They were generally aligned along the frontier. There were no preparations for a defense in depth or for a withdrawal into the heart of the country, the traditional method of defense against a strong enemy force. The massing of troops along the frontier would seem to indicate that Soviet Russia was herself prepared to launch an attack upon Germany. Yet we know that Stalin was surprised by Hitler's attack. It may be proper to conclude that Stalin was waiting for the appropriate time to launch his own offensive. We have no way of knowing—because true, accurate histories are not written in the Soviet Union. No individual or government agency could attempt the project because, in Russia today, history must conform to doctrine. For example, Stalin was depicted during and after World War II as the hero of the country, but was roundly denounced by his successor. The writing of history cannot be that flexible—and also be accurate. Therefore, since everything coming out of Russia is automatically suspect, we are forced to rely primarily upon German records for an account of these campaigns, and these records may be somewhat biased.

The Russian dispositions along the frontier were well known to the

Germans, who formulated their attack plans accordingly. The first objective would be the destruction of the Russian Army near the frontier. This meant rapid penetrations by armored columns, then a turning inward of these columns in pairs so as to form a pincers whose jaws would meet at some point well behind the Russian lines. Hard-marching infantry, following closely behind the armor and exerting pressure all along the front would reduce the pockets thus created, while the armored forces raced ahead to trap another group of the enemy. Hitler and his generals were in full agreement on this part of the plan. It was certainly the way to destroy and capture the largest possible number of the enemy before they could recover from their surprise. Of course a great many of the Russians would escape and begin to fight delaying actions as they retreated. Rapid pursuit and a continuation of such penetrations and envelopments would keep the Russians off balance as the Germans raced toward their objectives.

What should the objectives be after the frontier had been passed and the initial enemy forces destroyed? On this question Hitler and his generals disagreed completely. The military leaders of Germany were firmly convinced that there was only one primary objective: the destruction of the Russian Army. When the Russians began to retreat they would trade space for time. Opportunities would occur to cut off large numbers of the defenders as they retreated, but there was one place where they would surely stand and fight. At that point the Russian Army should be destroyed. In the generals' opinion that point was Moscow, which was not only the capital but also the greatest industrial center of the country, the heart of the armaments industry and the center point of the Russian railroad net. If the Russians lost Moscow they could not bring troops and supplies to the other fronts, which would then collapse. Therefore Stalin could not afford to abandon Moscow; he must accept battle in front of it.

Hitler, on the other hand, approached the problem from an entirely different point of view. He also wanted to destroy the Russian Army, but his idea was to strike at political and economic objectives which he felt the Russians would not dare to abandon. His attention was riveted on Leningrad, which he believed was sacred to communism, and on the Ukraine, which he needed for economic reasons.

In the first month the German forces achieved astounding results. The pockets created by the armored forces yielded immense numbers of prisoners. One pocket west of Minsk produced 290,000 men; an-

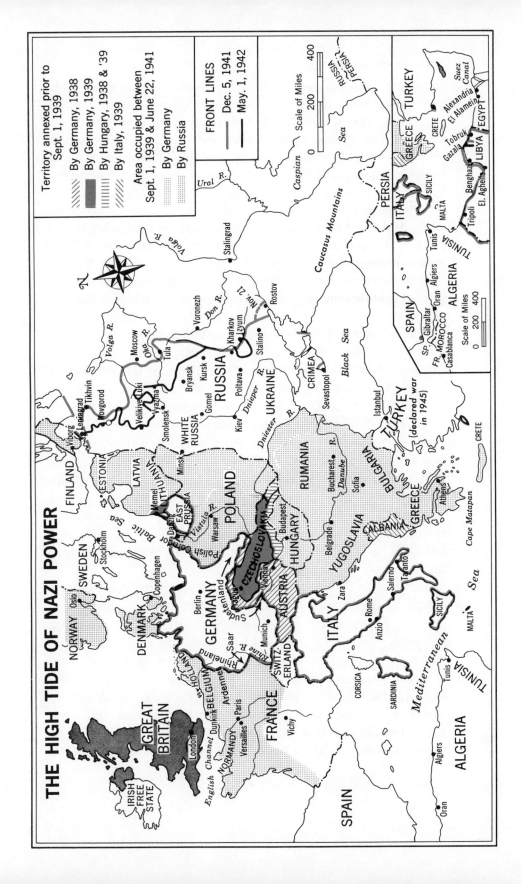

THE HIGH TIDE OF NAZI POWER

Territory annexed prior to Sept. 1, 1939

By Germany, 1938

By Germany, 1939

By Hungary, 1938 & '39

By Italy, 1939

Area occupied between Sept. 1, 1939 & June 22, 1941

By Germany

By Russia

FRONT LINES

Dec. 5, 1941

May. 1, 1942

Scale of Miles

0   200   400

IRISH FREE STATE

GREAT BRITAIN

London

English Channel

NORWAY   Oslo

SWEDEN

Stockholm

DENMARK

Copenhagen

Baltic Sea

North Sea

FINLAND

Viborg

Leningrad

Tikhvin

Novgorod

Velikiye Luki

ESTONIA

LATVIA

LITHUANIA

Memel

EAST PRUSSIA

Danzig

Polish Corridor

Vistula R.

Minsk

WHITE RUSSIA

Smolensk

Vyazma

Moscow

Oka R.

Tula

Volga R.

Volga R.

Stalingrad

Ural R.

HOLLAND

BELGIUM

Dunkirk

Ardennes

Paris

Versailles

NORMANDY

FRANCE

Vichy

Saar

Rhineland

Rhine R.

Munich

Sudetenland

Prague

GERMANY

Berlin

POLAND

Warsaw

CZECHOSLOVAKIA

Vienna

AUSTRIA

SWITZ-ERLAND

HUNGARY

Budapest

YUGOSLAVIA

Belgrade

Zara

ALBANIA

RUMANIA

Bucharest

Danube R.

BULGARIA

Sofia

GREECE

Athens

Cape Matapan

CRETE

Bryansk

Kursk

Gomel

Kiev

Poltava

Dnieper R.

UKRAINE

Dniester R.

Kharkov

Izyum

Stalino

Voronezh

Don R.

Rostov

Nov. 21

RUSSIA

CRIMEA

Sevastopol

Black Sea

Istanbul

TURKEY
(declared war in 1945)

Caucasus Mountains

Caspian Sea

CORSICA

ITALY

Rome

Anzio

Salerno

Taranto

SARDINIA

Mediterranean Sea

SICILY

MALTA

Tunis

TUNISIA

ALGERIA

Algiers

Oran

SPAIN

N

Scale of Miles

0   200   400

SPAIN

SP. Gibraltar

Oran   Algiers   Tunis

FR. MOROCCO

Casablanca

ALGERIA

TUNISIA

Tripoli

El Agheila

Benghazi

Gazala

Tobruk

LIBYA

EGYPT

El Alamein

Alexandria

Suez Canal

MALTA

SICILY

ITALY

GREECE

CRETE

TURKEY

PERSIA

RUSSIA

PERSIA

Sea

other near Smolensk gave up 100,000 prisoners. Furthermore, of the three army groups, the one in the center, driving toward Moscow, was gaining ground more swiftly than either of the other two. It was well over halfway toward the capital, and the Russians in its front were thoroughly disorganized. It appeared as if Russia were going to be defeated just as rapidly as all of the other countries in Europe had been.

At this point Hitler intervened. With victory in sight he ordered the armored forces of Army Group Center to turn and help the advance of Army Group North toward Leningrad, and aid Army Group South in its advance toward the Ukraine. The generals, knowing that this would delay the advance on Moscow and give the enemy time to prepare his defense and bring in additional troops to strengthen his lines, protested vigorously but to no avail. They then proceeded to execute the Führer's orders to the best of their ability, and their best was very good indeed. Fighting its way over extremely difficult terrain, Army Group North reached the outskirts of Leningrad; by this time Finnish troops had reached their old frontier on the other side of the city, and halted. In the south a huge pocket was created east of Kiev from which a total of 665,000 Russian prisoners was taken. Hitler was exultant. The complete conquest of the Ukraine was assured. He could now turn back toward Moscow. The victory had been tremendous, the number of prisoners taken unprecedented; but he had lost two months. Hitler did not seem to understand the value of the time he was losing, until it was too late. During these two months the Russians had strongly fortified their lines and had brought divisions to defend them from as far away as Siberia. The Germans were identifying divisions they had never known existed.

Yet, when the Germans attacked toward Moscow they again achieved surprise. In the first week of October they made another enormous haul, collecting 658,000 more prisoners at Vyazma and Bryansk. No matter how many errors Hitler made and how much time he lost, it began to appear as if the German Army and the German Air Force would somehow save him from paying for his mistakes. But they could not stop the rains that turned the primitive Russian roads into canals of mud. The army was almost brought to a halt, but by strenuous effort slowly forged forward to within forty miles from Moscow. In the north the Germans advanced well to the east of Leningrad to capture Tikhvin.

Army Group South was about to capture Rostov and had forced its way into the Crimea.

It was now mid-November. The military commanders could see the handwriting on the wall. Only a few of their troops had been equipped with winter clothing. Supplies of gasoline and oil were running low. Their trucks, guns, and tanks were badly in need of repair and maintenance. The supply lines stretched hundreds of miles back into Germany. It would take time to send replacements to the front and accumulate much-needed supplies. Now was the time to go on the defensive, consolidate their gains, and then prepare for a renewal of the attack in the spring. Hitler refused to consider such an idea. He had no conception whatever of the problems involved. These were details his generals had always before managed to solve for him; there was no reason, in his opinion, why they could not continue to do so. His was a campaign of the spirit that refused to take account of such problems. If his army was in difficulty, the Russians must also have their problems. He ordered a last final offensive in the firm belief that it would inevitably succeed. On December 5, with the thermometer reading thirty-five degrees below zero, the last attack stopped on the outskirts of Moscow, within sight of the towers of the Kremlin.

On the next day the Russians struck back. Their counterattack, planned and directed by Marshal Georgi Zhukov, who had recently taken command of the central front, was immediately successful. The invaders, fighting without winter clothing in subzero weather, were forced backward from Moscow. Under steadily increasing pressure from thousands of attacking Russian troops, including many hardened, well-trained Siberian divisions, Hitler at last agreed to let his army go on the defensive for the winter. It was almost too late. Throughout the remainder of December, 1941, all of January, and well into February, 1942, the German Army was in a desperate situation. Only two factors saved it from annihilation: the endurance and fighting ability of the trained German soldier, led by competent, courageous officers; and the fact that the Russian Army, having previously lost over one and a half million men, was far from being a well-organized, trained force.

During that winter the Russians, although they achieved no major victories, made several deep penetrations of the German lines, forced them well back from Moscow and destroyed the myth of the invincibility of the German Army. In its place arose another myth. Back in November, Field Marshal von Rundstedt's Army Group South had taken the city of Rostov, then had been counterattacked by Russian forces. Von Rundstedt had recommended a retreat. This was the same period during which the commanders on the central front were counseling a halt before Moscow. Hitler agreed, then ordered the retreat from Rostov stopped. When von Rundstedt objected, he was relieved from command. Up until that moment the German Army had always been going forward; it had never received a major setback. Hitler's orders to stand and fight had no more effect at Rostov in November than did his later directives issued in the middle of winter in front of Moscow. Despite orders to fight to the last man, never to yield an inch, the Germans were forced backward. Generals were relieved for retreating without authority or for failing to hold their ground. The fact was that the army itself well knew what its fate would be if the withdrawal became a rout; thoughts of Napoleon's disastrous retreat in 1812 haunted it. On the other hand, German officers understood the purpose of a strategic withdrawal, which Hitler never seemed to be able to grasp. The final result was that the army saved itself; but Hitler and many of his more ardent followers came to believe the myth that he had saved it by his insistence upon standing fast. After having accused his generals of blundering, lack of willpower, and even cowardice, he was later forced to recall some of the better ones such as von Rundstedt and General Guderian to try to save Germany. But from then until the end of the war he obstinately refused to ever permit a retreat, ordering his armies to stand fast and fight to the end rather than yield a foot of captured territory to the enemy. The results were to prove disastrous again and again in Russia, in North Africa, in Italy, in France, and finally along the Rhine in Germany.

Hitler's misguided military genius had saved Moscow for the Russians in 1941. Many authorities believe that this was the turning point of the war, but the German Army was by no means defeated. If properly employed, it still had the capability, when summer came, of again marching forward, inflicting severe defeats upon its enemy, capturing Moscow, and driving the Russians far back into the interior. Then it would have been difficult indeed for the Allies to have invaded Europe!

However great Hitler's military mistakes had been, he had made another error in an entirely different field that would in the long run prove possibly more disastrous to his war effort than any of his blunders on the battlefield. When the German armies attacked across the Russian frontiers, they were hailed as liberators by the oppressed people who were suffering under the Communist yoke. The people of Estonia, Latvia and Lithuania who had recently been absorbed by the Communists were not the only ones to greet the Germans with enthusiasm. The people of White Russia and the Ukraine also rose to rid themselves of Soviet rule. Hitler's answer was to proclaim the Germans as the master race, thus arousing the ancient enmity between the Teuton and the Slav, and to begin a process of extermination of the people who had welcomed his troops. Faced with this treatment the conquered peoples had no choice: naziism seemed even worse, for them, than communism. They, who had been willing and eager to fight for their German liberators, turned against them. Partisan bands, operating behind the lines, grew in ever-increasing numbers. German efforts to subdue them by terroristic methods failed completely. The partisans' reply was to conduct a regime of terror of their own. Thousands of German troops had to be withheld from the front line to guard their supply lines. The liberated peoples, who would gladly have fought for Germany and could have offset the tremendous Russian supply of manpower, thus became, instead, a drain upon the German manpower.

During the winter of 1941–42 the Russians had recaptured Tikhvin east of Leningrad, made deep penetrations toward Velikiye Luki and west of Izyum, and recaptured Rostov. In North Africa the British Eighth Army, commanded by General Auchinleck, had raised the siege of Tobruk and forced General Rommel's forces back across Libya to El Agheila. On December 7, 1941, the Japanese had made their surprise attack on Pearl Harbor so that the United States was now in the war. In early 1942, however, with Japan making tremendous strides in Asia and across the Pacific, Hitler was elated, rather than concerned with the future. Furthermore, British Commonwealth forces were being withdrawn from North Africa to help fight against the Japanese. German reinforcements were sent to Rommel, who resumed the offensive, recovering most of the ground he had lost.

For the next three months there was a lull in the action on all fronts while the Russians, the British and the Germans prepared for the coming battles. Early in May, General von Manstein, who was to play an outstanding role in the coming Stalingrad Campaign, began clearing the Crimea. By the beginning of July, Sevastopol had surrendered after a stout resistance which had lasted for nearly a month. Again Russian losses were phenomenal; a quarter of a million casualties were reported. Meanwhile the Russians had attempted an offensive toward Kharkov. It broke through the German lines, but a strong counterattack against the salient west of Izyum caused the Russians to withdraw. The net result was the loss by the Russian Army of another quarter of a million men, killed, wounded, and captured. In May also, General Rommel launched his assault against the Gazala line. After several days of severe fighting the Germans broke through, captured Tobruk, and in an astonishing advance reached El Alamein, where they were finally brought to a halt, less than seventy miles from Alexandria.

The main German offensive began at the end of June, 1942, and again it was aimed at economic objectives instead of toward Moscow where the major part of the Russian strength was concentrated. The principal target was the oilfields of the Caucasus hundreds of miles away from the nearest German forces. If the army reached that target it would mean stretching its flank outward to Voronezh, along the line of the Don, thence to Stalingrad and the Volga River. This long flank would be an open invitation to attack from the north by the Russians which, if successful, could cut off any Germans who had advanced farther to the east. The plan was obviously dangerous, but by this time Hitler's generals had concluded that it was useless to attempt to advise him. And any effort to tell him that his ambitious plan was impractical and beyond the capability of the army to execute would result only in abuse, being removed from command, or worse. All the senior officers of the army were well aware of the fact that the efficiency of the 1942 army was not so high as it had been in 1941. A number of divisions from the Balkan countries and from Italy had been added to bring the army up to strength, but these could not be relied upon to perform as well in battle as the German troops. Since it was hopeless to attempt to tell such unpleasant facts to Hitler, they might as well be left unsaid. The German commanders therefore took the only course of action left to them, which was to attempt, with the troops at their disposal, to make the plan succeed.

The campaign opened on June 28 with an attack toward Voronezh. The Germans then pushed southeast along the Don (keeping the river between themselves and their enemy) to meet another column attacking eastward from the Kharkov area. Then, according to the plan, they

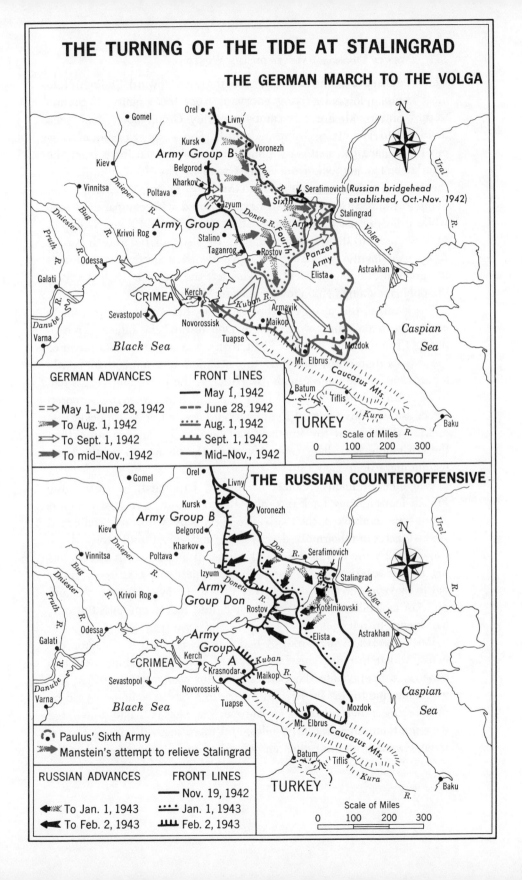

THE TURNING OF THE TIDE AT STALINGRAD

THE GERMAN MARCH TO THE VOLGA

Gomel • • Orel
Livny'
Kursk •
Belgorod • Voronezh
Army Group B
Kiev • Kharkov •
Vinnitsa • Poltava • Izyum
Army Group A Serafimovich *(Russian bridgehead established, Oct.-Nov. 1942)*
Sixth Army
Stalingrad
Donets R. Fourth Army
Krivoi Rog • Stalino •
Odessa • Taganrog • Rostov • Panzer Army
Galati • Elista • Astrakhan

CRIMEA Kerch
Sevastopol Novorossisk Kuban R. Armavik
Maikop
Varna Tuapse Mozdok Caspian Sea
Black Sea Mt. Elbrus Caucasus Mts.

GERMAN ADVANCES **FRONT LINES**
— May 1, 1942
⇒ May 1–June 28, 1942 --- June 28, 1942
➤ To Aug. 1, 1942 ⋯⋯ Aug. 1, 1942
⇨ To Sept. 1, 1942 ⊢⊢⊢ Sept. 1, 1942
➤ To mid–Nov., 1942 — Mid–Nov., 1942

Batum • Tiflis
TURKEY Kura
Scale of Miles
0   100   200   300
Baku •

THE RUSSIAN COUNTEROFFENSIVE

Gomel • Orel
Livny
Kursk •
Army Group B
Kiev • Belgorod •
Kharkov • Voronezh
Vinnitsa • Poltava • Don R. Serafimovich
Izyum Stalingrad
Army Group Don
Krivoi Rog • Donets R.
Odessa • Rostov • Kotelnikovski
Army Group A Elista • Astrakhan
Galati • Kerch
CRIMEA Krasnodar Kuban
Sevastopol Maikop
Novorossisk
Varna Tuapse Mozdok Caspian Sea
Black Sea Mt. Elbrus Caucasus Mts.

⟨ Paulus' Sixth Army
➤ Manstein's attempt to relieve Stalingrad

RUSSIAN ADVANCES **FRONT LINES**
— Nov. 19, 1942
◄ To Jan. 1, 1943 ⋯⋯ Jan. 1, 1943
◄ To Feb. 2, 1943 ⊥⊥⊥ Feb. 2, 1943

Batum • Tiflis
TURKEY Kura
Baku •
Scale of Miles
0   100   200   300

were supposed to continue alongside the Don toward Stalingrad to meet another column driving eastward from the vicinity of Stalino toward Stalingrad. For this campaign Army Group South had been divided into two Army Groups, A and B. The Voronezh column, now moving toward the southeast along the Don, and the force from the Kharkov area had come from Army Group B. The third column from the Stalino area was from Army Group A. At this moment, when Stalingrad could probably have been captured with comparative ease while the Russians were still retreating, Hitler turned Army Group A southeast toward the Caucasus oilfields. He also took the Fourth Panzer Army away from Army Group B to give the drive toward the Caucasus the greatest possible momentum. This left the German Sixth Army as the only remaining force moving toward Stalingrad.

The result of this change of direction was that Army Group A made extremely rapid progress across the Don toward the oilfields, recapturing Rostov easily, but the Sixth Army was slowed in its advance toward Stalingrad. By late July the situation was more than faintly reminiscent of the moves made by Hitler in the preceding year when he practically had Moscow in his grasp, but had turned his armored forces aside to drive toward Leningrad and create the great pocket east of Kiev. At Moscow the Russians had been given time to strengthen the city's defenses; they were now given the chance to do the same for Stalingrad.

When Hitler finally realized what had happened, he turned the Fourth Panzer Army back toward Stalingrad. During August the German forces continued their advance, very slowly toward Stalingrad against bitter, well-organized resistance, and very rapidly toward the Caucasus. By the end of the month Germans and Russians were fighting in the outskirts of the city. The grimmest, most savagely bitter battle of World War II, which was to last for over five months and grow in violence and intensity as each side fed troops into the city, had begun.

Farther south, Army Group A had actually reached the Maikop oilfields, which the Russians had wrecked before retreating, and had penetrated deeply into the Caucasus. Stalin was greatly alarmed and was clamoring for his British and American Allies to come to his aid by establishing a "second front" in Europe. The Germans had penetrated over three hundred and fifty miles, and there seemed no way to stop them. Actually, it was some sort of minor logistical miracle that the

German armies had managed to get this far. They were extremely short of gasoline, and now the force of their drive died away as Hitler diverted more and more of his troops and supporting air forces toward Stalingrad.

There the bitter struggle continued, day by day, all through the months of September, of October, and into November. Casualties mounted to alarming figures as Hitler exhorted his soldiers to fight on to the Volga, while Stalin insisted that his die in defense of the city. Slowly the Germans managed to forge ahead house by house, through the now completely ruined city.

Then, in rapid succession, Great Britain, the United States, and Soviet Russia dealt Hitler's armies three blows from which they never recovered. The first came at the Battle of El Alamein. There, in a furious thirteen-day battle lasting from October 23 to November 4, 1942, General Bernard Law Montgomery's British Commonwealth forces defeated General Rommel's German and Italian troops and began a long pursuit that would carry them all the way from Egypt, across Libya, and deep into Tunisia.

On November 8, United States and British troops, under the command of General Dwight D. Eisenhower, were landed on the shores of Morocco and Algeria. These landings and the victory at El Alamein were to spell the end of all German and Italian forces in North Africa.

On November 19, the Russian armies struck the exposed flank northwest of Stalingrad. On the following day they struck again south of the city. Swiftly they broke through the Rumanian forces opposing them, aiming toward a junction behind Stalingrad. General Friedrich von Paulus, commanding the German Sixth Army about to be trapped in the city, telegraphed the Führer, asking for permission to withdraw to save his army. Hitler's answer was a flat refusal, and a promise to supply the army by air, which was manifestly impossible. He then ordered General von Manstein to form a new group of armies, called Army Group Don, for the relief of Stalingrad. This was also an impossible task unless Hitler would permit von Paulus to break out to meet the relieving forces attempting to come to his aid. By mid-December, von Manstein was ready to make the attempt. It was a valiant effort that, in spite of determined Russian resistance, pushed seventy miles northeast from Kotelnikovski through snow and sleet and bitterly cold weather to within thirty miles of the beleaguered forces in Stalingrad. At that point von Manstein ordered von Paulus to force his way out of the city to meet him. When von Paulus failed to move because Hitler's permission had not been received, the relieving column was forced to turn back.

It is quite probable that von Paulus could have fought his way out of Stalingrad at the very beginning of the Russian attack in November or have joined von Manstein in December. Although he would surely have lost most of his heavy equipment, his army would have been saved. Now it was just a question of time until he would be forced to surrender. His troops were able to prolong the struggle for another month and a half until February 2, 1943, when the climactic battle ended with the German surrender.

In January, 1943, while the Battle of Stalingrad was at its height, President Roosevelt and Prime Minister Churchill with their Combined Chiefs of Staff met at Casablanca in Morocco. The military decisions agreed upon at this conference for the further prosecution of the war by the Allies were not as important as the joint declaration that they would insist upon unconditional surrender by Germany. The intent of the statement was obvious; they wished to ensure that in the future Germans would not claim, as they had at the end of World War I, that their army had never been defeated, that they had been "stabbed in the back."

This announcement at such an early date in the struggle was a great mistake because it played directly into the hands of the Nazis, who could now proclaim in all their propaganda that the Allies were waging war against the entire German people, not just the Nazi party. When the unconditional-surrender policy was followed by proposals for the occupation and dismemberment of Germany and by the announcement of the senseless plan, advocated by U.S. Secretary of the Treasury Henry Morgenthau, to convert Germany into an agrarian state, it placed all responsible, patriotic Germans in an impossible position. Even though the Morgenthau Plan was later abandoned, the seed had been planted in the minds of all the people of Germany and none could help but be suspicious of Allied intentions.

The Nazi propaganda machine made the most of it and stressed the point that, throughout history, temporary occupation of territory by Russia had always led to permanent occupation. Now, with the Communist party in control of Russia, no intelligent German needed to be told what occupation of Germany by Russia, temporary or otherwise, would mean. The Nazi propagandists did not need to describe to those who lived in eastern Germany the horrors that would follow upon a Russian victory after a war that was being waged with such hatred on both sides. The choice thus presented to patriotic Germans was somewhat similar to that given to the liberated peoples of Russia when Hitler's armies were followed by his political exterminators. No matter how much they might want to overthrow Hitler and the Nazis, they could not consider surrender to the Communists, and the "unconditional surrender" policy of the other Allies must be regarded with suspicion. It is therefore not at all surprising to find that the German armed forces chose to keep on fighting to the end.

After the surrender at Stalingrad in February, 1943, the Germans were never again strong enough to mount a full large-scale offensive against the Russians. By his failure to strike at the main Russian armies massed in the north near Moscow early enough in 1941, and not at all in 1942, Hitler had wasted the best years of the German Army when it could have defeated his enemy. Then the loss of close to 300,000 men, killed, wounded, captured, and missing, from August to February at Stalingrad was a blow from which his forces could not recover. The magnificent Russian defense of that city, the British victory at El Alamein, and the United States–British landings in North Africa placed Germany permanently on the defensive.

The German armies would fight to the bitter end, and it would be two long years before victory came in Europe. On the sea, while the Allied armies were completing the liberation of North Africa and preparing for invasion of Sicily and Italy, the Allied navies slowly turned the tide in the bitterly-contested Battle of the Atlantic. In 1943 and 1944 the Allied air forces struck deep into enemy territory to dislocate and destroy his military and industrial systems. In a series of violent air battles the strength of the *Luftwaffe* was broken, never again to be a serious menace. Then on June 6, 1944, two days after American troops had entered Rome, United States and British Commonwealth forces crossed the English Channel to storm the beaches of Normandy in the greatest amphibious operation recorded in history. Eleven months later, after smashing the last major German counteroffensive in the Ardennes in December, 1944, and January, 1945, the Allies swept across Germany to meet the advancing troops of Soviet Russia.

It would be pleasant to record, as Sir Edward Creasy was able to do, writing in 1851 in the Victorian Age, that the world had now entered upon a period of peace and prosperity. Unfortunately, this is far from being the case. The struggle between the forces of democracy and communism which, for lack of a better term, we call the "cold war" is in full swing. Unfortunately, also, during World War II man invented, and is continuing to improve, weapons of a far more destructive nature than any previously conceived.

After every war a new generation arises that has not known the horrors of war, and the passage of the years tends to cloud the memories of the older generation that lived through its terrors. Inevitably, then, it becomes easier for those who seek power to lead their people into another conflict. The principal deterrent today seems to be the possession by each side of nuclear weapons. The prospect of such a war seems too awful to contemplate, yet many prominent leaders talk and act as if the use of nuclear weapons will eventually be necessary. They may be correct in their assumptions, and surely the Free World cannot afford to neglect its nuclear armaments, but it is extremely harmful to imply that these weapons will be used too readily.

In this connection it may be noted, in passing, that World War II was the first war in history in which any large segment of the armed forces of a nation were involved in an impersonal way. There is something rather remote in the dropping of a bomb from 30,000 feet upon a city below. Now, with the introduction of guided missiles, there is still less connection with reality when "pressing a button" will launch a guided missile toward a target hundreds or thousands of miles away. Those who are responsible for the employment of these weapons are quite properly proud of the preparations they have made to use them if the necessity arises. Unfortunately, however, they tend to create the impression that the forces of democracy are fully prepared to wage nuclear war, but simultaneously, by their pronouncements, they raise doubts as to the ability of the democracies to fight in any other way. This impression does not inspire world confidence. It is too reminiscent of the situation in Europe preceding World War I.

Although ability to wage war of any kind will not, of course, have any effect upon the Communist plan to gain control of the nations of the world by peaceful means, it does appear that the threat of a nuclear war may deter Soviet Russia from active aggression upon the continent of Europe. On the other hand it seems to have little effect upon the Communists in China, where human life is a cheap commodity to be freely expended in the struggle for world domination. And both Soviet Russia and Communist China appear quite willing to embark upon aggressive enterprises against smaller countries. In such cases the Communist leaders have undoubtedly come to the conclusion that, for the protection of these countries, the democracies will not wage total war. And, as noted above, too many doubts have been raised as to whether or not the democracies are prepared to engage in limited wars.

There are many lessons to be learned from a study of world battles, not the least of which is the lesson that countries must be prepared to take a firm stand against aggressors from the very beginning. The quotation from Shakespeare given at the beginning of Chapter 14 is so apt that it is here repeated:

> *A little fire is quickly trodden out,*
> *Which, being suffered, rivers cannot quench.*

The next decisive battles of the world may come from a failure to heed this warning.

Bibliography

No one could possibly prepare a complete list of books covering over twenty-four hundred years of military history. A list as long as that given below could be compiled for any one of the wars described.

With the thought that a short listing would be more useful, this bibliography was purposely kept small and confined to those sources that proved most valuable for specific chapters, or were particularly helpful in the preparation of the synopses between chapters, although this meant omitting a great number of excellent books which I have read, or referred to from time to time over the years. Many of my favorites have been omitted simply because they dealt with battles or campaigns I did not consider as decisive to the history of mankind. For example, because I chose Vicksburg, many of the best studies on Chancellorsville and Gettysburg are not included in the list, despite the fact that these battles occurred while the Vicksburg Campaign was being fought. In like manner, books devoted to Tannenberg, the Dardanelles, and the Meuse-Argonne in World War I are not mentioned, nor are detailed accounts describing specific operations in North Africa, Italy, Normandy, or in the Pacific west of Midway in World War II.

The list does contain a somewhat higher percentage of general works relating to events of the last hundred years. This simply reflects the fact that I decided to adhere to the original fifteen battles chosen by Sir Edward Creasy, but was faced with the problem of selecting additional battles from among all those that had taken place since Waterloo.

Many of the sources mentioned by Creasy have been included. These not only contain the historical quotations used by him but also proved very helpful to me in understanding the viewpoint of the Victorian Age in which he wrote. Furthermore, except in those instances where additional research conducted during the last century has uncovered hitherto unknown facts, these sources contain a wealth of reliable information and detail of great value to the historian of today. Several of them have been republished a number of times. At this point it should be noted that Creasy's versions of what was originally written in Greek, Latin, French, German, or Spanish differ sometimes from those in the works cited. He may have used different translations, but one is inclined to suspect that in many cases he effected his own. The differences in wording, however, do not in any instance alter the meaning.

Finally, I should certainly mention that I often turned to *The Cambridge Ancient History, The Cambridge Medieval History,* and to standard encyclopedias to cross-check details and verify information. In many cases they led me on to other valuable source material.

Alison, Archibald. *The Military Life of John, Duke of Marlborough.* New York: Harper & Brothers, 1848.

———. *History of Europe from the Commencement of the French Revolution in 1789 to the Restoration of the Bourbons in 1815,* Vol. I. New York: Harper & Brothers, 1857.

The Army Air Forces in World War II. Office of Air Force History. Edited by Wesley F. Craven and James L. Cate. Chicago: University of Chicago Press, 1948–58.

Arnold, Thomas. *History of the Later Roman Commonwealth and of the Reign of Augustus with a Life of Trajan.* New York: D. Appleton & Co., 1846.

———. *The History of Rome.* New York: D. Appleton & Co., 1851.

Arrian. *Anabasis of Alexander.* Translated by E. Iliff Robson. New York: G. P. Putnam's Sons, 1929–32.

Atlas of World History. Edited by Robert R. Palmer, New York: Rand McNally & Co., 1957.

Bain, R. Nisbet. *Charles XII and the Collapse of the Swedish Empire.* New York: G. P. Putnam's Sons, 1895.

Belloc, Hilaire. *The Battle of Blenheim.* London: Stephen Swift & Co., 1911.

Bolingbroke, Henry St. John. *Letters VII and VIII on the Study and Use of History, The Works of Lord Bolingbroke,* Vol. II. Philadelphia: Carey & Hart, 1841.

Breasted, James H. *The Conquest of Civilization.* Edited by Edith W. Ware. New York: Harper & Brothers, 1938.

Bury, John B. *A History of Greece to the Death of Alexander the Great.* New York: The Modern Library, Random House, 1937.

———. *History of the Later Roman Empire.* New York: Dover Publications, 1958.

The Campaign of 1866 in Germany. Compiled by the Department of Military History of the Prussian Staff. Translated by Col. von Wright and Capt. Henry M. Hozier. London: Her Majesty's Stationery Office, 1872.

Carlyle, Thomas. *The French Revolution: A History.* New York: The Modern Library, Random House, 1934.

Carrington, Henry B. *Battles of the American Revolution.* New York: A. S. Barnes & Co., 1888.

Catton, Bruce. *This Hallowed Ground.* New York: Doubleday & Co., 1956.

Ceram, C. W. *Gods, Graves and Scholars.* Translated by E. B. Garside. New York: Alfred A. Knopf, 1951.

Churchill, Winston S. *The World Crisis.* New York: Charles Scribner's Sons, 1923–29.

Churchill, Winston S. *Marlborough, His Life and Times*. New York: Charles Scribner's Sons, 1933–35.

————. *The Second World War*. Boston: Houghton Mifflin Co., 1948–53.

————. *A History of the English-Speaking Peoples*. New York: Dodd, Mead & Co., 1956–58.

Clausewitz, Karl von. *On War*. Translated by O. J. Matthijs Jolles. Washington, D.C.: Combat Forces Press, 1953.

Coblentz, Stanton A. *Marching Men*. New York: Unicorn Press, 1927.

Conde, José A. *History of the Dominion of the Arabs in Spain*, Vol. I. Translated by Mrs. Jonathan Foster. London: Henry G. Bohn, 1854.

Corbett, Julian S. *Drake and the Tudor Navy*. New York: Longmans, Green & Co., 1898.

Creasy, Edward S. *The Fifteen Decisive Battles of the World*. New York: A. L. Burt, Publisher.

Curtius, Quintus. *History of Alexander*. Translated by John C. Rolfe, Cambridge, Mass.: Harvard University Press, 1956.

Dio, Cassius. *Cassius Dio's Roman History*. Translated by Herbert B. Foster. Troy, N.Y.: Pafraets Book Co., 1905–06.

Diodorus of Sicily. *Library of History*. Translated by C. H. Oldfather and others. New York: G. P. Putnam's Sons, 1933.

Dodge, Theodore A. *Great Captains, Alexander*. Boston and New York: Houghton Mifflin Co., 1890.

————. *Great Captains, Hannibal*. Boston and New York: Houghton Mifflin Co., 1891.

————. *Great Captains, Napoleon*. Boston and New York: Houghton Mifflin Co., 1904–07.

Edmonds, James E. *A Short History of World War I*. London: Oxford University Press, 1951.

Esposito, Vincent J. (Ed.). *The West Point Atlas of American Wars*. Compiled by the Department of Military Art and Engineering, U.S.M.A. New York: Frederick A. Praeger, 1959.

Falls, Cyril. *The Great War, 1914–1918*. New York: G. P. Putnam's Sons, 1959.

Fisher, Sidney G. *The Struggle for American Independence*. Philadelphia: J. B. Lippincott Co., 1908.

Fiske, John. *The American Revolution*. Boston and New York: Houghton Mifflin Co., 1891.

Fortescue, John W. *History of the British Army*. London and New York: The Macmillan Co., 1899–1930.

————. *Marlborough*. New York: D. Appleton & Co., 1932.

Freeman, Douglas S. *R. E. Lee: A Biography*. New York: Charles Scribner's Sons, 1934–35.

————. *George Washington*. New York: Charles Scribner's Sons, 1948–54.

Frothingham, Thomas G. *The Naval History of the World War*. Cambridge, Mass.: Harvard University Press, 1925.

Froude, James A. *The Spanish Story of the Armada*. London: Longmans, Green & Co., 1896.

Fuchida, Mitsuo, and Masatake Okumiya. *Midway, the Battle That Doomed Japan*. Annapolis, Md.: The United States Naval Institute, 1955.

Fuller, J. F. C. *A Military History of the Western World*. New York: Funk & Wagnalls Co., 1954–56.

Gibbon, Edward. *The Decline and Fall of the Roman Empire*. New York: The Modern Library, Random House, 1932.

Godley, Eveline. *Charles XII of Sweden*. London: W. Collins Sons, 1928.

Goerlitz, Walter. *History of the German General Staff*. Translated by Brian Battershaw. New York: Frederick A. Praeger, 1952.

Goethe, Johann Wolfgang von. *Campaign in France in the Year 1792*. Translated by Robert Farie. London: Chapman & Hall, 1849.

Gosnell, H. Allen. *Guns on the Western Waters*. Baton Rouge: Louisiana State University Press, 1949.

Grant, Ulysses S. *Personal Memoirs of U. S. Grant*. New York: Charles L. Webster & Co., 1885–86.

Grote, George. *History of Greece*. New York: The Bradley Co., 1846–58.

Grundy, George B. *The Great Persian War and Its Preliminaries*. New York: Charles Scribner's Sons;   London: John Murray, 1901.

———. *Thucydides and the History of His Age*. Oxford: Basil Blackwell, 1948.

Guderian, Heinz. *Panzer Leader*. Translated by Constantine Fitzgibbon. New York: E. P. Dutton & Co., 1952.

Guizot, François. Lectures on the *History of Civilization in Europe*, Vol. I. Translated by William Hazlitt. London: David Bogue, 1846.

Hakluyt, Richard. *The Principal Navigations, Voyages and Discoveries of the English Nation*, Vol. IV. Glasgow: James MacLehose & Sons, 1904.

Hallam, Henry. *View of the State of Europe During the Middle Ages*. London: John Murray, 1846.

———. *Constitutional History of England, Henry VII to George II*. New York: Everyman's Library, E. P. Dutton & Co., 1930.

Heeren, A. H. L. *Historical Researches into the Politics, Intercourse and Trade of the Carthaginians*. Translated from the German. Oxford: D. A. Talboys, 1832.

———. *A Manual of Ancient History*. Translated from the German. London: Henry G. Bohn, 1854.

Heinl, Robert D. *Marines at Midway*. Historical Section, Division of Public Information, Hq., U.S. Marine Corps, 1948.

Henderson, Bernard W. *The Great War Between Athens and Sparta*. New York: The Macmillan Company, 1927.

Henry, Robert S. *The Story of the Confederacy*. New York: Grosset & Dunlap, 1936.

Herbert, William. *Attila and His Predecessors*, historical treatise appended to *Attila, King of the Huns*. London: Henry G. Bohn, 1838.

Herodotus. *The History of Herodotus,* Vol. 6 of *Great Books of the Western World.* Translated by George Rawlinson. Chicago: William Benton, Publisher, Encyclopædia Britannica, 1952.

Houssaye, Henry. *1815 Waterloo.* Translated by S. R. Willis. Kansas City, Mo.: Franklin Hudson Publishing Co., 1905.

Howard, Michael. *The Franco-Prussian War.* New York: The Macmillan Company, 1962.

Hozier, Henry M. *The Seven Weeks' War.* London and New York: Macmillan & Co., 1871.

Hume, David. *The History of England from the Invasion of Julius Caesar to the Revolution in 1688.* Philadelphia: J. B. Lippincott & Co., 1859.

Johnson, Robert U. and Buel, Clarence C. (Eds.). *Battles and Leaders of the Civil War.* New York: The Century Co., 1884–87.

Jomini, Antoine H. *Jomini and His Summary of the Art of War.* Condensed, edited by J. D. Hittle. Harrisburg, Pa.: The Stackpole Co., 1958.

Jordanes. *The Origins and Deeds of the Goths.* Translated by Charles C. Mierow from Mommsen's text. Princeton, N.J.: Princeton University Press, 1908.

Karig, Walter. *Battle Report.* New York: Farrar & Rinehart, Rinehart & Co., 1944–52.

Keyes, Nelson B. *Story of the Bible World.* New York: C. S. Hammond & Co., 1959.

Kluck, Alexander von. *The March on Paris and the Battle of the Marne, 1914.* With maps and notes by the Historical Section (Military Branch of the Committee of Imperial Defence). London: Edward Arnold, 1920.

Klyuchevsky, Vasili. *Peter the Great.* Translated by Liliana Archibald. New York: Vintage Books, Random House, 1961.

Knox, Dudley W. *A History of the United States Navy.* New York: G. P. Putnam's Sons, 1948.

Kuhl, Hermann von. *The Marne Campaign, 1914.* Fort Leavenworth, Kans.: The Command & General Staff School Press, 1936.

Labberton, Robert H. *Labberton's Universal History.* New York: Silver, Burdett & Co., 1902.

Lamartine, Alphonse de. *History of the Girondists,* Vol. II. Translated by H. T. Ryde. New York: Harper & Brothers, 1848.

Lamb, Harold. *Genghis Khan: Emperor of all Men.* New York: Bantam Books, 1957.

———. *Hannibal: One Man Against Rome.* New York: Bantam Books, 1960.

Lang, Andrew. *The Maid of France.* New York: Longmans, Green & Co., 1908.

Langer, William L. (Ed.). *An Encyclopedia of World History.* Boston: Houghton Mifflin Co., 1948.

Leopold, Richard W. *The Growth of American Foreign Policy.* New York: Alfred A. Knopf, 1962.

Liddell Hart, B. H. *The German Generals Talk*. New York: William Morrow & Co., 1948.

Livy. *The History of Rome by Titus Livius*. Translated by D. Spillan, Cyrus Edmonds, and William A. M'Devitte. London: Bell & Daldy, 1878–81.

Lowell, Francis C. *Joan of Arc*. Boston and New York: Houghton Mifflin Co., 1896.

McEntee, Girard L. *Military History of the World War*. New York: Charles Scribner's Sons, 1937.

Mahan, Alfred T. *The Influence of Seapower upon History, 1660–1783*. Boston: Little, Brown & Co., 1890.

————. *Major Operations of the Navies in the War of American Independence*. Boston: Little, Brown & Co., 1913.

Malleson, G. B. *The Refounding of the German Empire, 1848–1871*. New York: Charles Scribner's Sons, 1893.

Manstein, Erich von. *Lost Victories*. Translated by Anthony G. Powell. Chicago: Henry Regnery Co., 1958.

Mattingly, Garrett. *The Armada*. Boston: Houghton Mifflin Co., 1962.

Michelet, Jules. *History of the Roman Republic*. Translated by William Hazlitt. London: David Bogue, 1847.

Miller, John C. *Triumph of Freedom, 1775–1783*. Boston: Little, Brown & Co., 1948.

Mitchell, Joseph B. *Decisive Battles of the Civil War*. New York: G. P. Putnam's Sons, 1955.

————. *Decisive Battles of the American Revolution*. New York: G. P. Putnam's Sons, 1962.

Mitchell, William A. *Outlines of the World's Military History*. Washington, D.C.: The Infantry Journal, 1931.

Mommsen, Theodor. *The History of Rome*. Translated from the German. Glencoe, Ill.: The Free Press, 1957.

Montholon, Charles Tristan. *History of the Captivity of Napoleon at St. Helena*, Vol. IV. Translated from the French. London: Henry Colburn, 1847.

Morison, Samuel E. *History of United States Naval Operations in World War II*. Boston: Little, Brown & Co., 1947–60.

Morris, Richard B. (Ed.). *Encyclopedia of American History*. New York: Harper & Brothers, 1953.

Neale, John E. *Essays in Elizabethan History*. New York: St. Martin's Press, 1958.

Nickerson, Hoffman. *The Turning Point of the Revolution*. Boston and New York: Houghton Mifflin Co., 1928.

Oman, Charles. *A History of the Art of War in the Middle Ages*. London: Methuen & Co., 1924.

Palgrave, Francis. *The History of Normandy and of England*, Vol. III. London: Macmillan & Co., 1864.

Palmer, Robert R. *A History of the Modern World.* New York: Alfred A. Knopf, 1950.

Peckham, Howard H. *The War for Independence.* Chicago: The University of Chicago Press, 1958.

Pemberton, John C. *Pemberton, Defender of Vicksburg.* Chapel Hill: The University of North Carolina Press, 1942.

Perroy, Edouard. *The Hundred Years War.* Translated by W. B. Wells. New York: Oxford University Press, 1951.

Plutarch. *Plutarch's Lives of the Noble Grecians and Romans.* Translated by John Dryden, revised by Arthur H. Clough. New York: The Modern Library, Random House, 1932.

Polybius. *The Histories of Polybius.* Translated by Evelyn S. Schuckburgh from the text of F. Hultsch. London and New York: Macmillan & Co., 1889.

Raleigh, Walter. *The History of the World.* His comments on sea warfare and the Spanish Armada are in Vol. V, in the sections devoted to the First Punic War. Edinburgh: Arnold Constable & Co., 1820.

Ranke, Leopold von. *History of the Popes of Rome During the 16th and 17th Centuries,* Vol. I. Translated by Sarah Austin. Philadelphia: Lea & Blanchard, 1841.

————. *History of the Reformation in Germany.* Translated by Sarah Austin. New York: E. P. Dutton & Co., 1905.

Rapin de Thoyras. *The History of England,* Vol. II. Translated by N. Tindal. London: James & John Knapton, 1731.

Ropes, John C. *The Campaign of Waterloo.* New York: Charles Scribner's Sons, 1892.

————. *The Story of the Civil War.* Continued by William R. Livermore. New York: G. P. Putnam's Sons, 1933.

Round, John H. *Feudal England.* London: S. Sonnenschein & Co., 1895.

Schlegel, Frederick von. *The Philosophy of History.* Translated by James B. Robertson. London: Saunders & Otley, 1835.

Schuyler, Eugene. *Peter the Great.* New York: Charles Scribner's Sons, 1884.

Shepherd, William R. *Historical Atlas.* New York: Henry Holt & Co., 1929.

Sherman, William T. *Memoirs of General William T. Sherman.* New York: D. Appleton & Co., 1875.

Shirer, William L. *The Rise and Fall of the Third Reich.* New York: Simon & Schuster, 1960.

Siborne, William. *History of the War in France and Belgium in 1815.* London: T. & W. Boone, 1848.

Stamps, T. Dodson, and Esposito, Vincent J. (Eds.). *A Military History of World War II.* Prepared by the Department of Military Art and Engineering, U.S.M.A., West Point, N.Y., 1953.

Steele, Matthew F. *American Campaigns.* Washington, D.C.: Byron S. Adams, 1909.

Suetonius. *Lives of the Caesars.* Translated by John C. Rolfe from the text of Maximilian Ihm. Cambridge, Mass.: Harvard University Press, 1951.

Tacitus. *The Annals and the Histories,* Vol. 15 of *Great Books of the Western World.* Translated by Alfred J. Church and William J. Brodribb. Chicago: William Benton, Publisher, Encyclopædia Britannica, 1952.

Taylor, Frank. *The Wars of Marlborough, 1702–1709.* Oxford: Basil Blackwell, 1921.

Thierry, Augustin. *History of the Conquest of England by the Normans.* Translated from the French. New York: Everyman's Library, E. P. Dutton & Co., 1927.

Thirlwall, Connop. *A History of Greece.* New York: Harper & Brothers, 1845.

Thompson, E. A. *A History of Attila and the Huns.* London: Oxford University Press, 1948.

Thucydides. *The History of the Peloponnesian War,* Vol. 6 of *Great Books of the Western World.* Translated by Richard Crawley. Chicago: William Benton, Publisher, Encyclopædia Britannica, 1952.

Trevelyan, George O. *The American Revolution.* London: Longmans, Green & Co., 1921.

Tuchman, Barbara W. *The Guns of August.* New York: The Macmillan Company, 1962.

Voltaire, François Marie Arouet de. *The Age of Louis XIV.* Translated by Martyn P. Pollack. New York: E. P. Dutton & Co., 1926.

Wace, Robert. *Master Wace, His Chronicle of the Norman Conquest from the Roman de Rou.* Translated by Edgar Taylor. London: William Pickering, 1837.

War of the Rebellion, Official Records of the Union and Confederate Armies. War Department, U.S. Government Printing Office, 1880–1901.

The War Reports of General of the Army George C. Marshall, General of the Army Henry H. Arnold, and Fleet Admiral Ernest J. King. New York: J. B. Lippincott Co., 1947.

Ward, Christopher. *The War of the Revolution.* New York: The Macmillan Company, 1952.

Whitton, Frederick E. *The Decisive Battles of Modern Times.* Boston and New York: Houghton Mifflin Co., 1923.

Williams, Kenneth P. *Lincoln Finds a General.* New York: The Macmillan Company, 1949–56.

Wilmot, Chester. *The Struggle for Europe.* New York: Harper & Brothers, 1952.

Index

As the index for this book was being prepared, it became obvious that a list of page numbers for certain countries would be of little value, because the references would be too numerous. Information concerning them would always be far more readily obtained by referring to place-names, leaders, battles, and other items. Therefore, Germany, ancient Greece, Italy, ancient Persia, Russia, Spain, and the United States are not given. Neither France nor Austria appear, but Gaul and the dual monarchy of Austria-Hungary are listed, and so is England prior to the Norman Conquest.

When an individual's rank or title is indicated, it is usually the highest attained during the battle or war described. Cross-references have been avoided wherever practicable. If a name appears in the book in more than one way, two or more entries were made below; for example, both John Churchill and the Duke of Marlborough are given, while Augustus Caesar (Octavian) is listed under all three names.